POEMS

By JOHN
GREENLEAF
WHITTIER

New York
Hurst & Company
Publishers

CONTENTS.

CONTENTS.

WHITTIER'S POEMS.

PROEM.

I LOVE the old melodious lays
Which softly melt the ages through,
   The songs of Spenser's golden days,
   Arcadian Sidney's silvery phrase,
Sprinkling our noon of time with freshest morning dew.

Yet, vainly in my quiet hours
To breathe their marvellous notes I try;
   I feel them, as the leaves and flowers
   In silence feel the dewy showers,
And drink with glad still lips the blessing of the sky.

The rigor of a frozen clime,
The harshness of an untaught ear,
   The jarring words of one whose rhyme
   Beat often Labor's hurried time,
Or Duty's rugged march through storm and strife, are here.

Of mystic beauty, dreamy grace,
No rounded art the lack supplies;
   Unskilled the subtle lines to trace
   Or softer shades of Nature's face,
I view her common forms with unanointed eyes.

Nor mine the seer-like power to show
The secrets of the heart and mind;
   To drop the plummet-line below
   Our common world of joy and woe,
A more intense despair or brighter hope to find.

Yet here at least an earnest sense
Of human right and weal is shown;
   A hate of tyranny intense,
   And hearty in its vehemence,
As if my brother's pain and sorrow were my own.

Oh Freedom! if to me belong
Nor mighty Milton's gift divine,
   Nor Marvel's wit and graceful song,
   Still with a love as deep and strong
As theirs, I lay, like them, my best gifts on thy shrine!

AMESBURY, 11*th month*, 1847.

7

MOGG MEGONE.

PART I.

[The story of MOGG MEGONE has been considered by the author only as a framework for sketches of the scenery of New England, and of its early inhabitants. In portraying the Indian character, he has followed, as closely as his story would admit, the rough but natural deline-ations of Church, Mayhew, Charlevoix, and Roger Williams ; and in so doing he has necessarily discarded much of the romance which poets and novelists have thrown around the ill-fated red man.—ED.]

WHO stands on that cliff, like a figure of stone,
  Unmoving and tall in the light of the sky,
  Where the spray of the cataract sparkles on high,
Lonely and sternly, save Mogg Megone ? *
Close to the verge of the rock is he,
  While beneath him the Saco its work is doing,
Hurrying down to its grave, the sea,
And slow through the rock its pathway hewing !
Far down, through the mist of the falling river,
Which rises up like an incense ever,

The splintered points of the crags are seen,
With water howling and vexed between,
While the scooping whirl of the pool beneath
Seems an open throat, with its granite teeth !
But Mogg Megone never trembled yet
Wherever his eye or his foot was set.
He is watchful : each form, in the moonlight dim,
Of rock or of tree, is seen of him :
He listens ; each sound from afar is caught,
The faintest shiver of leaf and limb :
But he sees not the waters, which foam and fret,
Whose moonlit spray has his moccasin wet—
And the roar of their rushing, he hears it not.

The moonlight, through the open bough
  Of the gnarl'd beech, whose naked root
  Coils like a serpent at his foot,
Falls, checkered, on the Indian's brow.
His head is bare, save only where
Waves in the wind one lock of hair,
  Reserved for him, whoe'er he be,
More mighty than Megone in strife,
  When breast to breast and knee to knee,
Above the fallen warrior's life
Gleams, quick and keen, the scalping-knife.

* MOGG MEGONE, or Hegone, was a leader among the Saco Indians, in the bloody war of 1677. He attacked and captured the garrison at Black Point, October 12th of that year ; and cut off, at the same time, a party of Englishmen near Saco River. From a deed signed by this Indian in 1664, and from other circumstances, it seems that, previous to the war, he had mingled much with the colonists. On this account, he was probably selected by the principal sachems as their agent, in the treaty signed in November, 1676.

Megone hath his knife and hatchet and gun,
And his gaudy and tasselled blanket on:
His knife hath a handle with gold inlaid,
And magic words on its polished blade—
'Twas the gift of Castine * to Mogg Megone,
For a scalp or twain from the Yengees torn:
His gun was the gift of the Tarrantine,
And Modocawando's wives had strung
The brass and the beads, which tinkle and shine
On the polished breech, and broad bright line
Of beaded wampum around it hung.

What seeks Megone ?   His foes are near—
Gray Jocelyn's † eye is never sleeping,
And the garrison lights are burning clear,
Where Phillips' ‡ men their watch are keeping.
Let him hie him away through the dank river fog,
Never rustling the boughs nor displacing the rocks,
For the eyes and the ears which are watching for Mogg,
Are keener than those of the wolf or the fox.

He starts—there's a rustle among the leaves:
Another—the click of his gun is heard !—
A footstep—is it the step of Cleaves,
With Indian blood on his English sword ?
Steals Harmon ‖ down from the sands of York,
With hand of iron and foot of cork ?
Has Scamman, versed in Indian wile,
For vengeance left his vine-hung isle ? §
Hark ! at that whistle, soft and low,
How lights the eye of Mogg Megone !
A smile gleams o'er his dusky brow—
"Boon welcome, Johnny Bonython ! "

* Baron de St. Castine came to Canada in 1644.   Leaving his civilized companions, he plunged into the great wilderness, and settled among the Penobscot Indians, near the mouth of their noble river.   He here took for his wives the daughters of the great Modocawando—the most powerful sachem of the east.   His castle was plundered by Governor Andros, during his reckless administration ; and the enraged Baron is supposed to have excited the Indians into open hostility to the English.

† The owner and commander of the garrison at Black Point, which Mogg attacked and plundered.   He was an old man at the period to which the tale relates.

‡ Major Phillips, one of the principal men of the Colony.   His garrison sustained a long and terrible siege by the savages.   As a magistrate and a gentleman, he exacted of his plebeian neighbors a remarkable degree of deference.   The Court Records of the settlement inform us that an individual was fined for the heinous offence of saying that " Major Phillips' mare was as lean an an Indian dog."

‖ Captain Harmon, of Georgeana, now York, was, for many years, the terror of the Eastern Indians.   In one of his expeditions up the Kennebec River, at the head of a party of rangers, he discovered twenty of the savages asleep by a large fire.   Cautiously creeping toward them, until he was certain of his aim, he ordered his men to single out their objects.   The first discharge killed or mortally wounded the whole number of the unconscious sleepers.

§ Wood island, near the mouth of the Saco.   It was visited by the Sieur De Monts and Champlain, in 1603.   The following extract, from the journal of the latter, relates to it. " Having left the Kennebec, we ran along the coast to the westward, and cast anchor under a small island, near the mainland, where we saw twenty or more natives.   I here visited an island, beautifully clothed with a fine growth of forest trees, particularly of the oak and walnut ; and overspread with vines, that, in their season, produce excellent grapes.   We named it the island of Bacchus."—*Les voyages de Sieur Champlain, Liv.* 2, c. 3.

Out steps, with cautious foot and slow,
And quick, keen glances to and fro,
    The hunted outlaw, Bonython!*
A low, lean swarthy man is he,
With blanket-garb and buskined knee,
    And naught of English fashion on;
For he hates the race from whence he sprung,
And he couches his words in the Indian tongue.

" Hush—let the Sachem's voice be weak;
The water-rat shall hear him speak—
The owl shall whoop in the white man's ear,
That Mogg Megone, with his scalps, is here!"
He pauses—dark, over cheek and brow,
A flush, as of shame, is stealing now:
" Sachem!" he says, " let me have the land,
Which stretches away upon either hand,
As far about as my feet can stray
In the half of a gentle summer's day,
    From the leaping brook † to the Saco River—
And the fair-haired girl, thou has sought of me,
Shall sit in the Sachem's wigwam, and be
    The wife of Mogg Megone forever."

There's a sudden light in the Indian's glance,
    A moment's trace of powerful feeling—
Of love or triumph, or both perchance,
    Over his proud, calm features stealing.
" The words of my father are very good;
He shall have the land, and water, and wood;
And he who harms the Sagamore John
Shall feel the knife of Mogg Megone;
But the fawn of the Yengees shall sleep on my breast
And the bird of the clearing shall sing in my nest."

---

* John Bonython was the son of Richard Bonython, Gent., one of the most efficient and able magistrates of the Colony. John proved to be " a degenerate plant." In 1635, we find, by the Court Records, that, for some offence, he was fined 40s. In 1640, he was fined for abuse toward R. Gibson, the minister, and Mary, his wife. Soon after, he was fined for disorderly conduct in the house of his father. In 1645, the " Great and General Court" adjudged " John Bonython outlawed, and incapable of any of his majesty's laws, and proclaimed him a rebel." [Court Records of the Province, 1645.] In 1651, he bade defiance to the laws of Massachusetts, and was again outlawed. He acted independently of all law and authority; and hence, doubtless, his burlesque title of " The Sagamore of Saco," which has come down to the present generation in the following epitaph:

" Here lies Bonython; the Sagamore of Saco,
He lived a rogue, and died a knave, and went to Hobomoko."

By some means or other, he obtained a large estate. In this poem, I have taken some liberties with him, not strictly warranted by historical facts, although the conduct imputed to him is in keeping with his general character. Over the last years of his life lingers a deep obscurity. Even the manner of his death is uncertain. He was supposed to have been killed by the Indians; but this is doubted by the indefatigable author of the history of Saco and Biddeford.—Part I., p. 115.

    † Foxwell's Brook flows from a marsh or bog, called the " Heath," in Saco, containing thirteen hundred acres. On this brook, and surrounded by wild and romantic scenery, is a beautiful waterfall, of more than sixty feet.

" But father!"—and the Indian's hand
  Falls gently on the white man's arm,
And with a smile as shrewdly bland
  As the deep voice is slow and calm—
" Where is my father's singing-bird—
  The sunny eye, and sunset hair ?
I know I have my father's word,
  And that his word is good and fair;
  But, will my father tell me where
Megone shall go and look for his bride ?—
For he sees her not by her father's side."

The dark, stern eye of Bonython
  Flashes over the features of Mogg Megone,
  In one of those glances which search within;
But the stolid calm of the Indian alone
  Remains where the trace of emotion has been.
" Does the Sachem doubt ? Let him go with me,
And the eyes of the Sachem his bride shall see."
Cautious and slow, with pauses oft,
And watchful eyes and whispers soft,
The twain are stealing through the wood,
Leaving the downward-rushing flood,
Whose deep and solemn roar behind,
Grows fainter on the evening wind.

Hark!—is that the angry howl
  Of the wolf, the hills among ?—
Or the hooting of the owl,
  On his leafy cradle swung ?—
Quickly glancing, to and fro,
Listening to each sound they go:
Round the columns of the pine,
  Indistinct, in shadow, seeming
Like some old and pillared shrine;
With the soft and white moonshine,
  Round the foliage-tracery shed
Of each column's branching head,
  For its lamps of worship gleaming !
And the sounds awakened there,
  In the pine leaves fine and small,
  Soft and sweetly musical,
By the fingers of the air,
For the anthem's dying fall
Lingering round some temple's wall!—
Niche and cornice round and round
Wailing like the ghost of sound !
Is not Nature's worship thus
  Ceaseless ever, going on ?
Hath it not a voice for us
  In the thunder, or the tone
Of the leaf-harp faint and small,

Speaking to the unsealed ear
    Words of blended love and fear,
Of the mighty Soul of all ?
Naught had the twain of thoughts like these
As they wound along through the crowded trees,
Where never had rung the axeman's stroke
On the gnarled trunk of the rough-barked oak ;—
Climbing the dead tree's mossy log,
    Breaking the mesh of the bramble fine,
    Turning aside the wild grape vine,
And lightly crossing the quaking bog
Whose surface shakes at the leap of the frog,
And out of whose pools the ghostly fog
    Creeps into the chill moonshine!

Yet even that Indian's ear had heard
The preaching of the Holy Word :
Sanchekantacket's isle of sand
Was once his father's hunting land,
Where zealous Hiacoomes * stood-—
The wild apostle of the wood,
Shook from his soul the fear of harm,
And trampled on the Powwaw's charm ;
Until the wizard's curses hung
Suspended on his palsying tongue,
And the fierce warrior, grim and tall,
Trembled before the forest Paul!

A cottage hidden in the wood—
    Red through its seams a light is glowing,
On rock and bough and tree-trunk rude,
    A narrow lustre throwing.
" Who's there ? " a clear, firm voice demands :
    " Hold, Ruth—'tis I, the Sagamore ! "
Quick, at the summons, hasty hands
    Unclose the bolted door ;
And on the outlaw's daughter shine
The flashes of the kindled pine.

Tall and erect the maiden stands,
    Like some young priestess of the wood,

---

* Hiacoomes, the first Christian preacher on Martha's Vineyard ; for a biography of whom the reader is referred to Increase Mayhew's account of the Praying Indians, 1726. The following is related of him : "One Lord's day, after meeting, where Hiacoomes had been preaching, there came in a Powwaw very angry, and said, ' I know all the meeting Indians are liars. You say you don't care for the Powwaws ; '—then, calling two or three of them by name, he railed at them, and told them they were deceived, for the Powwaws could kill all the meeting Indians, if they set about it. But Hiacoomes told him that he would be in the midst of all the Powwaws in the island, and they should do the utmost they could against him ; and when they should do their worst by their witchcraft to kill him, he would without fear set himself against them, by remembering Jehovah. He told them also he did put all the Powwaws under his heel. Such was the faith of this good man. Nor were these Powwaws ever able to do these Christian Indians any hurt, though others were frequently hurt and killed by them."—Mayhew's Book, pp. 6, 7, c. 1.

The free born child of Solitude,
　And bearing still the wild and rude,
Yet noble trace of Nature's hands.
Her dark brown cheek has caught its stain
More from the sunshine than the rain;
Yet, where her long fair hair is parting,
A pure white brow into light is starting;
And, where the folds of her blanket sever,
Are a neck and bosom as white as ever
The foam-wreaths rise on the leaping river.
But, in the convulsive quiver and grip
Of the muscles around her bloodless lip,
　There is something painful and sad to see;
And her eye has a glance more sternly wild
Than even that of a forest child
　In its fearless and untamed freedom should be.
Yet, seldom in hall or court are seen
So queenly a form and so noble a mien,
　As freely and smiling she welcomes them there!
Her outlawed sire and Mogg Megone:
　" Pray, father, how does thy hunting fare ?
And, Sachem, say—does Scamman wear,
In spite of thy promise, a scalp of his own ? "
Hurried and light is the maiden's tone;
　But a fearful meaning lurks within
Her glance, as it questions the eye of Megone—
　An awful meaning of guilt and sin!
The Indian hath opened his blanket, and there
Hangs a human scalp by its long damp hair!

With hand upraised, with quick-drawn breath.
She meets that ghastly sign of death.
In one long, glassy, spectral stare
The enlarging eye is fastened there,
As if that mesh of pale brown hair
　Had power to change at sight alone,
Even as the fearful locks which wound
Medusa's fatal forehead round,
　The gazer into stone.
With such a look Herodias read
The features of the bleeding head,
So looked the mad Moor on his dead,
Or the young Cenci as she stood,
O'er-dabbled with a father's blood!

Look!—feeling melts that frozen glance,
It moves that marble countenance,
As if at once within her strove
Pity with shame, and hate with love.
The Past recalls its joy and pain,
Old memories rise before her brain—
The lips which love's embraces met

The hand her tears of parting wet,
The voice whose pleading tones beguiled
The pleased ear of the forest-child,—
And tears she may no more repress
Reveal her lingering tenderness.

Oh! woman wronged can cherish hate
    More deep and dark than manhood may;
But, when the mockery of Fate
    Hath left Revenge its chosen way,
And the fell curse, which years have nursed,
Full on the spoiler's head hath burst—
When all her wrong, and shame, and pain,
Burns fiercely on his heart and brain—
Still lingers something of the spell
    Which bound her to the traitor's bosom—
Still, midst the vengeful fires of hell,
    Some flowers of old affection blossom.

John Bonython's eyebrows together are drawn
With a fierce expression of wrath and scorn—
He hoarsely whispers, "Ruth, beware!
    Is this the time to be playing the fool—
Crying over a paltry lock of hair,
    Like a love-sick girl at school?—
Curse on it!—an Indian can see and hear:
Away—and prepare our evening cheer!"

How keenly the Indian is watching now
Her tearful eye and her varying brow—
With a serpent eye, which kindles and burns,
    Like a fiery star in the upper air:
On sire and daughter his fierce glance turns:
    "Has my old white father a scalp to spare?
    For his young one loves the pale brown hair
Of the scalp of an English dog, far more
Than Mogg Megone, or his wigwam floor:
    Go—Mogg is wise: he will keep his land—
    And Sagamore John, when he feels with his hand,
Shall miss his scalp where it grew before."

The moment's gust of grief is gone—
    The lip is clenched—the tears are still—
God pity thee, Ruth Bonython!
    With what a strength of will
Are nature's feelings in thy breast,
As with an iron hand repressed!
And how, upon that nameless woe,
Quick as the pulse can come and go,
While shakes the unsteadfast knee, and yet
The bosom heaves—the eye is wet—
Has thy dark spirit power to stay

The heart's wild current on its way?
  And whence that baleful strength of guile,
Which, over that still working brow
And tearful eye and cheek, can throw
  The mockery of a smile?
Warned by her father's blackening frown,
With one strong effort crushing down
Grief, hate, remorse, she meets again
  The savage murderer's sullen gaze,
  And scarcely look or tone betrays
How the heart strives beneath its chain.

" Is the Sachem angry—angry with Ruth,
Because she cries with an ache in her tooth,*
Which would make a Sagamore jump and cry,
And look about with a woman's eye?
No—Ruth will sit in the Sachem's door,
And braid the mats for his wigwam floor,
And broil his fish and tender fawn,
And weave his wampum, and grind his corn,—
For she loves the brave and the wise, and none
Are braver and wiser than Mogg Megone ! "

The Indian's brow is clear once more:
  With grave, calm face, and half-shut eye,
He sits upon the wigwam floor,
  And watches Ruth go by,
Intent upon her household care;
  And ever and anon, the while,
Or on the maiden, or her fare,
Which smokes in grateful promise there,
  Bestows his quiet smile.

Ah, Mogg Megone!—what dreams are thine,
  But those which love's own fancies dress—
  The sum of Indian happiness!—
A wigwam, where the warm sunshine
Looks in among the groves of pine—
A stream, where, round thy light canoe,
The trout and salmon dart in view,
And the fair girl, before thee now,
Spreading thy mat with hand of snow,
Or plying, in the dews of morn,
Her hoe amidst thy patch of corn,
Or offering up, at eve, to thee,
Thy birchen dish of hominy !

From the rude board of Bonython,
Venison and succotash have gone—

---

* " The tooth-ache," says Roger Williams, in his observations upon the language and customs of the New England tribes, " is the only paine which will force their stoute hearts to cry." He afterwards remarks that even the Indian women never cry as he has heard " some of their men in this paine."

For long these dwellers of the wood
Have felt the gnawing want of food.
But untasted of Ruth is the frugal cheer—
With head averted, yet ready ear,
She stands by the side of her austere sire,
Feeding, at times, the unequal fire,
With the yellow knots of the pitch-pine tree,
Whose flaring light, as they kindle, falls
On the cottage-roof, and its black log walls,
And over its inmates three.

From Sagamore Bonython's hunting flask
    The fire-water burns at the lip of Megone:
" Will the Sachem hear what his father shall ask?
    Will he make his mark, that it may be known,
On the speaking-leaf, that he gives the land,
From the Sachem's own, to his father's hand ? "

The fire-water shines in the Indian's eyes,
    As he rises, the white man's bidding to do:
" Wuttamuttata—weekan! * Mogg is wise—
    For the water he drinks is strong and new,—
Mogg's heart is great!—will he shut his hand,
When his father asks for a little land ? "—

With unsteady fingers, the Indian has drawn
    On the parchment the shape of a hunter's bow:
" Boon water—boon water—Sagamore John!
    Wuttamuttata—weekan! our hearts will grow!"
He drinks yet deeper—he mutters low—
He reels on his bear-skin to and fro—
His head falls down on his naked breast—
He struggles, and sinks to a drunken rest.

" Humph—drunk as a beast!" and Bonython's brow
    Is darker than ever with evil thought—
" The fool has signed his warrant; but how
    And when shall the deed be wrought?
Speak Ruth! why, what the devil is here,
To fix thy gaze in that empty air ?—
Speak, Ruth!—by my soul, if I thought that tear,
Which shames thyself and our purpose here,
Were shed for that cursed and pale-faced dog,
Whose green scalp hangs from the belt of Mogg,
    And whose beastly soul is in Satan's keeping—
This—this!"—he dashes his hand upon
The rattling stock of his loaded gun—
    "Should send thee with him to do thy weeping!"

---

* *Wuttamuttata*, " Let us drink." *Weekan*, " It is sweet." *Vide* Roger Williams's *Key
to the Indian Language*, " in that parte of America called New England." London, 1643, p
35.

" Father ! "—the eye of Bonython
Sinks, at that low, sepulchral tone,
Hollow and deep, as it were spoken
  By the unmoving tongue of death—
Or from some statue's lips had broken—
  A sound without a breath !
" Father !—my life I value less
Than yonder fool his gaudy dress ;
And how it ends it matters not,
By heart-break or by rifle-shot :
But spare awhile the scoff and threat—
Our business is not finished yet."

" True, true, my girl—I only meant
To draw up again the bow unbent.
Harm thee, my Ruth ! I only sought
To frighten off thy gloomy thought ;—
Come—let's be friends !" He seeks to clasp
His daughter's cold, damp hand in his.
Ruth startles from her father's grasp,
As if each nerve and muscle felt,
Instinctively, the touch of guilt,
Through all their subtle sympathies.

He points her to the sleeping Mogg,
" What shall be done with yonder dog ?
Scamman is dead, and revenge is thine—
The deed is signed and the land is mine ;
  And this drunken fool is of use no more,
Save as thy hopeful bridegroom, and sooth,
'Twere Christian mercy, to finish him, Ruth,
  Now, while he lies like a beast on our floor,—
If not for thine, at least for his sake,
Rather than let the poor dog awake,
To drain my flask, and claim as his bride
Such a forest devil to run by his side—
Such a Wetuomanit * as thou wouldst make !"

He laughs at his jest. Hush—what is there ?—
  The sleeping Indian is striving to rise,
  With his knife in his hand, and glaring eyes !—
" Wagh !—Mogg will have the pale-face's hair,
  For his knife is sharp and his fingers can help
The hair to pull and the skin to peel—
Let him cry like a woman and twist like an eel,
  The great Captain Scamman must lose his scalp !

---

* *Wetuomanit*—a house god, or demon. "They—the Indians—have given me the names of
thirty-seven gods, which I have, all which in their solemne Worships they invocate ! "—R.
Williams's Briefe Observations of the Customs, Manners, Worships, &c., of the Natives, in
Peace and Warre, in Life and Death : on all which is added Spiritual Observations, General
and Particular, of Chiefe and Special use—upon all occasions—to all the English inhabiting
these parts ; yet Pleasant and Profitable to the view of all Mene, p, 110, c. 21,

And Ruth, when she sees it, shall dance with Mogg."
His eyes are fixed—but his lips draw in—
With a low, hoarse chuckle, and fiendish grin,—
   And he sinks again, like a senseless log.

Ruth does not speak—she does not stir;
But she gazes down on the murderer,
Whose broken and dreamful slumbers tell,
Too much for her ear, of that deed of hell.
She sees the knife, with its slaughter red,
And the dark fingers clenching the bear-skin bed!
What thoughts of horror and madness whirl
Through the burning brain of that fallen girl!

John Bonython lifts his gun to his eye,
   Its muzzle is close to the Indian's ear—
But he drops it again. "Some one may be nigh,
And I would not that even the wolves should hear."
He draws his knife from its deer-skin belt—
Its edge with his fingers is slowly felt;—
Kneeling down on one knee, by the Indian's side,
From his throat he opens the blanket wide;
And twice or thrice he feebly essays
A trembling hand with the knife to raise.

" I cannot "—he mutters—" did he not save
My life from a cold and wintry grave,
When the storm came down from Agioochook,
And the north-wind howled, and the tree-tops shook—
And I strove, in the drifts of the rushing snow,
Till my knees grew weak and I could not go,
And I felt the cold to my vitals creep,
And my heart's blood stiffen, and pulses sleep!
I cannot strike him—Ruth Bonython!
In the devil's name, tell me—what's to be done?"
Oh! when the soul, once pure and high,
Is stricken down from Virtue's sky,
As, with the downcast star of morn,
Some gems of light are with it drawn—
And, through its night of darkness, play
Some tokens of its primal day—
Some lofty feelings linger still—
   The strength to dare, the nerve to meet
   Whatever threatens with defeat
Its all-indomitable will!—
But lacks the mean of mind and heart,
   Though eager for the gains of crime,
   Oft, at this chosen place and time,
The strength to bear this evil part;
And, shielded by this very Vice,
Escapes from Crime by Cowardice.

Ruth starts erect—with bloodshot eye,
   And lips drawn tight across her teeth,
   Showing their locked embrace beneath,
In the red fire-light:—" Mogg must die!
Give me the knife ! "—The outlaw turns,
   Shuddering in heart and limb, away—
But, fitfully there, the hearth-fire burns,
   And he sees on the wall strange shadows play.
A lifted arm, a tremulous blade,
Are dimly pictured, in light and shade,
   Plunging down in the darkness.   Hark, that cry!
Again—and again—he sees it fall—
That shadowy arm down the lighted wall !
   He hears quick footsteps—a shape flits by !
The door on its rusted hinges creaks :—
   ' Ruth—daughter Ruth!" the outlaw shrieks,
But no sound comes back—he is standing alone
By the mangled corse of Mogg Megone!

Part II.

'Tis morning over Norridgewock—.
On tree and wigwam, wave and rock.
Bathed in the autumnal sunshine, stirred
At intervals by breeze and bird,
And wearing all the hues which glow
In heaven's own pure and perfect bow,
   That glorious picture of the air,
Which summer's light-robed angel forms.
On the dark ground of fading storms,
   With pencil dipped in sunbeams there—
And, stretching out, on either hand,
O'er all that wide and unshorn land,
   Till, weary of its gorgeousness,
The aching and the dazzled eye
Rests gladdened, on the calm blue sky—
   Slumbers the mighty wilderness!
The oak, upon the windy hill,
   Its dark green burthen upward heaves—
The hemlock broods above its rill,
Its cone-like foliage darker still,
   While the white birch's graceful stem
And the rough walnut bough receives
The sun upon their crowded leaves,
   Each colored like a topaz gem;
   And the tall maple wears with them
The coronal which autumn gives,
   The brief, bright sign of ruin near,
   The hectic of a dying year!

The hermit priest, who lingers now
On the Bald Mountain's shrubless brow

The gray and thunder smitten pile
Which marks afar the Desert Isle,*
    While gazing on the scene below,
May half forget the dreams of home,
That nightly with his slumbers come,—
The tranquil skies of sunny France,
The peasant's harvest song and dance,
The vines around the hillsides wreathing,
The soft airs midst their clusters breathing,
The winds which dipped, the stars which shone
Within thy bosom, blue Garonne!
And round the Abbey's shadowed wall,
At morning spring and even-fall,
    Sweet voices in the still air singing—
The chant of many a holy hymn—
    The solemn bell of vespers ringing—
And hallowed torch-light falling dim
On pictured saint and seraphim!
For here beneath him lies unrolled,
Bathed deep in morning's flood of gold,
A vision gorgeous as the dream
Of the beatified may seem
    When, as his Church's legends say,
Borne upward in ecstatic bliss,
    The rapt enthusiast soars away
Unto a brighter world than this:
A mortal's glimpse beyond the pale—
A moment's lifting of the veil!

Far eastward o'er the lovely bay,
Penobscot's clustered wigwams lay;
And gently from that Indian town
The verdant hillside slopes adown,
To where the sparkling waters play
    Upon the yellow sands below;
And shooting round the winding shores
    Of narrow capes, and isles which lie
    Slumbering to ocean's lullaby—
With birchen boat and glancing oars,
    The red men to their fishing go;
While from their planting ground is borne
The treasure of the golden corn,
By laughing girls, whose dark eyes glow
Wild through the locks which o'er them flow.
The wrinkled squaw, whose toil is done,
Sits on her bear-skin in the sun,
Watching the huskers, with a smile
For each full ear which swells the pile;
And the old chief, who never more

* Mt. Desert Island, the Bald Mountain which overlooks Frenchman's and Penobscot Bay
It was upon this island that the Jesuits made their earliest settlement.

May bend the bow or pull the oar,
Smokes gravely in his wigwam door,
Or slowly shapes, with axe of stone
The arrow-head from flint and bone.

Beneath the westward-turning eye
A thousand wooded islands lie—
Gems of the waters !—with each hue
Of brightness set in ocean's blue.
Each bears aloft its tuft of trees
   Touched by the pencil of the frost,
And, with the motion of each breeze,
   A moment seen—a moment lost—
   Changing and blent, confused and tossed,
The brighter with the darker crossed,
Their thousand tints of beauty glow
Down in the restless waves below,
   And tremble in the sunny skies,
As if, from waving bough to bough,
   Flitted the birds of paradise.
There sleep Placentia's group—and there
Père Breteaux marks the hour of prayer;
And there, beneath the sea-worn cliff,
   On which the Father's hut is seen,
The Indian stays his rocking skiff,
   And peers the hemlock boughs between,
Half trembling, as he seeks to look
Upon the Jesuit's Cross and Book.*
There, gloomily against the sky,
The Dark Isles rear their summits high;
And Desert Rock, abrupt and bare,
Lifts its gray turrets in the air—
Seen from afar, like some strong hold
Built by the ocean kings of old;
And, faint as smoke-wreath white and thin,
Swells in the north vast Katadin:
And, wandering from its marshy feet,
The broad Penobscot comes to meet
   And mingle with his own bright bay.
Slow sweep his dark and gathering floods,
Arched over by the ancient woods,
Which Time, in those dim solitudes,
   Wielding the dull axe of Decay,
   Alone hath ever shorn away.

Not thus, within the woods which hide
The beauty of thy azure tide,
   And with their falling timbers block
Thy broken currents, Kennebec!

* Father Hennepin, a missionary among the Iroquois, mentions that the Indians believed him to be a conjurer, and that they were particularly afraid of a bright silver chalice which he had in his possession. "The Indians," says Père Jerome Lallamant, "fear us as the greatest sorcerers on earth."

Gazes the white man on the wreck
　　Of the down-trodden Norridgewock—
In one lone village hemmed at length,
In battle shorn of half their strength,
Turned, like the panther in his lair,
　　With his fast flowing life-blood wet,
For one last struggle of despair,
　　Wounded and faint, but tameless yet!
Unreaped, upon the planting lands,
The scant, neglected harvest stands:
No shout is there—no dance—no song:
The aspect of the very child
Scowls with a meaning sad and wild
　　Of bitterness and wrong.
The almost infant Norridgewock
Essays to lift the tomahawk;
And plucks his father's knife away,
To mimic, in his frightful play,
　　The scalping of an English foe:
Wreathes on his lip a horrid smile,
Burns, like a snake's, his small eye, while
　　Some bough or sapling meets his blow.
The fisher, as he drops his line,
Starts, when he sees the hazels quiver
Along the margin of the river,
Looks up and down the rippling tide,
And grasps the firelock at his side.
For Bomazeen * from Tacconock
Has sent his runners to Norridgewock,
With tidings that Moulton and Harmon of York
　　Far up the river have come:
They have left their boats—they have entered the wood,
And filled the depths of the solitude
　　With the sound of the ranger's drum.

On the brow of a hill, which slopes to meet
The flowing river, and bathe its feet—
The bare-washed rock, and the drooping grass,
And the creeping vine, as the waters pass—
A rude and unshapely chapel stands,
Built up in that wild by unskilled hands;
Yet the traveler knows it a place of prayer,
For the holy sign of the cross is there:
And should he chance at that place to be,
　　Of a Sabbath morn, or some hallowed day,
When prayers are made and masses are said,
Some for the living and some for the dead,
Well might that traveler start to see
　　The tall dark forms, that take their way
From the birch canoe, on the river-shore,

---

* Bomazeen is spoken of by Penhallow as "the famous warrior and chieftain of Norridgewock." He was killed in the attack of the English upon Norridgewock, in 1724.

And the forest paths, to that chapel door;
And marvel to mark the naked knees
    And the dusky foreheads bending there,
While, in coarse white vesture, over these
    In blessing or in prayer,
Stretching abroad his thin pale hands,
Like a shrouded ghost, the Jesuit * stands.
Two forms are now in that chapel dim,
    The Jesuit, silent and sad and pale,
    Anxiously heeding some fearful tale,
Which a stranger is telling him.
That stranger's garb is soiled and torn,
And wet with dew and loosely worn;
Her fair neglected hair falls down
O'er cheeks with wind and sunshine brown;
Yet still, in that disordered face,
The Jesuit's cautious eye can trace
Those elements of former grace,
Which, half effaced, seem scarcely less,
Even now, than perfect loveliness.
With drooping head, and voice so low
    That scarce it meets the Jesuit's ears—
While through her clasp'd fingers flow,
From the heart's fountain, hot and slow,
    Her penitential tears—

---

* Père Ralle, or Rasles, was one of the most zealous and indefatigable of that band of Jesuit missionaries who, at the beginning of the seventeenth century, penetrated the forests of America, with the avowed object of converting the heathen. The first religious mission of the Jesuits, to the savages in North America, was in 1611. The zeal of the fathers for the conversion of the Indians to the Catholic faith knew no bounds. For this, they plunged into the depths of the wilderness; habituated themselves to all the hardships and privations of the natives; suffered cold, hunger, and some of them death itself, by the extremest tortures. Père Brebeuf, after laboring in the cause of his mission for twenty years, together with his companion, Père Lallamant, was burned alive. To these might be added the names of those Jesuits who were put to death by the Iroquois—Daniel, Garnier, Buteaux, La Riborerde, Goupil, Constantin, and Liegeouis. "For bed," says Father Lallamant, in his *Relation de ce qui s'est dans le pays des Hurons*, 1640, c. 3, "we have nothing but a miserable piece of bark of a tree; for nourishment, a handful or two of corn, either roasted or soaked in water, which seldom satisfies our hunger; and after all, not venturing to perform even the ceremonies of our religion, without being considered as sorcerers." Their success among the natives, however, by no means equaled their exertions. Père Lallamant says—" With respect to adult persons, in good health, there is little apparent success; on the contrary, there have been nothing but storms and whirlwinds from that quarter."

Sebastien Ralle established himself, some time about the year 1670, at Norridgewock, where he continued more than forty years. He was accused, and perhaps not without justice, of exciting his praying Indians against the English, whom he looked upon as the enemies not only of his king, but also of the Catholic religion. He was killed by the English, in 1724, at the foot of the cross, which his own hands had planted. This Indian church was broken up, and its members either killed outright or dispersed.

In a letter written by Ralle to his nephew, he gives the following account of his church, and his own labors. " All my converts repair to the church regularly twice every day; first, very early in the morning, to attend mass, and again in the evening, to assist in the prayers at sunset. As it is necessary to fix the imagination of savages, whose attention is easily distracted, I have composed prayers, calculated to inspire them with just sentiments of the august sacrifice of our altars: they chant, or at least recite them aloud, during mass. Besides preaching to them on Sundays and Saints' days, I seldom let a working day pass, without making a concise exhortation, for the purpose of inspiring them with horror at those vices to which they are most addicted, or to confirm them in the practice of some particular virtue." *Vide Lettres Edifiantes et Cur.*, vol. vi., p. 127.

She tells the story of the woe
    And evil of her years.

"Oh Father, bear with me; my heart
    Is sick and death-like, and my brain
    Seems girdled with a fiery chain,
Whose scorching links will never part,
    And never cool again.
Bear with me while I speak—but turn
    Away that gentle eye, the while—
The fires of guilt more fiercely burn
    Beneath its holy smile;
For half I fancy I can see
My mother's sainted look in thee.

"My dear lost mother! sad and pale,
Mournfully sinking day by day,
    And with a hold on life as frail
    As frosted leaves, that, thin and gray,
    Hang feebly on their parent spray,
And tremble in the gale;
Yet watching o'er my childishness
With patient fondness—not the less
For all the agony which kept
Her blue eye wakeful, while I slept;
And checking every tear and groan
That haply might have waked my own;
And bearing still, without offence,
My idle words, and petulance;
    Reproving with a tear—and, while
The tooth of pain was keenly preying
Upon her very heart, repaying
    My brief repentance with a smile.

"Oh, in her meek, forgiving eye
    There was a brightness not of mirth—
A light, whose clear intensity
    Was borrowed not of earth.
Along her cheek a deepening red
Told where the feverish hectic fed;
    And yet, each fatal token gave
To the mild beauty of her face
A newer and a dearer grace,
    Unwarning of the grave.
'Twas like the hue which autumn gives
To yonder changed and dying leaves,
    Breathed over by his frosty breath;
Scarce can the gazer feel that this
Is but the spoiler's treacherous kiss,
    The mocking-smile of Death!

"Sweet were the tales she used to tell
    When summer's eve was dear to us,

And, fading from the darkening dell,
The glory of the sunset fell
  On wooded Agamenticus,—
When, sitting by our cottage wall,
The murmur of the Saco's fall,
  And the south wind's expiring sighs
Came, softly blending, on my ear,
With the low tones I loved to hear.
  Tales of the pure—the good—the wise—
The holy men and maids of old,
In the all-sacred pages told;—
Of Rachel, stooped at Haran's fountains,
  Amid her father's thirsty flock,
Beautiful to her kinsman seeming
As the bright angels of his dreaming,
  On Padan-aran's holy rock;
Of gentle Ruth—and her who kept
  Her awful vigil on the mountains,
By Israel's virgin daughters wept;
Of Miriam, with her maidens, singing
  The song for grateful Israel meet,
While every crimson wave was bringing
  The spoils of Egypt at her feet;
Of her—Samaria's humble daughter,
  Who paused to hear, beside her well,
  Lessons of love and truth, which fell
Softly as Shiloh's flowing water;
  And saw, beneath his pilgrim guise,
The Promised One, so long foretold
By holy seer and bard of old,
Revealed before her wondering eyes!

"Slowly she faded. Day by day
Her step grew weaker in our hall,
And fainter, at each even-fall,
  Her sad voice died away.
Yet on her thin, pale lip, the while,
Sat Resignation's holy smile:
And even my father checked his tread,
And hushed his voice, beside her bed:
Beneath the calm and sad rebuke
Of her meek eye's imploring look,
The scowl of hate his brow forsook,
  And, in his stern and gloomy eye,
At times, a few unwonted tears
Wet the dark lashes, which for years
  Hatred and pride had kept so dry.

"Calm as a child to slumber soothed,
As if an angel's hand had smoothed
  The still, white features into rest,
Silent and cold, without a breath

To stir the drapery on her breast,
Pain, with its keen and poisoned fang,
The horror of the mortal pang,
The suffering look her brow had worn,
The fear, the strife, the anguish gone—
   She slept at last in death!

" Oh, tell me, father, *can* the dead
   Walk on the earth, and look on us,
And lay upon the living's head
   Their blessing or their curse ?
For, oh, last night she stood by me,
As I lay beneath the woodland tree!"

The Jesuit crosses himself in awe—
" Jesu! what was it my daughter saw ? "

"*She* came to me last night.
   The dried leaves did not feel her tread
She stood by me in the warm moonlight,
   In the white robes of the dead!
Pale, and very mournfully
She bent her light form over me.
I heard no sound, I felt no breath
Breathe o'er me from that face of death:
Its blue eyes rested on my own,
Rayless and cold as eyes of stone;
Yet, in their fixed, unchanging gaze,
Something, which spoke of early days—
A sadness in their quiet glare,
As if love's smile were frozen there—
Came o'er me with an icy thrill;
Oh God! I feel its presence still!"

The Jesuit makes the holy sign—
" How passed the vision, daughter mine ?"

" All dimly in the wan moonshine,
As a wreath of mist will twist and twine,
And scatter, and melt into the light—
So scattering—melting on my sight,
   The pale, cold vision passed;
But those sad eyes were fixed on mine
   Mournfully to the last."

" God help thee, daughter, tell me why
That spirit passed before thine eye!"

"Father, I know not, save it be
   That deeds of mine have summoned her
   From the unbreathing sepulchre,
To leave her last rebuke with me.
Ah, woe for me! my mother died
Just at the moment when I stood

Close on the verge of womanhood,
A child in everything beside;
And when my wild heart needed most
Her gentle counsels, they were lost.
" My father lived a stormy life,
Of frequent change and daily strife :
And—God forgive him! left his child
To feel, like him, a freedom wild;
To love the red man's dwelling place,
    The birch boat on his shaded floods,
The wild excitement of the chase
    Sweeping the ancient woods,
The camp-fire, blazing on the shore
    Of the still lakes, the clear stream, where
    The idle fisher sets his wear,
Or angles in the shade, far more
    Than that restraining awe I felt
Beneath my gentle mother's care,
    When nightly at her knee I knelt,
With childhood's simple prayer.

" There came a change. The wild, glad mood
    Of unchecked freedom passed.
Amid the ancient solitude
Of unshorn grass and waving wood,
    And waters glancing bright and fast,
A softened voice was in my ear,
    Sweet as those lulling sounds and fine
The hunter lifts his head to hear,
Now far and faint, now full and near—
    The murmur of the wind-swept pine.
A manly form was ever nigh,
A bold, free hunter, with an eye
    Whose dark, keen glance had power to wake
Both fear and love—to awe and charm;
    'Twas as the wizard rattlesnake,
Whose evil glances lure to harm—
Whose cold and small and glittering eye,
And brilliant coil, and changing dye,
Draw, step by step, the gazer near,
With drooping wing and cry of fear,
Yet powerless all to turn away,
A conscious, but a willing prey!

" Fear, doubt, thought, life itself, ere long
Merged in one feeling deep and strong.
Faded the world which I had known,
    A poor vain shadow, cold and waste,
In the warm present bliss alone
    Seemed I of actual life to taste.
Fond longings dimly understood,
The glow of passion's quickening blood,
And cherished fantasies which press

The young lip with a dream's caress,—
The heart's forecast and prophecy
Took form and life before my eye,
Seen in the glance which met my own,
Heard in the soft and pleading tone,
Felt in the arms around me cast,
And warm heart-pulses beating fast.
Ah! scarcely yet to God above
With deeper trust, with stronger love
Has prayerful saint his meek heart lent,
Or cloistered nun at twilight bent,
Than I, before a human shrine,
As mortal and as frail as mine,
With heart, and soul, and mind, and form,
Knelt madly to a fellow worm.

" Full soon, upon that dream of sin,
An awful light came bursting in.
The shrine was cold, at which I knelt ;
    The idol of that shrine was gone;
A humbled thing of shame and guilt,
    Outcast, and spurned and lone,
Wrapt in the shadows of my crime,
    With withering heart and burning brain,
    And tears that fell like fiery rain,
I passed a fearful time.

"There came a voice—it checked the tear—
    In heart and soul it wrought a change;—
My father's voice was in my ear;
    It whispered of revenge!
A new and fiercer feeling swept
    All lingering tenderness away;
And tiger passions, which had slept
    In childhood's better day,
Unknown, unfelt, arose at length
In all their own demoniac strength.

" A youthful warrior of the wild,
By words deceived, by smiles beguiled,
Of crime the cheated instrument,
Upon our fatal errands went.
    Through camp and town and wilderness
He tracked his victim; and, at last,
Just when the tide of hate had passed,
And milder thoughts came warm and fast,
Exulting, at my feet he cast
    The bloody token of success.

"Oh God ! with what an awful power
    I saw the buried past uprise,
And gather, in a single hour,
    Its ghost-like memories!

And then I felt—alas! too late—
That underneath the mask of hate,
That shame and guilt and wrong had thrown
O'er feelings which they might not own,
    The heart's wild love had known no change
And still, that deep and hidden love,
With its first fondness, wept above
    The victim of its own revenge!
There lay the fearful scalp, and there
The blood was on its pale brown hair!
I thought not of the victim's scorn,
    I thought not of his baleful guile,
My deadly wrong, my outcast name,
The characters of sin and shame
On heart and forehead drawn;
    I only saw that victim's smile—
The still, green places where we met—
The moonlit branches, dewy wet;
I only felt, I only heard
The greeting and the parting word—
The smile—the embrace—the tone, which made
An Eden of the forest shade.

" And oh, with what a loathing eye,
    With what a deadly hate, and deep,
I saw that Indian murderer lie
    Before me, in his drunken sleep!
What though for me the deed was done,
And words of mine had sped him on!
Yet when he murmured, as he slept.
    The horrors of that deed of blood,
The tide of utter madness swept
    O'er brain and bosom, like a flood.
And, father, with this hand of mine "—
    " Ha! what didst thou ?" the Jesuit cries,
Shuddering, as smitten with sudden pain,
    And shading, with one thin hand, his eyes,
With the other he makes the holy sign—
" I smote him as I would a worm;—
With heart as steeled—with nerves as firm:
    He never woke again ! "

" Woman of sin and blood and shame,
Speak—I would know that victim's name."

" Father," she gasped, " a chieftain, known
As Saco's Sachem—MOGG MEGONE ! "

Pale priest ! What proud and lofty dreams,
What keen desires, what cherished schemes,
What hopes, that time may not recall,
Are darkened by that chieftain's fall!
Was he not pledged, by cross and vow,

To lift the hatchet of his sire,
And, round his own, the Church's foe,
    To light the avenging fire?
Who now the Tarrantine shall wake,
For thine and for the Church's sake?
    Who summon to the scene
Of conquest and unsparing strife,
And vengeance dearer than his life,
    The fiery-souled Castine?*

Three backward steps the Jesuit takes—
His long, thin frame as ague shakes:
    And loathing hate is in his eye,
As from his lips these words of fear
Fall hoarsely on the maiden's ear—
    "The soul that sinneth shall surely die!"

She stands, as stands the stricken deer,
    Checked midway in the fearful chase,
When bursts, upon his eye and ear,
The gaunt, gray robber, baying near,
    Between him and his hiding-place;
While still behind, with yell and blow,
Sweeps, like a storm, the coming foe.
"Save me, O holy man!"—her cry
    Fills all the void, as if a tongue,
    Unseen, from rib and rafter hung,
Thrilling with mortal agony;
Her hands are clasping the Jesuit's knee,
    And her eye looks fearfully into his own;—
"Off, woman of sin?—nay, touch not me
    With those fingers of blood;—begone!"
With a gesture of horror, he spurns the form
That writhes at his feet like a trodden worm.

Ever thus the spirit must,
    Guilty in the sight of Heaven,
    With a keener woe be riven,
For its weak and sinful trust
In the strength of human dust;
    And its anguish thrill afresh
For each vain reliance given
    To the failing arm of flesh.

* The character of Ralle has probably never been correctly delineated. By his brethren of
the Romish Church, he has been nearly apotheosized. On the other hand, our Puritan his-
torians have represented him as a demon in human form. He was undoubtedly sincere in his
devotion to the interests of his church, and not overscrupulous as to the means of advancing
those interests. "The French," says the author of the History of Saco and Biddeford, "after
the peace of 1713, secretly promised to supply the Indians with arms and ammunition, if they
would renew hostilities. Their principal agent was the celebrated Ralle, the French Jesuit."—
p. 215.

Part III.

Ah, weary Priest!—with pale hands pressed
  On thy throbbing brow of pain,
Baffled in thy lifelong quest,
  Overworn with toiling vain,
How ill thy troubled musings fit
  The hold quiet of a breast
  With the Dove of Peace at rest,
Sweetly brooding over it!
Thoughts are thine which have no part
With the meek and pure of heart,
Undisturbed by outward things,
  Resting in the heavenly shade,
By the overspreading wings
  Of the Blessed Spirit made.
Thoughts of strife and hate and wrong
Sweep thy heated brain along—
Fading hopes, for whose success
  It were sin to breathe a prayer;—
Schemes which heaven may never bless—
  Fears which darken to despair.
Hoary priest! thy dream is done
Of a hundred red tribes won
  To the pale of Holy Church;
And the heretic o'erthrown,
And his name no longer known,
And thy weary brethren turning,
Joyful from their years of mourning,
  'Twixt the altar and the porch.

Hark! what sudden sound is heard
  In the wood and in the sky,
Shriller than the scream of bird—
  Than the trumpet's clang more high!
Every wolf-cave of the hills—
  Forest arch and mountain gorge,
  Rock and dell and river verge—
With an answering echo thrills.
Well does the Jesuit know that cry,
Which summons the Norridgewock to die,
And tells that the foe of his flock is nigh.
He listens, and hears the rangers come,
With loud hurrah, and jar of drum,
And hurrying feet (for the chase is hot),
And the short, sharp sound of rifle shot,
And taunt and menace—answered well
By the Indians' mocking cry and yell—
The bark of dogs—the squaw's mad scream—

The dash of paddles along the stream—
The whistle of shot as it cuts the leaves
Of the maples around the church's eaves—
And the gride of hatchets, fiercely thrown,
On wigwam-log and tree and stone.

Black with the grime of paint and dust,
    Spotted and streaked with human gore,
A grim and naked head is thrust
    Within the chapel door.
" Ha—Bomazeen!—In God's name say,
What mean these sounds of bloody fray ? "
Silent, the Indian points his hand
    To where across the echoing glen
Sweep Harmon's dreaded ranger-band,
    And Moulton with his men.
" Where are thy warriors, Bomazeen ?
Where are De Rouville * and Castine,
And where the braves of Sawga's queen ? "

" Let my father find the winter snow
Which the sun drank up long moons ago!
Under the falls of Tacconock,
The wolves are eating the Norridgewock;
Castine with his wives lies closely hid
Like a fox in the woods of Pemaquid!
On Sawga's banks the man of war
Sits in his wigwam like a squaw—
Squando has fled, and Mogg Megone,
Struck by the knife of Sagamore John,
Lies stiff and stark and cold as a stone."

Fearfully over the Jesuit's face,
Of a thousand thoughts, trace after trace,
Like swift cloud-shadows, each other chase.
One instant, his fingers grasp his knife,
For a last vain struggle for cherished life—
The next, he hurls the blade away,
And kneels at his altar's foot to pray;
Over his beads his fingers stray,
And he kisses the cross, and calls aloud
    On the Virgin and her Son;
For terrible thoughts his memory crowd
    Of evil seen and done—
Of scalps brought home by his savage flock
From Casco and Sawga and Sagadahock,
    In the Church's service won.
No shrift the gloomy savage brooks,

---

* Hertel de Rouville was an active and unsparing enemy of the English. He was the leader of the combined French and Indian forces which destroyed Deerfield, and massacred its inhabitants, in 1703. He was afterwards killed in the attack upon Haverhill. Tradition says that on examining his dead body, his head and face were found to be perfectly smooth without the slightest appearance of hair or beard.

As scowling on the priest he looks:
"Cowesass—cowesass—tawhich wessaseen?*
Let my father look upon Bomazeen—
My father's heart is the heart of a squaw,
But mine is so hard that it does not thaw:
Let my father ask his God to make
  A dance and a feast for a great sagamore,
When he paddles across the western lake
  With his dogs and his squaws to the spirit's shore.
Cowesass—cowesass—tawhich wessaseen?
Let my father die like Bomazeen!"

Through the chapel's narrow doors,
  And through each window in the walls,
Round the priest and warrior pours
  The deadly shower of English balls.
Low on his cross the Jesuit falls;
While at his side the Norridgewock,
With failing breath, essays to mock
And menace yet the hated foe—
Shakes his scalp-trophies to and fro
  Exultingly before their eyes—
Till, cleft and torn by shot and blow,
  Defiant still, he dies.

"So fare all eaters of the frog!
Death to the Babylonish dog!
  Down with the beast of Rome!"
With shouts like these, around the dead,
Unconscious on his bloody bed,
  The rangers crowding come.
Brave men! the dead priest cannot hear
The unfeeling taunt—the brutal jeer;—
Spurn—for he sees ye not—in wrath,
The symbol of your Saviour's death;—
  Tear from his death-grasp, in your zeal,
And trample, as a thing accursed,
The cross he cherished in the dust:
  The dead man cannot feel!

Brutal alike in deed and word,
  With callous heart and hand of strife,
How like a fiend may man be made,
Plying the foul and monstrous trade
  Whose harvest-field is human life,
Whose sickle is the reeking sword!
Quenching, with reckless hand, in blood,
Sparks kindled by the breath of God;
Urging the deathless soul, unshriven
  Of open guilt or secret sin,
Before the bar of that pure Heaven

* *Cowesass?—tawhich wessaseen?* Are you afraid?—why fear you?

The holy only enter in!
Oh! by the widow's sore distress,
The orphan's wailing wretchedness,
By Virtue struggling in the accursed
Embraces of polluting Lust,
By the fell discord of the Pit,
And the pained souls that people it,
And by the blessed peace which fills
    The Paradise of God forever,
Resting on all its holy hills,
    And flowing with its crystal river—
Let Christian hands no longer bear
    In triumph on his crimson car
    The foul and idol god of war;
No more the purple wreaths prepare
To bind amid his snaky hair;
Nor Christian bards his glories tell,
Nor Christian tongues his praises swell.

Through the gun-smoke wreathing white,
Glimpses on the soldiers' sight
A thing of human shape I ween,
For a moment only seen,
With its loose hair backward streaming,
And its eyeballs madly gleaming,
Shrieking, like a soul in pain,
    From the world of light and breath,
Hurrying to its place again,
    Spectre-like it vanisheth!

Wretched girl! one eye alone
Notes the way which thou hast gone.
That great Eye, which slumbers never,
Watching o'er a lost world ever,
Tracks thee over vale and mountain,
By the gushing forest-fountain,
Plucking from the vine its fruit,
Searching for the ground-nut's root,
Peering in the she wolf's den,
Wading through the marshy fen,
Where the sluggish water-snake
Basks beside the sunny brake,
Coiling in his slimy bed,
Smooth and cold against thy tread—
Purposeless, thy mazy way
Threading through the lingering day,
And at night securely sleeping
Where the dogwood's dews are weeping!
Still, though earth and man discard thee,
Doth thy heavenly Father guard thee—
He who spared the guilty Cain,
    Even when a brother's blood,
    Crying in the ear of God,

Gave the earth its primal stain—
He whose mercy ever liveth,
Who repenting guilt forgiveth,
And the broken heart receiveth;—
Wanderer of the wilderness,
    Haunted, guilty, crazed and wild,
He regardeth thy distress,
    And careth for his sinful child!

'Tis springtime on the eastern hills!
Like torrents gush the summer rills;
Through winter's moss and dry dead leaves
The bladed grass revives and lives,
Pushes the mouldering waste away,
And glimpses to the April day.
In kindly shower and sunshine bud
The branches of the dull gray wood;
Out from its sunned and sheltered nooks
The blue eye of the violet looks;
    The southwest wind is warmly blowing,
And odors from the springing grass,
The pine-tree and the sassafras,
    Are with it on its errands going.

A band is marching through the wood
Where rolls the Kennebec his flood—
The warriors of the wilderness,
Painted, and in their battle dress;
And with them one whose bearded cheek,
And white and wrinkled brow, bespeak
    A wanderer from the shores of France.
A few long locks of scattering snow
Beneath a battered morion flow,
And from the rivets of the vest
Which girds in steel his ample breast,
    The slanted sunbeams glance.
In the harsh outlines of his face
Passion and sin have left their trace;
Yet, save worn brow and thin gray hair,
No signs of weary age are there.
    His step is firm, his eye is keen,
Nor years in broil and battle spent,
Nor toil, nor wounds, nor pain have bent
    The lordly frame of old Castine.

No purpose now of strife and blood
    Urges the hoary veteran on:
The fire of conquest, and the mood
    Of chivalry have gone.

A mournful task is his—to lay
  Within the earth the bones of those
Who perished in that fearful day,
When Norridgewock became the prey
  Of all unsparing foes.
Sadly and still, dark thoughts between,
Of coming vengeance mused Castine,
Of the fallen chieftain Bomazeen,
Who bade for him the Norridgewocks
Dig up their buried tomahawks
  For firm defiance or swift attack;
And him whose friendship formed the tie
  Which held the stern self-exile back
From lapsing into savagery;
Whose garb and tone and kindly glance
  Recalled a younger, happier day,
  And prompted memory's fond essay,
  To bridge the mighty waste which lay
  Between his wild home and that gray,
Tall château of his native France,
Whose chapel bell, with far-heard din
Ushered his birth hour gayly in,
And counted with its solemn toll,
The masses for his father's soul.

Hark! from the foremost of the band
  Suddenly bursts the Indian yell;
For now on the very spot they stand
  Where the Norridgewocks fighting fell.
No wigwam smoke is curling there;
The very earth is scorched and bare:
And they pause and listen to catch a sound
  Of breathing life—but there comes not one,
Save the fox's bark and the rabbit's bound;
But here and there, on the blackened ground,
  White bones are glistening in the sun.
And where the house of prayer arose,
And the holy hymn, at daylight's close,
And the aged priest stood up to bless
The children of the wilderness,
There is naught save ashes sodden and dank;
  And the birchen boats of the Norridgewock,
  Tethered to tree and stump and rock,
Rotting along the river bank!
Blessed Mary!—who is she
Leaning against that maple tree?
The sun upon her face burns hot,
But the fixed eyelid moveth not;
The squirrel's chirp is shrill and clear
From the dry bough above her ear;
Dashing from rock and root its spray,
  Close at her feet the river rushes;

The black-bird's wing against her brushes,
And sweetly through the hazel bushes
    The robin's mellow music gushes ;—
God save her ! will she sleep alway ?

Castine hath bent him over the sleeper :
    " Wake, daughter—wake ! "—but she stirs no limb :
    The eye that looks on him is fixed and dim ;
And the sleep she is sleeping shall be no deeper,
    Until the angel's oath is said,
And the final blast of the trump goes forth
To the graves of the sea and the graves of earth.
    RUTH BONYTHON IS DEAD !

THE BRIDAL OF PENNACOOK.*

WE had been wandering for many days
Through the rough northern country. We had seen
The sunset, with its bars of purple cloud,
Like a new heaven, shine upward from the lake
Of Winnepiseogee ; and had felt
The sunrise breezes, midst the leafy aisles
Which stoop their summer beauty to the lips
Of the bright waters. We had checked our steeds,
Silent with wonder, where the mountain wall
Is piled to heaven ; and, through the narrow rift
Of the vast rocks, against whose rugged feet
Beats the mad torrent with perpetual roar,
Where noonday is as twilight, and the wind
Comes burdened with the everlasting moan
Of forests and of far-off waterfalls,
We had looked upward where the summer sky,
Tasselled with clouds light-woven by the sun,
Sprung its blue arch above the abutting crags
O'er-roofing the vast portal of the land
Beyond the wall of mountains. We had passed
The high source of the Saco : and, bewildered
In the dwarf spruce-belts of the Crystal Hills,
Had heard above us, like a voice in the cloud,

---

* Winnepurkit, otherwise called George, Sachem of Saugus married a daughter of Passacon-away, the great Pennacook chieftain, in 1662. The wedding took place at Pennacook (now Concord, N. H.), and the ceremonies closed with a great feast. According to the usages of the chiefs, Passaconaway ordered a select number of his men to accompany the newly-married couple to the dwelling of the husband, where in turn there was another great feast. Some time after, the wife of Winnepurkit expressing a desire to visit her father's house, was permitted to go accompanied by a brave escort of her husband's chief men. But when she wished to return, her father sent a messenger to Saugus, informing her husband, and asking him to come and take her away. He returned for answer that he had escorted his wife to her father's house in a style that became a chief, and that now if she wished to return, her father must send her back in the same way. This Passaconaway refused to do, and it is said that here terminated the con-nection of his daughter with the Saugus chief.—*Vide Morton's New Canaan.*

The horn of Fabyan sounding ; and atop
Of old Agioochook had seen the mountains
Piled to the northward, shagged with wood, and thick
As meadow mole hills—the far sea of Casco,
A white gleam on the horizon of the east ;
Fair lakes, embosomed in the woods and hills ;
Moosehillock's mountain range, and Kearsarge
Lifting his Titan forehead to the sun !

And we had rested underneath the oaks
Shadowing the bank, whose grassy spires are shaken
By the perpetual beating of the falls
Of the wild Ammonoosuc.   We had tracked
The winding Pemigewasset, overhung
By beechen shadows, whitening down its rocks,
Or lazily gliding through its intervals,
From waving rye-fields sending up the gleam
Of sunlit waters.   We had seen the moon
Rising behind Umbagog's eastern pines
Like a great Indian camp-fire ; and its beams
At midnight spanning with a bridge of silver
The Merrimack by Uncanoonuc's falls.

There were five souls of us whom travel's chance
Had thrown together in these wild north hills :—
A city lawyer, for a month escaping
From his dull office, where the weary eye
Saw only hot brick walls and close thronged streets—
Briefless as yet, but with an eye to see
Life's sunniest side, and with a heart to take
Its chances all as God-sends ; and his brother,
Pale from long pulpit studies, yet retaining
The warmth and freshness of a genial heart,
Whose mirror of the beautiful and true,
In Man and Nature, was as yet undimmed
By dust of theologic strife, or breath
Of sect, or cobwebs of scholastic lore ;
Like a clear crystal calm of water, taking
The hue and image of o'erleaning flowers,
Sweet human faces, white clouds of the noon,
Slant starlight glimpses through the dewy leaves,
And tenderest moonrise.   'Twas, in truth, a study,
To mark his spirit, alternating between
A decent and professional gravity
And an irreverent mirthfulness, which often
Laughed in the face of his divinity,
Plucked off the sacred ephod, quite unshrined
The oracle, and for the pattern priest
Left us the man.   A shrewd, sagacious merchant,
To whom the soiled sheet found in Crawford's inn,
Giving the latest news of city stocks
And sales of cotton had a deeper meaning
Than the great presence of the awful mountains

Glorified by the sunset ;—and his daughter,
A delicate flower on whom had blown too long
Those evil winds, which, sweeping from the ice
And winnowing the fogs of Labrador,
Shed their cold blight round Massachusetts' bay,
With the same breath which stirs Spring's opening leaves
And lifts her half-formed flower-bell on its stem,
Poisoning our seaside atmosphere.

                                        It chanced
That as we turned upon our homeward way,
A drear northeastern storm came howling up
The valley of the Saco ; and that girl
Who had stood with us upon Mount Washington,
Her brown locks ruffled by the wind which whirled
In gusts around its sharp cold pinnacle,
Who had joined our gay trout-fishing in the streams
Which lave that giant's feet ; whose laugh was heard
Like a bird's carol on the sunrise breeze
Which swelled our sail amidst the lake's green islands,
Shrank from its harsh, chill breath, and visibly drooped
Like a flower in the frost.   So, in that quiet inn
Which looks from Conway on the mountains piled
Heavily against the horizon of the north,
Like summer thunderclouds, we made our home :
And while the mist hung over dripping hills,
And the cold wind-driven raindrops, all day long
Beat their sad music upon roof and pane,
We strove to cheer our gentle invalid.
The lawyer in the pauses of the storm
Went angling down the Saco, and, returning,
Recounted his adventures and mishaps ;
Gave us the history of his scaly clients,
Mingling with ludicrous yet apt citations
Of barbarous law Latin, passages
From Izaak Walton's Angler, sweet and fresh
As the flower-skirted streams of Staffordshire
Where, under aged trees, the southwest wind
Of soft June mornings fanned the thin, white hair
Of the sage fisher.   And, if truth be told,
Our youthful candidate forsook his sermons,
His commentaries, articles and creeds
For the fair page of human loveliness—
The missal of young hearts, whose sacred text
Is music, its illumining sweet smiles.
He sang the songs she loved ; and in his low,
Deep earnest voice, recited many a page
Of poetry—the holiest, tenderest lines
Of the sad bard of Olney—the sweet songs,
Simple and beautiful as Truth and Nature,
Of him whose whitened locks on Rydal Mount
Are lifted yet by morning breezes blowing
From the green hills, immortal in his lays.

And for myself, obedient to her wish,
I searched our landlord's proffered library :
A well-thumbed Bunyan, with its nice wood pictures
Of scaly fiends and angels not unlike them—
Watts' unmelodious psalms—Astrology's
Last home, a musty file of Almanacs,
And an old chronicle of border wars
And Indian history.   And, as I read
A story of the marriage of the Chief
Of Saugus to the dusky Weetamoo,
Daughter of Passaconaway, who dwelt
In the old time upon Merrimack,
Our fair one, in the playful exercise
Of her prerogative—the right divine
Of youth and beauty,—bade us versify
The legend, and with ready pencil sketched
Its plan and outlines, laughingly assigning
To each his part, and barring our excuses
With absolute will.   So, like the cavaliers
Whose voices still are heard in the Romance
Of silver-tongued Boccaccio, on the banks
Of Arno, with soft tales of love beguiling
The ear of languid beauty, plague-exiled
From stately Florence, we rehearsed our rhymes
To their fair auditor, and shared by turns
Her kind approval and her playful censure.

It may be that these fragments owe alone
To the fair setting of their circumstances—
The associations of time, scene and audience—
Their place amid the pictures which fill up
The chambers of my memory.   Yet I trust
That some, who sigh, while wandering in thought,
Pilgrims of Romance o'er the olden world,
That our broad land—our sea-like lakes, and mountains
Piled to the clouds,—our rivers overhung
By forests which have known no other change
For ages, than the budding and the fall
Of leaves—our valleys lovelier than those
Which the old poets sang of—should but figure
On the apocryphal chart of speculation
As pastures, wood-lots, mill-sites, with the privileges,
Rights and appurtenances, which make up
A Yankee Paradise—unsung, unknown,
To beautiful tradition ; even their names,
Whose melody yet lingers like the last
Vibration of the red man's requiem,
Exchanged for syllables significant
Of cotton-mill and rail-car,—will look kindly
Upon this effort to call up the ghost
Of our dim Past, and listen with pleased ear
To the responses of the questioned Shade :

I.—THE MERRIMACK.

OH, child of that white-crested mountain whose springs
Gush forth in the shade of the cliff-eagle's wings,
Down whose slopes to the lowlands thy wild waters shine,
Leaping gray walls of rock, flashing through the dwarf pine.

From that cloud-curtained cradle so cold and so lone,
From the arms of that wintry-locked mother of stone,
By hills hung with forests, through vales wide and free,
Thy mountain-born brightness glanced down to the sea!

No bridge arched thy waters save that where the trees
Stretched their long arms above thee and kissed in the breeze:
No sound save the lapse of the waves on thy shores,
The plunging of otters, the light dip of oars.

Green-tufted, oak-shaded, by Amoskeag's fall
Thy twin Uncanoonucs rose stately and tall,
Thy Nashua meadows lay green and unshorn,
And the hills of Pentucket were tasselled with corn.

But thy Pennacook valley was fairer than these,
And greener its grasses and taller its trees,
Ere the sound of an axe in the forest had rung,
Or the mower his scythe in the meadows had swung.

In their sheltered repose looking out from the wood
The bark-builded wigwams of Pennacook stood,
There glided the corn-dance—the Council fire shone,
And against the red war-post the hatchet was thrown.

There the old smoked in silence their pipes, and the young
To the pike and the white perch their baited lines flung;
There the boy shaped his arrows, and there the shy maid
Wove her many-hued baskets and bright wampum braid.

Oh, Stream of the Mountains! if answer of thine
Could rise from thy waters to question of mine,
Methinks through the din of thy thronged banks a moan
Of sorrow would swell for the days which have gone.

Not for thee the dull jar of the loom and the wheel,
The gliding of shuttles, the ringing of steel;
But that old voice of waters, of bird and of breeze,
The dip of the wild-fowl, the rustling of trees!

II.—THE BASHABA.*

LIFT we the twilight curtains of the Past,
And turning from familiar sight and sound

---

* This was the name which the Indians of New England gave to two or three of their principal chiefs, to whom all their inferior sagamores acknowledged allegiance. Passaconaway seems to have been one of these chiefs. His residence was at Pennacook.—*Mass. Hist. Coll.,*

Sadly and full of reverence let us cast
  A glance upon tradition's shadowy ground,
Led by the few pale lights, which, glimmering round
  That dim, strange land of Eld, seem dying fast;
And that which history gives not to the eye,
The faded coloring of Time's tapestry,
Let fancy, with her dream-dipped brush supply.

Roof of bark and walls of pine,
Through whose chinks the sunbeams shine,
Tracing many a golden line
  On the ample floor within;

Where upon that earth-floor stark,
Lay the gaudy mats of bark,
With the bear's hide, rough and dark,
  And the red-deer's skin.

Window-tracery, small and slight,
Woven of the willow white,
Lent a dimly-checkered light,
  And the night-stars glimmered down,
Where the lodge-fire's heavy smoke,
Slowly through an opening broke,
In the low roof, ribbed with oak,
  Sheathed with hemlock brown.

Gloomed behind the changeless shade,
By the solemn pine-wood made;
Through the rugged palisade,
  In the open foreground planted,
Glimpses came of rowers rowing,
Stir of leaves and wild flowers blowing,
Steel-like gleams of water flowing,
  In the sunlight slanted.

Here the mighty Bashaba,
Held his long-unquestioned sway,
From the White Hills, far away,
  To the great sea's sounding shore;
Chief of chiefs, his regal word
All the river Sachems heard,
At his call the war-dance stirred,
  Or was still once more.

There his spoils of chase and war,
Jaw of wolf and black bear's paw,

vol. iii., pp. 21, 22. "He was regarded," says Hubbard, "as a great sorcerer, and his fame was widely spread. It was said of him that he could cause a green leaf to grow in winter, trees to dance, water to burn, etc. He was, undoubtedly, one of those shrewd and powerful men whose achievements are always regarded by a barbarous people as the result of supernatural aid. The Indians gave to such the names of Powahs or Panisees."

  "The Panisees are men of great courage and wisdom, and to these the Devill appeareth more familiarly than to others."—*Winslow's Relation.*

Panther's skin and eagle's claw,
 Lay beside his axe and bow ;
And, adown the roof-pole hung,
Loosely on a snake-skin strung,
In the smoke his scalp-locks swung
 Grimly to and fro.

Nightly down the river going,
Swifter was the hunter's rowing,
When he saw that lodge-fire glowing
 O'er the waters still and red ;
And the squaw's dark eye burned brighter,
And she drew her blanket tighter,
As, with quicker step and lighter,
 From that door she fled.

For that chief had magic skill,
And a Panisee's dark will,
Over powers of good and ill,
 Powers which bless and powers which ban—
Wizard lord of Pennacook,
Chiefs upon their war-path shook,
When they met the steady look
 Of that wise dark man.

Tales of him the gray squaw told,
When the winter night-wind cold
Pierced her blanket's thickest fold,
 And the fire burned low and small,
Till the very child a-bed,
Drew its bear-skin over head,
Shrinking from the pale lights shed
 On the trembling wall.

All the subtle spirits hiding
Under earth or wave, abiding
In the caverned rock, or riding
 Misty clouds or morning breeze ;
Every dark intelligence,
Secret soul, and influence
Of all things which outward sense
 Feels, or hears or sees,—

These the wizard's skill confessed,
At his bidding banned or blessed,
Stormful woke or lulled to rest
 Wind and cloud, and fire and flood ;
Burned for him the drifted snow,
Bade through ice fresh lilies blow,
And the leaves of summer grow
 Over winter's wood !

Not untrue that tale of old !
Now, as then, the wise and bold

All the powers of Nature hold
  Subject to their kingly will ;
From the wondering crowds ashore,
Treading life's wild waters o'er,
As upon a marble floor,
  Moves the strong man still.

Still, to such, life's elements
With their sterner laws dispense,
And the chain of consequence,
  Broken in their pathway lies ;
Time and change their vassals making,
Flowers from icy pillows waking,
Tresses of the sunrise shaking
  Over midnight skies.

Still, to earnest souls, the sun
Rests on towered Gibeon,
And the moon of Ajalon
  Lights the battle-grounds of life ;
To his aid the strong reverses,
Hidden powers and giant forces,
And the high stars in their courses
  Mingle in his strife !

III.—THE DAUGHTER.

THE soot-black brows of men—the yell
  Of women thronging round the bed—
The tinkling charm of ring and shell—
  The Powah whispering o'er the dead !—
All these the Sachem's home had known,
  When, on her journey long and wild
To the dim World of Souls, alone,
In her young beauty passed the mother of his child.

Three bow-shots from the Sachem's dwelling
  They laid her in the walnut shade,
Where a green hillock gently swelling
  Her fitting mound of burial made.
There trailed the vine in Summer hours—
  The tree-perched squirrel dropped his shell—
On velvet moss and pale-hued flowers,
Woven with leaf and spray, the softened sunshine fell !

The Indian's heart is hard and cold—
  It closes darkly o'er its care,
And, formed in Nature's sternest mold,
  Is slow to feel, and strong to bear.
The war-paint on the Sachem's face,
  Unwet with tears, shone fierce and red,
And, still in battle or in chase,
Dry leaf and snow-rime crisped beneath his foremost tread.

Yet, when her name was heard no more,
   And when the robe her mother gave,
And small, light moccasin she wore,
   Had slowly wasted on her grave,
Unmarked of him the dark maids sped
   Their sunset dance and moonlit play ;
No other shared his lonely bed,
No other fair young head upon his bosom lay.

A lone, stern man. Yet, as sometimes
   The tempest-smitten tree receives
From one small root the sap which climbs
   Its topmost spray and crowning leaves,
So from his child the Sachem drew
   A life of Love and Hope, and felt
His cold and rugged nature through
The softness and the warmth of her young being melt.

A laugh which in the woodland rang
   Bemocking April's gladdest bird—
A light and graceful form which sprang
   To meet him when his step was heard—
Eyes by his lodge-fire flashing dark,
   Small fingers stringing bead and shell
Or weaving mats of bright-hued bark,—
With these the household-god* had graced his wigwam wall.

Child of the forest !—strong and free,
   Slight-robed, with loosely flowing hair,
She swam the lake or climbed the tree,
   Or struck the flying bird in air.
O'er the heaped drifts of Winter's moon
   Her snow-shoes tracked the hunter's way ;
And dazzling in the Summer noon
The blade of her light oar threw off its shower of spray !

Unknown to her the rigid rule,
   The dull restraint, the chiding frown,
The weary torture of the school,
   The taming of wild nature down.
Her only lore, the legends told
   Around the hunter's fire at night ;
Stars rose and set, and seasons rolled,
Flowers bloomed and snowflakes fell, unquestioned in her sight.

Unknown to her the subtle skill
   With which the artist-eye can trace
In rock and tree and lake and hill
   The outlines of divinest grace ;
Unknown the fine soul's keen unrest

---

* " The Indians," says Roger Williams, " have a god whom they call Wetuomanit, who presides over the household."

Which sees, admires, yet yearns alway ;
Too closely on her mother's breast
To note her smiles of love the child of Nature lay !

It is enough for such to be
    Of common, natural things a part,
To feel with bird and stream and tree
    The pulses of the same great heart ;
But we, from Nature long exiled
    In our cold homes of Art and Thought,
Grieve like the stranger-tended child,
Which seeks its mother's arms, and sees but feels them not

The garden rose may richly bloom
    In cultured soil and genial air,
To cloud the light of Fashion's room
    Or droop in Beauty's midnight hair,
In lonelier grace, to sun and dew
    The sweet-briar on the hillside shows
Its single leaf and fainter hue,
Untrained and wildly free, yet still a sister rose !

Thus o'er the heart of Weetamoo
    Their mingling shades of joy and ill
The instincts of her nature threw,—
    The savage was a woman still.
Midst outlines dim of maiden schemes,
    Heart-colored prophecies of life,
Rose on the ground of her young dreams
The light of a new home—the lover and the wife !

IV.—THE WEDDING.

COOL and dark fell the Autumn night,
But the Bashaba's wigwam glowed with light,
For down from its roof by green withes hung
Flaring and smoking the pine-knots swung.

And along the river great wood fires
Shot into the night their long red spires,
Showing behind the tall, dark wood
Flashing before on the sweeping flood.

In the changeful wind, with shimmer and shade,
Now high, now low, that fire-light played,
On tree-leaves wet with evening dews,
On gliding water and still canoes.

The trapper that night on Turee's brook
And the weary fisher on Contoocook
Saw over the marshes and through the pine,
And down on the river the dance-lights shine.

For the Saugus Sachem had come to woo
The Bashaba's daughter Weetamoo,
And laid at her father's feet that night
His softest furs and wampum white.

From the Crystal Hills to the far South East
The river Sagamores came to the feast ;
And chiefs whose homes the sea-winds shook,
Sat down on the mats of Pennacook.

They came from Sunapee's shore of rock,
From the snowy sources of Snooganock,
And from rough Coös whose thick woods shake
Their pine-cones in Umbagog lake.

From Ammonoosuck's mountain pass
Wild as his home came Chepewass ;
And the Keenomps of the hills which throw
Their shade on the smile of Manito.

With pipes of peace and bows unstrung,
Glowing with paint came old and young,
In wampum and furs and feathers arrayed
To the dance and feast the Bashaba made.

Bird of the air and beast of the field,
All which the woods and waters yield
On dishes of birch and hemlock piled
Garnished and graced that banquet wild.

Steaks of the brown bear fat and large
From the rocky slopes of the Kearsarge ;
Delicate trout from Babboosuck brook,
And salmon spear'd in the Contoocook ;

Squirrels which fed where nuts fell thick
In the gravelly bed of the Otternic,
And small wild hens in reed-snares caught
From the banks of Sondagardee brought ;

Pike and perch from the Suncook taken,
Nuts from the trees of the Black Hills shaken,
Cramberries picked in the Squamscot bog,
And grapes from the vines of Piscataquog :

And, drawn from that great stone vase which stands
In the river scooped by a spirit's hands,*
Garnished with spoons of shell and horn,
Stood the birchen dishes of smoking corn.

* There are rocks in the River at the Falls of Amoskeag, in the cavities of which, tradition
says, the Indians formerly stored and concealed their corn.

Thus bird of the air and beast of the field,
All which the woods and the waters yield,
Furnished in that olden day
The bridal feast of the Bashaba.

And merrily when that feast was done
On the fire-lit green the dance begun,
With squaws' shrill stave, and deeper hum
Of old men beating the Indian drum.

Painted and plumed, with scalp locks flowing,
And red arms tossing and black eyes glowing,
Now in the light and now in the shade
Around the fires the dancers played.

The step was quicker, the song more shrill,
And the beat of the small drums louder still
Whenever within the circle drew
The Saugus Sachem and Weetamoo.

The moons of forty winters had shed
Their snow upon that chieftain's head,
And toil and care, and battle's chance
Had seamed his hard dark countenance.

A fawn beside the bison grim—
Why turns the bride's fond eye on him,
In whose cold look is naught beside
The triumph of a sullen pride?

Ask why the graceful grape entwines
The rough oak with her arm of vines ;
And why the gray rock's rugged cheek
The soft lips of the mosses seek :

Why, with wise instinct, Nature seems
To harmonize her wide extremes,
Linking the stronger with the weak,
The haughty with the soft and meek !

V.—THE NEW HOME.

A WILD and broken landscape, spiked with firs,
  Roughening the bleak horizon's northern edge,
Steep, cavernous hillside, where black hemlock spurs
  And sharp, gray splinters of the wind-swept ledge
Pierced the thin-glaz'd ice, or bristling rose,
Where the cold rim of the sky sunk down upon the snows.

And eastward cold, wide marshes stretched away,
  Dull, dreary flats without a bush or tree,
O'er-crossed by icy creeks, where twice a day
  Gurgled the waters of the moon-struck sea ;

And faint with distance came the stifled roar,
The melancholy lapse of waves on that low shore.

No cheerful village with its mingling smokes,
  No laugh of children wrestling in the snow,
No camp-fire blazing through the hillside oaks,
  No fishers kneeling on the ice below ;
Yet midst all desolate things of sound and view,
Through the long winter moons smiled dark-eyed Weetamoo.

Her heart had found a home ; and freshly all
  Its beautiful affections overgrew
Their rugged prop. As o'er some granite wall
  Soft vine leaves open to the moistening dew
And warm bright sun, the love of that young wife
Found on a hard cold breast the dew and warmth of life.

The steep bleak hills, the melancholy shore,
  The long dead level of the marsh between,
A coloring of unreal beauty wore
  Through the soft golden mist of young love seen,
For o'er those hills and from that dreary plain,
Nightly she welcomed home her hunter chief again.

No warmth of heart, no passionate burst of feeling
  Repaid her welcoming smile, and parting kiss,
No fond and playful dalliance half concealing,
  Under the guise of mirth, its tenderness ;
But, in their stead, the warrior's settled pride,
And vanity's pleased smile with homage satisfied.

Enough for Weetamoo, that she alone
  Sat on his mat and slumbered at his side ;
That he whose fame to her young ear had flown,
  Now looked upon her proudly as his bride ;
That he whose name the Mohawk trembling heard
Vouchsafed to her at times a kindly look or word.

For she has learned the maxims of her race,
  Which teach the woman to become a slave
And feel herself the pardonless disgrace
  Of love's fond weakness in the wise and brave—
The scandal and the shame which they incur,
Who give to woman all which man requires of her.

She passed the winter moons. The sun at last
  Broke link by link the frost chain of the rills,
And the warm breathings of the southwest passed
  Over the hoar rime of the Saugus hills,
The gray and desolate marsh grew green once more,
And the birch-tree's tremulous shade fell round the
    Sachem's door,

Then from far Pennacook swift runners came,
  With gift and greeting for the Saugus chief ;
Beseeching him in the great Sachem's name,
  That, with the coming of the flower and leaf,
The song of birds, the warm breeze and the rain,
Young Weetamoo might greet her lonely sire again.

And Winnepurkit called his chiefs together,
  And a grave council in his wigwam met,
Solemn and brief in words, considering whether
  The rigid rules of forest etiquette
Permitted Weetamoo once more to look
Upon her father's face and green-banked Pennacook.

With interludes of pipe-smoke and strong water,
  The forest sages pondered, and at length,
Concluded in a body to escort her
  Up to her father's home of pride and strength,
Impressing thus on Pennacook a sense
Of Winnepurkit's power and regal consequence.

So through old woods which Aukeetamit's * hand,
  A soft and many-shaded greenness lent,
Over high breezy hills, and meadow land
  Yellow with flowers, the wild procession went,
Till rolling down its wooded banks between,
A broad, clear, mountain stream, the Merrimack was seen.

The hunter leaning on his bow undrawn—
  The fisher lounging on the pebbled shores,
Squaws in the clearing dropping the seed-corn,
  Young children peering through the wigwam doors,
Saw with delight, surrounded by her train
Of painted Saugus braves, their Weetamoo again.

VI.—AT PENNACOOK.

THE hills are dearest which our childish feet
Have climbed the earliest ; and the streams most sweet,
Are ever those at which our young lips drank,
Stooped to their waters o'er the grassy bank :

Midst the cold dreary sea-watch, Home's hearth-light
Shines round the helmsman plunging through the night ;
And still, with inward eye, the traveller sees
In close, dark, stranger streets his native trees.

The homesick dreamer's brow is nightly fanned
By breezes whispering of his native land,
And, on the stranger's dim and dying eye,
The soft, sweet pictures of his childhood lie !

* The Spring God.—See Roger Williams's *Key*, etc.

Joy then for Weetamoo, to sit once more
A child upon her father's wigwam floor !
Once more with her old fondness to beguile
From his cold eye the strange light of a smile.

The long bright days of Summer swiftly passed,
The dry leaves whirled in Autumn's rising blast,
And evening cloud and whitening sunrise rime
Told of the coming of the winter time.

But vainly looked, the while, young Weetamoo,
Down the dark river for her chief's canoe ;
No dusky messenger from Saugus brought
The grateful tidings which the young wife sought.

At length a runner, from her father sent
To Winnepurkit's sea-cooled wigwam went :
" Eagle of Saugus,—in the woods the dove,
Mourns for the shelter of thy wings of love."

But the dark chief of Saugus turned aside
In the grim anger of hard-hearted pride ;
" I bore her as became a chieftain's daughter,
Up to her home beside the gliding water.

" If now no more a mat for her is found
Of all which line her father's wigwam round,
Let Pennacook call out his warrior train
And send her back with wampum gifts again."

The baffled runner turned upon his track,
Bearing the words of Winnepurkit back.
" Dog of the Marsh," cried Pennacook, " no more
Shall child of mine sit on his wigwam floor.

" Go—let him seek some meaner squaw to spread
The stolen bear-skin of his beggar's bed :
Son of a fish-hawk !—let him dig his clams
For some vile daughter of the Agawams,

" Or coward Nipmucks !—may his scalp dry black
In Mohawk smoke, before I send her back."
He shook his clenched hand toward the ocean wave,
While hoarse assent his listening council gave.

Alas poor bride !—can thy grim sire impart
His iron hardness to thy woman's heart ?
Or cold self-torturing pride like his atone
For love denied and life's warm beauty flown ?

On Autumn's gray and mournful grave the snow
Hung its white wreaths ; with stifled voice and low

The river crept, by one vast bridge o'ercrossed,
Built by the hoar-locked artisan of Frost.

And many a Moon in beauty newly born
Pierced the red sunset with her silver horn,
Or, from the east across her azure field,
Rolled the wide brightness of her full-orbed shield.

Yet Winnepurkit came not—on the mat
Of the scorned wife her dusky rival sat,
And he, the while, in Western woods afar—
Urged the long chase, or trod the path of war.

Dry up thy tears, young daughter of a chief!
Waste not on him the sacredness of grief;
Be the fierce spirit of thy sire thine own,
His lips of scorning, and his heart of stone.

What heeds the warrior of a hundred fights,
The storm-worn watcher through long hunting nights,
Cold, crafty, proud, of woman's weak distress,
Her home-bound grief and pining loneliness?

VII.—THE DEPARTURE.

THE wild March rains had fallen fast and long
The snowy mountains of the North among,
Making each vale a water-course—each hill
Bright with the cascade of some new made rill.

Gnawed by the sunbeams, softened by the rain,
Heaved underneath by the swollen current's strain,
The ice-bridge yielded, and the Merrimack
Bore the huge ruin crashing down its track.

On that strong turbid water, a small boat
Guided by one weak hand was seen to float,
Evil the fate which loosed it from the shore,
Too early voyager with too frail an oar!

Down the vexed center of that rushing tide,
The thick huge ice-blocks threatening either side,
The foam-white rocks of Amoskeag in view,
With arrowy swiftness sped that light canoe.

The trapper, moistening his moose's meat
On the wet bank by Uncanoonuc's feet,
Saw the swift boat flash down the troubled stream—
Slept he, or waked he?—was it truth or dream?

The straining eye bent fearfully before,
The small hand clenching on the useless oar,
The bead-wrought blanket trailing o'er the water—
He knew them all—woe for the Sachem's daughter!

Sick and aweary of her lonely life,
Heedless of peril the still faithful wife
Had left her mother's grave, her father's door,
To seek the wigwam of her chief once more.

Down the white rapids like a sear leaf whirled,
On the sharp rocks and piled up ices hurled,
Empty and broken, circled the canoe
In the vexed pool below—but, where was Weetamoo?

VIII.—SONG OF INDIAN WOMEN.

THE Dark eye has left us,
 The spring-bird has flown,
 On the pathway of spirits
  She wanders alone.
The song of the wood-dove has died on our shore
Mat wonck kunna-monee! *—we hear it no more!

Oh, dark water Spirit!
 We cast on thy wave
 These firs which may never
  Hang over her grave ;
Bear down to the lost one the robes that she wore,
Mat wonck kunna-monee!—We see her no more!

Of the strange land she walks in
 No Powah has told :
 It may burn with the sunshine,
  Or freeze with the cold.
Let us give to our lost one the robes that she wore,
Mat wonck kunna-monee!—We see her no more!

The path she is treading
 Shall soon be our own ;
 Each gliding in shadow
  Unseen and alone !—
In vain shall we call on the souls gone before—
Mat wonck kunna-monee!—They hear us no more!

Oh mighty Sowanna ! †
 Thy gateways unfold,
 From thy wigwam of sunset
  Lift curtains of gold !
Take home the poor Spirit whose journey is o'er
Mat wonck kunna-monee!—We see her no more!

So sang the Children of the Leaves beside
The broad, dark river's coldly-flowing tide,

---

* " Mat wonck kunna-monee."   We shall see thee or her no more.—*Vide* Roger Williams's *Key to the Indian Language*.
 † 'The Great South West God."—See Roger Williams's *Observations*, etc.

Now low, now harsh, with sob-like pause and swell
On the high wind their voices rose and fell.
Nature's wild music—sounds of wind-swept trees,
The scream of birds, the wailing of the breeze,
The roar of waters, steady, deep and strong,
Mingled and murmured in that farewell song.

LEGENDARY.

THE MERRIMACK.

[" The Indians speak of a beautiful river, far to the South, which they call Merrimack."—
SIEUR DE MONTS, 1604.]

STREAM of my fathers ! sweetly still
The sunset rays thy valley fill ;
Poured slantwise down the long defile,
Wave, wood, and spire beneath them smile.
I see the winding Powow fold
The green hill in its belt of gold,
And following down its wavy line,
Its sparkling waters blend with thine.
There's not a tree upon thy side,
Nor rock, which thy returning tide
As yet hath left abrupt and stark
Above thy evening water-mark ;
No calm cove with its rocky hem,
No isle whose emerald swells begem
Thy broad, smooth current; not a sail
Bowed to the freshening ocean gale ;
No small boat with its busy oars,
Nor gray wall sloping to thy shores ;
Nor farmhouse with its maple shade,
Or rigid poplar colonnade,
But lies distinct and full in sight,
Beneath this gush of sunset light.
Centuries ago, that harbor-bar,
Stretching its length of foam afar,
And Salisbury's beach of shining sand,
And yonder island's wave-smoothed strand,
Saw the adventurer's tiny sail
Flit, stooping from the eastern gale ; *
And o'er these woods and waters broke
The cheer from Britain's hearts of oak,
As brightly on the voyager's eye,
Weary of forest, sea, and sky,
Breaking the dull continuous wood,
The Merrimack rolled down his flood ;
Mingling that clear pellucid brook,
Which channels vast Agioochook
When springtime's sun and shower unlock
The frozen fountains of the rock,
And more abundant waters given
From that pure lake, " The Smile of Heaven," †
Tributes from vale and mountain side—
With ocean's dark, eternal tide !

On yonder rocky cape, which braves
The stormy challenge of the waves,

* The celebrated Captain Smith, after resigning the government of the colony in Virginia, in his capacity of " Admiral of New England," made a careful survey of the coast from Penobscot to Cape Cod, in the summer of 1614.
† Lake Winnipiseogee—*The Smile of the Great Spirit*—the source of one of the branches of the Merrimack.

Midst tangled vine and dwarfish
  wood,
The hardy Anglo-Saxon stood,
Planting upon the topmost crag
The staff of England's battle-flag ;
And, while from out its heavy
  fold
Saint George's crimson cross un-
  rolled,
Midst roll of drum and trumpet
  blare,
And weapons brandishing in air,
He gave to that lone promontory
The sweetest name in all his
  story ; *
Of her, the flower of Islam's
  daughters,
Whose harems look on Stamboul's
  waters—
Who, when the chance of war
  had bound
The Moslem chain his limbs
  around,
Wreathed o'er with silk that iron
  chain,
Soothed with her smiles his hours
  of pain,
And fondly to her youthful slave
A dearer gift than freedom gave.

But look !—the yellow light no
  more
Streams down on wave and ver-
  dant shore ;
And clearly on the calm air swells
The twilight voice of distant bells.
From Ocean's bosom, white and
  thin
The mists come slowly rolling in ;
Hills, woods, the river's rocky
  rim,
Amidst the sea-like vapor swim,
While yonder lonely coast-light set
Within its wave-washed minaret,
Half quenched, a beamless star
  and pale,
Shines dimly through its cloudy
  veil !

Home of my fathers !—I have
  stood

Where Hudson rolled his lordly
  flood :
Seen sunrise rest and sunset fade
Along his frowning Palisade ;
Looked down the Appalachian
  peak
On Juniata's silver streak ;
Have seen along his valley gleam
The Mohawk's softly winding
  stream ;
The level light of sunset shine
Through broad Potomac's hem of
  pine ;
And autumn's rainbow-tinted
  banner
Hang lightly o'er the Susque-
  hanna ;
Yet, wheresoe'er his step might
  be,
Thy wandering child looked back
  to thee !
Heard in his dreams thy river's
  sound
Of murmuring on its pebbly
  bound,
The unforgotten swell and roar
Of waves on thy familiar shore ;
And saw, amidst the curtained
  gloom
And quiet of his lonely room,
Thy sunset scenes before him
  pass ;
As, in Agrippa's magic glass,
The loved and lost arose to view,
Remembered groves in greenness
  grew,
Bathed still in childhood's morn-
  ing dew,
Along whose bowers of beauty
  swept
Whatever Memory's mourners
  wept,
Sweet faces, which the charnel
  kept,
Young, gentle eyes, which long
  had slept ;
And while the gazer leaned to
  trace,
More near, some dear familiar
  face,
He wept to find the vision flown—
A phantom and a dream alone !

* Captain Smith gave to the promontory, now called Cape Ann, the name of Tragabizanda, in memory of his young and beautiful mistress of that name, who, while he was a captive at Constantinople, like Desdemona, "loved him for the dangers he had passed."

THE NORSEMEN.

[Some three or four years since, a fragment of a statue, rudely chiselled from dark gray stone, was found in the town of Bradford, on the Merrimack. Its origin must be left entirely to conjecture. The fact that the ancient Northmen visited New England, some centuries before the discoveries of Columbus, is now very generally admitted.]

GIFT from the cold and silent
   Past!
A relic to the present cast;
Left on the ever-changing strand
Of shifting and unstable sand,
Which wastes beneath the steady
   chime
And beating of the waves of
   Time?
Who from its bed of primal rock
First wrenched thy dark, un-
   shapely block?
Whose hand, of curious skill un-
   taught,
Thy rude and savage outline
   wrought?

The waters of my native stream
Are glancing in the sun's warm
   beam:
From sail-urged keel and flashing
   oar
The circles widen to its shore;
And cultured field and peopled
   town
Slope to its willowed margin
   down.
Yet, while this morning breeze is
   bringing
The mellow sound of church-bells
   ringing,
And rolling wheel, and rapid
   jar
Of the fire-winged and steedless
   car,
And voices from the wayside
   near
Come quick and blended on my
   ear,
A spell is in this old gray stone—
My thoughts are with the Past
   alone!
A change!—The steepled town no
   more
Stretches along the sail-thronged
   shore;
Like palace-domes in sunset's
   cloud,

Fade sun-gilt spire and mansion
   proud!
Spectrally rising where they
   stood,
I see the old, primeval wood:
Dark, shadow-like, on either hand
I see its solemn waste expand:
It climbs the green and cultured
   hill,
It arches o'er the valley's rill;
And leans from cliff and crag, to
   throw
Its wild arms o'er the stream
   below.
Unchanged, alone, the same
   bright river
Flows on, as it will flow forever!
I listen, and I hear the low
Soft ripple where its waters go;
I hear behind the panther's cry,
The wild bird's scream goes thrill-
   ing by,
And shyly on the river's brink
The deer is stooping down to
   drink.

But hark!—from wood and rock
   flung back,
What sound comes up the Merrimack?
What sea-worn barks are those
   which throw
The light spray from each rushing prow?
Have they not in the North Sea's
   blast
Bowed to the waves the straining
   mast?
Their frozen sails the low, pale
   sun
Of Thulè's night has shone upon;
Flapped by the sea-wind's gusty
   sweep
Round icy drift, and headland
   steep.
Wild Jutland's wives and Loch-
   lin's daughters

Have watched them fading o'er
  the waters,
Lessening through driving mist
  and spray,
Like white-winged sea-birds on
  their way!
Onward they glide—and now I
  view
Their iron-armed and stalwart
  crew;
Joy glistens in each wild blue
  eye.
Turned to green earth and sum-
  mer sky:
Each broad, seamed breast has
  cast aside
Its cumbering vast of shaggy
  hide;
Bared to the sun and soft warm
  air,
Streams back the Norsemen's
  yellow hair.
I see the gleam of axe and spear,
The sound of smitten shields I
  hear,
Keeping a harsh and fitting time
To saga's chant, and Runic
  rhyme;
Such lays as Zetland's Skald has
  sung,
His gray and naked isles among;
Or muttered low at midnight
  hour
Round Odin's mossy stone of
  power.
The wolf beneath the Arctic
  moon
Has answered to that startling
  rune;
The Gaal has heard its stormy
  swell,
The light Frank knows its sum-
  mons well;
Iona's sable-stoled Culdee
Has heard it sounding o'er the
  sea,
And swept with hoary beard and
  hair
His altar's foot in trembling
  prayer!

'Tis past—the 'wildering vision
  dies

In darkness on my dreaming
  eyes!
The forest vanishes in air—
Hill-slope and vale lie starkly
  bare;
I hear the common tread of men,
And hum of work-day life again:
The mystic relic seems alone
A broken mass of common stone;
And if it be the chiselled limb
Of Berserkar or idol grim—
A fragment of Valhalla's Thor,
The stormy Viking's god of War,
Of Praga of the Runic lay,
Or love awakening Siona,
I know not—for no graven line,
Nor Druid mark, nor Runic sign,
Is left me here, by which to trace
Its name, or origin, or place.

Yet, for this vision of the Past,
This glance upon its darkness
  cast,
My spirit bows in gratitude
Before the Giver of all good,
Who fashioned so the human
  mind,
That, from the waste of Time be-
  hind
A simple stone, or mound of earth,
Can summon the departed forth;
Quicken the Past to life again—
The Present lose in what hath
  been,
And in their primal freshness
  show
The buried forms of long ago.
As if a portion of that Thought
By which the eternal will is
  wrought,
Whose impulse fills anew with
  breath
The frozen solitude of Death,
To mortal mind were sometimes
  lent,
To mortal musings sometimes
  sent,
To whisper—even when it seems
But Memory's phantasy of
  dreams—
Through the mind's waste of woe
  and sin,
Of an immortal origin!

CASSANDRA SOUTHWICK.

To the God of all sure mercies let my blessing rise to-day,
From the scoffer and the cruel He hath plucked the spoil away,—
Yea, He who cooled the furnace around the faithful three,
And tamed the Chaldean lions, hath set His handmaid free !

Last night I saw the sunset melt through my prison bars,
Last night across my damp earth-floor fell the pale gleam of stars ;
In the coldness and the darkness all through the long night time,
My grated casement whitened with Autumn's early rime.

Alone, in that dark sorrow, hour after hour crept by ;
Star after star looked palely in and sank adown the sky ;
No sound amid night's stillness, save that which seemed to be
The dull and heavy beating of the pulses of the sea ;

All night I sat unsleeping, for I knew that on the morrow
The ruler and the cruel priest would mock me in my sorrow,
Dragged to their place of market, and bargained for and sold,
Like a lamb before the shambles, like a heifer from the fold !

Oh, the weakness of the flesh was there—the shrinking and the shame ;
And the low voice of the Tempter like whispers to me came :
" Why sit'st thou thus forlornly ! " the wicked murmur said,
" Damp walls thy bower of beauty, cold earth thy maiden bed ?

" Where be the smiling faces, and voices soft and sweet,
Seen in thy father's dwelling, heard in the pleasant street ?
Where be the youths, whose glances the summer Sabbath through
Turned tenderly and timidly unto thy father's pew ?

" Why sit'st thou here, Cassandra ?—Bethink thee with what mirth
Thy happy schoolmates gather around the warm bright hearth ;
How the crimson shadows tremble on foreheads white and fair,
On eyes of merry girlhood, half hid in golden hair.

" Not for thee the hearth-fire brightens, not for thee kind words are
    spoken,
Not for thee the nuts of Wenham woods by laughing boys are broken,
No first-fruits of the orchard within thy lap are laid,
For thee no flowers of Autumn the youthful hunters braid.

" Oh ! weak, deluded maiden !—by crazy fancies led,
With wild and raving railers an evil path to tread ;
To leave a wholesome worship, and teaching pure and sound ;
And mate with maniac women, loose-haired and sack-cloth-bound.

" Mad scoffers of the priesthood, who mock at things divine,
Who rail against the pulpit, and holy bread and wine ;
Sore from their cart-tail scourgings, and from the pillory lame,
Rejoicing in their wretchedness, and glorying in their shame.

" And what a fate awaits thee ?—a sadly toiling slave,
Dragging the slowly lengthening chain of bondage to the grave !
Think of thy woman's nature, subdued in hopeless thrall,
The easy prey of any, the scoff and scorn of all ! "

Oh !—ever as the Tempter spoke, and feeble Nature's fears
Wrung drop by drop the scalding flow of unavailing tears,
I wrestled down the evil thoughts, and strove in silent prayer,
To feel, oh, Helper of the weak !—that Thou indeed wert there !

I thought of Paul and Silas, within Philippi's cell,
And how from Peter's sleeping limbs the prison-shackles fell,
Till I seemed to hear the trailing of an angel's robe of white,
And to feel a blessed presence invisible to sight.

Bless the Lord for all His mercies !—for the peace and love I felt,
Like dew of Hermon's holy hill, upon my spirit melt ;
When, " Get behind me, Satan ! " was the language of my heart,
And I felt the Evil Tempter with all his doubts depart.

Slow broke the gray cold morning ; again the sunshine fell,
Flecked with the shade of bar and grate within my lonely cell ;
The hoar frost melted on the wall, and upward from the street
Came careless laugh and idle word, and tread of passing feet.

At length the heavy bolts fell back, my door was open cast,
And slowly at the sheriff's side, up the long street I passed ;
I heard the murmur round me, and felt, but dared not see,
How, from every door and window, the people gazed on me.

And doubt and fear fell on me, shame burned upon my cheek,
Swam earth and sky around me, my trembling limbs grew weak :
" Oh, Lord ! support thy handmaid ; and from her soul cast out
The fear of man, which brings a snare—the weakness and the doubt."

Then the dreary shadows scattered like a cloud in morning's breeze,
And a low deep voice within me seemed whispering words like these :
" Though thy earth be as the iron, and thy heaven a brazen wall,
Trust still His loving kindness whose power is over all."

We paused at length, where at my feet the sunlit waters broke
On glaring reach of shining beach, and shingly wall of rock ;
The merchant-ships lay idly there, in hard clear lines on high,
Tracing with rope and slender spar their network on the sky.

And there were ancient citizens, cloak-wrapped and grave and cold,
And grim and stout sea-captains with faces bronzed and old,
And on his horse, with Rawson, his cruel clerk at hand,
Sat dark and haughty Endicott, the ruler of the land.

And poisoning with his evil words the ruler's ready ear,
The priest leaned o'er his saddle, with laugh and scoff and jeer ;
It stirred my soul, and from my lips the seal of silence broke,
As if through woman's weakness a warning spirit spoke.

I cried, " The Lord rebuke thee, thou smiter of the meek,
Thou robber of the righteous, thou trampler of the weak !
Go light the dark, cold hearth-stones—go turn the prison lock
Of the poor hearts thou hast hunted, thou wolf amid the flock ! "

Dark lowered the brows of Endicott, and with a deeper red
O'er Rawson's wine-empurpled cheek the flush of anger spread ;
" Good people," quoth the white-lipped priest, " heed not her words
    so wild,
Her Master speaks within her—the Devil owns his child ! "

But gray heads shook, and young brows knit, the while the sheriff read
That law the wicked rulers against the poor have made,
Who to their house of Rimmon and idol priesthood bring
No bended knee of worship, nor gainful offering.

Then to the stout sea-captains the sheriff turning said :
" Which of ye, worthy seamen, will take this Quaker maid ?
In the Isle of fair Barbadoes, or on Virginia's shore,
You may hold her at a higher price than Indian girl or Moor."

Grim and silent stood the captains ; and when again he cried,
" Speak out, my worthy seamen ! "—no voice, no sign replied ;
But I felt a hard hand press my own, and kind words met my ear :
" God bless thee, and preserve thee, my gentle girl and dear ! "

A weight seemed lifted from my heart, a pitying friend was nigh,
I felt it in his hard, rough hand, and saw it in his eye ;
And when again the sheriff spoke, that voice, so kind to me,
Growled back its stormy answer like the roaring of the sea :

" Pile my ships with bars of silver—pack with coins of Spanish gold,
From the keel-piece up the deck-plank, the roomage of her hold,
By the living God who made me !—I would sooner in your bay
Sink ship and crew and cargo, than bear this child away ! "

" Well answered, worthy captain, shame on their cruel laws ! "
Ran through the crowd in murmurs loud the people's just applause.
" Like the herdsmen of Tekoa, in Israel of old,
Shall we see the poor and righteous again for silver sold ? "

I looked on haughty Endicott ; with weapon half way drawn,
Swept round the throng his lion glare of bitter hate and scorn ;
Fiercely he drew his bridle rein, and turned in silence back,
And sneering priest and baffled clerk rode murmuring in his track.

Hard after them the sheriff looked, in bitterness of soul ;
Thrice smote his staff upon the ground, and crushed his parchment
    roll
" Good friends," he said, " since both have fled, the ruler and the
    priest,
Judge ye, if from their further work I be not well released,"

Loud was the cheer which, full and clear, swept round the silent bay,
As, with kind words and kinder looks, he bade me go my way ;
For He who turns the courses of the streamlet of the glen,
And the river of great waters, had turned the hearts of men.

Oh, at that hour the very earth seemed changed beneath my eye,
A holier wonder round me rose the blue walls of the sky,
A lovelier light on rock and hill, and stream and woodland lay,
And softer lapsed on sunnier sands the waters of the bay.

Thanksgiving to the Lord of life !—to Him all praises be,
Who from the hands of evil men hath set His handmaid free ;
All praise to him before whose power the mighty are afraid,
Who takes the crafty in the snare, which for the poor is laid !

Sing, oh, my soul, rejoicingly, on evening's twilight calm
Uplift the loud thanksgiving—pour forth the grateful psalm ;
Let all dear hearts with me rejoice, as did the saints of old,
When of the Lord's good angel the rescued Peter told.

And weep and howl, ye evil priests and mighty men of wrong,
The Lord shall smite the proud and lay His hand upon the strong.
Woe to the wicked rulers in His avenging hour !
Woe to the wolves who seek the flocks to raven and devour :

But let the humble ones arise,—the poor in heart be glad,
And let the mourning ones again with robes of praise be clad,
For He who cooled the furnace, and smoothed the stormy wave,
And tamed the Chaldean lions, is mighty still to save !

FUNERAL TREE OF THE SOKOKIS.*

AROUND Sebago's lonely lake
There lingers not a breeze to break
The mirror which its waters make.

The solemn pines along its shore,
The firs which hang its gray rocks o'er,
Are painted on its glassy floor.

The sun looks o'er, with hazy eye,
The snowy mountain-tops which lie
Piled coldly up against the sky.

* Polan, a chief of the Sokokis Indians, the original inhabitants of the country lying between Agamenticus and Casco Bay, was killed in a skirmish at Windham, on the Sebago lake, in the spring of 1756. He claimed all the lands on both sides of the Presumpscot River to its mouth at Casco, as his own. He was shrewd, subtle, and brave. After the white men had retired, the surviving Indians "swayed" or bent down a young tree until its roots were turned up, placed the body of their chief beneath them, and then released the tree to spring back to its former position.

Dazzling and white! save where the bleak,
Wild winds have bared some splintering peak,
Or snow-slide left its dusky streak.

Yet green are Saco's banks below,
And belts of spruce and cedar show,
Dark fringing round those cones of snow.

The earth hath felt the breath of spring,
Though yet on her deliverer's wing
The lingering frosts of winter cling.

Fresh grasses fringe the meadow-brooks,
And mildly from its sunny nooks
The blue eye of the violet looks.

And odors from the springing grass,
The sweet birch and the sassafras,
Upon the scarce-felt breezes pass.

Her tokens of renewing care
Hath Nature scattered everywhere,
In bud and flower, and warmer air.

But in their hour of bitterness,
What reck the broken Sokokis,
Beside their slaughtered chief, of this?

The turf's red stain is yet undried—
Scarce have the death-shot echoes died
Along Sebago's wooded side:

And silent now the hunters stand,
Grouped darkly, where a swell of land
Slopes upward from the lake's white sand.

Fire and the axe have swept it bare,
Save one lone beech, unclosing there
Its light leaves in the vernal air.

With grave, cold looks, all sternly mute,
They break the damp turf at its foot,
And bare its coiled and twisted root.

They heave the stubborn trunk aside,
The firm roots from the earth divide—
The rent beneath yawns dark and wide.

And there the fallen chief is laid,
In tasselled garb of skins arrayed,
And girded with his wampum-braid.

The silver cross he loved is pressed
Beneath the heavy arms, which rest
Upon his scarred and naked breast.*

'Tis done : the roots are backward sent,
The beechen tree stands up unbent—
The Indian's fitting monument !

When of that sleeper's broken race
Their green and pleasant dwelling-place
Which knew them once, retains no trace ;

O ! long may sunset's light be shed
As now upon that beech's head—
A green memorial of the dead !

There shall his fitting requiem be,
In northern winds, that, cold and free,
Howl nightly in that funeral tree.

To their wild wail the waves which break
Forever round that lonely lake
A solemn undertone shall make !

And who shall deem the spot unblest,
Where nature's younger children rest,
Lulled on their sorrowing mother's breast ?

Deem ye that mother loveth less
These bronzed forms of the wilderness
She foldeth in her long caress ?

As sweet o'er them her wild flowers blow,
As if with fairer hair and brow
The blue-eyed Saxon slept below.

What though the places of their rest
No priestly knee hath ever pressed—
No funeral rite nor prayer hath blessed ?

What though the bigot's ban be there,
And thoughts of wailing and despair,
And cursing in the place of prayer ! *

Yet Heaven hath angels watching round
The Indian's lowliest forest-mound—
And *they* have made it holy ground.

* The Sokokis were early converts to the Catholic faith. Most of them, prior to the year
756, had removed to the French settlements on the St. François.
* The brutal and unchristian spirit of the early settlers of New England toward the red man
s strikingly illustrated in the conduct of the man who shot down the Sokokis chief. He used
o say he always noticed the anniversary of that exploit, as "the day on which he sent the
evil a present."—Williamson's *History of Maine.*

There ceases man's frail judgment ; all
His powerless bolts of cursing fall
Unheeded on that grassy pall.

O, peeled, and hunted, and reviled,
Sleep on, dark tenant of the wild !
Great Nature owns her simple child !

And Nature's God, to whom alone
The secret of the heart is known—
The hidden language traced thereon ;

Who from its many cumberings
Of form and creed, and outward things,
To light the naked spirit brings ;

Not with our partial eye shall scan—
Not with our pride and scorn shall ban
The spirit of our brother man !

ST. JOHN.

"To the winds give our banner !
  Bear homeward again ! "
Cried the Lord of Acadia,
  Cried Charles of Estienne ;
From the prow of his shallop
  He gazed, as the sun,
From its bed in the ocean,
  Streamed up the St. John.

O'er the blue western waters
  That shallop had passed,
Where the mists of Penobscot
  Clung damp on her mast.
St. Saviour * had look'd
  On the heretic sail,
As the songs of the Huguenot
  Rose on the gale.

The pale, ghostly fathers
  Remembered her well
And had cursed her while passing,
  With taper and bell,
But the men of Monhegan,†
  Of Papists abhorr'd,
Had welcomed and feasted
  The heretic Lord.

They had loaded his shallop
  With dun-fish and ball,
With stores for his larder,
  And steel for his wall.
Pemequid, from her bastions
  And turrets of stone,
Had welcomed his coming
  With banner and gun.

And the prayers of the elders
  Had followed his way,
As homeward he glided,
  Down Pentecost Bay.
Oh ! well sped La Tour !
  For, in peril and pain,
His lady kept watch
  For his coming again.

O'er the Isle of the Pheasant
  The morning sun shone,
On the plane trees which shaded
  The shores of St. John.
" Now, why from yon battlements
  Speaks not my love !
Why waves there no banner
  My fortress above ? "

---

* The settlement of the Jesuits on the island of Mount Desert was called St. Saviour.
† The isle of Monhegan was one of the first settled on the coast of Maine.

Dark and wild, from his deck
St. Estienne gazed about,
On fire-wasted dwellings,
And silent redoubt ;
From the low, shattered walls
Which the flame had o'errun,
There floated no banner,
There thunder'd no gun !

But, beneath the low arch
Of its doorway there stood
A pale priest of Rome,
In his cloak and his hood.
With the bound of a lion,
La Tour sprang to land,
On the throat of the Papist
He fastened his hand.

" Speak, son of the Woman,
Of scarlet and sin !
What wolf has been prowling
My castle within ? "
From the grasp of the soldier
The Jesuit broke,
Half in scorn, half in sorrow,
He smiled as he spoke :

" No wolf, Lord of Estienne,
Has ravaged thy hall,
But thy red-handed rival,
With fire, steel, and ball !
On an errand of mercy
I hitherward came,
While the walls of thy castle
Yet spouted with flame.

" Pentagoet's dark vessels
Were moored in the bay,
Grim sea-lions, roaring
Aloud for their prey."
" But what of my lady ? "
Cried Charles of Estienne :
" On the short-crumbled turret
Thy lady was seen :

" Half-veiled in the smoke-cloud,
Her hand grasped thy pennon,
While her dark tresses swayed
In the hot breath of cannon !
But woe to the heretic,
Evermore woe !
When the son of the church
And the cross is his foe !

" In the track of the shell,
In the path of the ball,
Pentagoet swept over
The breach of the wall !
Steel to steel, gun to gun,
One moment—and then
Alone stood the victor,
Alone with his men !

" Of its sturdy defenders,
Thy lady alone
Saw the cross-blazon'd banner
Float over St. John."
" Let the dastard look to it ! "
Cried fiery Estienne,
" Were D'Aulney King Louis,
I'd free her again ! "

" Alas, for thy lady !
No service from thee
Is needed by her
Whom the Lord hath set free :
Nine days, in stern silence,
Her thraldom she bore,
But the tenth morning came,
And Death opened her door ! "

As if suddenly smitten
La Tour stagger'd back ;
His hand grasped his sword-hilt,
His forehead grew black.
He sprang on the deck
Of his shallop again :
" We cruise now for vengeance !
Give way ! " cried Estienne,

" Massachusetts shall hear
Of the Huguenot's wrong,
And from island and creek-side
Her fishers shall throng !
Pentagoet shall rue
What his Papists have done,
When his palisades echo
The Puritan's gun ! "

O ! the loveliest of heavens
Hung tenderly o'er him,
There were waves in the sun-
shine,
And green isles before him :
But a pale hand was beckoning
The Huguenot on ;
And in blackness and ashes
Behind was St. John !

PENTUCKET.

[The village of Haverhill, on the Merrimack, called by the Indians Pentucket, was for nearly
seventeen years a frontier town, and during thirty years endured all the horrors of savage warfare. In the year 1708, a combined body of French and Indians, under the command of De
Challions, and Hertel de Rouville, the famous and bloody sacker of Deerfield, made an attack
upon the village, which at that time contained only thirty houses. Sixteen of the villagers were
massacred, and a still larger number made prisoners. About thirty of the enemy also fell, and
among them Hertel de Rouville. The minister of the place, Benjamin Rolfe, was killed by a
shot through his own door.]

How sweetly on the wood-girt town
The mellow light of sunset shone!
Each small, bright lake, whose waters still
Mirror the forest and the hill,
Reflected from its waveless breast
The beauty of a cloudless West,
Glorious as if a glimpse were given
Within the western gates of Heaven,
Left, by the spirit of the star
Of sunset's holy hour, ajar!

Beside the river's tranquil flood
The dark and low-wall'd dwellings stood,
Where many a rood of open land
Stretch'd up and down on either hand,
With corn-leaves waving freshly green
The thick and blacken'd stumps between.
Behind, unbroken, deep and dread,
The wild, untravel'd forest spread,
Back to those mountains, white and cold,
Of which the Indian trapper told,
Upon whose summits never yet
Was mortal foot in safety set.
Quiet and calm, without a fear
Of danger darkly lurking near,
The weary laborer left his plough—
The milkmaid carrol'd by her cow—
From cottage door and household hearth
Rose songs of praise, or tones of mirth.
At length the murmur died away,
And silence on that village lay—
So slept Pompeii, tower and hall,
Ere the quick earthquake swallow'd all,
Undreaming of the fiery fate
Which made its dwellings desolate!

Hours pass'd away. By moonlight sped
The Merrimack along his bed.
Bathed in the pallid lustre, stood
Dark cottage-wall and rock and wood,
Silent, beneath that tranquil beam,
As the hush'd grouping of a dream.

Yet on the still air crept a sound—
No bark of fox—nor rabbit's bound—
Nor stir of wings—nor waters flowing—
Nor leaves in midnight breezes blowing.

Was that the tread of many feet,
Which downward from the hillside beat?
What forms were those which darkly stood
Just on the margin of the wood?—
Charr'd tree-stumps in the moonlight dim,
Or paling rude, or leafless limb?
No—through the trees fierce eyeballs glow'd,
Dark human forms in sunshine show'd,
Wild from their native wilderness,
With painted limbs and battle-dress!
A yell, the dead might wake to hear,
Swell'd on the night air, far and clear—
Then smote the Indian tomahawk
On crashing door and shattering lock—
Then rang the rifle-shot—and then
The shrill death-scream of stricken men—
Sank the red axe in woman's brain,
And childhood's cry arose in vain—
Bursting through roof and window came,
Red, fast and fierce, the kindled flame;
And blended fire and moonlight glared
On still dead men and weapons bared.

The morning sun looked brightly through
The river willows, wet with dew.
No sound of combat fill'd the air,—
No shout was heard,—nor gun-shot there:
Yet still the thick and sullen smoke
From smouldering ruins slowly broke;
And on the greensward many a stain,
And, here and there, the mangled slain
Told how that midnight bolt had sped,
Pentucket, on thy fated head!

Even now the villager can tell
Where Rolfe beside his hearth-stone fell,
Still show the door of wasting oak
Through which the fatal death-shot broke,
And point the curious stranger where
De Rouville's corse lay grim and bare—
Whose hideous head, in death still fear'd,
Bore not a trace of hair or beard—
And still, within the churchyard ground,
Heaves darkly up the ancient mound,
Whose grass-grown surface overlies
The victims of that sacrifice.

THE FAMILIST'S HYMN.

[The " Pilgrims " of New England, even in their wilderness home, were not exempted from the sectarian contentions which agitated the mother country after the downfall of Charles the First, and of the established Episcopacy. The Quakers, Baptists, and Catholics were banished, on pain of death, from the Massachusetts Colony. One Samuel Gorton, a bold and eloquent declaimer, after preaching for a time in Boston, against the doctrines of the Puritans, and declaring that their churches were mere human devices, and their sacrament and baptism an abomination, was driven out of the State's jurisdiction, and compelled to seek a residence among the savages. He gathered round him a considerable number of converts, who, like the primitive Christians, shared all things in common. His opinions, however, were so troublesome to the leading clergy of the Colony, that they instigated an attack upon his " Family " by an armed force, which seized upon the principal men in it, and brought them into Massachusetts, where they were sentenced to be kept at hard labor in several towns (one only in each town), during the pleasure of the General Court, they being forbidden, under severe penalties, to utter any of their religious sentiments, except to such ministers as might labor for their conversion. They were unquestionably sincere in their opinions, and, whatever may have been their errors, deserved to be ranked among those who have in all ages suffered for the freedom of conscience.]

FATHER! to thy suffering poor
  Strength and grace and faith
    impart,
And with Thy own love restore
  Comfort to the broken heart!
Oh, the failing ones confirm
  With a holier strength of zeal!—
Give Thou not the feeble worm
  Helpless to the spoiler's heel!
Father! for Thy holy sake
  We are spoiled and hunted thus;
Joyful, for Thy truth we take
  Bonds and burthens unto us:
Poor, and weak, and robbed of all,
  Weary with our daily task,
That Thy truth may never fall
  Through our weakness, Lord,
    we ask.

Round our fired and wasted homes
  Flits the forest-bird unscared,
And at noon the wild beast comes
  Where our frugal meal was
    shared;
For the song of praises there
  Shrieks the crow the livelong
    day,
For the sound of evening prayer
  Howls the evil beast of prey !

Sweet the songs we loved to sing
  Underneath Thy holy sky—
Words and tones that used to bring
  Tears of joy in every eye,—
Dear the wrestling hours of prayer,
  When we gathered knee to knee,

Blameless youth and hoary hair,
  Bow'd, O God, alone to Thee.

As Thine early children, Lord,
  Shared their wealth and daily
    bread,
Even so, with one accord,
  We, in love, each other fed.
Not with us the miser's hoard,
  Not with us his grasping hand;
Equal round a common board,
  Drew our meek and brother
    band !

Safe our quiet Eden lay
  When the war-whoop stirred the
    land,
And the Indian turn'd away
  From our home his bloody hand.
Well that forest-ranger saw,
  That the burthen and the curse
Of the white man's cruel law
  Rested also upon us.

Torn apart, and driven forth
  To our toiling hard and long,
Father! from the dust of earth
  Lift we still our grateful song!
Grateful—that in bonds we share
  In Thy love which maketh free
Joyful—that the wrongs we bear,
  Draw us nearer, Lord, to Thee!

Grateful!—that where'er we toil—
  By Wachuset's wooded side,

On Nantucket's sea-worn isle,
  Or by wild Neponset's tide—
Still, in spirit, we are near,
  And our evening hymns which rise
Separate and discordant here,
  Meet and mingle in the skies!

Let the scoffer scorn and mock,
  Let the proud and evil priest
Rob the needy of his flock,
  For his wine-cup and his feast,—
Redden not Thy bolts in store
  Through the blackness of Thy skies?
For the sighing of the poor
  Wilt Thou not, at length, arise?

Worn and wasted, oh, how long,
  Shall Thy trodden poor complain?
In Thy name they bear the wrong,
  In Thy cause the bonds of pain!
Melt oppression's heart of steel,
  Let the haughty priesthood see,
And their blinded followers feel,
  That in us they mock at Thee!

In Thy time, O Lord of hosts,
  Stretch abroad that hand to save
Which of old, on Egypt's coasts,
  Smote apart the Red Sea's wave!
Lead us from this evil land,
  From the spoiler set us free,
And once more our gather'd band,
  Heart to heart, shall worship Thee!

THE FOUNTAIN.

[On the declivity of a hill, in Salisbury, Essex County, is a beautiful fountain of clear water, gushing out from the very roots of a majestic and venerable oak. It is about two miles from the junction of the Powow River with the Merrimack.]

TRAVELER! on thy journey toiling
  By the swift Powow,
With the summer sunshine falling
  On thy heated brow,
Listen, while all else is still
To the brooklet from the hill.

Wild and sweet the flowers are blowing
  By that streamlet's side,
And a greener verdure showing
  Where its waters glide—
Down the hill-slope murmuring on,
Over root and mossy stone.

Where yon oak his broad arms flingeth
  O'er the sloping hill,
Beautiful and freshly springeth
  That soft-flowing rill,
Through its dark roots wreath'd and bare,
Gushing up to sun and air.

Brighter waters sparkled never
  In that magic well,
Of whose gift of life forever
  Ancient legends tell,—
In the lonely desert wasted,
And by mortal lip untasted.

Waters which the proud Castilian*
  Sought with longing eyes,
Underneath the bright pavilion
  Of the Indian skies;
Where his forest pathway lay
Through the blooms of Florida.

Years ago a lonely stranger,
  With the dusky brow
Of the outcast forest-ranger,
  Crossed the swift Powow;
And betook him to the rill,
And the oak upon the hill.

O'er his face of moody sadness
  For an instant shone

* De Soto, in the sixteenth century, penetrated into the wilds of the new world in search of gold and the fountain of perpetual youth.

Something like a gleam of glad-
        ness,
    As he stooped him down
To the fountain's grassy side
And his eager thirst supplied.

With the oak its shadow throwing
    O'er his mossy seat,
And the cool, sweet waters flowing
    Softly at his feet,
Closely by the fountain's rim
That lone Indian seated him.

Autumn's earliest frost had given
    To the woods below
Hues of beauty, such as Heaven
    Lendeth to its bow;
And the soft breeze from the west
Scarcely broke their dreamy rest.

Far behind was Ocean striving
    With his chains of sand;
Southward, sunny glimpses giving,
    'Twixt the swells of land,
Of its calm and silvery track,
Rolled the tranquil Merrimack.

Over village, wood and meadow,
    Gazed that stranger man
Sadly, till the twilight shadow
    Over all things ran,
Save where spire and westward
        pane
Flashed the sunset back again.

Gazing thus upon the dwelling
    Of his warrior sires,
Where no lingering trace was
        telling
    Of their wigwam fires,
Who the gloomy thoughts might
        know
Of that wandering child of woe?

Naked lay, in sunshine glowing,
    Hills that once had stood,
Down their sides the shadows
        throwing

Of a mighty wood,
Where the deer his covert kept,
And the eagle's pinion swept!

Where the birch canoe had glided
    Down the swift Powow,
Dark and gloomy bridges strided
    Those clear waters now;
And where once the beaver swam,
Jarred the wheel and frowned the
        dam.

For the wood-bird's merry singing,
    And the hunter's cheer,
Iron clang and hammer's ringing
    Smote upon his ear;
And the thick and sullen smoke
From the blackened forges broke.

Could it be, his fathers ever,
    Loved to linger here?
These bare hills—this conquer'd
        river—
    Could they hold them dear,
With their native loveliness
Tamed and tortured into this?

Sadly, as the shades of even
    Gathered o'er the hill,
While the western half of Heaven
    Blushed with sunset still,
From the fountain's mossy seat
Turned the Indian's weary feet.

Year on year hath flown forever,
    But he came no more
To the hillside or the river
    Where he came before.
But the villager can tell
Of that strange man's visit well.

And the merry children, laden
    With their fruits or flowers—
Roving boy and laughing maiden,
    In their school-day hours,
Love the simple tale to tell
Of the Indian and his well.

THE EXILES.

[The incidents upon which the following ballad has its foundation, occurred about the year 1660. Thomas Macey was one of the first, if not *the* first white settler of Nantucket. A quaint description of his singular and perilous voyage, in his own handwriting, is still preserved.]

THE goodman sat beside his door
  One sultry afternoon,
With his young wife singing at his
    side
  An old and goodly tune.

A glimmer of heat was in the air,—
  The dark green woods were still;
And the skirts of a heavy thunder-
    cloud
  Hung over the western hill.

Black, thick, and vast, arose that
    cloud
  Above the wilderness,
As some dark world from upper air
  Were stooping over this.

At times, the solemn thunder
    pealed,
  And all was still again,
Save a low murmur in the air
  Of coming wind and rain.

Just as the first big raindrop fell,
  A weary stranger came,
And stood before the farmer's door,
  With travel soiled and lame.

Sad seemed he, yet sustaining hope
  Was in his quiet glance,
And peace, like autumn's moon-
    light, clothed
  His tranquil countenance.

A look, like that his Master wore
  In Pilate's council-hall :
It told of wrongs—but of a love
  Meekly forgiving all.

" Friend ! wilt thou give me shelter
    here ? "
  The stranger meekly said;
And, leaning on his oaken staff,
  The goodman's features read.

" My life is hunted—evil men
  Are following in my track ;
The traces of the torturer's whip
  Are on my aged back.

" And much, I fear, 'twill peril
    thee
  Within thy doors to take
A hunted seeker of the Truth,
  Oppressed for conscience' sake."

Oh, kindly spoke the goodman's
    wife—
  " Come in, old man ! " quoth
    she,—
" We will not leave thee to the
    storm,
  Whoever thou may'st be."

Then came the aged wanderer in,
  And silent sat him down;
While all within grew dark as
    night
  Beneath the storm-cloud's frown.

But while the sudden lightning's
    blaze
  Filled every cottage nook,
And with the jarring thunder-roll
  The loosened casement shook,

A heavy tramp of horses' feet
  Came sounding up the lane,
And half a score of horse, or more,
  Came plunging through the rain.

" Now, Goodman Macey, ope thy
    door,—
  We would not be house-breakers;
A rueful deed thou'st done this
    day,
  In harboring banished Quakers."

Out looked the cautious goodman
    then,
  With much of fear and awe,

For there, with broad wig drenched
    with rain,
  The parish priest he saw.

"Open thy door, thou wicked
    man,
  And let thy pastor in,
And give God thanks, if forty
    stripes
  Repay thy deadly sin."

"What seek ye?" quoth the good-
    man,—
  "The stranger is my guest;
He is worn with toil and grievous
    wrong,—
  Pray let the old man rest."

"Now, out upon thee, canting
    knave!"
  And strong hands shook the
    door,
"Believe me, Macey," quoth the
    priest,—
  "Thou'lt rue thy conduct sore."

Then kindled Macey's eye of fire:
  "No priest who walks the earth,
Shall pluck away the stranger-
    guest
  Made welcome to my hearth."

Down from his cottage wall he
    caught
  The matchlock, hotly tried
At Preston-pans and Marston-moor,
  By fiery Ireton's side;

Where Puritan, and Cavalier,
  With shout and psalm contended;
And Rupert's oath, and Crom-
    well's prayer,
  With battle-thunder blended.

Up rose the ancient stranger then:
  "My spirit is not free
To bring the wrath and violence
  Of evil men on thee:

"And for thyself, I pray forbear,—
  Bethink thee of thy Lord,

Who healed again the smitten ear,
  And sheathed his follower's
    sword.

"I go, as to the slaughter led:
  Friends of the poor, farewell!"
Beneath his hand the oaken door
  Back on its hinges fell.

"Come forth, old gray-beard, yea
    and nay;"
  The reckless scoffers cried,
As to a horseman's saddle-bow
  The old man's arms were tied.

And of his bondage hard and long
  In Boston's crowded jail,
Where suffering woman's prayer
    was heard,
  With sickening childhood's wail,

It suits not with our tale to tell:
  Those scenes have passed away—
Let the dim shadows of the past
  Brood o'er that evil day.

"Ho, sheriff!" quoth the ardent
    priest—
  "Take goodman Macey too;
The sin of this day's heresy,
  His back or purse shall rue."

And priest and sheriff, both to-
    gether
  Upon his threshold stood,
When Macey, through another
    door,
  Sprang out into the wood.

"Now, goodwife, haste thee!"
    Macey cried,
  She caught his manly arm:—
Behind, the parson urged pursuit,
  With outcry and alarm,

Ho! speed the Maceys, neck or
    naught,—
  The river course was near:—
The plashing on its pebbled shore
  Was music to their ear.

A gray rock, tasselled o'er with
    birch,

Above the waters hung,
And at its base, with every wave,
  A small light wherry swung.

A leap—they gain the boat—and there
  The goodman wields his oar :
"Ill luck betide them all"—he cried,—
  "The laggards upon the shore."

Down through the crashing under-
    wood,
  The burly sheriff came:—
"Stand, goodman Macey—yield
    thyself;
  Yield in the King's own name."

"Now out upon thy hangman's
    face!"
  Bold Macey answered then,—
"Whip *women* on the village green
  But meddle not with *men*."

The priest came panting to the
    shore,—
  His grave cocked hat was gone :
Behind him, like some owl's nest,
    hung
  His wig upon a thorn.

"Come back—come back!" the
    parson cried,
  "The church's curse beware."
"Curse and thou wilt," said Macey,
    "but
  Thy blessing prithee spare."

"Vile scoffer!" cried the baffled
    priest,—
  "Thou'lt yet the gallows see."
"Who's born to be hanged, will
    not be drowned,"
  Quoth Macey merrily;

"And so, sir sheriff and priest,
    good-bye!"
  He bent him to his oar,
And the small boat glided quietly
  From the twain upon the shore.

Now in the west, the heavy clouds
  Scattered and fell asunder,
While feebler came the rush of rain,
  And fainter growled the thun-
    der.

And through the broken clouds,
    the sun
  Looked out serene and warm,
Painting its holy symbol-light
  Upon the passing storm.

Oh, beautiful! that rainbow span,
  O'er dim Crane-neck was bend-
    ed;—
One bright foot touched the eastern
    hills,
  And one with ocean blended.

By green Pentucket's southern
    slope
  The small boat glided fast,—
The watchers of "the Block-house"
    saw
  The strangers as they passed.

That night a stalwart garrison
  Sat shaking in their shoes,
To hear the dip of Indian oars,—
  The glide of birch canoes.

The fisher-wives of Salisbury,
  (The men were all away),
Looked out to see the stranger oar
  Upon their waters play.

Deer-Island's rocks and fir-trees
    threw
  Their sunset-shadows o'er them,
And Newbury's spire and weather-
    cock
  Peered o'er the pines before them.

Around the Black Rocks, on their
    left,
  The marsh lay broad and green;
And on their right, with dwarf
    shrubs crowned,
  Plum Island's hills were seen.

With skilful hand and wary eye
  The harbor-bar was crossed;—

A plaything of the restless wave,
 The boat on ocean tossed.

The glory of the sunset heaven
 On land and water lay,—
On the steep hills of Agawam,
 On cape, and bluff, and bay.

They passed the gray rocks of Cape
  Ann,
 And Gloucester's harbor-bar;
The watch-fire of the garrison
 Shone like a setting star.

How brightly broke the morning
 On Massachusetts' Bay!
Blue wave, and bright green island,
 Rejoicing in their day.

On passed the bark in safety
 Round isle and headland steep—
No tempest broke above them,
 No fog-cloud veiled the deep.

Far round the bleak and stormy
  Cape
 The vent'rous Macey passed,
And on Nantucket's naked isle,
 Drew up his boat at last.

And how, in log-built cabin,
 They braved the rough sea-
  weather;

And there, in peace and quietness,
 Went down life's vale together:

How others drew around them,
 And how their fishing sped,
Until to every wind of heaven
 Nantucket's sails were spread:

How pale want alternated
 With plenty's golden smile;
Behold, is it not written
 In the annals of the isle?

And yet that isle remaineth
 A refuge of the free,
As when true-hearted Macey
 Beheld it from the sea.

Free as the winds that winnow
 Her shrubless hills of sand—
Free as the waves that batter
 Along her yielding land.

Than hers, at duty's summons,
 No loftier spirit stirs,—
Nor falls o'er human suffering
 A readier tear than hers.

God bless the sea-beat island!—
 And grant for evermore,
That charity and freedom dwell,
 As now upon her shore!

THE NEW WIFE AND THE OLD.

[The following Ballad is founded upon one of the marvellous legends connected with the famous General M., of Hampton, N. H., who was regarded by his neighbors as a Yankee Faust, in league with the adversary. I give the story, as I heard it when a child, from a venerable family visitant.]

DARK the halls, and cold the feast—
Gone the bridemaids, gone the
  priest!
All is over—all is done,
Twain of yesterday are one!
Blooming girl and manhood gray,
Autumn in the arms of May!

Hushed within and hushed without,
Dancing feet and wrestlers' shout;

Dies the bonfire on the hill;
All is dark and all is still,
Save the starlight, save the breeze
Moaning through the grave-yard
  trees;
And the great sea-waves below,
Like the night's pulse, beating
  slow.

From the brief dream of a bride
She hath wakened, at his side.

With half uttered shriek and start—
Feels she not his beating heart?
And the pressure of his arm,
And his breathing near and warm?

Lightly from the bridal bed
Springs that fair dishevelled head,
And a feeling, new, intense,
Half of shame, half innocence,
Maiden fear and wonder speaks
Through her lips and changing
   cheeks.

From the oaken mantel glowing
Faintest light the lamp is throwing
On the mirror's antique mould,
High-backed chair, and wainscot
   old,
And, through faded curtains steal-
   ing,
His dark sleeping face revealing.

Listless lies the strong man there,
Silver-streaked his careless hair;
Lips of love have left no trace
On that hard and haughty face;
And that forehead's knitted
   thought
Love's soft hand hath not un-
   wrought.

"Yet," she sighs, "he loves me
   well,
More than these calm lips will tell.
Stooping to my lowly state,
He hath made me rich and great,
And I bless him, though he be
Hard and stern to all save me!"

While she speaketh, falls the light
O'er her fingers small and white;
Gold and gem, and costly ring
Back the timid lustre fling—
Love's selectest gifts, and rare,
His proud hand had fastened there.

Gratefully she marks the glow
From those tapering lines of snow;
Fondly o'er the sleeper bending
His black hair with golden blend-
   ing,

In her soft and light caress,
Cheek and lip together press.

Ha!—that start of horror!—Why
That wild stare and wilder cry,
Full of terror, full of pain?
Is there madness in her brain?
Hark! that gasping, hoarse and
   low :
"Spare me—spare me—let me go!"

God have mercy!—Icy cold
Spectral hands her own enfold,
Drawing silently from them
Love's fair gifts of gold and gem,
"Waken! save me!" still as death
At her side he slumbereth.

Ring and bracelet all are gone,
And that ice-cold hand withdrawn;
But she hears a murmur low,
Full of sweetness, full of woe,
Half a sigh and half a moan :
"Fear not! give the dead her
   own!"

Ah!—the dead wife's voice she
   knows!
That cold hand whose pressure
   froze,
Once in warmest life had borne
Gem and band her own hath worn,
"Wake thee! wake thee!" Lo,
   his eyes
Open with a dull surprise.

In his arms the strong man folds
   her,
Closer to his breast he holds her;
Trembling limbs his own are meet-
   ing,
And he feels her heart's quick
   beating :
"Nay, my dearest, why this fear?"
"Hush!" she saith, "the dead is
   here!"

"Nay, a dream—an idle dream."
But before the lamp's pale gleam
Tremblingly her hand she raises,—
There no more the diamond blazes,

Clasp of pearl, or ring of gold,—
"Ah!" she sighs, "her hand was
   cold !"

Broken words of cheer he saith,
But his dark lip quivereth,
And as o'er the past he thinketh,
From his young wife's arms he
   shrinketh;
Can those soft arms round him lie,
Underneath his dead wife's eye ?

She her fair young head can rest
Soothed and child-like on his breast,
And in trustful innocence
Draw new strength and courage
   thence;
He, the proud man, feels within
But the cowardice of sin!

She can murmur in her thought
Simple prayers her mother taught,
And his blessed angels call,
Whose great love is over all;

He, alone, in prayerless pride,
Meets the dark Past at her side !

One, who living shrank with dread
From his look, or word, or tread,
Unto whom her early grave
Was as freedom to the slave,
Moves him at this midnight hour,
With the dead's unconscious power!

Ah, the dead, the unforgot !
From their solemn homes of
   thought,
Where the cypress shadows blend
Darkly over foe and friend,
Or in love or sad rebuke,
Back upon the living look.

And the tenderest ones and weak-
   est,
Who their wrongs have borne the
   meekest,
Lifting from those dark, still places
Sweet and sad-remembered faces,
O'er the guilty hearts behind
An unwitting triumph find.

VOICES OF FREEDOM.

TOUSSAINT L'OUVERTURE.

[TOUSSAINT L'OUVERTURE, the black chieftain of Hayti, was a slave on the plantation " of
Libertas," belonging to M. BAYOU. When the rising of the negroes took place, in 1791, TOU
SAINT refused to join them until he had aided M. BAYOU and his family to escape to Baltimor
The white man had discovered in TOUSSAINT many noble qualities, and had instructed him
some of the first branches of education; and the preservation of his life was owing to the negro
gratitude for this kindness.

In 1797, TOUSSAINT L'OUVERTURE was appointed, by the French government, General-
Chief of the armies of St. Domingo, and, as such, signed the Convention with General MAI
LAND, for the evacuation of the island by the British. From this period until 1801, the islan
under the government of TOUSSAINT was happy, tranquil, and prosperous. The miserable a
tempt of NAPOLEON to reëstablish slavery in St. Domingo, although it failed of its intende
object, proved fatal to the negro chieftain. Treacherously seized by LE CLERC, he was hurri
on board a vessel by night, and conveyed to France, where he was confined in a cold subte
ranean dungeon, at Besançon, where, in April, 1803, he died. The treatment of TOUSSAIN
finds a parallel only in the murder of the Duke D'ENGHIEN. It was the remark of GODWI
in his Lectures, that the West India Islands, since their first discovery by COLUMBUS, could n
boast of a single name which deserves comparison with that of TOUSSAINT L'OUVERTURE.]

'TWAS night. The tranquil moonlight smile
   With which Heaven dreams of Earth, shed down
   Its beauty on the Indian isle—
     On broad green field and white-walled town;

An inland waste of rock and wood,
In searching sunshine, wild and rude,
Rose, mellowed through the silver gleam,
Soft as the landscape of a dream,
All motionless and dewy wet,
Tree, vine, and flower in shadow met:
The myrtle with its snowy bloom,
Crossing the nightshade's solemn gloom—
The white cecropia's silver rind
Relieved by deeper green behind,—
The orange with its fruit of gold,—
The lithe paullinia's verdant fold,—
The passion-flower, with symbol holy,
Twining its tendrils long and lowly,—
The rhexias dark, and cassia tall,
And proudly rising over all,
The kingly palm's imperial stem,
Crowned with its leafy diadem,—
Star-like, beneath whose sombre shade,
The fiery-winged cucullo played!

Yes—lovely was thine aspect, then,
    Fair island of the Western Sea!
Lavish of beauty, even when
Thy brutes were happier than thy men,
    For they, at least, were free!
Regardless of thy glorious clime,
    Unmindful of thy soil of flowers,
The toiling negro sighed, that Time
    No faster sped his hours.
For, by the dewy moonlight still,
He fed the weary-turning mill,
Or bent him in the chill morass,
To pluck the long and tangled grass,
And hear above his scar-worn back
The heavy slave-whip's frequent crack;
While in his heart one evil thought
In solitary madness wrought,—
One baleful fire surviving still
    The quenching of the immortal mind—
One sterner passion of his kind,
Which even fetters could not kill,—
The savage hope, to deal, ere long,
A vengeance bitterer than his wrong!

Hark to that cry!—long, loud, and shrill,
From field and forest, rock and hill,
Thrilling and horrible it rang,
    Around, beneath, above;—
The wild beast from his cavern sprang—
    The wild bird from her grove!

Nor fear, nor joy, nor agony
Were mingled in that midnight cry;
But, like the lion's growl of wrath,
When falls that hunter in his path,
Whose barbed arrow, deeply set,
Is rankling in his bosom yet,
It told of hate, full, deep, and strong,—
Of vengeance kindling out of wrong;
It was as if the crimes of years—
The unrequited toil—the tears—
The shame and hate, which liken well
Earth's garden to the nether hell,
Had found in Nature's self a tongue,
On which the gathered horror hung;
As if from cliff, and stream, and glen,
Burst, on the startled ears of men,
That voice which rises unto God,
Solemn and stern—the cry of blood!
It ceased—and all was still once more,
Save ocean chafing on his shore,
The sighing of the wind between
The broad banana's leaves of green,
Or bough by restless plumage shook,
Or murmuring voice of mountain brook,

Brief was the silence.   Once again
   Pealed to the skies that frantic yell—
Glowed on the heavens a fiery stain,
   And flashes rose and fell;
And, painted on the blood-red sky,
Dark, naked arms were tossed on high;
And, round the white man's lordly hall,
   Trode, fierce and free, *the brute he made;*
And those who crept along the wall,
And answered to his lightest call
   With more than spaniel dread—
The creatures of his lawless beck—
Were trampling on his very neck!
And, on the night-air, wild and clear,
Rose woman's shriek of more than fear;
For bloodied arms were round her thrown,
And dark cheeks pressed against her own!

Then, injured Afric!—for the shame
Of thy own daughters, vengeance came
Full on the scornful hearts of those,
Who mocked thee in thy nameless woes,
And to thy hapless children gave
One choice—pollution, or the grave !

Where then was he, whose fiery zeal
Had taught the trampled heart to feel,

Until despair itself grew strong,
And vengeance fed its torch from wrong?
Now—when the thunderbolt is speeding:
Now—when oppression's heart is bleeding,
Now—when the latent curse of Time
   Is raining down in fire and blood—
That curse which, through long years of crime,
   Has gathered, drop by drop, its flood—
Why strikes he not, the foremost one,
Where murder's sternest deeds are done?

He stood the aged palms beneath,
   That shadowed o'er his humble door,
Listening, with half-suspended breath,
To the wild sounds of fear and death—
   Toussaint L'Ouverture!
What marvel that his heart beat high!
   The blow for freedom had been given;
And blood had answered to the cry
   Which earth sent up to Heaven!
What marvel, that a fierce delight
Smiled grimly o'er his brow of night,
As groan, and shout, and bursting flame,
Told where the midnight tempest came,
With blood and fire along its van,
And death behind!—he was a MAN!

Yes, dark-souled chieftain!—if the light
   Of mild Religion's heavenly ray
Unveiled not to thy mental sight
   The lowlier and the purer way,
In which the Holy Sufferer trod,
   Meekly amidst the sons of crime,—
That calm reliance upon God
   For justice, in his own good time,—
That gentleness, to which belongs
Forgiveness for its many wrongs.
Even as the primal martyr, kneeling
For mercy on the evil-dealing,—
Let not the favored white man name
Thy stern appeal, with words of blame.
Has *he* not, with the light of heaven
   Broadly around him, made the same?
Yea, on his thousand war-fields striven,
   And gloried in his ghastly shame?—
Kneeling amidst his brother's blood,
To offer mockery unto God,
As if the High and Holy One
Could smile on deeds of murder done!—
As if a human sacrifice
Were purer in his Holy eyes,

Though offered up by Christian hands,
Than the foul rites of Pagan lands!

*   *   *

Sternly, amidst his household band,
His carbine grasped within his hand,
  The white man stood, prepared and still,
Waiting the shock of maddened men,
Unchained, and fierce as tigers, when
  The horn winds through their caverned hill.
And one was weeping in his sight—
  The sweetest flower of all the isle,—
The bride who seemed but yesternight
  Love's fair embodied smile.
And, clinging to her trembling knee,
Looked up the form of infancy,
With tearful glance in either face,
The secret of its fear to trace.
"Ha—stand, or die!" The white man's eye
  His steady musket gleamed along,
As a tall Negro hastened nigh,
  With fearless step and strong.
"What, ho, Toussaint!" A moment more,
His shadow crossed the lighted floor.
"Away," he shouted; "fly with me,—
The white man's bark is on the sea;—
Her sails must catch the seaward wind,
For sudden vengeance sweeps behind.
Our brethren from their grave have spoken,
The yoke is spurned—the chain is broken;
On all the hills our fires are glowing—
Through all the vales red blood is flowing!
No more the mocking White shall rest
His foot upon the Negro's breast;
No more, at morn or eve, shall drip
The warm blood from the driver's whip;
Yet, though Toussaint has vengeance sworn
For all the wrongs his race have borne,—
Though for each drop of Negro blood
The white man's veins shall pour a flood;
Not all alone the sense of ill
Around his heart is lingering still,
Nor deeper can the white man feel
The generous warmth of grateful zeal.
Friends of the Negro! fly with me—
The path is open to the sea:
Away, for life!"—He spoke, and pressed
The young child to his manly breast,
As, headlong, through the cracking cane,
Down swept the dark insurgent train—
Drunken and grim, with shout and yell
Howled through the dark, like sounds from hell!

Far out, in peace, the white man's sail
Swayed free before the sunrise gale.
Cloud-like that island hung afar,
  Along the bright horizon's verge,
O'er which the curse of servile war
  Rolled its red torrent, surge on surge.
And he—the Negro champion—where
  In the fierce tumult, struggled he?
Go trace him by the fiery glare
Of dwellings in the midnight air—
The yells of triumph and despair—
  The streams that crimson to the sea!

Sleep calmly in thy dungeon-tomb,
  Beneath Besançon's alien sky,
Dark Haytien!—for the time shall come,
  Yea, even now is nigh—
When, everywhere, thy name shall be
Redeemed from *color's infamy;*
And men shall learn to speak of thee,
As one of earth's great spirits, born
In servitude, and nursed in scorn,
Casting aside the weary weight
And fetters of its low estate,
In that strong majesty of soul,
  Which knows no color, tongue or clime—
Which still hath spurned the base control
  Of tyrants through all time!
Far other hands than mine may wreathe
The laurel round thy brow of death,
And speak thy praise, as one whose word
A thousand fiery spirits stirred,—
Who crushed his foeman as a worm—
Whose step on human hearts fell firm:—*
Be mine the better task to find
A tribute for thy lofty mind,
Amidst whose gloomy vengeance shone
Some milder virtues all thine own,—

* The reader may, perhaps, call to mind the beautiful sonnet of William **Wordsworth**, addressed to Toussaint L'Ouverture, during his confinement in France.

> " Toussaint!—thou most unhappy man of men !
>   Whether the whistling rustic tends his plough
>   Within thy hearing, or thou liest now
> Buried in some deep dungeon's earless den ;
> Oh, miserable chieftain !—where and when
>   Wilt thou find patience?—Yet, die not ; do thou
>   Wear rather in thy bonds a cheerful brow:
> Though fallen thyself, never to rise again,
> Live and take comfort. Thou hast left behind
>   Powers that will work for thee ; air, earth, and skies,—
> There's not a breathing of the common wind
>   That will forget thee: thou hast great allies,
>   Thy friends are exultations, agonies,
> And love, and man's unconquerable mind,"

Some gleams of feeling pure and warm,
  Like sunshine on a sky of storm,—
Proofs that the Negro's heart retains
  Some nobleness amidst its chains,—
That kindness to the wronged is never
    Without its excellent reward,—
Holy to human-kind, and ever
    Acceptable to God.

THE SLAVE SHIPS.

"That fatal, that perfidious bark,
Built i' the eclipse, and rigged with curses dark."

Milton's Lycidas.

[The French ship LE RODEUR, with a crew of twenty-two men, and with one hundred and sixty negro slaves, sailed from Bonny, in Africa, April, 1819. On approaching the line, a terrible malady broke out—an obstinate disease of the eyes—contagious, and altogether beyond the resources of medicine. It was aggravated by the scarcity of water among the slaves (only half a wine-glass per day being allowed to an individual), and by the extreme impurity of the air in which they breathed. By the advice of the physician, they were brought upon deck occasionally; but some of the poor wretches, locking themselves in each other's arms, leaped overboard, in the hope, which so universally prevails among them, of being swiftly transported to their own homes in Africa. To check this, the captain ordered several, who were stopped in the attempt, to be shot, or hanged, before their companions. The disease extended to the crew; and one after another were smitten with it, until only *one* remained unaffected. Yet even this dreadful condition did not preclude calculation: to save the expense of supporting slaves rendered unsalable, and to obtain grounds for a claim against the underwriters, *thirty-six of the negroes, having become blind, were thrown into the sea and drowned!*

In the midst of their dreadful fears lest the solitary individual, whose sight remained unaffected, should also be seized with the malady, a sail was discovered. It was the Spanish slaver, LEON. The same disease had been there; and, horrible to tell, all the crew had become blind! Unable to assist each other, the vessels parted. The Spanish ship has never since been heard of. The RODEUR reached Gaudaloupe on the 21st of June; the only man who had escaped the disease, and had thus been enabled to steer the slaver into port, caught it in three days after its arrival.—*Speech of M. Benjamin Constant, in the French Chamber of Deputies,* June 17, 1820.]

"ALL ready?" cried the captain;
  "Ay, ay!" the seamen said;
"Heave up the worthless lubbers—
  The dying and the dead."
Up from the slave-ship's prison
  Fierce, bearded heads were thrust—
"Now let the sharks look to it—
  Toss up the dead ones first!"

Corpse after corpse came up,—
  Death had been busy there;
Where every blow is mercy,
  Why should the spoiler spare?
Corpse after corpse they cast
  Sullenly from the ship,
Yet bloody with the traces
  Of fetter-link and whip.

Gloomily stood the captain,
  With his arms upon his breast,
With his cold brow sternly knotted,
  And his iron lip compressed.
"Are all the dead dogs over?"
  Growled through that matted lip—
"The blind ones are no better,
  Let's lighten the good ship."

Hark! from the ship's dark bosom,
  The very sounds of hell!
The ringing clank of iron—
  The maniac's short, sharp yell!—
The hoarse, low curse, throat-stifled—
  The starving infant's moan—
The horror of a breaking heart
  Poured through a mother's groan!

Up from that loathsome prison
  The stricken blind ones came:

Below, had all been darkness—
　Above, was still the same.
Yet the holy breath of heaven
　Was sweetly breathing there,
And the heated brow of fever
　Cooled in the soft sea air.

"Overboard with them, ship-
　mates!"
Cutlass and dirk were plied ;
Fettered and blind, one after one,
　Plunged down the vessel's side.
The sabre smote above—
　Beneath, the lean shark lay, .
Waiting with wide and bloody jaw
　His quick and human prey.

God of the earth ! what cries
　Rang upward unto Thee ?
Voices of agony and blood,
　From ship-deck and from sea.
The last dull plunge was heard—
　The last wave caught its stain—
And the unsated shark looked up
　For human hearts in vain.

　　*　　*　　*　　*　　*

Red glowed the western waters—
　The setting sun was there,
Scattering alike on wave and cloud
　His fiery mesh of hair.
Amidst a group in blindness,
　A solitary eye
Gazed, from the burdened slaver's
　deck,
　Into that burning sky.

"A storm," spoke out the gazer,
　"Is gathering and at hand—
Curse on't—I'd give my other eye
　For one firm rood of land."
And then he laughed—but only
　His echoed laugh replied—
For the blinded and the suffering
　Alone were at his side.

Night settled on the waters,
　And on a stormy heaven,
While fiercely on that lone ship's
　track
　The thunder-gust was driven.
"A sail!—thank God, a sail!"
And, as the helmsman spoke,
Up through the stormy murmur,
　A shout of gladness broke.

Down came the stranger vessel
　Unheeding on her way,
So near, that on the slaver's deck
　Fell off her driven spray.
"Ho! for the love of mercy—
　We're perishing and blind !"
A wail of utter agony
　Came back upon the wind :

"Help us ! for we are stricken
　With blindness every one ;
Ten days we've floated fearfully,
　Unnoting star or sun.
Our ship's the slaver Leon—
　We've but a score on board—
Our slaves are all gone over—
　Help—for the love of God!"

On livid brows of agony
　The broad red lightning shone—
But the roar of wind and thunder
　Stifled the answering groan.
Wailed from the broken waters
　A last despairing cry,
As, kindling in the stormy light,
　The stranger ship went by.

　　*　　*　　*　　*

In the sunny Guadaloupe
　A dark-hulled vessel lay—
With a crew who noted never
　The nightfall or the day.
The blossom of the orange
　Was white by every stream,
And tropic leaf, and flower, and
　bird
　Were in the warm sunbeam.

And the sky was bright as ever,
　And the moonlight slept as well
On the palm trees by the hillside,
　And the streamlet of the dell;
And the glances of the Creole
　Were still as archly deep,
And her smiles as full as ever
　Of passion and of sleep.

But vain were bird and blossom,
　The green earth and the sky,
And the smile of human faces,
　To the slaver's darkened eye;
At the breaking of the morning,
　At the starlit evening time,
O'er a world of light and beauty
　Fell the blackness of his crime

STANZAS.

[" The despotism which our fathers could not bear in their native country is expiring, and the sword of justice in her reformed hands has applied its exterminating edge to slavery. Shall the United States—the free United States, which could not bear the bonds of a king, cradle the bondage which a king is abolishing? Shall a Republic be less free than a Monarchy? Shall we, in the vigor and buoyancy of our manhood, be less energetic in righteousness than a kingdom in its age?"—*Dr. Follen's Address.*

" Genius of America!—Spirit of our free institutions—where art thou?—How art thou fallen, O Lucifer! son of the morning—how art thou fallen from Heaven! Hell from beneath is moved for thee, to meet thee at thy coming!—The kings of the earth cry out to thee, Aha! Aha!—ART THOU BECOME LIKE UNTO US?"—*Speech of Samuel J. May.*]

OUR fellow countrymen in chains!
　　Slaves—in a land of light and law!
Slaves—crouching on the very plains
　　Where rolled the storm of Freedom's war!
A groan from Eutaw's haunted wood—
　　A wail where Camden's martyrs fell—
By every shrine of patriot blood,
　　From Moultrie's wall and Jasper's well!

By storied hill and hallowed grot,
　　By mossy wood and marshy glen,
Whence rang of old the rifle-shot,
　　And hurrying shout of Marion's men!
The groan of breaking hearts is there—
　　The falling lash—the fetter's clank!
Slaves—SLAVES are breathing in that air,
　　Which old De Kalb and Sumter drank!

What, ho!—*our* countrymen in chains!
　　The whip on WOMAN's shrinking flesh!
Our soil yet reddening with the stains,
　　Caught from her scourging, warm and fresh!
What! mothers from their children riven!
　　What! God's own image bought and sold!
AMERICANS to market driven,
　　And bartered as the brute for gold!

Speak! shall their agony of prayer
　　Come thrilling to our hearts in vain?
To us whose fathers scorned to bear
　　The paltry *menace* of a chain;
To us, whose boast is loud and long
　　Of holy Liberty and Light—
Say, shall these writhing slaves of Wrong
　　Plead vainly for their plundered Right?

What! shall we send, with lavish breath,
　　Our sympathies across the wave,
Where Manhood, on the field of death,
　　Strikes for his freedom, or a grave?

Shall prayers go up, and hymns be sung
  For Greece, the Moslem fetter spurning,
And millions hail with pen and tongue
  Our light on all her altars burning ?

Shall Belgium feel, and gallant France,
  By Vendôme's pile and Schoenbrun's wall,
And Poland, gasping on her lance,
  The impulse of our cheering call ?
And shall the SLAVE, beneath our eye,
  Clank o'er *our* fields his hateful chain ?
And toss his fettered arms on high,
  And groan for Freedom's gift, in vain ?

Oh, say, shall Prussia's banner be
  A refuge for the stricken slave ?
And shall the Russian serf go free
  By Baïkal's lake and Neva's wave ?
And shall the wintry-bosomed Dane
  Relax the iron hand of pride,
And bid his bondman cast the chain
  From fettered soul and limb, aside ?

Shall every flap of England's flag
  Proclaim that all around are free,
From " farthest Ind " to each blue crag
  That beetles o'er the Western Sea ?
And shall we scoff at Europe's kings,
  When Freedom's fire is dim with us,
And round our country's altar clings
  The damning shade of Slavery's curse ?

Go—let us ask of Constantine
  To loose his grasp on Poland's throat ;
And beg the lord of Mahmoud's line
  To spare the struggling Suliote—
Will not the scorching answer come
  From turbaned Turk, and scornful Russ
"Go, loose your fettered slaves at home,
  Then turn, and ask the like of us ! "·

Just God ! and shall we calmly rest,
  The Christian's scorn—the heathen's mirth—
Content to live the lingering jest
  And by-word of a mocking Earth ?
Shall our own glorious land retain
  That curse which Europe scorns to bear ?
Shall our own brethren drag the chain
  Which not even Russia's menials wear ?

Up, then, in Freedom's manly part,
  From gray-beard eld to fiery youth,
And on the nation's naked heart
  Scatter the living coals of Truth !

Up—while ye slumber, deeper yet
    The shadow of our fame is growing !
Up—while ye pause, our sun may set
    In blood, around our altars flowing !

Oh ! rouse ye, ere the storm comes forth—
    The gathered wrath of God and man—
Like that which wasted Egypt's earth,
    When hail and fire above it ran.
Hear ye no warnings in the air ?
    Feel ye no earthquake underneath ?
Up—up—why will ye slumber where
    The sleeper only wakes in death ?

Up *now* for Freedom !—not in strife
    Like that your sterner fathers saw—
The awful waste of human life—
    The glory and the guilt of war :
But break the chain—the yoke remove,
    And smite to earth Oppression's rod,
With those mild arms of Truth and Love,
    Made mighty through the living God !

Down let the shrine of Molock sink,
    And leave no traces where it stood ;
Nor longer let its idol drink
    His daily cup of human blood :
But rear another altar there,
    To Truth and Love and Mercy given,
And Freedom's gift, and Freedom's prayer,
    Shall call an answer down from Heaven !

THE YANKEE GIRL.

She sings by her wheel, at that low cottage-door,
Which the long evening shadow is stretching before,
With a music as sweet as the music which seems
Breathed softly and faint in the ear of our dreams !

How brilliant and mirthful the light of her eye,
Like a star glancing out from the blue of the sky!
And lightly and freely her dark tresses play
O'er a brow and a bosom as lovely as they!

Who comes in his pride to that low cottage-door—
The haughty and rich to the humble and poor ?
'Tis the great Southern planter—the master who waves
His whip of dominion o'er hundreds of slaves.

" Nay, Ellen—for shame ! Let those Yankee fools spin,
Who would pass for our slaves with a change of their skins;

Let them toil as they will at the loom or the wheel,
Too stupid for shame, and too vulgar to feel!

" But thou art too lovely and precious a gem
To be bound to their burdens and sullied by them—
For shame, Ellen, shame!—cast thy bondage aside,
And away to the South, as my blessing and pride.

" Oh, come where no winter thy footsteps can wrong,
But where flowers are blossoming all the year long,
Where the shade of the palm-tree is over my home,
And the lemon and orange are white in their bloom !

" Oh, come to my home, where my servants shall all
Depart at thy bidding and come at thy call;
They shall heed thee as mistress with trembling and awe,
And each wish of thy heart shall be felt as a law."

Oh, could ye have seen her—that pride of our girls—
Arise and cast back the dark wealth of her curls,
With a scorn in her eye which the gazer could feel,
And a glance like the sunshine that flashes on steel!

" Go back, haughty Southron! thy treasures of gold
Are dim with the blood of the hearts thou hast sold;
Thy home may be lovely, but round it I hear
The crack of the whip and the footsteps of fear!

" And the sky of thy South may be brighter than ours,
And greener thy landscapes, and fairer thy flowers;
But, dearer the blast round our mountains which raves,
Than the sweet summer zephyr which breathes over slaves!

" Full low at thy bidding thy negroes may kneel,
With the iron of bondage on spirit and heel;
Yet know that the Yankee girl sooner would be
In fetters with them, than in freedom with thee!"

TO W. L. G.

CHAMPION of those who groan beneath
  Oppression's iron hand:
In view of penury, hate and death,
  I see thee fearless stand,
Still bearing up thy lofty brow,
  In the steadfast strength of truth,
In manhood sealing well the vow
  And promise of thy youth.

Go on!—for thou hast chosen well;
  On in the strength of God !

Long as one human heart shall swell
  Beneath the tyrant's rod.
Speak in a slumbering nation's ear,
  As thou hast ever spoken,
Until the dead in sin shall hear—
  The fetter's link be broken!

I love thee with a brother's love,
  I feel my pulses thrill,
To mark thy spirit soar above
  The cloud of human ill.

My heart hath leaped to answer
    thine,
    And echo back thy words,
As leaps the warrior's at the shine
    And flash of kindred swords!

They tell me thou art rash and
    vain—
A searcher after fame—
That thou art striving but to gain
    A long-enduring name—
That thou hast nerved the Afric's
    hand,
    And steeled the Afric's heart,
To shake aloft his vengeful brand,
    And rend his chain apart.

Have I not known thee well, and
    read
    Thy mighty purpose long!

And watched the trials which have
    made
    Thy human spirit strong?
And shall the slanderer's demon
    breath
    Avail with one like me,
To dim the sunshine of my faith
    And earnest trust in thee?

Go on—the dagger's point may
    glare
    Amid thy pathway's gloom—
The fate which sternly threatens
    there
    Is glorious martyrdom!
Then onward with a martyr's
    zeal—
    Press on to thy reward—
The hour when man shall only
    kneel
    Before his Father—God.

SONG OF THE FREE.

[" Living, I shall assert the right of FREE DISCUSSION ; dying, I shall assert it ; and, should I leave no other inheritance to my children, by the blessing of God I will leave them the inheritance of FREE PRINCIPLES, and the example of a manly and independent defence of them."— *Daniel Webster.*]

PRIDE of New England!
    Soul of our fathers!
Shrink we all craven-like,
    When the storm gathers?
What though the tempest be
    Over us lowering,
Where's the New Englander
    Shamefully cowering?
Graves green and holy
    Around us are lying,—
Free were the sleepers all,
    Living and dying!

Back with the Southerner's
    Padlocks and scourges!
Go—let him fetter down
    Ocean's free surges!
Go—let him silence
    Winds, clouds, and waters—
Never New England's own
    Free sons and daughters!
Free as our rivers are
    Ocean-ward going—
Free as the breezes are
    Over us blowing.

Up to our altars, then,
    Haste we, and summon
Courage and loveliness,
    Manhood and woman!
Deep let our pledges be:
    Freedom forever!
Truce with oppression,
    Never, oh! never!
By our own birthright-gift,
    Granted of Heaven—
Freedom for heart and lip,
    Be the pledge given!

If we have whispered truth,
    Whisper no longer;
Speak as the tempest does,
    Sterner and stronger;
Still be the tones of truth,
    Louder and firmer,
Startling the haughty South
    With the deep murmur:
God and our charter's right,
    Freedom forever!
Truce with oppression,
    Never, oh! never!

THE HUNTERS OF MEN.

Written on reading the report of the proceedings of the American Colonization Society, at its annual meeting in 1834.

HAVE ye heard of our hunting, o'er mountain and glen,
Through cane-crake and forest—the hunting of men?
The lords of our land to this hunting have gone,
As the fox-hunter follows the sound of the horn:
Hark!—the cheer and the hallo!—the crack of the whip,
And the yell of the hound as he fastens his grip!
All blithe are our hunters, and noble their match—
Though hundreds are caught, there are millions to catch.
So speed to their hunting, o'er mountain and glen,
Through cane-brake and forest—the hunting of men!

Gay luck to our hunters!—how nobly they ride
In the glow of their zeal, and the strength of their pride!—
The priest with his cassock flung back on the wind,
Just screening the politic statesman behind—
The saint and the sinner, with cursing and prayer—
The drunk and the sober, ride merrily there.
And woman—kind woman—wife, widow, and maid—
For the good of the hunted, is lending her aid:
Her foot's in the stirrup—her hand on the rein—
How blithely she rides to the hunting of men!

Oh! goodly and grand is our hunting to see,
In this "land of the brave and this home of the free."
Priest, warrior, and statesman, from Georgia to Maine,
All mounting the saddle—all grasping the rein—
Right merrily hunting the black man, whose sin
Is the curl of his hair and the hue of his skin!
Woe, now, to the hunted who turns him at bay!
Will our hunters be turned from their purpose and prey?
Will their hearts fail within them?—their nerves tremble, when
All roughly they ride to the hunting of men?

Ho!—ALMS for our hunters! all weary and faint
Wax the curse of the sinner and prayer of the saint.
The horn is wound faintly—the echoes are still,
Over cane-brake and river, and forest and hill.
Haste—alms for our hunters! the hunted once more
Have turned from their flight with their backs to the shore:
What right have *they* here in the home of the white,
Shadowed o'er by *our* banner of Freedom and Right?
Ho!—alms for the hunters! or never again
Will they ride in their pomp to the hunting of men!

ALMS—ALMS for our hunters! why *will* ye delay,
When their pride and their glory are melting away?
The parson has turned; for, on charge of his own,
Who goeth a warfare, or hunting, alone?

The politic statesman looks back with a sigh—
There is doubt in his heart—there is fear in his eye.
Oh! haste, lest that doubting and fear shall prevail,
And the head of his steed take the place of the tail.
Oh! haste, ere he leave us! for who will ride then,
For pleasure or gain, to the hunting of men?

CLERICAL OPPRESSORS.

[In the Report of the celebrated pro-slavery meeting in Charleston S. C., on the 4th of the 9th month, 1835, published in the "Courier" of that city, it is stated, "*The* CLERGY *of all denominations attended in a body*, LENDING THEIR SANCTION TO THE PROCEEDINGS, and adding by their presence to the impressive character of the scene!"]

JUST God!—and these are they
Who minister at Thine altar, God of Right!
Men who their hands with prayer and blessing lay
  On Israel's Ark of light!

What! preach and kidnap men?
Give thanks—and rob Thy own afflicted poor?
Talk of Thy glorious liberty, and then
  Bolt hard the captive's door?

What! servants of Thy own
Merciful Son, who came to seek and save
The homeless and the outcast,—fettering down
  The tasked and plundered slave!

Pilate and Herod, friends!
Chief priests and rulers, as of old, combine!
Just God and holy! is that church, which lends
  Strength to the spoiler, Thine?

Paid hypocrites, who turn
Judgment aside, and rob the Holy Book
Of those high words of truth which search and burn
  In warning and rebuke;

Feed fat, ye locusts, feed!
And, in your tasselled pulpits, thank the Lord
That, from the toiling bondsman's utter need,
  Ye pile your own full board.

How long, O Lord! how long
Shall such a priesthood barter truth away,
And, in Thy name, for robbery and wrong
  At Thy own altars pray?

Is not Thy hand stretched forth
Visibly in the heavens, to awe and smite?
Shall not the living God of all the earth,
  And heaven above, do right?

Woe, then, to all who grind
Their brethren of a common Father down!
To all who plunder from the immortal mind
Its bright and glorious crown!

Woe to the priesthood! woe
To those whose hire is with the price of blood—
Perverting, darkening, changing as they go,
The searching truths of God!

Their glory and their might
Shall perish; and their very names shall be
Vile before all the people, in the light
Of a world's liberty.

Oh! speed the moment on
When Wrong shall cease—and Liberty, and Love,
And Truth, and Right, throughout the earth be known
As in their home above.

THE CHRISTIAN SLAVE.

[In a late publication of L. F. TASISTRO, " Random Shots and Southern Breezes," is a description of a slave auction at New Orleans, at which the auctioneer recommended the woman on the stand as " A GOOD CHRISTIAN! "]

A CHRISTIAN! going, gone!
Who bids for God's own image?—for His grace
Which that poor victim of the market-place
Hath in her suffering won?

My God! can such things be?
Hast thou not said that whatsoe'er is done
Unto Thy weakest and Thy humblest one,
Is even done to Thee?

In that sad victim, then,
Child of Thy pitying love, I see Thee stand—
Once more the jest-word of a mocking band,
Bound, sold, and scourged again!

A Christian up for sale!
Wet with her blood your whips—o'ertask her frame,
Make her life loathsome with your wrong and shame.
Her patience shall not fail!

A heathen hand might deal
Back on your heads the gathered wrong of years,
But her low, broken prayer and nightly tears
Ye neither heed nor feel.

Con well thy lesson o'er,
Thou *prudent* teacher—tell the toiling slave

No dangerous tale of Him who came to save
    The outcast and the poor.

    But wisely shut the ray
Of God's free Gospel from her simple heart,
And to her darkened mind alone impart
    One stern command—" OBEY!" *

    So shalt thou deftly raise
The market price of human flesh; and while
On thee, their pampered guest, the planters smile
    Thy church shall praise.

    Grave, reverend men shall tell
From Northern pulpits how thy work was blest,
While in that vile South Sodom, first and best,
    Thy poor disciples sell.

    Oh, shame! the Moslem thrall,
Who, with his master, to the Prophet kneels,
While turning to the sacred Kebla feels
    His fetters break and fall.

    Cheers for the turbaned Bey
Of robber-peopled Tunis! he hath torn
The dark slave-dungeons open, and hath borne
    Their inmates into day:

    But our poor slave in vain
Turns to the Christian shrine his aching eyes—
Its rites will only swell his market price,
    And rivet on his chain.†

    God of all right! how long
Shall priestly robbers at Thine altar stand,
Lifting in prayer to Thee, the bloody hand
    And haughty brow of wrong?

    Oh, from the fields of cane,
From the low rice-swamp, from the trader's cell—
From the black slave-ship's foul and loathsome hell,
    And coffle's weary chain,—

    Hoarse, horrible, and strong,
Rises to Heaven that agonizing cry,
Filling the arches of the hollow sky,
    How LONG, OH GOD, HOW LONG?

---

* There is in Liberty County, Georgia, an Association for the religious instruction of Negroes. Their seventh annual report contains an address by the *Rev.* Josiah Spry Law, from which we extract the following:—" There is a growing interest, in this community, in the religious instruction of Negroes. There is a conviction that religious instruction promotes the *quiet* and *order* of the people, and the pecuniary *interest* of the owners."

† We often see advertisements in the Southern papers, in which individual slaves, or several of a lot, are recommended as "*pious*," or as "*members of churches*." Lately we saw a slave advertised, who, among other qualifications, was described as "*a Baptist preacher*."

STANZAS FOR THE TIMES.

Is this the land our fathers loved,
    The freedom which they toiled to win?
Is this the soil whereon they moved?
    Are these the graves they slumber in?
Are *we* the sons by whom are borne
The mantles which the dead have worn?

And shall we crouch above these graves,
    With craven soul and fettered lip?
Yoke in with marked and branded slaves,
    And tremble at the driver's whip?
Bend to the earth our pliant knees,
And speak—but as our masters please?

Shall outraged Nature cease to feel?
    Shall mercy's tears no longer flow?
Shall ruffian threats of cord and steel—
    The dungeon's gloom—the assassin's blow,
Turn back the spirit roused to save
The Truth, our Country, and the Slave?

Of human skulls that shrine was made,
    Round which the priests of Mexico
Before their loathsome idol prayed—
    Is Freedom's altar fashioned so?
And must we yield to Freedom's God,
As offering meet, the negro's blood?

Shall tongues be mute, when deeds are wrought
    Which well might shame extremest hell?
Shall freemen lock the indignant thought?
    Shall Pity's bosom cease to swell?
Shall Honor bleed?—Shall Truth succumb?
Shall pen, and press, and soul be dumb?

No—by each spot of haunted ground,
    Where Freedom weeps her children's fall—
By Plymouth's rock, and Bunker's mound—
    By Griswold's stained and shattered wall—
By Warren's ghost—by Langdon's shade—
By all the memories of our dead!

By their enlarging souls, which burst
    The bands and fetters round them set—
By the free Pilgrim spirit nursed
    Within our inmost bosoms, yet,—
By all above—around—below—
Be ours the indignant answer—NO!

No—guided by our country's laws,
   For truth, and right, and suffering man,
Be ours to strive in Freedom's cause,
   As Christians *may*—as freemen *can!*
Still pouring on unwilling ears
That truth oppression only fears.

What! shall we guard our neighbor still,
   While woman shrieks beneath his rod,
And while he tramples down at will
   The image of a common God!
Shall watch and ward be round him set,
Of Northern nerve and bayonet?

And shall we know and share with him
   The danger and the growing shame?
And see our Freedom's light grow dim,
   Which should have filled the world with flame?
And, writhing, feel, where'er we turn,
A world's reproach around us burn?

Is 't not enough that this is borne?
   And asks our hearty neighbor more?
Must fetters which his slaves have worn,
   Clank round the Yankee farmer's door?
Must he be told, beside his plough,
What he must speak, and when, and how?

Must he be told his freedom stands
   On Slavery's dark foundations strong—
On breaking hearts and fettered hands,
   On robbery, and crime, and wrong?
That all his fathers taught is vain—
That Freedom's emblem is the chain?

Its life—its soul, from slavery drawn?
   False—foul—profane! Go—teach as well
Of holy Truth from Falsehood born!
   Of Heaven refreshed by airs from Hell!
Of Virtue in the arms of Vice!
Of Demons planting Paradise!

Rail on, then, " brethren of the South "—
   Ye shall not hear the truth the less—
No seal is on the Yankee's mouth,
   No fetters on the Yankee press!
From our Green Mountains to the Sea,
One voice shall thunder—WE ARE FREE!

LINES

Written on reading the spirited and manly remarks of Governor RITNER, of Pennsylvania, in his Message of 1836, on the subject of Slavery.

THANK God for the token!—one lip is still free—
One spirit untrammelled—unbending one knee !
Like the oak of the mountain, deep-rooted and firm,
Erect, when the multitude bends to the storm ;
When traitors to Freedom, and Honor, and God,
Are bowed at an Idol polluted with blood ;
When the recreant North has forgotten her trust,
And the lip of her honor is low in the dust,—
Thank God, that one arm from the shackle has broken!
Thank God, that one man, as a *freeman,* has spoken !

O'er thy crags, Alleghany, a blast has been blown!
Down thy tide, Susquehanna, the murmur has gone!
To the land of the South—of the charter and chain—
Of Liberty sweetened with Slavery's pain;
Where the cant of Democracy dwells on the lips
Of the forgers of fetters, and wielders of whips !
Where " chivalric " honor means really no more
Than scourging of women, and robbing the poor !
Where the Moloch of Slavery sitteth on high,
And the words which he utters are—WORSHIP, OR DIE!

Right onward, oh, speed it !   Wherever the blood
Of the wronged and the guiltless is crying to God;
Wherever a slave in his fetters is pining;
Wherever the lash of the driver is twining;
Wherever from kindred, torn rudely apart,
Comes the sorrowful wail of the broken of heart;
Wherever the shackles of tyranny bind,
In silence and darkness, the God-given mind ;
There, God speed it onward!—its truth will be felt—
The bonds shall be loosened—the iron shall melt!

And oh, will the land where the free soul of PENN
Still lingers and breathes over mountain and glen—
Will the land where a BENEZET's spirit went forth
To the peeled, and the meted, and outcast of Earth—
Where the words of the Charter of Liberty first
From the soul of the sage and the patriot burst—
Where first for the wronged and the weak of their kind,
The Christian and statesman their efforts combined—
Will that land of the free and the good wear a chain ?
Will the call to the rescue of Freedom be vain ?

No, RITNER !—her " Friends," at thy warning shall stand
Erect for the truth, like their ancestral band ;
Forgetting the feuds and the strife of past time,
Counting coldness injustice, and silence a crime;

Turning back from the cavil of creeds, to unite
Once again for the poor in defence of the Right;
Breasting calmly, but firmly, the full tide of Wrong,
Overwhelmed, but not borne on its surges along;
Unappalled by the danger, the shame, and the pain,
And counting each trial for Truth as their gain!

And that bold-hearted yeomanry, honest and true,
Who, haters of fraud, give to labor its due;
Whose fathers, of old, sang in concert with thine,
On the banks of Swetara, the songs of the Rhine—
The German-born pilgrims, who first dared to brave
The scorn of the proud in the cause of the slave:*—
Will the sons of such men yield the lords of the South
One brow for the brand—for the padlock one mouth?
They cater to tyrants?—they rivet the chain,
Which their fathers smote off, on the negro again?

No, never!—one voice, like the sound in the cloud,
When the roar of the storm waxes loud and more loud,
Wherever the foot of the freeman hath pressed
From the Delaware's marge to the Lake of the West,
On the South-going breezes shall deepen and grow
Till the land it sweeps over shall tremble below!
The voice of a PEOPLE—uprisen—awake—
Pennsylvania's watchword, with Freedom at stake,
Thrilling up from each valley, flung down from each height,
" OUR COUNTRY AND LIBERTY!—GOD FOR THE RIGHT!"

LINES.

Written on reading the famous " PASTORAL LETTER " of the Massachusetts General Association, 1837.

So, this is all—the utmost reach
    Of priestly power the mind to fetter!
When laymen think—when women preach—
    A war of words—a " Pastoral Letter!*"
Now, shame upon ye, parish Popes!
    Was it thus with those, your predecessors,
Who sealed with racks, and fire, and ropes
    Their loving kindness to transgressors?

A " Pastoral Letter," grave and dull—
    Alas! in hoof and horns and features,
How different is your Brookfield bull,
    From him who bellows from St. Peter's!
Your pastoral rights and powers from harm,
    Think ye, Can words alone preserve them?
Your wiser fathers taught the arm
    And sword of temporal power to serve them.

* It is a remarkable fact that the first testimony of a religious body against negro slavery was that of a Society of German " Friends " in Pennsylvania.

Oh, glorious days—when church and state
  Were wedded by your spiritual fathers!
And on submissive shoulders sat
  Your Wilsons and your Cotton Mathers.
No vile "itinerant" then could mar
  The beauty of your tranquil Zion,
But at his peril of the scar
  Of hangman's whip and branding-iron.

Then, wholesome laws relieved the church
  Of heretic and mischief-maker,
And priest and bailiff joined in search,
  By turns, of Papist, witch, and Quaker!
The stocks were at each church's door,
  The gallows stood on Boston Common,
A Papist's ears the pillory bore,—
  The gallows-rope, a Quaker woman!

Your fathers dealt not as ye deal
  With "non-professing" frantic teachers;
They bored the tongue with red-hot steel,
  And flayed the backs of female preachers."
Old Newbury, had her fields a tongue,
  And Salem's streets, could tell their story,
Of fainting woman dragged along,
  Gashed by the whip, accursed and gory!

And will ye ask me, why this taunt
  Of memories sacred from the scorner?
And why with reckless hand I plant
  A nettle on the graves ye honor?
Not to reproach New England's dead
  This record from the past I summon,
Of manhood to the scaffold led,
  And suffering and heroic woman.

No—for yourselves alone, I turn
  The pages of intolerance over,
That, in their spirit, dark and stern,
  Ye haply may your own discover!
For, if ye claim the "pastoral right"
  To silence Freedom's voice of warning,
And from your precincts shut the light
  Of Freedom's day around ye dawning;

If when an earthquake voice of power,
  And signs in earth and heaven are showing
That, forth, in its appointed hour,
  The Spirit of the Lord is going!
And, when that Spirit, Freedom's light
  On kindred, tongue, and people breaking,
Whose slumbering millions, at the sight,
  In glory and in strength are waking!

When for the sighing of the poor,
   And for the needy, God hath risen,
And chains are breaking, and a door
   Is opening for the souls in prison !
If then ye would, with puny hands,
  —Arrest the very work of Heaven,
And bind anew the evil bands
   Which God's right arm of power hath riven—

What marvel that, in many a mind,
   Those darker deeds of bigot madness
Are closely with your own combined,
   Yet " less in anger than in sadness " ?
What marvel, if the people learn
   To claim the right of free opinion ?
What marvel, if at times they spurn
   The ancient yoke of your dominion ?

Oh, how contrast, with such as ye,
   A LEAVITT's free and generous bearing !
A PERRY's calm integrity.
   A PHELP's zeal and Christian daring !
A FOLLENS' soul of sacrifice,
   And MAY's with kindness overflowing !
How green and lovely in the eyes
   Of freemen are their graces growing !

Ay, there's a glorious remnant yet,
   Whose lips are wet at Freedom's fountains,
The coming of whose welcome feet
   Is beautiful upon our mountains !
Men, who the gospel tidings bring
   Of Liberty and Love forever,
Whose joy is one abiding spring,
   Whose peace is as a gentle river !

But ye, who scorn the thrilling tale
   Of Carolina's high-souled daughters,
Which echoes here the mournful wail
   Of sorrow from Edisto's waters,
Close while ye may the public ear—
   With malice vex, with slander wound them—
The pure and good shall throng to hear,
   And tried and manly hearts surround them.

Oh, ever may the power which led
   Their way to such a fiery trial,
And strengthened womanhood to tread
   The wine-press of such self-denial,
Be round them in an evil land,
   With wisdom and with strength from Heaven,
With Miriam's voice, and Judith's hand,
   And Deborah's song for triumph given !

And what are ye who strive with God,
   Against the ark of his salvation,
Moved by the breath of prayer abroad,
   With blessings for a dying nation?
What, but the stubble and the hay
   To perish, even as flax consuming,
With all that bars His glorious way,
   Before the brightness of His coming?

And thou sad Angel, who so long
   Hast waited for the glorious token,
That Earth from all her bonds of wrong
   To liberty and light has broken—
Angel of Freedom! soon to thee
   The sounding trumpet shall be given,
And over Earth's full jubilee
   Shall deeper joy be felt in Heaven!

LINES.

Written for the Meeting of the Anti-Slavery Society, at Chatham Street Chapel, **N. Y.,** held on the 4th of the 7th month, 1834.

O THOU, whose presence went before
   Our fathers in their weary way,
As with thy chosen moved of yore
   The fire by night—the cloud by day!

When from each temple of the free,
   A nation's song ascends to Heaven,
Most Holy Father! unto Thee
   May not our humble prayer be given?

Thy children all—though hue and form
   Are varied in thine own good will—
With Thy own holy breathings warm,
   And fashioned in Thine image still

We thank Thee, Father!—hill and plain
   Around us wave their fruits once more,
And clustered vine, and blossomed grain,
   Are bending round each cottage door.

And peace is here; and hope and love
   Are round us as a mantle thrown,
And unto Thee, supreme above,
   The knee of prayer is bowed alone.

But oh, for those this day can bring,
   As unto us, no joyful thrill—
For those who, under Freedom's wing,
   Are bound in Slavery's fetters still:

For those to whom Thy living word
  Of light and love is never given—
For those whose ears have never heard
  The promise and the hope of Heaven!

For broken heart, and clouded mind,
  Whereon no human mercies fall—
Oh, be Thy gracious love inclined,
  Who, as a father, pitiest all!

And grant, O Father! that the time
  Of Earth's deliverance may be near,
When every land, and tongue, and clime,
  The message of Thy love shall hear—

When, smitten as with fire from heaven,
  The captive's chain shall sink in dust,
And to his fettered soul be given
  The glorious freedom of the just!

LINES

Written for the celebration of the Third Anniversary of British Emancipation, at the Broadway Tabernacle, N. Y., "First of August," 1837.

O HOLY FATHER!—just and true
  Are all Thy works and words and ways,
And unto Thee alone are due
  Thanksgiving and eternal praise!
As children of Thy gracious care,
  We veil the eye—we bend the knee,
With broken words of praise and prayer,
  Father and God, we come to Thee.

For Thou hast heard, O God of Right,
  The sighing of the island slave;
And stretched for him the arm of might,
  Not shortened that it could not save.
The laborer sits beneath his vine,
  The shackled soul and hand are free—
Thanksgiving!—for the work is Thine!
  Praise!—for the blessing is of Thee!

And oh, we feel Thy presence here—
  Thy awful arm in judgment bare!
Thine eye hath seen the bondman's tear—
  Thine ear hath heard the bondman's prayer!
Praise!—for the pride of man is low.
  The counsels of the wise are naught,
The fountains of repentance flow;
  What hath our God in mercy wrought?

Speed on Thy work, Lord God of Hosts!
    And when the bondman's chain is riven,
And swells from all our guilty coasts
    The anthem of the free to Heaven,
Oh, not to those whom Thou hast led,
    As with Thy cloud and fire before,
But unto Thee, in fear and dread,
    Be praise and glory evermore.

LINES

Written for the Anniversary celebration of the First of August, at Milton, 1840.

A FEW brief years have passed away
    Since Britain drove her million slaves
Beneath the tropic's fiery ray:
God willed their freedom; and to-day
    Life blooms above those island graves!

He spoke! across the Carib sea,
    We heard the clash of breaking chains,
And felt the heart-throb of the free,
The first, strong pulse of liberty
    Which thrilled along the bondman's veins.

Though long delayed, and far, and slow,
    The Briton's triumph shall be ours:
Wears slavery here a prouder brow
Than that which twelve short years ago
    Scowled darkly from her island bowers?

Mighty alike for good or ill
    With mother-land, we fully share
The Saxon strength—the nerve of steel—
The tireless energy of will,—
    The power to do, the pride to dare.

What she has done can we not do?
    Our hour and men are both at hand;
The blast which Freedom's angel blew
O'er her green islands, echoes through
    Each valley of our forest land.

Hear it, old Europe! we have sworn
    The death of slavery.—When it falls
Look to your vassals in their turn,
Your poor dumb millions, crushed and worn,
    Your prisons and your palace walls!

Oh kingly mockers!—scoffing show
    What deeds in Freedom's name we do;
Yet know that every taunt ye throw
Across the waters, goads our slow
    Progression toward the right and true.

Not always shall your outraged poor,
  Appalled by democratic crime,
Grind as their fathers ground before,—
The hour which sees our prison door
  Swing wide shall be *their* triumph time.

On then, my brothers! every blow
  Ye deal is felt the wide earth through;
Whatever here uplifts the low
Or humbles Freedom's hateful foe,
  Blesses the Old World through the New.

Take heart! The promised hour draws near—
  I hear the downward beat of wings,
And Freedom's trumpet sounding clear—
Joy to the people!—woe and fear
  To new world tyrants, old world kings!

THE FAREWELL

OF A VIRGINIA SLAVE MOTHER TO HER DAUGHTERS, SOLD INTO SOUTHERN BONDAGE.

GONE, gone—sold and gone,
  To the rice-swamp dank and lone.
Where the slave-whip ceaseless swings,
Where the noisome insect stings,
Where the fever demon strews
Poison with the falling dews,
Where the sickly sunbeams glare
Through the hot and misty air,—
  Gone, gone—sold and gone,
  To the rice-swamp dank and lone,
  From Virginia's hills and waters,—
  Woe is me, my stolen daughters!

Gone, gone—sold and gone,
  To the rice-swamp dank and lone.
There no mother's eye is near them,
There no mother's ear can hear them;
Never, when the torturing lash
Seams their back with many a gash,
Shall a mother's kindness bless them,
Or a mother's arms caress them.
  Gone, gone—sold and gone,
  To the rice-swamp dank and lone,
  From Virginia's hills and waters—
  Woe is me, my stolen daughters!

Gone, gone—sold and gone,
  To the rice-swamp dank and lone.

Oh, when weary, sad, and slow,
From the fields at night they go,
Faint with toil, and racked with pain,
To their cheerless homes again—
There no brother's voice shall greet them—
There no father's welcome meet them.
    Gone, gone—sold and gone,
    To the rice-swamp dank and lone,
    From Virginia's hills and waters—
    Woe is me, my stolen daughters!

    Gone, gone—sold and gone,
    To the rice-swamp dank and lone,
From the tree whose shadow lay
On their childhood's place of play—
From the cool spring where they drank—
Rock, and hill, and rivulet bank—
From the solemn house of prayer,
And the holy counsels there—
    Gone, gone—sold and gone,
    To the rice-swamp dank and lone,
    From Virginia's hills and waters,—
    Woe is me, my stolen daughters!

    Gone, gone—sold and gone,
    To the rice-swamp dank and lone—
Toiling through the weary day,
And at night the spoiler's prey.
Oh, that they had earlier died,
Sleeping calmly, side by side,
Where the tyrant's power is o'er
And the fetter galls no more!
    Gone, gone—sold and gone,
    To the rice-swamp dark and lone,
    From Virginia's hills and waters,—
    Woe is me, my stolen daughters!

    Gone, gone—sold and gone,
    To the rice-swamp dark and lone.
By the holy love He beareth—
By the bruised reed He spareth—
Oh, may He, to whom alone
All their cruel wrongs are known,
Still their hope and refuge prove,
With a more than a mother's love,
    Gone, gone—sold and gone,
    To the rice-swamp dank and lone,
    From Virginia's hills and waters,—
    Woe is me, my stolen daughters!

ADDRESS

Written for the opening of " PENNSYLVANIA HALL," dedicated to Free Discussion, Virtue, Liberty, and Independence, of the 15th of the 5th month, 1838.

NOT with the splendors of the days of old,
The spoil of nations, and " barbaric gold "—
No weapons wrested from the fields of blood,
Where dark and stern the unyielding Roman stood
And the proud eagles of his cohorts saw
A world, war-wasted, crouching to his law—
Nor blazoned car—nor banners floating gay,
Like those which swept along the Appian way,
When to the welcome of imperial Rome,
The victor warrior came in triumph home,
And trumpet-peal, and shoutings wild and high,
Stirred the blue quiet of the Italian sky;
But calm and grateful, prayerful and sincere,
As Christian freemen, only, gathering here,
We dedicate our fair and lofty Hall,
Pillar and arch, entablature and wall,
As Virtue's shrine—as Liberty's abode—
Sacred to Freedom, and to Freedom's God!

Oh! loftier halls, 'neath brighter skies than these,
Stood darkly mirrored in the Ægean seas,
Pillar and shrine—and lifelike statues seen,
Graceful and pure, the marble shafts between,
Where glorious Athens from her rocky hill
Saw Art and Beauty subject to her will—
And the chaste temple, and the classic grove—
The hall of sages—and the bowers of love,
Arch, fane, and column, graced the shores, and gave
Their shadows to the blue Saronic wave;
And statelier rose, on Tiber's winding side,
The Pantheon's dome—the Coliseum's pride—
The Capitol, whose arches backward flung
The deep, clear cadence of the Roman tongue,
Whence stern decrees, like words of fate, went forth
To the awed nations of a conquered earth,
Where the proud Cæsars in their glory came,
And Brutus lightened from his lips of flame!

Yet in the porches of Athena's halls,
And in the shadows of her stately walls,
Lurked the sad bondman, and his tears of woe
Wet the cold marble with unheeded flow;
And fetters clanked beneath the silver dome
Of the proud Pantheon of imperious Rome.
Oh! not for him—the chained and stricken slave—
By Tiber's shore, or blue Ægina's wave,

In the thronged forum, or the sage's seat,
The bold lip pleaded, and the warm heart beat;
No soul of sorrow melted at his pain,
No tear of pity rusted on his chain!

But this fair Hall, to Truth and Freedom given,
Pledged to the Right before all Earth and Heaven,
A free arena for the strife of mind,
To caste, or sect, or color unconfined,
Shall thrill with echoes, such as ne'er of old
From Roman hall, or Grecian temple rolled;
Thoughts shall find utterance, such as never yet
The Propylaea or the Forum met.
Beneath its roof no gladiator's strife
Shall win applauses with the waste of life;
No lordly lictor urge the barbarous game—
No wanton Lais glory in her shame.
But here the tear of sympathy shall flow,
As the ear listens to the tale of woe;
Here, in stern judgment of the oppressor's wrong—
Shall strong rebukings thrill on Freedom's tongue—
No partial justice hold the unequal scale—
No pride of caste a brother's rights assail—
No tyrant's mandates echo from this wall,
Holy to Freedom and the Rights of All!
But a fair field, where mind may close with mind,
Free as the sunshine and the chainless wind;
Where the high trust is fixed on Truth alone,
And bonds and fetters from the soul are thrown;
Where wealth, and rank, and worldly pomp, and might,
Yield to the presence of the True and Right.

And fitting is it that this Hall should stand
Where Pennsylvania's Founder led his band,
From thy blue waters, Delaware!—to press
The virgin verdure of the wilderness.
Here, where all Europe with amazement saw
The soul's high freedom trammelled by no law;
Here, where the fierce and warlike forest-men
Gathered in peace, around the home of PENN,
Awed by the weapons Love alone had given,
Drawn from the holy armory of Heaven;
Where Nature's voice against the bondman's wrong
First found an earnest and indignant tongue;
Where LAY's bold message to the proud was borne
And KEITH's rebuke, and FRANKLIN's manly scorn—
Fitting it is that here, where Freedom first
From her fair feet shook off the Old World's dust,
Spread her white pinions to our Western blast,
And her free tresses to our sunshine cast,
One Hall should rise redeemed from Slavery's ban—
One Temple sacred to the Rights of Man!

Oh! if the spirits of the parted come,
Visiting angels, to their olden home;
If the dead fathers of the land look forth
From their far dwellings, to the things of earth—
Is it a dream, that with their eyes of love,
They gaze now on us from the bowers above?
LAY's ardent soul—and BENEZET the mild,
Steadfast in faith, yet gentle as a child—
Meek-hearted WOOLMAN,—and that brother-band,
The sorrowing exiles from their "FATHERLAND,"
Leaving their homes in Krieshiem's bowers of vine,
And the blue beauty of their far glorious Rhine,
To seek amidst our solemn depths of wood
Freedom from man and holy peace with God;
Who first.of all their testimonial gave
Against the oppressor,—for the outcast slave,—
Is it a dream that such as these look down,
And with their blessing our rejoicings crown?

Let us rejoice, that, while the pulpit's door
Is barred against the pleaders for the poor;
While the church, wrangling upon points of faith,
Forgets her bondmen suffering unto death;
While crafty traffic and the lust of gain
Unite to forge oppression's triple chain,
One door is open, and one Temple free—
As a resting place for hunted Liberty!
Where men may speak, unshackled and unawed,
High words of truth, for Freedom and for God.

And when that truth its perfect work hath done,
And rich with blessings o'er our land hath gone;
When not a slave beneath his yoke shall pine,
From broad Potomac to the far Sabine;
When unto angel-lips at last is given
The silver trump of Jubilee to Heaven;
And from Virginia's plains—Kentucky's shades,
And through the dim Floridian everglades,
Rises, to meet that angel-trumpet's sound,
The voice of millions from their chains unbound—
Then, though this Hall be crumbling in decay,
Its strong walls blending with the common clay,
Yet, round the ruins of its strength shall stand
The best and noblest of a ransomed land—
Pilgrims, like those who throng around the shrine
Of Mecca, or of holy Palestine!—
A prouder glory shall that ruin own
Than that which lingers round the Parthenon.

Here shall the child of after years be taught
The work of Freedom which his fathers wrought—
Told of the trials of the present hour,
Our weary strife with prejudice and power,—

How the high errand quickened woman's soul,
And touched her lip as with a living coal—
How Freedom's martyrs kept their lofty faith,
True and unwavering, unto bonds and death.—
The pencil's art shall sketch the ruined Hall,
The Muses' garland crown its aged wall,
And History's pen for after times record
Its consecration unto FREEDOM'S GOD !

THE MORAL WARFARE.

WHEN Freedom, on her natal day,
Within her war-rocked cradle lay,
An iron race around her stood,
Baptized her infant brow in blood
And, through the storm which
  round her swept,
Their constant ward and watching
  kept.

Our fathers to their graves have
  gone;
Their strife is past—their triumph
  won;
But sterner trials wait the race
Which rises in their honored place—
A moral warfare with the crime
And folly of an evil time.

Then, where our quiet herds re-
  pose,
The roar of baleful battle rose,
And brethren of a common tongue
To mortal strife as tigers sprung,
And every gift on Freedom's
  shrine
Was man for beast, and blood for
  wine !

So let it be. In God's own might
We gird us for the coming fight,
And, strong in Him whose cause is
  ours
In conflict with unholy powers,
We grasp the weapons He has
  given,—
The Light, and Truth, and Love of
  Heaven !

THE RESPONSE.

["To agitate the question (Slavery) anew, is not only impolitic, but it is a virtual breach of good faith to our brethren of the South ; an unwarrantable interference with their domestic relations and institutions." "I can never, in the official station which I occupy, consent to *countenance* a course which may jeopard the peace and harmony of the Union."—*Governor Porter's Inaugural Message*, 1838.]

No "countenance" of his, forsooth !
  Who asked it at his vassal hands ?
Who looked for homage done to Truth,
  By party's vile and hateful bands ?
Who dreamed that one by them possessed,
Would lay for her his spear in rest ?

His "countenance"! well, let it light
  The human robber to his spoil !—
Let those who track the bondsman's flight,
  Like bloodhounds o'er our once free soil,
Bask in its sunshine while they may,
And howl its praises on their way ;

We ask no boon : our rights we claim—
　　Free press and thought—free tongue and pen—
The right to speak in Freedom's name,
　　As Pennsylvanians and as men ;
To do, by Lynch law unforbid,
What our own Rush and Franklin did.

Ay, there we stand, with planted feet,
　　Steadfast, where those old worthies stood :—
Upon us let the tempest beat,
　　Around us swell and surge the flood :
We fail or triumph on that spot ;
God helping us, we falter not.

" A breach of plighted faith ? " For shame !—
　　Who voted for that " breach "!　Who gave
In the state councils, vote and name
　　For freedom for the District slave ?
Consistent patriot !　go, forswear,
Blot out, " expunge " the record there ! *

Go, eat thy words.　Shall H——C——
　　Turn round—a moral harlequin ?
And arch V——B——wipe away
　　The stains of his Missouri sin ?
And shall that one unlucky vote
Stick, burr-like, in *thy* honest throat ?

No—do thy part in *" putting down "* †
　　The friends of Freedom :—summon out
The parson in his saintly gown,
　　To curse the outlawed roundabout,
In concert with the Belial brood—
The Balaam of " the brotherhood " !

Quench every free discussion light—
　　Clap on the legislative snuffers,
And caulk with " resolutions " tight
　　The ghastly rents the Union suffers!
Let church and state brand Abolition
As heresy and rank sedition.

Choke down, at once, each breathing thing,
　　That whispers of the Rights of Man:—
Gag the free girl who dares to sing
　　Of freedom o'er her dairy pan:—
Dog the old farmer's steps about,
And hunt his cherished treason out.

---

* It ought to be borne in mind that DAVID R. PORTER voted in the Legislature to instruct the congressional delegation of Pennsylvania to use their influence for the abolition of slavery in the District of Columbia.

† " He [MartinVan Buren] thinks the abolitionists may be put down."--*Richmond (Va.) Enquirer.*

Go, hunt sedition.—Search for that
  In every pedler's cart of rags ;
Pry into every Quaker's hat,
  And DOCTOR FUSSELL's saddle bags !
Lest treason wrap, with all its ills,
Around his powders and his pills.

Where Chester's oak and walnut shades
  With slavery-laden breezes stir,
And on the hills, and in the glades
  Of Bucks and honest Lancaster,
Are heads which think and hearts which feel—
Flints to the Abolition steel !

Ho ! send ye down a corporal's guard
  With flow of flag and beat of drum—
Storm LINDLEY COATES's poultry yard,
  Beleaguer THOMAS WHITSON's home !
Beat up the Quaker quarters—show
Your valor to an unarmed foe !

Do more. Fill up your loathsome jails
  With faithful men and women—set
The scaffold up in these green vales,
  And let their verdant turf be wet
With blood of unresisting men—
Ay, do all this, and more,—WHAT THEN ?

Think ye, one heart of man and child
  Will falter from his lofty faith,
At the mob's tumult, fierce and wild—
  The prison cell—the shameful death ?
No!—nursed in storm and trial long,
The weakest of our band is strong !

Oh! while before us visions come
  Of slave ships on Virginia's coast—
Of mothers in their childless home,
  Like Rachel, sorrowing o'er the lost—
The slave-gang scourged upon its way—
The bloodhound and his human prey—

We cannot falter ! Did we so,
  The stones beneath would murmur out,
And all the winds that round us blow
  Would whisper of our shame about.
No ! let the tempest rock the land,
Our faith shall live—our truth shall stand.

True as the Vaudois hemmed around
  With Papal fire and Roman steel—
Firm as the Christian heroine bound
  Upon Domitian's torturing wheel,
We 'bate no breath—we curb no thought—
Come what may come, WE FALTER NOT !

THE WORLD'S CONVENTION

Of the Friends of Emancipation, Held in London in 1840.

Yes, let them gather!—Summon forth
The pledged philanthropy of Earth,
From every land, whose hills have heard
  The bugle blast of Freedom waking;
Or shrieking of her symbol-bird
  From out his cloudy eyrie breaking;
Where Justice hath one worshipper,
Or truth one altar built to her;
Where'er a human eye is weeping
  O'er wrongs which Earth's sad children know—
Where'er a single heart is keeping
  Its prayerful watch with human woe:
Thence let them come, and greet each other,
And know in each, a friend and brother!

Yes, let them come! from each green vale
  Where England's old baronial halls
  Still bear upon their storied walls
The grim crusader's rusted mail,
Battered by Paynim spear and brand
On Malta's rock or Syria's sand!
And mouldering pennon-staves once set
  Within the soil of Palestine,
By Jordan and Gennesaret;
  Or borne with England's battle line,
O'er Acre's shattered turrets stooping,
Or, midst the camp their banners drooping,
  With dews from hallowed Hermon wet,
A holier summons now is given
  Than that gray hermit's voice of old,
Which unto all the winds of heaven
  The banners of the Cross unrolled!
Not for the long deserted shrine,—
  Not for the dull unconscious sod,
Which tells not by one lingering sigh
  That there the hope of Israel trod;—
But for the TRUTH, for which alone
  In pilgrim eyes are sanctified
The garden moss, the mountain stone,
Whereon His holy sandals pressed—
The fountain which His lip hath blessed—
Whate'er hath touched His garment's hem
At Bethany or Bethlehem,
  Or Jordan's riverside.
For FREEDOM, in the name of Him
  Who came to raise Earth's drooping poor

To break the chain from every limb—
  The bolt from every prison door!
For these, o'er all the Earth hath passed
An ever-deepening trumpet blast,
As if an angel's breath had lent
Its vigor to the instrument.

And Wales, from Snowden's mountain wall,
Shall startle at that thrilling call,
  As if she heard her bards again;
And Erin's "harp on Tara's wall"
  Give out its ancient strain,
Mirthful and sweet, yet sad withal—
  The melody which Erin loves,
When o'er that harp, mid bursts of gladness
And slogan cries and lyke-wake sadness,
  The hand of her O'Connell moves:
Scotland, from lake and tarn and rill,
And mountain hold, and heathery hill,
  Shall catch and echo back the note.
As if she heard upon her air
Once more her Cameronian's prayer
  And song of Freedom float.
And cheering echoes shall reply
From each remote dependency,
Where Britain's mighty sway is known,
In tropic sea or frozen zone;
Where'er her sunset flag is furling,
Or morning gun-fire's smoke is curling;
From Indian Bengal's groves of palm
And rosy fields and gales of balm,
Where Eastern pomp and power are rolled
Through regal Ava's gates of gold;
And from the lakes and ancient woods
And dim Canadian solitudes,
Whence, sternly from her rocky throne,
Queen of the North, Quebec looks down;
And from those bright and ransomed Isles
Where all unwonted Freedom smiles,
And the dark laborer still retains
The scar of slavery's broken chains!

From the hoar Alps, which sentinel
The gateways of the land of Tell,
Where morning's keen and earliest glance
  On Jura's rocky wall is thrown,
And from the olive bowers of France
  And vine groves garlanding the Rhone,—
"Friends of the Blacks," as true and tried
As those who stood by Oge's side—
Brissot and eloquent Grégoire—
When with free lip and heart of fire

The Haytien told his country's wrong,
Shall gather at that summons strong—
Broglie, Passy, and him, whose song
Breathed over Syria's holy sod,
And in the paths which Jesus trod,
And murmured midst the hills which hem
Crownless and sad Jerusalem,
Hath echoes whereso'er the tone
Of Israel's prophet-lyre is known.

Still let them come—from Quito's walls,
    And from the Orinoco's tide,
From Lima's Inca-haunted halls,
From Santa Fe and Yucatan,—
    Men who by swart Guerrero's side
Proclaimed the deathless RIGHTS OF MAN,
    Broke every bond and fetter off,
    And hailed in every sable serf
A free and brother Mexican!
Chiefs who across the Andes' chain
    Have followed Freedom's flowing pennon
And seen on Junin's fearful plain,
Glare o'er the broken ranks of Spain,
    The fire-burst of Bolivar's cannon!
And Hayti, from her mountain land,
    Shall send the sons of those who hurled
Defiance from her blazing strand—
The war-gage from her Pétion's hand,
    Alone against a hostile world.

Nor all unmindful, thou, the while,
Land of the dark and mystic Nile!—
    Thy Moslem mercy yet may shame
    All tyrants of a Christian name—
When in the shade of Gezeh's pile,
Or, where from Abyssinian hills
El Gerek's upper fountain fills,
Or where from mountains of the Moon
El Abiad bears his watery boon,
Where'er thy lotos blossoms swim
    Within their ancient hollowed waters—
Where'er is heard thy prophet's hymn,
    Or song of Nubia's sable daughters,—
The curse of SLAVERY and the crime,
Thy bequest from remotest time,
At thy dark Mehemet's decree
For evermore shall pass from thee;
    And chains forsake each captive's limb
Of all those tribes, whose hills around
Have echoed back the cymbal sound
    And victor horn of Ibraham.

And thou whose glory and whose crime
To earth's remotest bound and clime,
In mingled tones of awe and scorn,
The echoes of a world have borne,
My country! glorious at thy birth,
A day-star flashing brightly forth—
   The herald-sign of Freedom's dawn !
Oh! who could dream that saw thee then,
   And watched thy rising from afar,
That vapors from oppression's fen
   Would cloud the upward-tending star ?
Or, that earth's tyrant powers, which heard,
   Awe-struck, the shout which hailed thy dawning,
Would rise so soon, prince, peer, and king,
To mock thee with their welcoming,
Like Hades when her thrones were stirred
   To greet the down-cast Star of Morning!
"Aha! and art thou fallen thus ?
Art THOU become as one of *us ?* "

Land of my fathers!—there will stand,
Amidst that world-assembled band,
Those owning thy maternal claim
Unweakened by thy crime and shame,—
The sad reprovers of thy wrong—
The children thou hast spurned so long.
Still with affection's fondest yearning
To their unnatural mother turning.
No traitors they!—but tried and leal,
Whose own is but thy general weal,
Still blending with the patriot's zeal
The Christian's love for human kind,
To caste and climate unconfined.

A holy gathering!—peaceful all—
No threat of war—no savage call
   For vengeance on an erring brother;
But in their stead the God-like plan
To teach the brotherhood of man
   To love and reverence one another,
As sharers of a common blood—
The children of a common God!—
Yet, even at its lightest word,
Shall Slavery's darkest depths be stirred;
Spain watching from her Moro's keep
Her slave-ships traversing the deep,
And Rio, in her strength and pride,
Lifting, along her mountain side,
Her snowy battlements and towers—
Her lemon groves and tropic bowers,
With bitter hate and sullen fear
Its freedom-giving voice shall hear;

And where my country's flag is flowing,
On breezes from Mount Vernon blowing
  Above the Nation's council-halls,
Where Freedom's praise is loud and long,
    While, close beneath the outward walls,
The driver plies his reeking thong--
    The hammer of the man-thief falls,
O'er hypocritic cheek and brow
The crimson flush of shame shall glow:
And all who for their native land
Are pledging life and heart and hand—
Worn watchers o'er her changing weal,
Who for her tarnished honor feel—
Through cottage-door and council-hall
Shall thunder an awakening call.
The pen along its page shall burn
With all intolerable scorn—
And eloquent rebuke shall go
On all the winds that Southward blow;
From priestly lips, now sealed and dumb,
Warning and dread appeal shall come,
Like those which Israel heard from him,
The Prophet of the Cherubim—
Or those which sad Esaias hurled
Against a sin-accursed world !
Its wizard-leaves the Press shall fling
Unceasing from its iron wing,
With characters inscribed thereon,
    As fearful in the despot's hall
As to the pomp of Babylon
    The fire-sign on the palace wall !
And, from her dark iniquities,
Methinks I see my country rise :
Not challenging the nations round
    To note her tardy justice done—
Her captives from their chains unbound,
    Her prisons opening to the sun ;—
But tearfully her arms extending
Over the poor and unoffending;
Her legal emblem now no longer
A bird of prey, with talons reeking,
Above the dying captive shrieking,
But, spreading out her ample wing—
A broad, impartial covering—
    The weaker sheltered by the stronger!—
Oh ! then to Faith's anointed eyes
    The promised token shall be given ;
And on a nation's sacrifice,
    Atoning for the sin of years,
And wet with penitential tears—
The fire shall fall from Heaven !

NEW HAMPSHIRE.—1845.

GOD bless New Hampshire!—from her granite peaks
Once more the voice of Stark and Langdon speaks.
The long bound vassal of the exulting South
    For very shame her self-forged chain has broken—
Torn the black seal of slavery from her mouth,
    And in the clear tones of her old time spoken !
Oh, all undreamed of, all unhoped-for changes !—
    The tyrant's ally proves his sternest foe;
To all his biddings, from her mountain ranges,
    New Hampshire thunders an indignant No !
Who is it now despairs ? Oh, faint of heart,
    Look upward to those Northern mountains cold,
    Flouted by Freedom's victor-flag unrolled,
And gather strength to bear a manlier part!
All is not lost.   The angel of God's blessing
    Encamps with Freedom on the field of fight;
Still to her banner, day by day, are pressing,
    Unlooked for allies, striking for the right!
Courage, then, Northern hearts!—Be firm, be true:
What one brave State hath done, can ye not also do ?

THE NEW YEAR.

ADDRESSED TO THE PATRONS OF THE PENNSYLVANIA FREEMAN.

THE wave is breaking on the shore—
    The echo fading from the chime—
Again the shadow moveth o'er
    The dial-plate of time !

Oh, seer-seen Angel! waiting now
    With weary feet on sea and shore,
Impatient for the last dread vow
    That time shall be no more!—

Once more across thy sleepless eye
    The semblance of a smile has passed;
The year departing leaves more nigh
    Time's fearfullest and last.

Oh! in that dying year hath been
    The sum of all since time began—
The birth and death, the joy and pain,
    Of Nature and of Man.

Spring, with the change of sun and shower,
    And streams released from winter's chain,

And bursting bud, and opening flower,
   And greenly-growing grain;

And Summer's shade, and sunshine warm,
   And rainbows o'er the hilltops bowed,
And voices in her rising storm—
   God speaking from his cloud !—

And Autumn's fruits and clustering sheaves,
   And soft, warm days of golden light,
The glory of her forest leaves,
   And harvest-moon at night;

And Winter with her leafless grove,
   And prisoned stream, and drifting snow,
The brilliance of her heaven above
   And of her earth below :—

And man—in whom an angel's mind
   With earth's low instincts finds abode—
The highest of the links which bind
   Brute nature to her God;

His infant eye hath seen the light,
   His childhood's merriest laughter rung,
And active sports to manlier might
   The nerves of boyhood strung !

And quiet love, and passion's fires,
   Have soothed or burned in manhood's breast,
And lofty aims and low desires
   By turns disturbed his rest.

The wailing of the newly-born
   Has mingled with the funeral knell;
And o'er the dying's ear has gone
   The merry marriage-bell.

And Wealth has filled his halls with mirth,
   While Want, in many a humble shed,
Toiled, shivering by her cheerless hearth,
   The live-long night for bread.

And worse than all—the human slave—
   The sport of lust, and pride, and scorn!
Plucked off the crown his Maker gave—
   His regal manhood gone!

Oh! still my country! o'er thy plains,
   Blackened with slavery's blight and ban,
That human chattel drags his chains—
   An uncreated man!

And still, where'er to sun and breeze,
  My country, is thy flag unrolled,
With scorn, the gazing stranger sees
  A stain on every fold.

Oh, tear the gorgeous emblem down!
  It gathers scorn from every eye,
And despots smile, and good men frown,
  Whene'er it passes by.

Shame! shame! its starry splendors glow
  Above the slaver's loathsome jail—
Its folds are ruffling even now
  His crimson flag of sale.

Still round our country's proudest hall
  The trade of human flesh is driven,
And at each careless hammer-fall
  A human heart is riven.

And this, too, sanctioned by the men,
  Vested with power to shield the right,
And throw each vile and robber den
  Wide open to the light.

Yet shame upon them!—there they sit,
  Men of the North, subdued and still;
Meek, pliant poltroons, only fit
  To work a master's will.

Sold—bargained off for Southern votes—
  A passive herd of Northern mules,
Just braying through their purchased throats
  Whate'er their owner rules.

And he *—the basest of the base—
  The vilest of the vile—whose name,
Embalmed in infinite disgrace,
  Is deathless in its shame!—

A tool—to bolt the people's door
  Against the people clamoring there,—
An ass—to trample on their floor
  A people's right of prayer!

Nailed to the self-made gibbet fast,
  Self-pilloried to the public view—
A mark for every passing blast
  Of scorn to whistle through;

* The Northern author of the Congressional rule against receiving petitions of the people on the subject of Slavery.

There let him hang, and hear the boast
  Of Southrons o'er their pliant tool—
A St. Stylites on his post,
  " Sacred to ridicule !"

Look we at home !—our noble hall,
  To Freedom's holy purpose given,
Now rears its black and ruined wall,
  Beneath the wintry heaven—

Telling the story of its doom—
  The fiendish mob—the prostrate law—
The fiery jet through midnight's gloom,
  Our gazing thousands saw.

Look to our State—the poor man's right
  Torn from him :—and the sons of those
Whose blood in Freedom's sternest fight
  Sprinkled the Jersey snows,

Outlawed within the land of Penn,
  That Slavery's guilty fears might cease.
And those whom God created men,
  Toil on as brutes in peace.

Yet o'er the blackness of the storm,
  A bow of promise bends on high,
And gleams of sunshine, soft and warm,
  Break through our clouded sky.

East, West, and North, the shout is heard
  Of freemen rising for the right:
Each valley hath its rallying word—
  Each hill its signal light.

O'er Massachusetts' rocks of gray,
  The strengthening light of freedom shines,
Rhode Island's Narragansett Bay—
  And Vermont's snow-hung pines!

From Hudson's frowning palisades
  To Alleghany's laurelled crest,
O'er lakes and prairies, streams and glades,
  It shines upon the West.

Speed on the light to those who dwell
  In Slavery's land of woe and sin,
And through the blackness of that hell
  Let Heaven's own light break in.

So shall the Southern conscience quake,
  Before that light poured full and strong,

So shall the Southern heart awake
  To all the bondman's wrong.

And from that rich and sunny land
  The song of grateful millions rise,
Like that of Israel's ransomed band
  Beneath Arabia's skies:

And all who now are bound beneath
  Our banner's shade—our eagle's wing,
From Slavery's night of moral death
  To light and life shall spring.

Broken the bondman's chain—and gone
  The master's guilt, and hate, and fear,
And unto both alike shall dawn,
  A New and Happy Year.

MASSACHUSETTS TO VIRGINIA.

[Written on reading an account of the proceedings of the citizens of Norfolk, Va., in reference to GEORGE LATIMER, the alleged fugitive slave, the result of whose case in Massachusetts will probably be similar to that of the negro SOMERSET in England, in 1772.]

THE blast from Freedom's Northern hills, upon its Southern way,
Bears greeting to Virginia from Massachusetts Bay:—
No word of haughty challenging, nor battle bugle's peal,
Nor steady tread of marching files, nor clang of horsemen's steel.

No trains of deep-mouthed cannon along our highways go—
Around our silent arsenals untrodden lies the snow;
And to the land breeze of our ports, upon their errands far,
A thousand sails of commerce swell, but none are spread for war.

We hear thy threats, Virginia! thy stormy words and high,
Swell harshly on the Southern winds which melt along our sky;
Yet, not one brown, hard hand foregoes its honest labor here—
No hewer of our mountain oaks suspends his axe in fear.

Wild are the waves which lash the reefs along St. George's bank—
Cold on the shore of Labrador the fog lies white and dank;
Through storm, and wave, and blinding mist, stout are the hearts which
    man
The fishing-smacks of Marblehead, the sea boats of Cape Ann.

The cold north light and wintry sun glare on their icy forms,
Bent grimly o'er their straining lines or wrestling with the storms;
Free as the winds they drive before, rough as the waves they roam,
They laugh to scorn the slaver's threat against their rocky home.

What means the Old Dominion? Hath she forgot the day
When o'er her conquered valleys swept the Briton's steel array?

How side by side, with sons of hers, the Massachusetts men
Encountered Tarleton's charge of fire, and stout Cornwallis, then?

Forgets she how the Bay State, in answer to the call
Of her old House of Burgesses, spoke out from Faneuil Hall?
When, echoing back her Henry's cry, came pulsing on each breath
Of Northern winds, the thrilling sounds of " LIBERTY OR DEATH!"

What asks the Old Dominion? If now her sons have proved
False to their fathers' memory—false to the faith they loved;
If she can scoff at Freedom, and its great charter spurn,
Must we of Massachusetts from truth and duty turn?

We hunt your bondmen, flying from Slavery's hateful hell—
Our voices, at your bidding, take up the blood-hound's yell—
We gather, at your summons, above our fathers' graves,
From Freedom's holy altar-horns to tear your wretched slaves!

Thank God! not yet so vilely can Massachusetts bow;
The spirit of her early time is with her even now;
Dream not because her Pilgrim blood moves slow, and calm, and cool,
She thus can stoop her chainless neck, a sister's slave and tool!

All that a *sister* State should do, all that a *free* State may,
Heart, hand, and purse we proffer, as in our early day;
But that one dark loathsome burden ye must stagger with alone,
And reap the bitter harvest which ye yourselves have sown!

Hold, while ye may, your struggling slaves, and burden God's free air
With woman's shriek beneath the lash, and manhood's wild despair;
Cling closer to the " cleaving curse " that writes upon your plains
The blasting of Almighty wrath against a land of chains.

Still shame your gallant ancestry, the cavaliers of old,
By watching round the shambles where human flesh is sold—
Gloat o'er the new-born child, and count his market value, when
The maddened mother's cry of woe shall pierce the slaver's den!

Lower than plummet soundeth, sink the Virginian name;
Plant, if ye will, your fathers' graves with rankest weeds of shame;
Be, if ye will, the scandal of God's fair universe—
We wash our hands forever, of your sin, and shame, and curse.

A voice from lips whereon the coal from Freedom's shrine hath been,
Thrilled, as but yesterday, the hearts of Berkshire's mountain men:
The echoes of that solemn voice are sadly lingering still
In all our sunny valleys, on every wind-swept hill.

And when the prowling man-thief came hunting for his prey
Beneath the very shadow of Bunker's shaft of gray,
How, through the free lips of the son, the father's warning spoke;
How, from its bonds of trade and sect, the Pilgrim city broke!

A hundred thousand right arms were lifted up on high,—
A hundred thousand voices sent back their loud reply;

Through the thronged towns of Essex the startling summons rang,
And up from bench and loom and wheel her young mechanics sprang!

The voice of free, broad Middlesex—of thousands as of one—
The shaft of Bunker calling to that of Lexington—
From Norfolk's ancient villages; from Plymouth's rocky bound
To where Nantucket feels the arms of ocean close her round;—

From rich and rural Worcester, where through the calm repose
Of cultured vales and fringing woods the gentle Nashua flows,
To where Wachuset's wintry blasts the mountain larches stir,
Swelled up to Heaven the thrilling cry of "God save Latimer!"

And sandy Barnstable rose up, wet with the salt sea spray—
And Bristol sent her answering shout down Narragansett Bay!
Along the broad Connecticut old Hampden felt the thrill,
And the cheer of Hampshire's woodmen swept down from Holyoke Hill.

The voice of Massachusetts! Of her free sons and daughters—
Deep calling unto deep aloud—the sound of many waters!
Against the burden of that voice what tyrant power shall stand?
No fetters in the Bay State! No slave upon her land!

Look to it well, Virginians! In calmness we have borne,
In answer to our faith and trust, your insult and your scorn;
You've spurned our kindest counsels—you've hunted for our lives—
And shaken round our hearths and homes your manacles and gyves!

We wage no war—we lift no arm—we fling no torch within
The fire-damps of the quaking mine beneath your soil of sin;
We leave ye with your bondmen, to wrestle, while ye can,
With the strong upward tendencies and God-like soul of man!

But for us and for our children, the vow which we have given
For freedom and humanity, is registered in Heaven;
No slave-hunt in our borders—no pirate on our strand!
No fetters in the Bay State—no slave upon our land!

THE RELIC.

[PENNSYLVANIA HALL, dedicated to Free Discussion and the cause of Human Liberty, was
destroyed by a mob in 1838. The following was written on receiving a cane wrought from a
fragment of the wood-work which the fire had spared.]

TOKEN of friendship true and tried,
   From one whose fiery heart of youth
With mine has beaten, side by side,
   For Liberty and Truth;
With honest pride the gift I take,
And prize it for the giver's sake.

But not alone because it tells
   Of generous hand and heart sincere;

Around that gift of friendship dwells
   A memory doubly dear—
Earth's noblest aim—man's holiest thought,
   With that memorial frail inwrought !

Pure thoughts and sweet, like flowers unfold
   And precious memories round it cling,
Even as the Prophet's rod of old
   In beauty blossoming :
And buds of feeling pure and good
Spring from its cold unconscious wood.

Relic of Freedom's shrine !—a brand
   Plucked from its burning!—let it be
Dear as a jewel from the hand
   Of a lost friend to me!—
Flower of a perished garland left,
Of life and beauty unbereft!

Oh! if the young enthusiast bears,
   O'er weary waste and sea, the stone
Which crumbled from the Forum's stairs,
   Or round the Parthenon ;
Or olive bough from some wild tree
Hung over old Thermopylæ :

If leaflets from some hero's tomb,
   Or moss-wreath torn from ruins hoary,—
Or faded flowers whose sisters bloom
   On fields renowned in story,—
Or fragment from the Alhambra's crest,
Or the gray rock by druids blessed ;

Sad Erin's shamrock greenly growing
   Where Freedom led her stalwart kern,
Or Scotia's "rough burr thistle" blowing
   On Bruce's Bannockburn—
Or Runnymede's wild English rose,
Or lichen plucked from Sempach's snows!—

If it be true that things like these
   To heart and eye bright visions bring,
Shall not far holier memories
   To this memorial cling ?
Which needs no mellowing mist of time
To hide the crimson stains of crime!

Wreck of a temple, unprofaned—
   Of courts where Peace with Freedom trod,
Lifting on high, with hands unstained,
   Thanksgiving unto God ;
Where Mercy's voice of love was pleading
For human hearts in bondage bleeding!—

Where midst the sound of rushing feet
  And curses on the night air flung,
That pleading voice rose calm and sweet
  From woman's earnest tongue;
And Riot turned his scowling glance,
Awed, from her tranquil countenance!

That temple now in ruin lies!—
  The fire-stain on its shattered wall,
And open to the changing skies
  Its black and roofless hall,
It stands before a nation's sight,
A grave-stone over buried Right!

But from that ruin, as of old,
  The fire-scorched stones themselves are crying,
And from their ashes white and cold
  Its timbers are replying!
A voice which slavery cannot kill
Speaks from the crumbling arches still!

And even this relic from thy shrine,
  Oh, holy Freedom!—hath to me
A potent power, a voice and sign
  To testify of thee;
And, grasping it, methinks I feel
A deeper faith, a stronger zeal.

And not unlike that mystic rod,
  Of old stretched o'er the Egyptian wave,
Which opened, in the strength of God,
  A pathway for the slave,
It yet may point the bondman's way,
And turn the spoiler from his prey.

STANZAS FOR THE TIMES.—1844.

[Written on reading the sentence of JOHN L. BROWN of South Carolina, to be executed on the 25th of 4th month, 1844, for the crime of assisting a female slave to escape from bondage. The sentence was afterward commuted.].

Ho! thou who seekest late and long
  A license from the Holy Book
For brutal lust and hell's red wrong,
  Man of the pulpit, look!—
Lift up those cold and atheist eyes,
  This ripe fruit of thy teaching see;
And tell us how to Heaven will rise
The incense of this sacrifice—
  This blossom of the Gallows Tree!—

Search out for SLAVERY's hour of need
    Some fitting text of sacred writ; *
Give Heaven the credit of a deed
    Which shames the nether pit.
Kneel, smooth blasphemer, unto Him
    Whose truth is on thy lips a lie,
Ask that His bright-winged cherubim
May bend around that scaffold grim
    To guard and bless and sanctify!—

Ho! champion of the people's cause—
    Suspend thy loud and vain rebuke
Of foreign wrong and Old World laws,
    Man of the Senate, look!—
Was this the promise of the free,—
    The great hope of our early time,—
That Slavery's poison vine should be
Upborne by Freedom's prayer-nursed tree,
    O'erclustered with such fruits of crime?—

Send out the summons, East and West,
    And South and North, let all be there,
Where he who pitied the oppressed
    Swings out in sun and air.
Let not a democratic hand
    The grisly hangman's task refuse;
There let each loyal patriot stand
Awaiting Slavery's command
    To twist the rope and draw the noose!

But vain is irony—unmeet
    Its cold rebuke for deeds which start
In fiery and indignant beat
    The pulses of the heart.
Leave studied wit, and guarded phrase;
    And all that kindled heart can feel
Speak out in earnest words which raise,
Where'er they fall, an answering blaze,
    Like flints which strike the fire from steel.

Still let a mousing priesthood ply
    Their garbled text and gloss of sin,
And make the lettered scroll deny
    Its living soul within;
Still let the place-feed titled knave
    Plead Robbery's right with purchased lips,
And tell us that our fathers gave
For Freedom's pedestal, a slave,
    For frieze and moulding, chains and whips!—

* Three new publications, from the pens of Dr. Junkin, President of Miami College, Alexander McCaine of the Methodist Protestant church, and of a clergyman of the Cincinnati Synod, defending Slavery on Scriptural ground, have recently made their appearance.

But ye who own that higher law
 Whose tables in the heart are set,
Speak out in words of power and awe
 That God is living yet!
Breathe forth once more those tones sublime
 Which thrilled the burdened prophet's lyre,
And in a dark and evil time
Smote down on Israel's fast of crime
 And gift of blood, a rain of fire!

Oh, not for us the graceful lay,
 To whose soft measures lightly move
The Dryad and the woodland Fay,
 O'erlooked by Mirth and Love;
But such a stern and startling strain
 As Britain's hunted bards flung down
From Snowden, to the conquered plain,
Where harshly clanked the Saxon chain
 On trampled field and smoking town.

By Liberty's dishonored name,
 By man's lost hope, and failing trust,
By words and deeds, which bow with shame
 Our foreheads to the dust,—
By the exulting tyrant's sneer,
 .Borne to us from the Old World's thrones,
And by their grief, who pining hear,
In sunless mines and dungeons drear,
 How Freedom's land her faith disowns;—

Speak out in *acts ;* the time for words
 Has passed, and deeds alone suffice;
In the loud clang of meeting swords
 The softer music dies!
Act—act, in God's name, while ye may,
 Smite from the church her leprous limb,
Throw open to the light of day
The bondman's cell, and break away
 The chains the state has bound on him.

Ho! every true and living soul,
 To Freedom's perilled altar bear
The freeman's and the Christian's whole,
 Tongue, pen, and vote, and prayer!
One last great battle for the Right,—
 One short, sharp struggle to be free!—
To do is to succeed—our fight
Is waged in Heaven's approving sight—
 The smile of God is Victory!

THE BRANDED HAND.

[CAPTAIN JONATHAN WALKER, of Harwich, Mass., was solicited by several fugitive slaves Pensacola, Florida, to convey them in his vessel to the British West Indies. Although we aware of the hazard of the enterprise, he attempted to comply with their request. He was seize by an American vessel, consigned to the American authorities at Key West, and by them take back to Florida—where, after a long and rigorous imprisonment, he was brought to trial. H was sentenced to be branded on the right hand with the letters "S. S." ("Slave Stealer" and amerced in a heavy fine. He was released on the payment of his fine in the 6th month 1845.]

WELCOME home again, brave seaman! with thy thoughtful brow an
    gray,
And the old heroic spirit of our earlier, better day—
With that front of calm endurance, on whose steady nerve, in vain
Pressed the iron of the prison, smote the fiery shafts of pain!

Is the tyrant's brand upon thee? Did the brutal cravens aim
To make God's truth thy falsehood, His holiest work thy shame?
When, all blood-quenched, from the torture the iron was withdrawn,
How laughed their evil angel the baffled fools to scorn!

They change to wrong, the duty which God hath written out
On the great heart of humanity too legible for doubt!
They, the loathsome moral lepers, blotched from footsole up to crown,
Give to shame what God hath given unto honor and renown!

Why, that brand is highest honor!—than its traces never yet
Upon old armorial hatchments was a prouder blazon set;
And thy unborn generations, as they tread our rocky strand,
Shall tell with pride the story of their father's BRANDED HAND!

As the Templar home was welcomed, bearing back from Syrian wars
The scars of Arab lances, and of Paynim scimitars.
The pallor of the prison and the shackle's crimson span,
So we meet thee, so we greet thee, truest friend of God and man!

He suffered for the ransom of the dear Redeemer's grave,
Thou for His living presence in the bound and bleeding slave;
He for a soil no longer by the feet of angels trod,
Thou for the true Shechinah, the present home of God!

For, while the jurist sitting with the slave-whip o'er him swung,
From the tortured truths of freedom the lie of slavery wrung,
And the solemn priest to Moloch, on each God-deserted shrine,
Broke the bondman's heart for bread, poured the bondman's blood fo
    wine—

While the multitude in blindness to a far-off Saviour knelt,
And spurned, the while, the temple where a present Saviour dwelt;
Thou beheld'st Him in the task-field, in the prison shadows dim,
And thy mercy to the bondman, it was mercy unto Him!

In the lone and long night watches, sky above and wave below,
Thou did'st learn a higher wisdom than the babbling school-men know

God's stars and silence taught thee, as His angels only can,
That the one, sole sacred thing beneath the cope of heaven is Man!

That he who treads profanely on the scrolls of law and creed,
In the depth of God's great goodness may find mercy in his need;
But woe to him who crushes the SOUL with chain and rod,
And herds with lower natures the awful form of God!

Then lift that manly right hand, bold ploughman of the wave!
Its branded palm shall prophesy, "SALVATION TO THE SLAVE!"
Hold up its fire-wrought language, that whoso reads may feel
His heart swell strong within him, his sinews change to steel.

Hold it up before our sunshine, up against our Northern air—
Ho! men of Massachusetts, for the love of God look there!
Take it henceforth for your standard—like the Bruce's heart of yore,
In the dark strife closing round ye, let that hand be seen before!

And the tyrants of the slave-land shall tremble at that sign,
When it points its finger Southward along the Puritan line:
Woe to the State-gorged leeches, and the Church's locust band,
When they look from slavery's ramparts on the coming of that hand!

TEXAS.

VOICE OF NEW ENGLAND.

Up the hillside, down the glen,
Rouse the sleeping citizen;
Summon out the might of men!

Like a lion growling low—
Like a night-storm rising slow—
Like the tread of unseen foe—

It is coming—it is nigh!
Stand your homes and altars by;
On your own free thresholds die!

Clang the bells in all your spires;
On the gray hills of your sires
Fling to heaven your signal fires!

From Wachuset, lone and bleak,
Unto Berkshire's tallest peak,
Let the flame-tongued heralds speak!

All for God and duty stand,
Heart to heart and hand to hand,
Round the old graves of the land!

Whoso shrinks or falters now,
Whoso to the yoke would bow,
Brand the craven on his brow!

Freedom's soil hath only place
For a free and fearless race—
None for traitors false and base.

Perish party—perish clan;
Strike together while ye can,
Like the arm of one strong man!

Like that angel's voice sublime,
Heard above a world of crime.
Crying of the end of time—

With one heart and with one mouth,
Let the North unto the South
Speak the word befitting both:

"What though Issachar be strong!
Ye may load his back with wrong
Overmuch and over long

" Patience with her cup o'errun,
 With her weary thread outspun,
 Murmurs that her work is done.

" Make our Union-bond a chain,
 Weak as tow in Freedom's strain
 Link by link shall snap in twain.

" Vainly shall your sand-wrought
 rope
 Bind the starry cluster up,
 Shattered over heaven's blue
 cope !

" Give us bright though broken
 rays,
 Rather than eternal haze,
 Clouding o'er the full-orbed-
 blaze !

" Take your land of sun and bloom ;
 Only leave to Freedom room
 For her plough, and forge, and
 loom ;

" Take your slavery-blackened
 vales :
 Leave us but our own free gales,
 Blowing on our thousand sails !

" Boldly, or with treacherous art,
 Strike the blood-wrought chain
 apart ;
 Break the Union's mighty heart ;

" Work the ruin, if ye will :
 Pluck upon your heads an ill
 Which shall grow and deepen
 still !

" With your bondman's right arm
 bare,
 With his heart of black despair,
 Stand alone, if stand ye dare !

" Onward with your fell design ;
 Dig the gulf and draw the line :
 Fire beneath your feet the mine :

" Deeply, when the wide abyss
 Yawns between your land and
 this,
 Shall ye feel your helplessness.

" By the hearth, and in the bed,
 Shaken by a look or tread,
 Ye shall own a guilty dread.

" And the curse of unpaid toil,
 Downward   through   your
 generous soil
 Like a fire shall burn and spoil.

" Our bleak hills shall bud and
 blow,
 Vines our rocks shall overgrow,
 Plenty in our valleys flow ;—

" And when vengeance clouds your
 skies,
 Hither shall ye turn your eyes,
 As the lost on Paradise !

" We but ask our rocky strand,
 Freedom's true and brother band
 Freedom's strong and honest
 hand,—

" Valleys by the slave untrod,
 And the Pilgrim's mountain sod
 Blessed of our fathers' God ! "

TO FANEUIL HALL

MEN !—if manhood still ye claim,
 If the Northern pulse can thrill
Roused by wrong or stung by
 shame,
 Freely, strongly still :—
Let the sounds of traffic die :
 Shut the mill-gate—leave the
 stall—
Fling the axe and hammer by—
 Throng to Faneuil Hall !

Wrongs which   freemen   never
 brooked—
 Dangers grim and fierce as they
Which, like couching lions, looked
 On your fathers' way ;—
These your instant zeal demand,
 Shaking with their earthquake
 call
Every rood of Pilgrim land—
 Ho, to Faneuil Hall !

'rom your capes and sandy bars—
From your mountain-ridges cold,
'hrough whose pines the westering
    stars
  Stoop their crowns of gold—
'ome, and with your footsteps
    wake
  Echoes from that holy wall:
nce again, for Freedom's sake,
  Rock your fathers' hall!

p, and tread beneath your feet
  Every cord by party spun;
et your hearts together beat
  As the heart of one.
anks and tariffs, stocks and trade,
  Let them rise or let them fall:
reedom asks your common aid—
  Up, to Faneuil Hall!

p, and let each voice that speaks
  Ring from thence to Southern
    plains,
arply as the blow which breaks
  Prison-bolts and chains!
)eak as well becomes the free—
  Dreaded more than steel or ball,
all your calmest utterance be,
  Heard from Faneuil Hall!

ive they wronged us? Let us
    then
Render back nor threats nor
    prayers;
ive they chained our free-born
    men?
LET US UNCHAIN THEIRS!
) ! your banner leads the van,
  Blazoned "Liberty for all!"
nish what your sires began—
  Up, to Faneuil Hall!

TO MASSACHUSETTS.

RITTEN DURING THE PENDING OF
    THE TEXAS QUESTION.

HAT though around thee blazes
  No fiery rallying sign?
om all thy own high places,
  }ive heaven the light of thine!

What though unthrilled, unmov-
    ing,
  The statesman stands apart,
And comes no warm approving
  From Mammon's crowded mart?

Still let the land be shaken
  By a summons of thine own !
By all save truth forsaken,
  · Why, stand with that alone!
Shrink not from strife unequal!
  With the best is always hope;
And ever in the sequel
  God holds the right side up!

But when, with thine uniting,
  Come voices long and loud,
And far-off hills are writing
  Thy fire-words on the cloud:
When from Penobscot's fountains
  A deep response is heard,
And across the Western mountains
  Rolls back thy rallying word;

Shall thy line of battle falter,
  With its allies just in view ?
Oh, by hearth and holy altar,
  My Fatherland, be true!
Fling abroad thy scrolls of Free-
    dom!
  Speed them onward far and fast!
Over hill and valley speed them,
  Like the Sibyl's on the blast!

Lo! the Empire State is shaking
  The shackles from her hand;
With the rugged North is waking
  The level sunset land!
On they come—the free battalions !
  East and West and North they
    come,
And the heart-beat of the millions
  Is the beat of Freedom's drum.

" To the tyrant's plot no favor!
  No heed to place-fed knaves!
Bar and bolt the door forever
  Against the land of Slaves!"
Hear it, mother Earth, and hear it,
  The Heavens above us spread!
The land is roused—its spirit
  Was sleeping, but not dead!

THE PINE TREE.

LIFT again the stately emblem on the Bay State's rusted shield,
Give to Northern winds the Pine Tree on our banner's tattered field,
Sons of men who sat in council with their Bibles round the board,
Answering England's royal missive with a firm, "THUS SAITH TH
    LORD!"
Rise again for home and freedom!—set the battle in array!—
What the fathers did of old time we their sons must do to-day.

Tell us not of banks and tariffs—cease your paltry pedler cries,—
Shall the good State sink her honor that your gambling stocks may rise
Would ye barter man for cotton?—That your gains may be the same,
Must we kiss the feet of Moloch, pass our children through the flame?
Is the dollar only real?—God and truth and right a dream?
Weighed against your lying ledgers must our manhood kick the beam

Oh, my God!—for that free spirit, which of old in Boston town
Smote the Province House with terror, struck the crest of Andros down!—
For another strong-voiced Adams in the city's streets to cry:
"Up for God and Massachusetts!—Set your feet on Mammon's lie!
Perish banks and perish traffic—spin your cotton's latest pound—
But in Heaven's name keep your honor—keep the heart o' the Bay Sta
    sound!"

Where's the MAN for Massachusetts?—Where's the voice to speak h
    free?—
Where's the hane to light up bonfires from her mountains to the sea?
Beats her Pilgrim pulse no longer?—Sits she dumb in her despair?—
Has she none to break the silence?—Has she none to do and dare?
Oh my God! for one right worthy to lift up her rusted shield,
And to plant again the Pine Tree in her banner's tattered field!

LINES.

SUGGESTED BY A VISIT TO THE CITY OF WASHINGTON IN THE 12T
MONTH OF 1845.

WITH a cold and wintry noon-light,
    On its roofs and steeples shed,
Shadows weaving with the sunlight
    From the gray sky overhead,
Broadly, vaguely, all around me, lies the half-built town out
    spread.

Through this broad street, restless ever,
    Ebbs and flows a human tide,
Wave on wave a living river;
    Wealth and fashion side by side;
Toiler, idler, slave and master, in the same quick current
    glide.

Underneath yon dome, whose coping
Springs above them, vast and tall,
Grave men in the dust are groping
For the largest, base and small,
Which the hand of Power is scattering, crumbs which from its
table fall.

Base of heart! They vilely barter
Honor's wealth for party's place:
Step by step on Freedom's charter
Leaving footprints of disgrace ;
For to-day's poor pittance turning from the great hope of their
race.

Yet, where festal lamps are throwing
Glory round the dancer's hair,
Gold-tressed, like an angel's flowing
Backward on the sunset air;
And the low quick pulse of music beats its measures sweet and
rare:

There to-night shall woman's glances,
Star-like, welcome give to them,
Fawning fools with shy advances
Seek to touch their garments' hem,
With the tongue of flattery glozing deeds which God and Truth
condemn.

From this glittering lie my vision
Takes a broader, sadder range,
Full before me have arisen
Other pictures dark and strange;
From the parlor to the prison must the scene and witness change.

Hark ! the heavy gate is swinging
On its hinges, harsh and slow;
One pale prison lamp is flinging
On a fearful group below
Such a light as leaves to terror whatsoe'er it does not show.

Pitying God!—Is that a WOMAN
On whose wrists the shackles clash ?
Is that shriek she utters human,
Underneath the stinging lash ?
Are they MEN whose eyes of madness from that sad procession
flash ?

Still the dance goes gaily onward!
What is it to Wealth and Pride,
That without the stars are looking
On a scene which earth should hide ?
That the SLAVE-SHIP lies in waiting, rocking on Potomac's tide!

Vainly to that mean Ambition
　　Which, upon a rival's fall,
Winds above its old condition,
　　With a reptile's slimy crawl,
Shall the pleading voice of sorrow, shall the slave in anguish
　　　　call.

Vainly to the child of Fashion,
　　Giving to ideal woe
Graceful luxury of compassion,
　　Shall the stricken mourner go;
Hateful seems the earnest sorrow, beautiful the hollow show!

Nay, my words are all too sweeping:
　　In this crowded human mart
Feeling is not dead, but sleeping;
　　Man's strong will and woman's heart,
In the coming strife for Freedom, yet shall bear their generous
　　　　part.

And from yonder sunny valleys,
　　Southward in the distance lost,
Freedom yet shall summon allies
　　Worthier than the North can boast,
With the Evil by their hearth-stones grappling at severer cost.

Now, the soul alone is willing:
　　Faint the heart and weak the knee;
And as yet no lip is thrilling
　　With the mighty words "BE FREE!'
Tarrieth long the land's Good Angel, but his advent is to be!

Meanwhile, turning from the revel
　　To the prison-cell my sight,
For intenser hate of evil,
　　For a keener sense of right,
Shaking off thy dust, I thank thee, City of the Slaves, to-night!

" To thy duty now and ever!
　　Dream no more of rest or stay;
Give to Freedom's great endeavor
　　All thou art and hast to-day:"
Thus, above the city's murmur, saith a Voice or seems to say.

Ye with heart and vision gifted
　　To discern and love the right,
Whose worn faces have been lifted
　　To the slowly-growing light,
Where from Freedom's sunrise drifted slowly back the murk
　　　　of night!—

Ye who through long years of trial
　　Still have held your purpose fast,

While a lengthening shade the dial
From the westering sunshine cast,
And of hope each hour's denial seemed an echo of the last!—

Oh, my brothers! oh, my sisters!
Would to God that ye were near,
Gazing with me down the vistas
Of a sorrow strange and drear;
Would to God that ye were listening to the Voice I seem to hear!

With the storm above us driving,
With the false earth mined below—
Who shall marvel if thus striving
We have counted friend as foe;
Unto one another giving in the darkness blow for blow?

Well it may be that our natures
Have grown sterner and more hard,
And the freshness of their features
Somewhat harsh and battle-scarred,
And their harmonies of feeling overtasked and rudely jarred.

Be it so. It should not swerve us
From a purpose true and brave;
Dearer Freedom's rugged service
Than the pastime of the slave;
Better is the storm above it than the quiet of the grave.

Let us then, uniting, bury
All our idle feuds in dust,
And to future conflicts carry
Mutual faith and common trust;
Always he who most forgiveth in his brother is most just.

From the eternal shadow rounding
All our sun and starlight here,
Voices of our lost ones sounding
Bid us be of heart and cheer,
Through the silence, down the spaces, falling on the inward ear.

Know we not our dead are looking
Downward with a sad surprise,
All our strife of words rebuking
With their mild and loving eyes?
Shall we grieve the holy angels? Shall we cloud their blessed
skies?

Let us draw their mantles o'er us
Which have fallen in our way;
Let us do the work before us,
Cheerly, bravely, while we may,
Ere the long night-silence cometh, and with us it is not day!

LINES

From a Letter to a Young Clerical Friend.

A STRENGTH Thy service cannot tire—
　　A faith which doubt can never dim—
A heart of love, a lip of fire—
　　Oh! Freedom's God! be Thou to him!

Speak through him words of power and fear,
　　As through Thy prophet bards of old,
And let a scornful people hear
　　Once more Thy Sinai-thunders rolled.

For lying lips Thy blessing seek,
　　And hands of blood are raised to Thee,
And on thy children, crushed and weak,
　　The oppressor plants his kneeling knee.

Let then, oh, God! Thy servant dare
　　Thy truth in all its power to tell,
Unmask the priestly thieves, and tear
　　The Bible from the grasp of hell!

From hollow rite and narrow span
　　Of law and sect by Thee released,
Oh! teach him that the Christian man
　　Is holier than the Jewish priest.

Chase back the shadows, gray and old,
　　Of the dead ages, from his way,
And let his hopeful eyes behold
　　The dawn of Thy millennial day;—

That day, when fettered limb and mind
　　Shall know the truth which maketh free,
And he alone who loves his kind
　　Shall, childlike, claim the love of Thee!

YORKTOWN.

[DR. THATCHER, surgeon in SCAMMEL's regiment, in his description of the siege of Yorktown says: "The labor on the Virginia plantations is performed altogether by a species of the human race cruelly wrested from their native country, and doomed to perpetual bondage, while their masters are manfully contending for freedom and the natural rights of man Such is the inconsistency of human nature." Eighteen hundred slaves were found at Yorktown, after its surrender, and restored to their masters. Well was it said by DR. BARNES, in his late work on Slavery: "No slave was any nearer his freedom after the surrender of Yorktown, than when PATRICK HENRY first taught the notes of liberty to echo among the hills and vales of Virginia."

FROM Yorktown's ruins, ranked and still,
Two lines stretch far o'er vale and hill:
Who curbs his steed at head of one?
Hark! the low murmur: Washington!

Who bends his keen, approving glance
Where down the gorgeous line of France
Shine knightly star and plume of snow ?
Thou too art victor, Rochambeau!

The earth which bears this calm array
Shook with the war-charge yesterday,
Ploughed deep with hurrying hoof and wheel,
Shot-sown and bladed thick with steel;
October's clear and noonday sun
Paled in the breath-smoke of the gun.
And down night's double blackness fell,
Like a dropped star, the blazing shell.

Now all is hushed : the gleaming lines
Stand moveless as the neighboring pines;
While through them, sullen, grim, and slow,
The conquered hosts of England go:
O'Hara's brow belies his dress,
Gay Tarlton's troop ride bannerless:
Shout, from thy fired and wasted homes,
Thy scourge, Virginia, captive comes!

Nor thou alone: with one glad voice
Let all thy sister States rejoice;
Let Freedom, in whatever clime
She waits with sleepless eye her time,
Shouting from cave and mountain wood,
Make glad her desert solitude,
While they who hunt her quail with fear:
The New World's chain lies broken here!

But who are they, who, cowering, wait
Within the shattered fortress gate?
Dark tillers of Virginia's soil,
Classed with the battle's common spoil,
With household stuffs, and fowl, and swine,
With Indian weed and planters' wine,
With stolen beeves, and foraged corn—
Are they not men, Virginian born?

Oh! veil your faces, young and brave!
Sleep, Scammel, in thy soldier grave!
Sons of the North-land, ye who set
Stout hearts against the bayonet,
And pressed with steady footfall near
The moated battery's blazing tier,
Turn your scarred faces from the sight,
Let shame do homage to the right !

Lo! threescore years have passed; and where
The Gallic timbrel stirred the air,

With Northern drum-roll, and the clear,
Wild horn-blow of the mountaineer,
While Britain grounded on that plain
The arms she might not lift again,
As abject as in that old day
The slave still toils his life away.

Oh! fields still green and fresh in story,
Old days of pride, old names of glory,
Old marvels of the tongue and pen,
Old thoughts which stirred the hearts of men,
Ye spared the wrong; and over all
Behold the avenging shadow fall!
Your world-wide honor stained with shame—
Your freedom's self a hollow name!

Where's now the flag of that old war?
Where flows its stripe? Where burns its star?
Bear witness, Palo Alto's day,
Dark Vale of Palms, red Monterey,
Where Mexic Freedom, young and weak,
Fleshes the Northern eagle's beak:
Symbol of terror and despair,
Of chains and slaves, go seek it there!

Laugh, Prussia, midst thy iron ranks!
Laugh, Russia, from thy Neva's banks!
Brave sport to see the fledgling born
Of Freedom by its parent torn!
Safe now is Spielberg's dungeon cell,
Safe drear Siberia's frozen hell:
With slavery's flag o'er both unrolled,
What of the New World fears the Old?

EGO.

WRITTEN IN THE BOOK OF A FRIEND.

On page of thine I cannot trace
The cold and heartless commonplace
A statue's fixed and marble grace.

Forever as these lines are penned,
Still with the thought of thee will blend
That of some loved and common friend—

Who in life's desert track has made
His pilgrim tent with mine, or strayed
Beneath the same remembered shade.

And hence my pen unfettered moves
In freedom which the heart approves—
The negligence which friendship loves.

And wilt thou prize my poor gift less
For simple air and rustic dress,
And sign of haste and carelessness ?—

Oh ! more than specious counterfeit
Of sentiment, or studied wit,
A heart like thine should value it.

Yet half I fear my gift will be
Unto thy book, if not to thee,
Of more than doubtful courtesy.

A banished name from Fashion's sphere,
A lay unheard of Beauty's ear,
Forbid, disowned,—what do they here ?—

Upon my ear not all in vain
Came the sad captive's clanking chain—
The groaning from his bed of pain.

And sadder still, I saw the woe
Which only wounded spirits know
When Pride's strong footsteps o'er them go.

Spurned not alone in walks abroad,
But from the " temples of the Lord "
Thrust out apart, like things abhorred.

Deep as I felt, and stern and strong,
In words which Prudence smothered long,
My soul spoke out against the wrong ;

Not mine alone the task to speak
Of comfort to the poor and weak,
And dry the tear on Sorrow's cheek ;

But, mingled in the conflict warm,
To pour the fiery breath of storm
Through the harsh trumpet of Reform ;

To brave Opinion's settled frown,
From ermined robe and saintly gown,
While wrestling reverenced Error down.

Founts gushed beside my pilgrim way,
Cool shadows on the greensward lay,
Flowers swung upon the bending spray.

And, broad and bright, on either hand,
Stretched the green slopes of Fairy land,
With Hope's eternal sunbow spanned;

Whence voices called me like the flow,
Which on the listener's ear will grow,
Of forest streamlets soft and low,

And gentle eyes, which still retain
Their picture on the heart and brain,
Smiled, beckoning from that path of pain

In vain !—nor dream, nor rest, nor pause
Remain for him who round him draws
The battered mail of Freedom's cause.

From youthful hopes—from each green spot
Of young Romance, and gentle Thought,
Where storm and tumult enter not—

From each fair altar, where belong
The offerings Love requires of Song
In homage to her bright-eyed throng—

With soul and strength, with heart and hand,
I turned to Freedom's struggling band—
To the sad Helots of our land.

What marvel then that Fame should turn
Her notes of praise to those of scorn—
Her gifts reclaimed—her smiles withdrawn ?

What matters it !—a few years more,
Life's surge so restless heretofore
Shall break upon the unknown shore!

In that far land shall disappear
The shadows which we follow here—
The mist-wreaths of our atmosphere!

Before no work of mortal hand,
Of human will or strength expand
The pearl gates of the Better Land ;

Alone in that great love which gave
Life to the sleeper of the grave,
Resteth the power to " seek and save."

Yet, if the spirit gazing through
The vista of the past can view
One deed to Heaven and virtue true—

If through the wreck of wasted powers,
Of garlands wreathed from Folly's bowers,
Of idle aims and misspent hours—

The eye can note one sacred spot
By Pride and Self profaned not—
A green place in the waste of thought—

Where deed or word hath rendered less
" The sum of human wretchedness,"
And Gratitude looks forth to bless—

The simple burst of tenderest feeling
From sad hearts worn by evil-dealing,
For blessing on the hand of healing,—

Better than Glory's pomp will be
That green and blessed spot to me—
A palm-shade in Eternity!—

Something of Time which may invite
The purified and spiritual sight
To rest on with a calm delight.

And when the summer winds shall sweep
With their light wings my place of sleep,
And mosses round my head-stone creep—

If still, as Freedom's rallying sign,
Upon the young heart's altars shine
The very fires they caught from mine—

If words my lips once uttered still,
In the calm faith and steadfast will
Of other hearts, their work fulfil—

Perchance with joy the soul may learn
These tokens, and its eye discern
The fires which on those altars burn—

A marvellous joy that even then,
The spirit hath its life again,
In the strong hearts of mortal men.

Take, lady, then, the gift I bring,
No gay and graceful offering—
No flower-smile of the laughing spring.

Midst the green buds of Youth's fresh **May,**
With Fancy's leaf-enwoven bay,
My sad and sombre gift I lay.

And if it deepens in thy mind
A sense of suffering human kind—
The outcast and the spirit-blind:

Oppressed and spoiled on every side,
By Prejudice, and Scorn, and Pride,
Life's common courtesies denied;

Sad mothers mourning o'er their trust,
Children by want and misery nursed,
Tasting life's bitter cup at first;

If to their strong appeals which come
From fireless hearth, and crowded room,
And the close alley's noisome gloom—

Though dark the hands upraised to thee
In mute beseeching agony,
Thou lend'st thy woman's sympathy—

Not vainly on thy gentle shrine,
Where Love, and Mirth, and Friendship twine
Their varied gifts, I offer mine.

TO GOV. M'DUFFIE.

"The patriarchal institution of slavery,"—" the corner stone of our republican edifice."
Gov. M'Duffie.

KING of Carolina—hail!
    Last champion of Oppression's battle!
Lord of rice-tierce and cotton-bale!
    Of sugar-box and human cattle!
Around thy temples, green and dark,
    Thy own tobacco-wreath reposes;
Thyself, a brother Patriarch
    Of Isaac, Abraham, and Moses!

Why not?—Their household rule is thine,
    Like theirs, thy bondmen feel its rigor;
And thine, perchance, as concubine,
    Some swarthy counterpart of Hagar.
Why not?—Like patriarchs of old,
    The priesthood is thy chosen station;
Like them thou payest thy rites to gold—
    An Aaron's calf of Nullification.

All fair and softly!—Must we, then,
    From Ruin's open jaws to save us,
Upon our own free workingmen
    Confer a master's special favors?
Whips for the back—chains for the heels—
    Hooks for the nostrils of Democracy,
Before it spurns as well as feels
    The riding of the Aristocracy!

Ho!—fishermen of Marblehead!
    Ho!—Lynn cordwainers, leave your leather
And wear the yoke in kindness made,
    And clank your needful chains together!
Let Lowell mills their thousands yield,
    Down let the rough Vermonter hasten,
Down from the workshop and the field,
    And thank us for each chain we fasten.

SLAVES in the rugged Yankee land!
    I tell thee, Carolinian, never!
Our rocky hills and iron strand
    Are free, and shall be free forever.

The surf shall wear that strand away,
  Our granite hills in dust shall moulder,
Ere Slavery's hateful yoke shall lay,
  Unbroken, on a Yankee's shoulder!

No, George M'Duffie!—keep thy words
  For the mail plunderers of thy city,
Whose robber-right is in their swords;
  For recreant Priest and Lynch-Committee!
Go, point thee to thy cannon's mouth,
  And swear its brazen lips are better,
To guard "the interests of the South."
  Than parchment scroll, or Charter's letter.*

We fear not. Streams which brawl most loud
  Along their course, are oftenest shallow;
And loudest to a doubting crowd
  The coward publishes his valor.
Thy courage has at least been shown
  In many a bloodless Southern quarrel,
Facing, with hartshorn and cologne,
  The Georgian's harmless pistol-barrel.†

No, Southron! not in Yankee land
  Will threats, like thine, a fear awaken ;
The men, who on their charter stand
  For truth and right, may not be shaken.
Still shall that truth assail thine ear:
  Each breeze, from Northern mountains blowing,
The tones of Liberty shall bear
  God's "free incendiaries" going!

We give thee joy!—thy name is heard
  With reverence on the Neva's borders;
And "turban'd Turk," and Poland's lord,
  And Metternich are thy applauders.
Go—if thou lov'st *such* fame, and share
  The mad Ephesian's base example—
The holy bonds of UNION tear,
  And clap the torch to FREEDOM's temple !

Do this—Heaven's frown, thy country's curse
  Guilt's fiery torture ever burning—
The quenchless thirst of Tantalus,
  And Ixion's wheel forever turning—
A name, for which " the pain'dest fiend
  Below " his own would barter never,—
These shall be thine unto the end
  Thy damning heritage forever!

* See Speech of Gov. M'D. to an artillery company in Charleston, S. C.
† Most of our readers will recollect the "chivalrous" affair between M'Duffie and Col. Cummings, of Georgia, some years ago, in which the parties fortified themselves with spirits of hartshorn and *eau de Cologne.*

LINES.

Written on reading "WRIGHT AND WRONG IN BOSTON;" containing an account of the meeting of the Boston Female Anti-Slavery Society, and the MOB which followed, on the 21st of the 10th month, 1835.

UNSHRINKING from the storm,
  Well have ye borne your part,
With WOMAN'S fragile form,
  But more than manhood's heart!
Faithful to Freedom, when
  Its name was held accursed—
Faithful, midst ruffian men,
  Unto your holy trust.

Oh—steadfast in the Truth!
  Not for yourselves alone,
Matron and gentle youth,
  Your lofty zeal was shown:
For the bondman of all climes—
  For Freedom's last abode—
For the hope of future times—
  For the birthright gift of God—

For scorn'd and broken laws—
  For honor and the right—
For the staked and peril'd cause
  Of liberty and light—
For the holy eyes above
  On a world of evil cast—
For the CHILDREN of your love—
  For the MOTHERS of the past!

Worthy of THEM are ye—
  The Pilgrim wives who dared
The waste and unknown sea,
  And the hunter's perils shared.

Worthy of her * whose mind,
  Triumphant over all,
Ruler nor priest could bind,
  Nor banishment appal.

Worthy of her † who died
  Martyr of Freedom, where
Your " Commons' " verdant pride,
  Opens to sun and air:
Upheld at that dread hour
  By strength which could not fail;
Before whose holy power
  Bigot and priest turn'd pale,

God give ye strength to run,
  Unawed by Earth or Hell,
The race ye have begun
  So gloriously and well,
Until the trumpet-call
  Of Freedom has gone forth,
With joy and life to all
  The bondmen of the earth!

Until IMMORTAL MIND
  Unshackled walks abroad,
And chains no longer bind
  The image of our God
Until no captive one
  Murmurs on land or wave;
And, in his course, the sun
  Looks down upon NO SLAVE!

LINES.

Written on the adoption of Pinckney's Resolutions, in the House of Representatives, and th passage of Calhoun's "Bill of Abominations" to a second reading, in the Senate of the Unite States.

Now, by our fathers' ashes! where's the spirit
  Of the true-hearted and the unshackled gone?
Sons of old freemen, do we but inherit
      Their *names* alone?

* Mrs. Hutchinson, who was banished from the Massachusetts Colony, as the easiest meth of confuting her doctrines.
† Mary Dyer, the Quaker Martyr, who was hanged in Boston in 1659 for worshiping G according to the dictates of her conscience.

Is the old Pilgrim spirit quench'd within us?
  Stoops the proud manhood of our souls so low,
That Mammon's lure or Party's wile can win us
                    To silence now?

No. When our land to ruin's brink is verging,
  In God's name, let us speak while there is time!
Now, when the padlocks for our lips are forging,
                    SILENCE IS CRIME!

What! shall we henceforth humbly ask as favors
  Rights all our own? In madness shall we barter,
For treacherous peace, the FREEDOM Nature gave us,
                    God and our charter?

Here shall the statesman seek the free to fetter?
  Here Lynch law light its horrid fires on high?
And, in the church, their proud and skill'd abettor,
                    Make truth a lie?

Torture the pages of the hallow'd Bible,
  To sanction crime, and robbery, and blood?
And, in Oppression's hateful service, libel
                    Both man and God?

Shall our New England stand erect no longer,
  But stoop in chains upon her downward way,
Thicker to gather on her limbs and stronger
                    Day after day ?

Oh, no; methinks from all her wild, green mountains—
  From valleys where her slumbering fathers lie—
From her blue rivers and her welling fountains,
                    And clear, cold sky—

From her rough coast, and isles, which hungry Ocean
  Gnaws with his surges—from the fisher's skiff,
With white sail swaying to the billows' motion
                    Round rock and cliff—

From the free fireside of her unbought farmer—
  From her free laborer at his loom and wheel—
From the brown smith-shop, where, beneath the hammer,
                    Rings the red steel—

From each and all, if God hath not forsaken
  Our land, and left us to an evil choice,
Loud as the summer thunderbolt shall waken
                    A PEOPLE'S VOICE!

Startling and stern! the Northern winds shall bear it
  Over Potomac's to St. Mary's wave ;

And buried Freedom shall awake to hear it
                    Within her grave.

Oh, let that voice go forth! The bondman sighing
  By Santee's wave, in Mississippi's cane,
Shall feel the hope, within his bosom dying,
                  Revive again.

Let it go forth ! The millions who are gazing
  Sadly upon us from afar, shall smile,
And unto God devout thanksgiving raising,
                  Bless us the while.

Oh, for your ancient freedom, pure and holy,
  For the deliverance of a groaning earth,
For the wrong'd captive, bleeding, crush'd, and
    lowly,
                  Let it go forth !

Sons of the best of fathers! will ye falter
  With all they left ye peril'd and at stake ?
Ho! once again on Freedom's holy altar
                  The fire awake!

Prayer-strengthen'd for the trial, come together,
  Put on the harness for the moral fight,
And, with the blessing of your heavenly Father,
             MAINTAIN THE RIGHT !

MISCELLANEOUS.

PALESTINE.

BLEST land of Judea! thrice hallowed of song
Where the holiest of memories pilgrim-like throng;
In the shade of thy palms, by the shores of thy sea,
On the hills of thy beauty, my heart is with thee.

With the eye of a spirit I look on that shore,
Where pilgrim and prophet have lingered before;
With the glide of a spirit I traverse the sod
Made bright by the steps of the angels of God.

Blue sea of the hills!—in my spirit I hear
Thy waters, Gennesaret, chime on my ear;
Where the Lowly and Just with the people sat down,
And thy spray on the dust of His sandals was thrown.

Beyond are Bethulia's mountains of green,
And the desolate hills of the wild Gadarene;
And I pause on the goat-crags of Tabor to see
The gleam of thy waters, O dark Galilee!

Hark, a sound in the valley! where, swollen and strong,
Thy river, O Kishon, is sweeping along;
Where the Canaanite strove with Jehovah in vain,
And thy torrent grew dark with the blood of the slain.

There down from his mountains stern Zebulon came,
And Naphtali's stag, with his eye-balls of flame,
And the chariots of Jabin rolled harmlessly on,
For the arm of the Lord was Abinoam's son !

There sleep the still rocks and the caverns which rang
To the song which the beautiful prophetess sang,
When the princes of Issachar stood by her side,
And the shout of a host in its triumph replied.

Lo, Bethlehem's hill-site before me is seen,
With the mountains around, and the valleys between;
There rested the shepherds of Judah, and there
The song of the angels rose sweet on the air.

And Bethany's palm trees in beauty still throw
Their shadows at noon on the ruins below;
But where are the sisters who hastened to greet
The lowly Redeemer, and sit at His feet ?

I tread where the TWELVE in their way-faring trod;
I stand where they stood with the CHOSEN OF GOD—
Where His blessing was heard and His lessons were taught,
Where the blind were restored and the healing was wrought.

Oh, here with His flock the sad Wanderer came—
These hills He toiled over in grief, are the same—
The founts where He drank by the wayside still flow,
And the same airs are blowing which breathed on His brow!

And throned on her hills sits Jerusalem yet,
But with dust on her forehead, and chains on her feet;
For the crown of her pride to the mocker hath gone,
And the Holy Shechinah is dark where it shone.

But wherefore this dream of the earthly abode
Of Humanity clothed in the brightness of God?
Where my spirit but turned from the outward and dim,
It could gaze, even now, on the presence of Him!

Not in clouds and in terrors, but gentle as when,
In love and in meekness, He moved among men;
And the voice which breathed peace to the waves of the sea,
In the hush of my spirit would whisper to me!

And what if my feet may not tread where He stood,
Nor my ears hear the dashing of Galilee's flood,
Nor my eyes see the cross which He bowed him to bear,
Nor my knees press Gethsemane's garden of prayer?

Yet loved of the Father, Thy Spirit is near
To the meek, and the lowly, and penitent here;
And the voice of Thy love is the same even now,
As at Bethany's tomb, or on Olivet's brow.

Oh, the outward hath gone!—but in glory and power,
The SPIRIT surviveth the things of an hour;
Unchanged, undecaying, its Pentecost flame
On the heart's secret altar is burning the same!

EZEKIEL.

CHAPTER XXXIII. 30–33.

THEY hear thee not, O God! nor see:
Beneath Thy rod they mock at Thee;
The princes of our ancient line
Lie drunken with Assyrian wine;
The priests around Thy altar speak
The false words which their hearers seek;
And hymn which Chaldea's wanton maids
Have sung in Dura's idol-shades,
Are with the Levites' chant ascending,
With Zion's holiest anthems blending!

On Israel's bleeding bosom set,
The heathen heel is crushing yet;
The towers upon our holy hill
Echo Chaldean footsteps still.
Our wasted shrines—who weeps for them?
Who mourneth for Jerusalem?
Who turneth from his gains away?
Whose knee with mine is bowed to pray?
Who, leaving feast and purpling cup,
Takes Zion's lamentation up?

A sad and thoughtful youth, I went
With Israel's early banishment;
And where the sullen Chebar crept,
The ritual of my fathers kept.
The water for the trench I drew,
The firstling of the flock I slew,
And, standing at the altar's side,
I shared the Levites' lingering pride,
That still amidst her mocking foes,
The smoke of Zion's offering rose.

In sudden whirlwind, cloud and flame,
The Spirit of the Highest came!
Before mine eyes a vision passed,
A glory terrible and vast;
With dreadful eyes of living things,
And sounding sweep of angel wings,
With circling light and sapphire throne,
And flame-like form of One thereon,
And voice of that dread Likeness sent
Down from the crystal firmament!

The burden of a prophet's power
Fell on me in that fearful hour;
From off unutterable woes
The curtain of the future rose;
I saw far down the coming time
The fiery chastisement of crime;
With noise of mingling hosts, and jar
Of falling towers and shouts of war,
I saw the nations rise and fall,
Like fire-gleams on my tent's white wall.

In dream and trance, I saw the slain
Of Egypt heaped like harvest grain;
I saw the walls of sea-born Tyre
Swept over by the spoiler's fire;
And heard the low, expiring moan
Of Edom on his rocky throne;
And, woe is me! the wild lament
From Zion's desolation sent;
And felt within my heart each blow
Which laid her holy places low.

In bonds and sorrow, day by day,
Before the pictured tile I lay;
And there, as in a mirror, saw
The coming of Assyria's war,—
Her swarthy lines of spearmen pass
Like locusts through Bethhoron's grass;
I saw them draw their stormy hem
Of battle round Jerusalem;
And, listening, heard the Hebrew wail
Blend with the victor-trump of Baal!

Who trembled at my warning word?
Who owned the prophet of the Lord?
How mocked the rude—how scoffed the vile—
How stung the Levites' scornful smile,
As o'er my spirit, dark and slow,
The shadow crept of Israel's woe,
As if the angel's mournful roll
Had left its record on my soul,
And traced in lines of darkness there
The picture of its great despair!

Yet ever at the hour I feel
My lips in prophecy unseal.
Prince, priest, and Levite, gather near,
And Salem's daughters haste to hear,
On Chebar's waste and alien shore,
The harp of Judah swept once more.
They listen, as in Babel's throng
The Chaldeans to the dancer's song,
Or wild sabbeka's nightly play,
As careless and as vain as they.

―――――

And thus, oh Prophet-bard of old,
Hast thou thy tale of sorrow told!
The same which earth's unwelcome seers
Have felt in all succeeding years.
Sport of the changeful multitude,
Nor calmly heard nor understood,
Their song has seemed a trick of art,
Their warnings but the actors' part.
With bonds, and scorn, and evil will,
The world requites its prophets still.

So was it when the Holy One
The garments of the flesh put on!
Men followed where the Highest led
For common gifts of daily bread,
And gross of ear, of vision dim,
Owned not the Godlike power of Him.
Vain as a dreamer's words to them
His wail above Jerusalem,

And meaningless the watch He kept
Through which His weak disciples slept.

Yet shrink not thou, whoe'er thou art,
For God's great purpose set apart,
Before whose far discerning eyes,
The Future as the Present lies!
Beyond a narrow-bounded age
Stretches thy prophet-heritage,

Through Heaven's dim spaces angel-trod,
Through arches round the throne of God!
Thy audience, worlds!—all Time to be
The witness of the Truth in thee!

THE WIFE OF MANOAH TO HER HUSBAND.

AGAINST the sunset's glowing wall
The city towers rise black and tall,
Where Zorah on its rocky height
Stands like an armed man in the light.

Down Eshtaol's vales of ripened grain
Falls like a cloud the night amain,
And up the hillsides climbing slow
The barley reapers homeward go.

Look, dearest! how our fair child's head
The sunset light hath hallowed,
Where at this olive's foot he lies,
Uplooking to the tranquil skies.

Oh! while beneath the fervent heat
Thy sickle swept the bearded wheat,
I've watched with mingled joy and dread,
Our child upon his grassy bed.

Joy, which the mother feels alone
Whose morning hope like mine had flown,
When to her bosom, ever blessed,
A dearer life than hers is pressed.

Dread, for the future dark and still,
Which shapes our dear one to its will;
Forever in his large calm eyes,
I read a tale of sacrifice.—

The same foreboding awe I felt
When at the altar's side we knelt,
And he, who as a pilgrim came,
Rose, winged and glorious, through the flame!

I slept not, though the wild bees made
A dreamlike murmuring in the shade,
And on me the warm-fingered hours
Pressed with the drowsy smell of flowers.

Before me, in a vision, rose
The hosts of Israel's scornful foes,—
Rank over rank, helm, shield, and spear,
Glittered in noon's hot atmosphere.

I heard their boast, and bitter word,
Their mockery of the Hebrew's Lord,
I saw their hands His ark assail,
Their feet profane His holy veil.

No angel down the blue space spoke,
No thunder from the still sky broke,
But in their midst, in power and awe,
Like God's waked wrath, OUR CHILD I saw!

A child no more!—harsh-browed and strong
He towered a giant in the throng,
And down his shoulders, broad and bare,
Swept the black terror of his hair.

He raised his arm—he smote amain,
As round the reaper falls the grain,
So the dark host around him fell,
So sank the foes of Israel!

Again I looked.   In sunlight shone
The towers and domes of Askelon.
Priests, warrior, slave, a mighty crowd
Within her idol temple bowed.

Yet one knelt not; stark, gaunt, and blind,
His arms the massive pillars twined,—
An eyeless captive, strong with hate,
He stood there like an evil Fate.

The red shrines smoked—the trumpets pealed—
He stooped—the giant columns reeled—
Reeled tower and fane, sank arch and wall,
And the thick dust-cloud closed o'er all!

Above the shriek, the crash, the groan
Of the fallen pride of Askelon,
I heard, sheer down the echoing sky,
A voice as of an angel cry.—

The voice of him, who at our side
Sat through the golden eventide,

Of him, who on thy altar's blaze
Rose fire-winged, with his song of praise!

"Rejoice o'er Israel's broken chain,
  Gray mother of the mighty slain!
Rejoice!" it cried, "He vanquisheth!
The strong in life is strong in death!

"To him shall Zorah's daughters raise
  Through coming years their hymns of praise,
And gray old men, at evening tell
Of all he wrought for Israel.

"And they who sing and they who hear
  Alike shall hold thy memory dear,
And pour their blessings on thy head,
Oh, mother of the mighty dead!"

It ceased: and though a sound I heard
As if great wings the still air stirred,
I only saw the barley sheaves,
And hills half hid by olive leaves.

I bowed my face, in awe and fear,
On the dear child who slumbered near,
"With me, as with my only son,
Oh God!" I said, "THY WILL BE DONE!"

THE CITIES OF THE PLAIN.

"GET ye up from the wrath of God's terrible day!
Ungirded, unsandalled, arise and away!
'Tis the vintage of blood—'tis the fulness of time,
And vengeance shall gather the harvest of crime!"

The warning was spoken—the righteous had gone,
And the proud ones of Sodom were feasting alone;
All gay was the banquet—the revel was long,
With the pouring of wine and the breathing of song.

'Twas an evening of beauty; the air was perfume,
The earth was all greenness, the trees were all bloom;
And softly the delicate viol was heard,
Like the murmur of love or the notes of a bird.

And beautiful maidens moved down in the dance,
With the magic of motion and sunshine of glance;
And white arms wreathed lightly, and tresses fell free,
As the plumage of birds in some tropical tree.

Where the shrines of foul idols were lighted on high,
And wantonness tempted the lust of the eye;
Midst rites of obsceneness, strange, loathsome, abhorred,
The blasphemer scoffed at the name of the Lord.

Hark! the growl of the thunder—the quaking of earth!
Woe—woe to the worship, and woe to the mirth!
The black sky has opened—there's flame in the air—
The red arm of vengeance is lifted and bare!

Then the shriek of the dying rose wild where the song
And the low tone of love had been whispered along;
For the fierce flames went lightly o'er palace and bower,
Like the red tongues of demons, to blast and devour!

Down—down, on the fallen, the red ruin rained,
And the reveller sank with his wine-cup undrained;
The foot of the dancer, the music's loved thrill,
And the shout and the laughter grew suddenly still.

The last throb of anguish was fearfully given;
The last eye glared forth in its madness on Heaven!
The last groan of horror rose wildly and vain,
And death brooded over the pride of the Plain!

THE CRUCIFIXION.

SUNLIGHT upon Judea's hills!
    And on the waves of Galilee—
On Jordan's stream, and on the rills
    That feed the dead and sleeping sea!
Most freshly from the greenwood springs
The light breeze on its scented wings;
And gayly quiver in the sun
The cedar tops of Lebanon!

A few more hours—a change hath come!
    The sky is dark without a cloud!
The shouts of wrath and joy are dumb,
    And proud knees unto earth are bowed.
A change is on the hill of Death,
The helmed watchers pant for breath,
And turn with wild and maniac eyes
From the dark scene of sacrifice!

That Sacrifice!—the death of Him—
    The High and ever Holy One!
Well may the conscious Heaven grow dim,
    And blacken the beholding Sun!
The wonted light hath fled away,
Night settles on the middle day,
And earthquake from his caverned bed
Is waking with a thrill of dread!

The dead are waking underneath !
　　Their prison door is rent away!
And, ghastly with the seal of death,
　　They wander in the eye of day!
The temple of the Cherubim,
The House of God is cold and dim;
A curse is on its trembling walls,
Its mighty veil asunder falls!

Well may the cavern-depths of Earth
　　Be shaken, and her mountains nod ;
Well may the sheeted dead come forth
　　To gaze upon a suffering God!
Well may the temple-shrine grow dim,
And shadows veil the Cherubim,
When He, the chosen one of Heaven,
A sacrifice for guilt is given !

And shall the sinful heart, alone,
　　Behold unmoved the atoning hour,
When Nature trembles on her throne,
　　And Death resigns his iron power ?
Oh, shall the heart—whose sinfulness
Gave keenness to His sore distress,
And added to His tears of blood—
Refuse its trembling gratitude!

THE STAR OF BETHLEHEM.

Where Time the measure of his hours
　　By changeful bud and blossom keeps,
And like a young bride crowned with flowers,
　　Fair Shiraz in her garden sleeps;

Where, to her poet's turban stone,
　　The Spring her gift of flowers imparts,
Less sweet than those his thoughts have sown
　　In the warm soil of Persian hearts:

There sat the stranger, where the shade
　　Of scattered date-trees thinly lay,
While in the hot clear heaven delayed
　　The long, and still, and weary day.

Strange trees and fruits above him hung,
　　Strange odors filled the sultry air,
Strange birds upon the branches swung,
　　Strange insect voices murmured there.

And strange bright blossoms shone around,
　　Turned sunward from the shadowy bowers,
As if the Gheber's soul had found
　　A fitting home in Iran's flowers.

Whate'er he saw, whate'er he heard,
　　Awakened feelings new and sad,—
No Christian garb, nor Christian word,
　　Nor church with Sabbath bell chimes glad,

But Moslem graves, with turban stones,
　　And mosque-spires gleaming white, in view,
And gray-beard Mollahs in low tones
　　Chanting their Koran service through.

The flowers which smiled on either hand
　　Like tempting fiends, were such as they
Which once, o'er all that Eastern land,
　　As gifts on demon altars lay.

As if the burning eye of Baal
　　The servant of his Conqueror knew,
From skies which knew no cloudy veil,
　　The Sun's hot glances smote him through.

" Ah me!" the lonely stranger said,
　　" The hope which led my footsteps on,
And light from Heaven around them shed,
　　O'er weary wave and waste, is gone!

" Where are the harvest fields all white,
　　For Truth to thrust her sickle in ?
Where flock the souls, like doves in flight,
　　From the dark hiding place of sin ?

" A silent horror broods o'er all—
　　The burden of a hateful spell—
The very flowers around recall
　　The hoary magi's rites of hell.

" And what am I, o'er such a land
　　The banner of the Cross to bear ?
Dear Lord uphold me with thy hand,
　　Thy strength with human weakness share! "

He ceased; for at his very feet
　　In mild rebuke a floweret smiled—
How thrilled his sinking heart to greet
　　The Star-flower of the Virgin's child!

Sown by some wandering Frank, it drew
　　Its life from alien air and earth,
And told to Paynim sun and dew
　　The story of the Saviour's birth.

From scorching beams, in kindly mood,
　　The Persian plants its beauty screened;
And on its pagan sisterhood,
　　In love, the Christian floweret leaned.

With tears of joy the wanderer felt
   The darkness of his long despair
Before that hallowed symbol melt,
   Which God's dear love had nurtured there.

From Nature's face, that simple flower
   The lines of sin and sadness swept,
And Magian pile and Paynim bower
   In peace like that of Eden slept.

Each Moslem tomb, and cypress old,
   Looked holy through the sunset air:
And angel like, the Muezzin told
   From tower and mosque the hour of prayer.

With cheerful steps, the morrow's dawn
   From Shiraz saw the stranger part;
The Star-flower of the Virgin-Born
   Still blooming in his hopeful heart!

CHRIST IN THE TEMPEST.

STORM on the heaving waters!—The vast sky
   Is stooping with its thunder. Cloud on cloud
   Rolls heavily in the darkness, like a shroud
Shaken by midnight's Angel from on high,
Through the thick sea-mist, faintly and afar,
Chorazin's watch-light glimmers like a star,
And, momently, the ghastly cloud-fires play
On the dark sea-wall of Capernaum's bay,
And tower and turret into light spring forth
Like spectres starting from the storm-swept earth
And, vast and awful, Tabor's mountain form,
Its Titan forehead naked to the storm,
Towers for one instant, full and clear, and then
Blends with the blackness and the cloud again.

And it is very terrible!—The roar
   Ascendeth unto heaven, and thunders back,
   Like the response of demons, from the black
Rifts of the hanging tempest—yawning o'er
The wild waves in their torment. Hark!—the cry
   Of strong man in peril, piercing through
The uproar of the waters and the sky,
   As the rent bark one moment rides to view,
On the tall billows, with the thunder cloud
Closing around, above her, like a shroud!
He stood upon the reeling deck—His form
Made visible by the lightning, and His brow
Pale, and uncover'd to the rushing storm,
   Told of a triumph man may never know—
Power underived and mighty—" PEACE—BE STILL! "
   The great waves heard Him, and the storm's loud tone

Went moaning into silence at His will;
   And the thick clouds, where yet the lightning shone,
   And slept the latent thunder, roll'd away,
Until no trace of tempest lurk'd behind,
Changing, upon the pinions of the wind,
   To stormless wanderers, beautiful and gay.

Dread Ruler of the tempest!   Thou before
   Whose presence boweth the uprisen storm—
To whom the waves do homage round the shore
   Of many an Island empire!—if the form
Of the frail dust beneath Thine eye, may claim
   Thy infinite regard—oh, breathe upon
The storm and darkness of man's soul the same
Quiet, and peace, and humbleness which came
   O'er the roused waters, where Thy voice had gone
A minister of power—to conquer in Thy name!

"KNOWEST THOU THE ORDINANCES OF HEAVEN?"

—Job XXXVIII. 33.

Look unto heaven!
The still and solemn stars are burning there,
Like altars lighted in the upper air,
And to the worship of the great God given,
Where the pure spirits of the unsinning dead,
Redeem'd and sanctified from Earth, might shed
   The holiness of prayer.

Look ye above!
The Earth is glorious with its summer wreath
The tall trees bend with verdure; and, beneath,
Young flowers are blushing like unwhisper'd love.
Yet *these* will change—Earth's glories be no more,
And all her bloom and greenness fade before
   The ministry of Death.

Then gaze not there.
God's constant miracle—the star-wrought sky
Bends o'er ye, lifting silently on high,
As with an Angel's hand, the soul of prayer,
And heaven's own language to the pure of Earth,
Written in stars at Nature's mighty birth,
   Burns on the gazing eye.

Oh! turn ye, then,
And bend the knee of worship; and the eyes
Of the pure stars shall smile, with glad surprise
At the deep reverence of the sons of men.
Oh! bend in worship, till those stars grow dim
And the skies vanish, at the thought of Him
   Whose light beyond them lies!

HYMNS.

FROM THE FRENCH OF LAMARTINE.

ONE hymn more, O my lyre!
    Praise to the God above,
    Of joy and life and love,
Sweeping its strings of fire!

Oh! who the speed of bird and wind
    And sunbeam's glance will lend to me,
That, soaring upward, I may find
    My resting place and home in Thee ?—
Thou, whom my soul, midst doubt and gloom,
    Adoreth with a fervent flame—
Mysterious spirit! unto whom
    Pertain nor sign nor name!

Swiftly my lyre's soft murmurs go,
    Up from the cold and joyless earth,
Back to the God who bade them flow,
    Whose moving spirit sent them forth.
But as for me, O God! for me,
    The lowly creature of Thy will,
Lingering and sad, I sigh to Thee
    An earth-bound pilgrim still!

Was not my spirit born to shine
    Where yonder stars and suns are glowing?
To breathe with them the light divine,
    From God's own holy altar flowing?
To be, indeed, whate'er the soul
    In dreams hath thirsted for so long—
A portion of Heaven's glorious whole
    Of loveliness and song?

Oh! watchers of the stars at night,
    Who breathe their fire, as we the air—
Suns, thunders, stars, and rays of light,
    Oh! say, is He, the Eternal, there?
Bend there around His awful throne
    The seraph's glance, the angel's knee?
Or are thy inmost depths his own,
    O wild and mighty sea?

Thoughts of my soul, how swift ye go!
    Swift as the eagle's glance of fire,
Or arrows from the archer's bow,
    To the far aim of your desire!
Thought after thought, ye thronging rise,
    Like spring-doves from the startled wood,
Bearing like them your sacrifice
    Of music unto God!

And shall these thoughts of joy and love
    Come back again no more to me ?—
Returning like the Patriarch's dove
    Wing-weary from the eternal sea,
To bear within my longing arms
    The promise-bough of kindlier skies,
Plucked from the green, immortal palms
    Which shadow Paradise ?

All-moving spirit !—freely forth
    At Thy command the strong wind goes;
Its errand to the passive earth,
    Nor art can stay, nor strength oppose,
Until it folds its weary wing
    Once more within the hand divine;
So, weary from its wandering,
    My spirit turns to Thine!

Child of the sea, the mountain stream,
    From its dark caverns, hurries on,
Ceaseless, by night and morning's beam,
    By evening's star and noontide's sun,
Until at last it sinks to rest,
    O'erwearied, in the waiting sea,
And moans upon its mother's breast—
    So turns my soul to Thee!

O Thou who bidst the torrent flow,
    Who lendest wings unto the wind—
Mover of all things! where art Thou ?
    Oh, whither shall I go to find
The secret of Thy resting place ?
    Is there no holy wing for me,
That, soaring, I may search the space
    Of highest Heaven for Thee ?

Oh, would I were as free to rise
    As leaves on Autumn's whirlwind borne—
The arrowy light of sunset skies,
    Or sound, or ray, or star of morn
Which melts in heaven at twilight's close,
    Or aught which soars unchecked and free
Through Earth and Heaven; that I might lose
    Myself in finding Thee!

    When the BREATH DIVINE is flowing,
    Zephyr-like o'er all things going,
    And as the touch of viewless fingers,
    Softly on my soul it lingers,
    Open to a breath the lightest,
    Conscious of a touch the slightest—
    As some calm still lake, whereon
    Sinks the snowy-bosomed swan,

And the glistening water-rings
Circle round her moving wings:
When my upward gaze is turning
Where the stars of heaven are burning
Through the deep and dark abyss—
Flowers of midnight's wilderness,
Blowing with the evening's breath
Sweetly in their Maker's path:

When the breaking day is flushing
All the East, and light is gushing
Upward through the horizon's haze,
Sheaf-like, with its thousand rays
Spreading, until all above
Overflows with joy and love,
And below, on earth's green bosom,
All is changed to light and blossom:

When my waking fancies over,
Forms of brightness flit and hover,
Holy as the seraphs are,
Who by Zion's fountains wear
On their foreheads, white and broad,
"HOLINESS UNTO THE LORD!"
When, inspired with rapture high,
It would seem a single sigh
Could a world of love create—
That my life could know no date,
And my eager thoughts could fill
Heaven and earth, o'erflowing still!—

Then, O Father!—Thou alone,
From the shadow of Thy throne,
To the sighing of my breast
And its rapture answerest.
All my thoughts, which, upward winging,
Bathe where Thy own light is springing—
All my yearnings to be free
Are as echoes answering Thee!

Seldom upon lips of mine,
Father! rests that name of Thine—
Deep within my inmost breast,
  In the secret place of mind,
  Like an awful presence shrined,
Doth the dread idea rest!
Hushed and holy dwells it there—
Prompter of the silent prayer,
Lifting up my spirit's eye
And its faint, but earnest cry,
From its dark but cold abode,
Unto Thee, my Guide and God!

THE FEMALE MARTYR.

[MARY G———, aged eighteen, a "SISTER OF CHARITY," died in one of our Atlantic cities,
during the prevalence of the Indian Cholera, while in voluntary attendance upon the sick.]

"BRING out your dead!" the midnight street
    Heard and gave back the hoarse, low call;
Harsh fell the tread of hasty feet—
Glanced through the dark the coarse white sheet—
    Her coffin and her pall.
"What—only one!" The brutal hackman said,
As, with an oath, he spurned away the dead.

How sunk the inmost hearts of all,
    As rolled that dead-cart slowly by,
With creaking wheel and harsh hoof-fall!
The dying turned him to the wall,
    To hear it and to die!—
Onward it rolled; while oft its driver stayed,
And hoarsely clamored, "Ho!—bring out your dead."

It paused beside the burial-place;
    "Toss in your load!"—and it was done.—
With quick hand and averted face,
Hastily to the grave's embrace
    They cast them, one by one—
Stranger and friend—the evil and the just,
Together trodden in the church-yard dust!

And thou, young martyr!—thou wast there—
    No white-robed sisters round thee trod—
Nor holy hymn nor funeral prayer
Rose through the damp and noisome air,
    Giving thee to thy God;
Nor flower, nor cross, nor hallowed taper gave
Grace to the dead, and beauty to the grave!

Yet, gentle sufferer!—there shall be.
    In every heart of kindly feeling,
A rite as holy paid to thee
As if beneath the convent-tree
    Thy sisterhood were kneeling,
At vesper hours, like sorrowing angels, keeping
Their tearful watch around thy place of sleeping.

For thou wast one in whom the light
    Of Heaven's own love was kindled well,
Enduring with a martyr's might,
Through weary day and wakeful night,
    Far more than words may tell:
Gentle, and meek, and lowly, and unknown—
Thy mercies measured by thy God alone!

Where manly hearts were failing,—where
  The throngful street grew foul with death,
O high-souled martyr!—thou was there,
Inhaling from the loathsome air,
  Poison with every breath.
Yet shrinking not from offices of dread
For the wrung dying, and the unconscious dead.

And, where the sickly taper shed
  Its light through vapors, damp, confined,
Hushed as a seraph's fell thy tread—
A new Electra by the bed
  Of suffering human-kind!
Pointing the spirit, in its dark dismay,
To that pure hope which fadeth not away.

Innocent teacher of the high
  And holy mysteries of Heaven!
How turned to thee each glazing eye,
In mute and awful sympathy,
  As thy low prayers were given;
And the o'er-hovering Spoiler wore, the while,
An angel's features—a deliverer's smile!

A blessed task!—and worthy one
  Who, turning from the world, as thou,
Before life's pathway had begun
To leave its springtime flower and sun,
  Had sealed her early vow;
Giving to God her beauty and her youth,
Her pure affections and her guileless truth.

Earth may not claim thee. Nothing here
  Could be for thee a meet reward;
Thine is a treasure far more dear—
Eye hath not seen it, nor the ear
  Of living mortal heard,—
The joys prepared—the promised bliss above—
The holy presence of Eternal Love!

Sleep on in peace. The earth has not
  A nobler name than thine shall be.
The deeds by martial manhood wrought,
The lofty energies of thought,
  The fire of poesy—
These have but frail and fading honors;—thine
Shall Time unto Eternity consign.

Yea, and when thrones shall crumble down,
  And human pride and grandeur fall,—
The herald's line of long renown—
The mitre and the kingly crown—
  Perishing glories all !
The pure devotion of thy generous heart
Shall live in Heaven, of which it was a part!

THE FROST SPIRIT.

He comes—he comes—the Frost Spirit comes! You may trace his foot-
    steps now
On the naked woods and the blasted fields and the brown hill's withered
    brow.
He has smitten the leaves of the gray old trees where their pleasant
    green came forth,
And the winds, which follow wherever he goes, have shaken them down
    to earth.

He comes—he comes—the Frost Spirit comes!—from the frozen
    Labrador—
From the icy bridge of the Northern seas, which the white bear
    wanders o'er—
Where the fisherman's sail is stiff with ice, and the luckless form
    below
In the sunless cold of the lingering night into marble statues grow!

He comes—he comes—the Frost Spirit comes!—On the rushing Northern
    blast,
And the dark Norwegian pines have bowed as his fearful breath went
    past.
With an unscorched wing he was hurried on, where the fires of Hecla
    glow
On the darkly beautiful sky above and the ancient ice below.

He comes—he comes—the Frost Spirit comes!—and the quiet lake shall
    feel
The torpid touch of his glazing breath and ring to the skater's heel;
And the streams which danced on the broken rocks, or sang to the
    leaning grass,
Shall bow again to their winter chain, and in mournful silence pass.

He comes—he comes—the Frost Spirit comes!—let us meet him as we
    may,
And turn with the light of the parlor-fire his evil power away;
And gather closer the circle round, when that firelight dances high,
And laugh at the shriek of the baffled Fiend as his sounding wing
    goes by!

THE VAUDOIS TEACHER.

["The manner in which the WALDENSES and heretics disseminated their principles among the CATHOLIC gentry, was by carrying with them a box of trinkets, or articles of dress. Having entered the houses of the gentry, and disposed of some of their goods, they cautiously intimated that they had commodities far more valuable than these—inestimable jewels, which they would show if they could be protected from the clergy. They would then give their purchasers a bible or testament; and thereby many were deluded into heresy."—*R. Saccho.*]

"Oh, lady fair, these silks of mine are beautiful and rare—
The richest web of the Indian loom, which beauty's queen might wear;
And my pearls are pure as thy own fair neck, with whose radiant light
    they vie;
I have brought them with me a weary way,—will my gentle lady buy?"

And the lady smiled on the worn old man through the dark and cluster-
    ing curls,
Which veiled her brow as she bent to view his silks and glittering pearls;
And she placed their price in the old man's hand, and lightly turned
    away,
But she paused at the wanderer's earnest call—"My gentle lady, stay!"

"Oh, lady fair, I have yet a gem which a purer lustre flings,
Than the diamond flash of the jewelled crown on the lofty brow of kings—
A wonderful pearl of exceeding price, whose virtue shall not decay,
Whose light shall be as a spell to thee and a blessing on thy way!"

The lady glanced at the mirroring steel where her form of grace was
    seen,
Where her eye shone clear, and her dark locks waved their clasping
    pearls between;—
"Bring forth thy pearl of exceeding worth, thou traveller gray and old—
And name the price of thy precious gem, and my page shall count thy
    gold."

The cloud went off from the pilgrim's brow, as a small and meagre book,
Unchased with gold or gem of cost, from his folding robe he took!
"Here, lady fair, is the pearl of price, may it prove as such to thee!
Nay—keep thy gold—I ask it not, for the word of God is free!"

The hoary traveller went his way, but the gift he left behind
Hath had its pure and perfect work on that high-born maiden's mind,
And she hath turned from the pride of sin to the lowliness of truth,
And given her human heart to God in its beautiful hour of youth!

And she hath left the gray old halls, where an evil faith had power,
The courtly knights of her father's train, and the maidens of her bower;
And she hath gone to the Vaudois vales by lordly feet untrod,
Where the poor and needy of earth are rich in the perfect love of God!

THE CALL OF THE CHRISTIAN.

Not always as the whirlwind's rush
  On Horeb's mount of fear,
Not always as the burning bush
  To Midian's shepherd seer,
Nor as the awful voice which came
  To Israel's prophet bards,
Nor as the tongues of cloven flame,
  Nor gift of fearful words—

Not always thus, with outward sign
  Of fire or voice from Heaven,
The message of a truth divine,
  The call of God is given!
Awaking in the human heart
  Love for the true and right—
Zeal for the Christian's "better part,"
  Strength for the Christian's fight.

Nor unto manhood's heart alone
  The holy influence steals:
Warm with a rapture not its own, .
  The heart of woman feels!
As she who by Samaria's wall
  The Saviour's errand sought—
As those who with the fervent Paul
  And meek Aquila wrought:

Or those meek ones whose martyrdom
  Rome's gathered grandeur saw:
Or those who in their Alpine home
  Braved the Crusader's war,
When the green Vaudois, trembling, heard,
  Through all its vales of death,
The martyr's song of triumph poured
  From woman's failing breath.

And gently, by a thousand things
  Which o'er our spirits pass,
Like breezes o'er the harp's fine strings,
  Or vapors o'er a glass,
Leaving their token strange and new
  Of music or of shade,
The summons to the right and true
  And merciful is made.

Oh, then, if gleams of truth and light
  Flash o'er thy waiting mind,
Unfolding to thy mental sight
  The wants of human kind;

If brooding over human grief,
    The earnest wish is known
To soothe and gladden with relief
    An anguish not thine own:

Though heralded with naught of fear,
    Or outward sign, or show:
Though only to the inward ear
    It whispers soft and low;
Though dropping, as the manna fell,
    Unseen, yet from above,
Noiseless as dew-fall, heed it well—
    Thy Father's call of love!

MY SOUL AND I.

STAND still, my soul, in the silent dark
    I would question thee,
Alone in the shadow drear and stark
    With God and me!

What, my soul, was thy errand here?
    Was it mirth or ease,
Or heaping up dust from year to year?
    "Nay, none of these!"

Speak, soul, aright in His holy sight
    Whose eye looks still
And steadily on thee through the night:
    "To do His will!"

What hast thou done, oh soul of mine
    That thou tremblest so?—
Hast thou wrought His task, and kept the line
    He bade thee go?

What, silent all!—art sad of cheer?
    Art fearful now?
When God seemed far and men were near
    How brave wert thou?

Ah! thou tremblest!—well I see
    Thou'rt craven grown.
Is it so hard with God and me
    To stand alone?—

Summon thy sunshine bravery back,
    Oh, wretched sprite!
Let me hear thy voice through this deep and black
    Abysmal night.

What hast thou wrought for Right and Truth,
    For God and Man,
From the golden hours of bright-eyed youth
    To life's mid span ?

Ah, soul of mine, thy tones I hear,
    But weak and low,
Like far sad murmurs on my ear
    They come and go.

" I have wrestled stoutly with the Wrong,
    And borne the Right
From beneath the footfall of the throng
    To life and light.

" Wherever Freedom shivered a chain,
    God speed, quoth I;
To Error amidst her shouting train
    I gave the lie."

Ah, soul of mine ! ah, soul of mine !
    Thy deeds are well :
Were they wrought for Truth's sake or for thine ?
    My soul, pray tell.

" Of all the work my hand hath wrought
    Beneath the sky,
Save a place in kindly human thought,
    No gain have I."

Go to, go to !—for thy very self
    Thy deeds were done:
Thou for fame, the miser for pelf,
    Your end is one !

And where art thou going, soul of mine ?
    Canst see the end ?
And whither this troubled life of thine
    Evermore doth tend ?

What daunts thee now ?—what shakes thee so ?
    My sad soul say.
" I see a cloud like a curtain low
    Hang o'er my way.

" Whither I go I cannot tell:
    That cloud hangs black,
High as the heaven and deep as hell,
    Across my track.

" I see its shadow coldly enwrap
    The souls before,
Sadly they enter it, step by step,
    To return no more.

"They shrink, they shudder, dear God! they kneel
    To thee in prayer.
They shut their eyes on the cloud, but feel
    That it still is there.

" In vain they turn from the dread Before
    To the Known and Gone;
For while gazing behind them evermore
    Their feet glide on.

" Yet, at times, I see upon sweet pale faces
    A light begin
To tremble, as if from holy places
    And shrines within.

" And at times methinks their cold lips move
    With hymn and prayer,
As if somewhat of awe, but more of love
    And hope were there.

" I call on the souls who have left the light
    To reveal their lot;
I bend mine ear to that wall of night,
    And they answer not.

" But I hear around me sighs of pain
    And the cry of fear,
And a sound like the slow sad dropping of rain,
    Each drop a tear!

" Ah, the cloud is dark, and day by day,
    I am moving thither :
I must pass beneath it on my way—
    God pity me!—WHITHER ?"

Ah soul of mine ! so brave and wise
    In the life-storm loud,
Fronting so calmly all human eyes
    In the sunlit crowd!

Now standing apart with God and me
    Thou art weakness all,
Gazing vainly after the things to be
    Through Death's dread wall.

But never for this, never for this
    Was thy being lent;
For the craven's fear is but selfishness,
    Like his merriment.

Folly and Fear are sisters twain:
    One closing her eyes,
The other peopling the dark inane
    With spectral lies.

Know well, my soul, God's hand controls
    Whate'er thou fearest;
Round Him in calmest music rolls
    Whate'er thou hearest.

What to thee is shadow, to Him is day,
    And the end He knoweth,
And not on a blind and aimless way
    The spirit goeth.

Man sees no future—a phantom show
    Is alone before him;
Past Time is dead, and the grasses grow,
    And flowers bloom o'er him.

Nothing before, nothing behind:
    The steps of Faith
Fall on the seeming void, and find
    The rock beneath.

The Present, the Present is all thou hast
    For thy sure possessing;
Like the patriarch's angel hold it fast
    Till it gives its blessing.

Why fear the night? why shrink from Death,
    That phantom wan?
There is nothing in Heaven or earth beneath
    Save God and man.

Peopling the shadows we turn from Him
    And from one another;
All is spectral and vague and dim
    Save God and our brother!

Like warp and woof all destinies
    Are woven fast,
Linked in sympathy like the keys
    Of an organ vast.

Pluck one thread, and the web ye mar;
    Break but one
Of a thousand keys, and the paining jar
    Through all will run.

Oh, restless spirit! wherefore strain
    Beyond thy sphere?—
Heaven and hell, with their joy and pain
    Are now and here.

Back to thyself is measured well
    All thou hast given;
Thy neighbor's wrong is thy present hell,
    His bliss thy heaven.

And in life, in death, in dark and light
  All are in God's care ;
Sound the black abyss, pierce the deep of night,
  And He is there !

All which is real now remaineth,
  And fadeth never:
The hand which upholds it now, sustaineth
  The soul forever.

Leaning on Him, make with reverent meekness
  His own thy will,
And with strength from Him shall thy utter weak-
  ness
  Life's task fulfil ;

And that cloud itself, which now before thee
  Lies dark in view,
Shall with beams of light from the inner glory
  Be stricken through.

And like meadow mist through Autumn's dawn
  Uprolling thin,
Its thickest folds when about thee drawn
  Let sunlight in.

Then of what is to be, and of what is done
  Why queriest thou ?—
The past and the time to be are one,
  And both are NOW !

TO A FRIEND,

ON HER RETURN FROM EUROPE.

How smiled the land of France
Under thy blue eye's glance,
  Light-hearted rover ?
Old walls of châteaux gray,
Towers of an early day,
Which the Three Colors play
  Flauntingly over.

Now midst the brilliant train
Thronging the banks of Seine:
  Now midst the splendor
Of the wild Alpine range,
Waking with change on change
Thoughts in thy young heart
  strange,
  Lovely, and tender

Vales, soft Elysian,
Like those in the vision
  Of Mirza, when, dreaming,
He saw the long hollow dell,
Touched by the prophet's spell,
Into an ocean swell
  With its isles teeming.

Cliffs wrapped in snows of years,
Splintering with icy spears
  Autumn's blue heaven:
Loose rock and frozen slide,
Hung on the mountain side,
Waiting their hour to glide
  Downward, storm-driven!

Rhine stream, by castle old,
Baron's and robber's hold,
    Peacefully flowing;
Sweeping through vineyards green
Or where the cliffs are seen
O'er the broad wave between
    Grim shadows throwing.

Or where St. Peter's dome
Swells o'er eternal Rome,
    Vast, dim, and solemn, —
Hymns ever chanting low—
Censers swung to and fro—
Sable stoles sweeping slow
    Cornice and column!

Oh, as from each and all
Will there not voices call
    Evermore back again?
In the mind's gallery
Wilt thou not always see
Dim phantoms beckon thee
    O'er that old track again?

New forms thy presence haunt—
New voices softly chant—
    New faces greet thee!—
Pilgrims from many a shrine
Hallowed by poet's line,
At memory's magic sign,
    Rising to meet thee.

And when such visions come
Unto thy olden home,
    Will they not waken
Deep thoughts of Him whose hand
Led thee o'er sea and land
Back to the household band
    Whence thou wast taken?

While, at the sunset time,
Swells the cathedral's chime,
    Yet, in thy dreaming,
While to thy spirit's eye
Yet the vast mountains lie
Piled in the Switzer's sky,
    Icy and gleaming:

Prompter of silent prayer,
Be the wild picture there
    In the mind's chamber,
And, through each coming day
Him, who, as staff and stay,
Watched o'er thy wandering way,
    Freshly remember.

So, when the call shall be
Soon or late unto thee,
    As to all given,
Still may that picture live,
All its fair forms survive,
And to thy spirit give
    Gladness in Heaven!

THE ANGEL OF PATIENCE.

A Free Paraphrase of the German.

To weary hearts, to mourning homes,
God's meekest Angel gently comes:
No power has he to banish pain,
Or give us back our lost again;
And yet in tenderest love, our dear
And Heavenly Father sends him here.

There's quiet in that Angel's glance,
There's rest in his still countenance!
He mocks no grief with idle cheer,
Nor wounds with words the mourner's ear;
But ills and woes he may not cure
He kindly trains us to endure.

Angel of Patience! sent to calm
Our feverish brows with cooling palm

To lay the storms of hope and fear,
And reconcile life's smile and tear;
The throbs of wounded pride to still,
And make our own our Father's will !

Oh! thou who mournest on thy way,
With longings for the close of day;
He walks with thee, that Angel kind,
And gently whispers "Be resigned:
Bear up, bear on, the end shall tell
The dear Lord ordereth all things well !"

FOLLEN.

ON READING HIS ESSAY ON THE "FUTURE STATE."

FRIEND of my soul !—as with moist eye
I look up from this page of thine,
Is it a dream that thou art nigh,
Thy mild face gazing into mine ?

That presence seems before me now,
A placid heaven of sweet moonrise,
When dew-like, on the earth below
Descends the quiet of the skies.

The calm brow through the parted hair,
The gentle lips which knew no guile,
Softening the blue eye's thoughtful care
With the bland beauty of their smile.

Ah me!—at times that last dread scene
Of Frost and Fire and moaning Sea,
Will cast its shade of doubt between
The failing eyes of Faith and thee.

Yet, lingering o'er thy charmèd page,
Where through the twilight air of earth,
Alike enthusiast and sage,
Prophet and bard, thou gazest forth;

Lifting the Future's solemn veil;
The reaching of a mortal hand
To put aside the cold and pale
Cloud-curtains of the Unseen Land;

In thoughts which answer to my own,
In words which reach my inward ear,
Like whispers from the void Unknown,
I feel thy living presence here.

The waves which lull thy body's rest,
　　The dust thy pilgrim footsteps trod,
Unwasted, through each change, attest
　　The fixed economy of God.

Shall these poor elements outlive
　　The mind whose kingly will they wrought?
Their gross unconsciousness survive
　　Thy Godlike energy of thought?

THOU LIVEST, FOLLEN!—not in vain
　　Hath thy fine spirit meekly borne
The burden of Life's cross of pain,
　　And the thorned crown of suffering worn.

Oh! while Life's solemn mystery glooms
　　Around us like a dungeon's wall—
Silent earth's pale and crowded tombs,
　　Silent the heaven which bends o'er all!—

While day by day our loved ones glide
　　In spectral silence, hushed and lone,
To the cold shadows which divide
　　The living from the dread Unknown;

While even on the closing eye,
　　And on the lip which moves in vain,
The seals of that stern mystery
　　Their undiscovered trust retain;—

And only midst the gloom of death,
　　Its mournful doubts and haunting fears,
Two pale, sweet angels, Hope and Faith,
　　Smile dimly on us through their tears;

'Tis something to a heart like mine
　　To think of thee as living yet;
To feel that such a light as thine
　　Could not in utter darkness set.

Less dreary seems the untried way
　　Since thou hast left thy footprints there,
And beams of mournful beauty play
　　Round the sad Angel's sable hair.

Oh!—at this hour when half the sky
　　Is glorious with its evening light,
And fair broad fields of summer lie
　　Hung o'er with greenness in my sight;

While through these elm boughs wet with rain
　　The sunset's golden walls are seen,

With clover bloom and yellow grain
    And wood-draped hill and stream between;

I long to know if scenes like this
    Are hidden from an angel's eyes;
If earth's familiar loveliness
    Haunts not thy heaven's serener skies.

For sweetly here upon thee grew
    The lesson which that beauty gave,
The ideal of the Pure and True
    In earth and sky and gliding wave.

And it may be that all which lends
    The soul an upward impulse here,
With a diviner beauty blends,
    And greets us in a holier sphere.

Through groves where blighting never fell
    The humbler flowers of earth may twine;
And simple draughts from childhood's well
    Blend with the angel tasted wine.

But be the prying vision veiled,
    And let the seeking lips be dumb,—
Where even seraph eyes have failed
    Shall mortal blindness seek to come?

We only know that thou hast gone,
    And that the same returnless tide
Which bore thee from us still glides on,
    And we who mourn thee with it glide.

On all thou lookest we shall look,
    And to our gaze ere long shall turn
That page of God's mysterious book
    We so much wish, yet dread to learn.

With Him, before whose awful power
    Thy spirit bent its trembling knee,—
Who, in the silent greeting flower,
    And forest leaf, looked out on thee,—

We leave thee, with a trust serene,
    Which Time, nor Change, nor Death can move,
While with thy childlike faith we lean
    On Him whose dearest name is Love!

TO THE REFORMERS OF ENGLAND.

God bless ye, brothers!—in the fight
  Ye're waging now, ye cannot
For better is your sense of right
  Than kingcraft's triple mail.

Than tyrant's law, or bigot's ban
  More mighty is your simplest word;
The free heart of an honest man
  Than crosier or the sword.

Go—let your bloated Church rehearse
  The lesson it has learned so well;
It moves not with its prayer or curse
  The gates of Heaven or hell.

Let the State scaffold rise again—
  Did Freedom die when Russell died?
Forget ye how the blood of Vane
  From earth's green bosom cried ?

The great hearts of your olden time
  Are beating with you, full and strong;
All holy memories and sublime
  And glorious round ye throng.

The bluff, bold men of Runnymede
  Are with ye still in times like these;
The shades of England's mighty dead,
  Your cloud of witnesses!

The truths ye urge are borne abroad
  By every wind and every tide;
The voice of Nature and of God
  Speaks out upon your side.

The weapons which your hands have found
  Are those which Heaven itself hath wrought,
Light, Truth, and Love;—your battle ground
  The free, broad field of Thought.

No partial, selfish purpose breaks
  The simple beauty of your plan,
Nor lie from throne or altar shakes
  Your steady faith in man.

The languid pulse of England starts
  And bounds beneath your words of power:
The beating of her million hearts
  Is with you at this hour!

Oh, ye who, with undoubting eyes,
    Through present cloud and gathering storm,
Behold the span of Freedom's skies,
    And sunshine soft and warm,—

Press bravely onward!—not in vain
    Your generous trust in human kind;
The good which bloodshed could not gain
    Your peaceful zeal shall find.

Press on!—the triumph shall be won
    Of common rights and equal laws,
The glorious dream of Harrington,
    And Sidney's good old cause.

Blessing the cotter and the crown,
    Sweetening worn Labor's bitter cup;
And, plucking not the highest down,
    Lifting the lowest up.

Press on!—and we who may not share
    The toil or glory of your fight,
May ask, at least, in earnest prayer,
    God's blessing on the right!

THE QUAKER OF THE OLDEN TIME.

THE Quaker of the olden time!—
    How calm and firm and true,
Unspotted by its wrong and crime,
    He walked the dark earth through!
The lust of power, the love of gain,
    The thousand lures of sin
Around him, had no power to stain
    The purity within.

With that deep insight which detects
    All great things in the small,
And knows how each man's life affects
    The spiritual life of all,
He walked by faith and not by sight,
    By love and not by law;
The presence of the wrong or right
    He rather felt than saw.

He felt that wrong with wrong partakes,
    That nothing stands alone,
That whoso gives the motive, makes
    His brother's sin his own.
And, pausing not for doubtful choice
    Of evils great or small,

He listened to that inward voice
  Which called away from all.

Oh! Spirit of that early day,
  So pure and strong and true,
Be with us in the narrow way
  Our faithful fathers knew.
Give strength the evil to forsake,
  The cross of Truth to bear,
And love and reverent fear to make
  Our daily lives a prayer!

THE REFORMER.

ALL grim and soiled and brown with tan,
  I saw a Strong One, in his wrath,
Smiting the godless shrines of man
    Along his path.

The Church beneath her trembling dome
  Essayed in vain her ghostly charm:
Wealth shook within his gilded home
    With strange alarm.

Fraud from his secret chambers fled
  Before the sunlight bursting in:
Sloth drew her pillow o'er her head
    To drown the din.

"Spare," Art implored, "yon holy pile;
  That grand, old, time-worn, turret spare;"
Meek Reverence, kneeling in the aisle,
    Cried out, "Forbear!"

Gray-bearded Use, who, deaf and blind,
  Groped for his old accustomed stone,
Leaned on his staff, and wept, to find
    His seat o'erthrown.

Young Romance raised his dreamy eyes,
  O'erhung with paly locks of gold:
"Why smite," he asked in sad surprise,
    "The fair, the old?"

Yet louder rang the Strong One's stroke,
  Yet nearer flashed his axe's gleam;
Shuddering and sick of heart I woke,
    As from a dream.

I looked: aside the dust cloud rolled—
  The Waster seemed the Builder too;

Upspringing from the ruined Old
    I saw the New.

'Twas but the ruin of the bad—
    The wasting of the wrong and ill;
Whate'er of good the old time had
    Was living still.

Calm grew the brows of him I feared;
    The frown which awed me passed away,
And left behind a smile which cheered
    Like breaking day.

The grain grew green on battle-plains,
    O'er swarded war-mounds grazed the cow;
The slave stood forging from his chains
    The spade and plough.

Where frowned the fort, pavilions gay
    And cottage windows, flower-entwined,
Looked out upon the peaceful bay
    And hills behind.

Through vine-wreathed cups with wine once red,
    The lights on brimming crystal fell,
Drawn, sparkling, from the rivulet head
    And mossy well.

Through prison walls, like Heaven-sent hope,
    Fresh breezes blew, and sunbeams strayed,
And with the idle gallows-rope
    The young child played.

Where the doomed victim in his cell
    Had counted o'er the weary hours,
Glad schoolgirls, answering to the bell,
    Came crowned with flowers.

Grown wiser for the lesson given,
    I fear no longer, for I know
That, where the share is deepest driven,
    The best fruits grow.

The outworn rite, the old abuse,
    The pious fraud transparent grown,
The good held captive in the use
    Of wrong alone—

These wait their doom, from that great law
    Which makes the past time serve to-day;
And fresher life the world shall draw
    From their decay.

Oh! backward-looking son of time!—
    The new is old, the old is new,

The cycle of a change sublime
    Still sweeping through.

So wisely taught the Indian seer;
    Destroying Seva, forming Brahm,
Who wake by turns Earth's love and fear,
    Are one, the same.

As idly as, in that old day
    Thou mournest, did thy sires repine,
So, in his time, thy child, grown gray,
    Shall sigh for thine.

Yet, not the less for them or thou
    The eternal step of Progress beats
To that great anthem, calm and slow,
    Which God repeats !

Take heart!—the Waster builds again—
    A charmed life old goodness hath;
The tears may perish—but the grain
    Is not for death.

God works in all things; all obey
    His first propulsion from the night:
Ho, wake and watch!—the world is gray
    With morning light!

THE PRISONER FOR DEBT.

Look on him!—through his dungeon grate
    Feebly and cold, the morning light
Comes stealing round him, dim and late,
    As if it loathed the sight,
Reclining on his strawy bed,
His hand upholds his drooping head—
His bloodless cheek is seamed and hard,
Unshorn his gray, neglected beard;
And o'er his bony fingers flow
His long, dishevelled locks of snow.

No grateful fire before him glows,
    And yet the winter's breath is chill;
And o'er his half-clad person goes
    The frequent ague thrill!
Silent, save ever and anon,
A sound, half murmur and half groan,
Forces apart the painful grip
Of the old sufferer's bearded lip;
O sad and crushing is the fate
Of old age chained and desolate!

Just God! why lies that old man there?
  A murderer shares his prison bed,
Whose eyeballs, through his horrid hair,
  Gleam on him, fierce and red;
And the rude oath and heartless jeer
Fall ever on his loathing ear,
And, or in wakefulness or sleep,
Nerve, flesh, and pulses thrill and creep
Whene'er that ruffian's tossing limb,
Crimson with murder, touches him!

What has the gray-haired prisoner done?
  Has murder stained his hands with gore?
Not so; his crime's a fouler one:
  GOD MADE THE OLD MAN POOR!
For this he shares a felon's cell—
The fittest earthly type of hell!
For this, the boon for which he poured
His young blood on the invader's sword,
And counted light the fearful cost—
His blood-gained liberty is lost!

And so, for such a place of rest,
  Old prisoner, dropped thy blood as rain
On Concord's field, and Bunker's crest,
  And Saratoga's plain?
Look forth, thou man of many scars,
Through thy dim dungeon's iron bars;
It must be joy, in sooth, to see
Yon monument upreared to thee—
Piled granite and a prison cell—
The land repays thy service well!

Go, ring the bells and fire the guns,
  And fling the starry banner out;
Shout "Freedom!" till your lisping ones
  Give back their cradle-shout:
Let boastful eloquence declaim
Of honor, liberty and fame;
Still let the poet's strain be heard,
With glory for each second word,
And everything with breath agree
To praise "our glorious liberty!"

But when the patriot cannon jars
  That prison's cold and gloomy wall,
And through its grates the stripes and stars
  Rise on the wind and fall—
Think ye that prisoner's aged ear
Rejoices in the general cheer?
Think ye his dim and failing eye
Is kindled at your pageantry?
Sorrowing of soul, and chained of limb,
What is your carnival to him?

Down with the LAW that binds him thus !
    Unworthy freemen, let it find
No refuge from the withering curse
    Of God and human kind !
Open the prison's living tomb,
And usher from its brooding gloom
The victims of your savage code,
To the free sun and air of God ;
No longer dare as crime to brand
The chastening of the Almighty's hand.

LINES

Written on Reading Several Pamphlets Published by Clergymen against the Abolition of the Gallows.

I.

THE suns of eighteen centuries have shone
    Since the Redeemer walked with man, and made
The fisher's boat, the cavern's floor of stone,
    And mountain moss, a pillow for his head ;
And He, who wandered with the peasant Jew,
    And broke with publicans the bread of shame,
    And drank, with blessings in His Father's name,
The water which Samaria's outcast drew,
Hath now His temples upon every shore,
    Altar and shrine and priest,—and incense dim
Evermore rising, with low prayer and hymn,
From lips which press the temple's marble floor,
Or kiss the gilded sign of the dread Cross He bore !

II.

Yet as of old, when, meekly "doing good,"
He fed a blind and selfish multitude,
And even the poor companions of His lot
With their dim earthly vision knew Him not,
    How ill are His high teachings understood !
Where he hath spoken Liberty, the priest
    At His own altar binds the chain anew ;
Where He hath bidden to Life's equal feast,
    The starving many wait upon the few ;
Where He hath spoken Peace, His name hath been
The loudest war-cry of contending men ;
Priests, pale with vigils, in His name have blessed
The unsheathed sword, and laid the spear in rest,
Wet the war-banner with their sacred wine,
And crossed its blazon with the holy sign ;
Yea, in His name who bade the erring live,
And daily taught his lesson—to forgive !—
    Twisted the cord and edged the murderous steel ;

And, with His words of mercy on their lips,
Hung gloating o'er the pincer's burning grips,
    And the grim horror of the straining wheel ;
Fed the slow flame which gnawed the victim's limb
Who saw before his searing eyeballs swim
    The image of *their* Christ, in cruel zeal,
Through the black torment-smoke, held mockingly to him !

III.

The blood which mingled with the desert sand
    And beaded with its red and ghastly dew
The vines and olives of the Holy Land—
    The shrieking curses of the hunted Jew—
The white-sown bones of heretics, where'er
They sank beneath the Crusade's holy spear—
Goa's dark dungeons—Malta's sea-washed cell,
    Where with the hymns the ghostly fathers sung
    Mingled the groans by subtle torture wrung,
Heaven's anthem blending with the shriek of hell!
The midnight of Bartholomew—the stake
Of Smithfield, and that thrice-accursed flame
Which Calvin kindled by Geneva's lake—
New England's scaffold, and the priestly sneer
Which mocked its victims in that hour of fear,
    When guilt itself a human tear might claim,—
Bear witness, O Thou wronged and merciful One!
That Earth's most hateful crimes have in Thy name been done!

IV.

Thank God! that I have lived to see the time
    When the great truth begins at last to find
    An utterance from the deep heart of mankind,
Earnest and clear, that ALL REVENGE is CRIME!
That man is holier than a creed,—that all
    Restraint upon him must consult his good,
Hope's sunshine linger on his prison wall,
    And Love look in upon his solitude.
The beautiful lesson which our Saviour taught
Through long, dark centuries its way hath wrought
Into the common mind and popular thought;
And words, to which by Galilee's lake shore
The humble fishers listened with hushed oar,
Have found an echo in the general heart,
And of the public faith become a living part.

V.

Who shall arrest this tendency ?—Bring back
The cells of Venice and the bigot's rack ?
Harden the softening human heart again
To cold indifference to a brother's pain ?

Ye most unhappy men !—who, turned away
From the mild sunshine of the Gospel day,
    Grope in the shadows of Man's twilight time,
What mean ye, that with ghoul-like zest ye brood
O'er those foul altars streaming with warm blood,
    Permitted in another age and clime ?
Why cite that law with which the bigot Jew
Rebuked the Pagan's mercy, when he knew
No evil in the Just One ?—Wherefore turn
To the dark cruel past ?—Can ye not learn
From the pure Teacher's life, how mildly free
Is the great Gospel of Humanity ?
The Flamen's knife is bloodless, and no more
Mexitli's altars soak with human gore,
No more the ghastly sacrifices smoke
Through the green arches of the Druid's oak ;
And ye of milder faith, with your high claim
Of prophet-utterance in the Holiest name,
Will ye become the Druids of *our* time ?
    Set up your scaffold-altars in *our* land,
And consecrators of Law's darkest clime,
    Urged to its loathsome work the hangman's hand ?
Beware—lest human nature, roused at last,
From its peeled shoulder your encumbrance cast,
    And, sick to loathing of your cry for blood,
Rank ye with those who led their victims round
The Celt's red altar and the Indian's mound,
    Abhorred of Earth and Heaven—a pagan brotherhood !

THE WORSHIP OF NATURE.

" It hath beene as it were especially rendered unto mee and made plaine and legible to m
understandynge that a great worshipp is going on among the thyngs of God."—*Gratt.*

THE Ocean looketh up to Heaven,
    As't were a living thing,
The homage of its waves is given
    In ceaseless worshipping.

They kneel upon the sloping sand,
    As bends the human knee,
A beautiful and tireless band,
    The Priesthood of the Sea !

They pour the glittering treasures out
    Which in the deep have birth,
And chant their awful hymns about
    The watching hills of earth.

The green earth sends its incense up
    From every mountain shrine,

From every flower and dewy cup
  That greeteth the sunshine.

The mists are lifted from the rills
  Like the white wing of prayer,
They lean above the ancient hills
  As doing homage there.

The forest tops are lowly cast
  O'er breezy hill and glen,
As if a prayerful spirit pass'd
  On Nature as on men.

The clouds weep o'er the fallen world
  E'en as repentant love;
Ere to the blessed breeze unfurl'd
  They fade in light above.

The sky is as a temple's arch,
  The blue and wavy air
Is glorious with the spirit-march
  Of messengers of prayer.

The gentle moon—the kindling sun—
  The many stars are given,
As shrines to burn earth's incense on—
  The altar-fires of Heaven!

LINES

Written in the Commonplace Book of a young lady.

" Write, write!" Dear Cousin, since thy word,
Like that my ancient namesake heard
  On Patmos, may not be denied,
I offer for thy page a lay
Breathing of Beauty pass'd away
Of Grace and Genius, Love and Truth,
All which can add a charm to youth,
  To virtue and to Heaven allied.
Forgive me if the lay be such
  As may not suit thy hours of gladness,
Forgive me, if it breathe too much
  Of mourning and of sadness.
It may be well that tears, at whiles,
Should take the place of Folly's smiles,
  When 'neath some Heaven-directed blow,
  Like those of Horeb's rock, they flow,
  For sorrows are in mercy given
  To fit the chasten'd soul for Heaven:

Prompting, with woe and weariness,
   Our yearning for that better sky,
Which, as the shadows close on this,
   Grows brighter to the longing eye.
For each unwelcome blow may break,
   Perchance, some chain which binds us here;
And clouds around the heart may make
   The vision of our Faith more clear ;
As through the shadowy veil of even
The eye looks farthest into Heaven,
On gleams of star and depths of blue
The fervid sunshine never knew!

————"The parted spirit,
Knoweth it not our sorrow ? Answereth not
Its blessing to our tears?"

The circle is broken—one seat is forsaken,—
One bud from the tree of our friendship is shaken—
One heart from among us no longer shall thrill
With the spirit of gladness, or darken with ill.

Weep!—Lonely and lowly, are slumbering now
The light of her glances, the pride of her brow.
Weep!—Sadly and long shall we listen in vain
To hear the soft tones of her welcome again.

Give our tears to the dead ! For humanity's claim
From its silence and darkness is ever the same;
The hope of that World whose existence is bliss
May not stifle the tears of the mourners of this.

For, oh! if one glance the freed spirit can throw
On the scene of its troubled probation below,
Than the pride of the marble—the pomp of the dead—
To that glance will be dearer the tears which we shed.

Oh, who can forget the rich light of her smile,
Over lips moved with music and feeling the while—
The eye's deep enchantment, dark, dream-like, and clear,
In the glow of its gladness—the shade of its tear.

And the charm of her features, while over the whole
Play'd the hues of the heart and the sunshine of soul,—
And the tones of her voice, like the music which seems
Murmur'd low in our ears by the Angel of dreams!

But holier and dearer our memories hold
Those treasures of feeling, more precious than gold—
The love and the kindness,—the pity which gave
Fresh hopes to the living and wreaths for the grave—

The heart ever open to Charity's claim,
Unmoved from its purpose by censure and blame,

While vainly alike on her eye and her ear
Fell the scorn of the heartless, the jesting and jeer.

For, though spotless herself, she could sorrow for them
Who sullied with evil the spirit's pure gem;
And a sigh or a tear could the erring reprove,
And the sting of reproof was still temper'd by love.

As a cloud of the sunset, slow melting in heaven,
As a star that is lost when the daylight is given,
As a glad dream of slumber, which wakens in bliss,
She hath pass'd to the world of the holy from this.

She hath pass'd!—but, oh! sweet as the flowerets that bloom
From her last lonely dwelling—the dust of her tomb—
The charm of her virtues, as Heaven's own breath,
Shall rise like an incense from darkness and death.

THE WATCHER.

"And Rizpah, the daughter of Aiah, took sackcloth, and spread it for her upon the rock,
from the beginning of harvest until water dropped upon them out of Heaven, and suffered
either the birds of the air to rest on them by day, nor the beasts of the field by night."—
Sam. xxi. 10.

TALL men and kingly-brow'd!—they led them forth
Bound for the sacrifice. It was high noon;
And ancient Gibeah, emptied of her life,
Rose silently before the harvest sun.
Her dwellers had gone out before the walls,
With a stern purpose; and her maidens lean'd
Breathless for its fulfilment, from the hills,
Uncheer'd by reaper's song. The harvest lay
Stinted and sere upon their parched tops.
The streams had perish'd in their goings on;
And the deep fountains fail'd. The fervent sun,
Unchasten'd by a cloud, for months had shone
A lidless eye in heaven; and all the sky
Glow'd as a furnace, and the prodigal dew
With the scorch'd earth held no companionship.
A curse was over Israel. Unjudged crime
Had wrought it in the elements. Her soil
Was unbless'd as the heathen's; and the plagues
Of those who know not God, and bow them down
To a strange worship, had been meted her.

The sacrifice was finish'd. Gibeon roll'd
Back like a torrent through the city gates
Her gather'd thousands; and her victims lay
Naked beneath the brazen arch of heaven,
On the stain'd Rock of Sacrifice. The sun
Went down his heated pathway with a slow

And weary progress, as he loved to gaze
On the dark horror of his burning noon—
The sacrifice of Innocence for Guilt,
Whose blood had sent its sleepless murmur up
To the Avenger's ear, until fierce wrath
Burn'd over earth and heaven, and Vengeance held
The awful mastery of the elements.

Who stealeth from the city, in the garb
Which tokens the heart's sorrow, and which seems
Around her wasted form to shadow forth
The visitation of dark grief within?
Lo!—she hath pass'd the valley, and her foot
Is on the Rock of Sacrifice—and now
She stoopeth over the unburied dead.
And moves her lip, but speaks not. It is strange
And very fearful! The descending sun
Is pausing like a fire-wing'd Angel on
The bare hills of the West, and, fierce and red,
His last rays fall aslant the place of blood,
Coloring its dark stains deeper. Lo! she kneels
To cover, with a trembling hand, the cold
And ghastly work of death—those desecrate
And darken'd temples of the living soul!

Her task was finish'd, and she went away
A little distance, and, as night stole on
With dim starlight and shadow, she sat down
Upon a jutting fragment of the rock—
A solitary watcher. The red glow
That wrestled with the darkness, and sent up
Its spear-like lines of light until they waned
Into the dark blue zenith, pass'd away,
And, from the broad and shadow'd West, the stars
Shone through substantial blackness. Midnight came;
The wind was groaning on the hills and through
The naked branches of their perishing trees,
And strange sounds blended with it. The gaunt wolf,
Scenting the place of slaughter, with his long
And most offensive howl did ask for blood;
And the hyena sat upon the cliff,
His red eye glowing terribly; and low,
But frequent and most fearfully, his growl
Came to the watcher's ear. Alone she sat,
Unmoving as her resting-place of rock.
Fear for herself she felt not—every tie
That once took hold on life with aught of love
Was broken utterly. Her eye was fix'd,
Stony and motionless, upon the pall
Which veil'd her princely dead. And this was love

In its surpassing power—yea, love as strong
As that which binds the peopled Universe,
And pure as angel-worship, when the just
And beautiful of Heaven are bow'd in prayer!

The night stole into morning, and the sun,
Red and unwelcome, rose without a cloud,
And there was Rizpah still, woe-worn and pale;
And yet in her dark eye and darker hair,
And in the marble and uplifted brow,
And the much wasted figure, might be seen
A wreck of perfect beauty, such as bow'd
The throned one of Israel at her feet,
Low as the trampled Philistine had knelt
Before his mailed presence. Not a tear
Glisten'd on eye or cheek, but still she gazed
On the dark veil of sackcloth with a strange
And fixed earnestness. The sky again
Redden'd with heat, and the unmoisten'd earth
Was like the ashen surface of the hush'd
But perilous volcano. Rizpah bore
The fever of the noon-time, with a stern
And awful sense of duty nerving her,
In her devotedness. She might not leave
The high place of her watching for the shade
Of cluster'd palm-trees; and the lofty rocks,
Casting their grim and giant shadows down,
Might not afford her shelter; for the sweep
Of heavy wings went over her like clouds
Crossing the sunshine, and most evil birds,
Dark and obscene,—the jaguars of the air!—
From all the hills had gather'd. Far and shy
The sombre raven sat upon his rock,
And his vile mate did mock him. The vast wing
Of the great eagle, stooping from the sun,
Winnow'd the cliffs above her!

Day by day,
Beneath the scorching of the unveil'd sun,
And the unweeping solitude of night,
Pale Rizpah kept her vigils; and her prayer
Went up at morn and eventide, that Earth
Might know the gentle visitings of rain
And be accurs'd no more. And when at last
God thunder'd in the heavens, and clouds came up
From their long slumber, and the great rain fell,
And the parch'd earth drank deeply, Rizpah knew
Her prayers were answer'd, and she knelt again;
In earnest gratitude; and when the storm
Roll'd off before the sunshine, kindly hands
Convey'd away her wasted charge, and gave
The sons of Saul a sepulchre with him,

THE CITY OF REFUGE.

JOSHUA, CHAPTER XX.

" Away from thy people, thou shedder of blood—
Away to the refuge appointed of God!
Nay, pause not to look for thy household or kin,
For Death is behind thee, thou worker of sin.

" Away!—look not back, though that sorrowful one,
The mother who bore thee, shall wail for her son,
Nor stay when thy wife, as a beautiful blossom,
Shall clasp thy fair child to her desolate bosom.

" Away, with thy face to the refuge afar
In the glow of the sun—in the eye of the star;
Though the Simoom breathe o'er thee, oppressive and warm,
Rest not by the fountain nor under the palm.

" Away! for the kinsman of him thou hast slain
Has breathed on thy head the dark curses of Cain;
The cry of his vengeance shall follow thy path—
The tramp of his footstep, the shout of his wrath."

And the slayer sprang up as the warning was said,
And the stones of the altar rang out to his tread;
The wail of his household was lost on his ear—
He spoke not, he paused not, he turn'd not to hear.

He fled to the desert—he turn'd him not back
When the rush of the sand-storm grew loud in his track,
Nor paused till his vision fell, grateful and glad,
On the green hills of Gilead—the white tents of Gad.

Oh, thus, when the crimes and the errors of Earth
Have driven her children as wanderers forth,
To the bow'd and the broken of spirit is given
The hope of a refuge—the refuge of Heaven!

THE HUMAN SACRIFICE.

I.

Far from his close and noisome cell,
    By grassy lane and sunny stream,
Blown clover field and strawberry dell,
And green and meadow freshness, fell
    The footsteps of his dream.

Again from careless feet the dew
  Of summer's misty morn he shook;
Again with merry heart he threw
  His light line in the rippling brook.
Back crowded all his school-day joys—
  He urged the ball and quoit again,
And heard the shout of laughing boys
  Come ringing down the walnut glen.
Again he felt the western breeze,
  With scent of flowers and crisping hay;
And down again through wind-stirred trees
  He saw the quivering sunlight play.
An angel in home's vine-hung door,
  He saw his sister smile once more;
Once more the truant's brown-locked head
Upon his mother's knee was laid,
And sweetly lulled to slumber there,
With evening's holy hymn and prayer.

II.

He woke. At once on heart and brain
The present Terror rushed again—
Clanked on his limbs the felon's chain!
He woke, to hear the church-tower tell
Time's foot-fall on the conscious bell,
And, shuddering, feel that clanging din
His life's LAST HOUR had ushered in;
To see within his prison yard,
Through the small window, iron-barred,
The gallows shadow rising dim
Between the sunrise heaven and him,—
A horror in God's blessed air—
  A blackness in His morning light—
Like some foul devil-altar there
  Built up by demon hands at night.
And, maddened by that evil sight,
Dark, horrible, confused, and strange,
A chaos of wild, weltering change,
All power of check and guidance gone,
Dizzy and blind, his mind swept on.
In vain he strove to breathe a prayer,
  In vain he turned the Holy Book,
He only heard the gallows-stair
  Creak as the wind its timbers shook.
No dream for him of sin forgiven,
  While still that baleful spectre stood,
  With its hoarse murmur, " *Blood for Blood* "
Between him and the pitying Heaven!

III.

Low on his dungeon floor he knelt,
   And smote his breast, and on his chain,
Whose iron clasp he always felt,
   His hot tears fell like rain;
And near him, with the cold, calm look
   And tone of one whose formal part,
   Unwarmed, unsoftened of the heart,
Is measured out by rule and book,
With placid lip and tranquil blood,
The hangman's ghostly ally stood,
Blessing with solemn text and word
The gallows-drop and strangling cord;
Lending the sacred Gospel's awe
And sanction to the crime of Law.

IV.

He saw the victim's tortured brow—
   The sweat of anguish starting there—
The record of a nameless woe
   In the dim eye's imploring stare,
   Seen hideous through the long, damp hair—
Fingers of ghastly skin and bone
Working and writhing on the stone!—
And heard, by mortal terror wrung
From heaving breast and stiffened tongue,
   The choking sob and low hoarse prayer;
As o'er his half-crazed fancy came
A vision of the eternal flame—
Its smoking cloud of agonies—
Its devil-worm that never dies—
The everlasting rise and fall
Of fire-waves round the infernal wall;
While high above that dark red flood,
Black, giant-like, the gallows stood:
Two busy fiends attending there;
One with cold mocking rite and prayer,
The other, with impatient grasp,
Tightening the death-rope's strangling clasp!

V.

The unfelt rite at length was done—
   The prayer unheard at length was said—
An hour had passed—the noonday sun
   Smote on the features of the dead!
And he who stood the doomed beside,
Calm gauger of the swelling tide
Of mortal agony and fear,
Heeding with curious eye and ear
Whate'er revealed the keen excess

Of man's extremest wretchedness:
And who in that dark anguish saw
    An earnest of the victim's fate,
The vengeful terrors of God's law,
    The kindlings of Eternal hate—
The first drops of that fiery rain
Which beats the dark red realm of pain,—
Did he uplift his earnest cries
    Against the crime of Law, which gave
    His brother to that fearful grave,
Whereon Hope's moonlight never lies,
    And Faith's white blossoms never wave
To the soft breath of Memory's sighs;—
Which sent a spirit marred and stained,
By fiends of sin possessed, profaned,
In madness and in blindness stark,
Into the silent, unknown dark?
No—from the wild and shrinking dread
With which he saw the victim led
    Beneath the dark veil which divides
Ever the living from the dead,
    And Nature's solemn secret hides,
The man of prayer can only draw
New reasons for his bloody law;
New faith in staying Murder's hand
By murder at that Law's command;
New reverence for the gallows-rope,
As human nature's latest hope;
Last relic of the good old time,
When Power found license for its crime,
And held a writhing world in check
By that fell cord about its neck;
Stifled Sedition's rising shout,
Choked the young breath of Freedom out,
And timely checked the words which sprung
From Heresy's forbidden tongue;
While in its noose of terror bound,
The Church its cherished union found,
Conforming, on the Moslem plan,
The motley-colored mind of man,
Not by the Koran and the Sword,
But by the Bible and the Cord!

VI.

Oh, Thou! at whose rebuke the grave
Back to warm life its sleeper gave,
Beneath whose sad and tearful glance
The cold and changed countenance
Broke the still horror of its trance,
And waking, saw with joy above,

A brother's face of tenderest love;
Thou, unto whom the blind and lame,
The sorrowing and the sin-sick came,
And from thy very garment's hem
Drew life and healing unto them,
The burden of Thy holy faith
Was love and life, not hate and death,
Man's demon ministers of pain,
  The fiends of his revenge, were sent
  From Thy pure Gospel's element
To their dark home again.
Thy name is Love! What, then, is he,
  Who in that name the gallows rears,
An awful altar built to Thee,
  With sacrifice of blood and tears?
Oh, once again Thy healing lay
  On the blind eyes which know Thee not;
And let the light of Thy pure day
  Melt in upon his darkened thought.
Soften his hard, cold heart, and show
  The power which in forbearance lies,
And let him feel that mercy now
  Is better than old sacrifice!

VII.

As on the White Sea's* charmed shore,
  The Parsee sees his holy hill
With dunnest smoke-clouds curtained o'er,
Yet knows beneath them, evermore,
  The low pale fire is quivering still,
So underneath its clouds of sin,
  The heart of man retaineth yet
Gleams of its holy origin;
  And half-quenched stars that never set,
Dim colors of its faded bow,
And early beauty, linger there,
And o'er its wasted desert blow
  Faint breathings of its morning air.
Oh! never yet upon the scroll
Of the sin-stained, but priceless soul,
  Hath Heaven inscribed " DESPAIR! "
Cast not the clouded gem away,
Quench not the dim but living ray—
  My brother man, Beware!
With that deep voice which from the skies
Forbade the Patriarch's sacrifice,
  God's angel cries, FORBEAR!

* Among the Tartars, the Caspian is known as *Akdingis*, that is, White Sea. Baku, on the Persian side, is remarkable for its perpetual fire, scarcely discoverable under the pitchy clouds of smoke from the bitumen which feeds it. It is the natural fire-altar of the old Persian worship.

RANDOLPH OF ROANOKE.

ı, Mother Earth! upon thy lap
Thy weary ones receiving,
ıd o'er them, silent as a dream,
Thy grassy mantle weaving,
ıld softly in thy long embrace
That heart so worn and broken,
ıd cool its pulse of fire beneath
Thy shadows old and oaken.

ut out from him the bitter word
And serpent hiss of scorning;
ır let the storms of yesterday
Disturb his quiet morning.
eathe over him forgetfulness
Of all save deeds of kindness,
ıd, save to smiles of grateful
   eyes,
Press down his lids in blindness.

cre, where with living ear and
   eye
Ie heard Potomac's flowing,
ıd, through his tall ancestral
   trees,
Saw Autumn's sunset glowing,
   sleeps—still looking to the
   West,
Beneath the dark wood shadow,
if he still would see the sun
ınk down on wave and meadow.

rd, Sage, and Tribune!—in himself
ıll moods of mind contrasting—
e tenderest wail of human woe,
The scorn like lightning blasting;
e pathos which from rival eyes
Unwilling tears could summon,
e stinging taunt, the fiery burst
ıf hatred scarcely human!

th, sparkling like a diamond
   shower
rom lips of life-long sadness;
ar picturings of majestic
   thought
pon a ground of madness;
ı over all Romance and Song
, classic beauty throwing,

And laurelled Clio at his side
   Her storied pages showing.

All parties feared him: each in turn
   Beheld its schemes disjointed,
As right or left his fatal glance
   And spectral finger pointed.
Sworn foe of Cant, he smote it
   down
   With trenchant wit unsparing,
And, mocking, rent with ruthless
   hand
   The robe Pretence was wearing.

Too honest or too proud to feign
   A love he never cherished,
Beyond Virginia's border line
   His patriotism perished.
While others hailed in distant skies
   Our eagle's dusky pinion,
He only saw the mountain bird
   Stoop o'er his Old Dominion!

Still through each change of for-
   tune strange,
   Racked nerve, and brain all
   burning,
His loving faith of Mother-land
   Knew never shade of turning;
By Britain's lakes, by Neva's wave,
   Whatever sky was o'er him,
He heard her rivers' rushing sound,
   Her blue peaks rose before him.

He held his slaves, yet made withal
   No false and vain pretences,
Nor paid a lying priest to seek
   For scriptural defences.
His harshest words of proud re-
   buke,
   His bitterest taunt and scorning,
Fell fire-like on the Northern brow
   That bent to him in fawning.

He held his slaves· yet kept the
   while
   His reverence for the Human;
In the dark vassals of his will
   He saw but Man and Woman!

No hunter of God's outraged poor
  His Roanoke valley entered;
No trader in the souls of men
  Across his threshold ventured.*

And when the old and wearied man
  Laid down for his last sleeping,
And at his side, a slave no more,
  His brother man stood weeping,
His latest thought, his latest breath,
  To Freedom's duty giving,
With failing tongue and trembling
    hand
  The dying blest the living.

Oh! never bore his ancient State
  A truer son or braver!
None trampling with a calmer
    scorn
  On foreign hate or favor.
He knew her faults, yet never
    stooped
  His proud and manly feeling
To poor excuses of the wrong
  Or meanness of concealing.

But none beheld with clearer eye
  The plague-spot o'er her spread-
    ing,
None heard more sure the steps of
    Doom
  Along her future treading.

For her as for himself he spake,
  When, his gaunt frame upbr
    ing,
He traced with dying hand "I
    MORSE!" †
  And perished in the tracing.

As from the grave where He
    sleeps,
  From Vernon's weeping will
And from the grassy pall wh
    hides
  The Sage of Monticello,
So from the leaf-strewn burial-st
  Of Randolph's lowly dwelling
Virginia! o'er thy land of slave
  A warning voice is swelling!

And hark! from thy deserted fie
  Are sadder warnings spoken,
From quenched hearths, where t
    exiled sons
    Their household gods h
    broken.
The curse is on thee—wolves
    men,
  And briars for corn-sheaves g
    ing!
Oh! more than all thy dead reno
  Were now one hero living!

DEMOCRACY.

["All things whatsoever ye would that men should do to you, do ye even so to them
Matthew vii. 12.]

    BEARER of Freedom's holy light,
      Breaker of Slavery's chain and rod,
    The foe of all which pains the light,
      Or wounds the generous ear of God!

    Beautiful yet thy temples rise,
      Though there profaning gifts are thrown;
    And fires unkindled of the skies
      Are glaring round thy altar-stone.

    Still sacred—though thy name be breathed
      By those whose hearts thy truth deride;
    And garlands, plucked from thee, are wreathed
      Around the haughty brows of Pride.

* Randolph had a hearty hatred of slave traders, and it is said treated some of them
roughly, who ventured to cheapen his "chattels personal."
† See the remarkable statement of Dr. Parish, his medical attendant.

O, ideal of my boyhood's time!
  The faith in which my father stood,
Even when the sons of Lust and Crime
  Had stained thy peaceful courts with blood!

Still to those courts my footsteps turn,
  For through the mists which darken there,
I see the flame of Freedom burn—
  The Kebla of the patriot's prayer!

The generous feeling, pure and warm,
  Which owns the rights of *all* divine—
The pitying heart—the helping arm—
  The prompt self-sacrifice—are thine.

Beneath thy broad, impartial eye,
  How fade the lines of caste and birth!
How equal in their suffering lie
  The groaning multitudes of earth!

Still to a stricken brother true,
  Whatever clime hath nurtured him;
As stooped to heal the wounded Jew
  The worshipper of Gerizim.

By misery unrepelled, unawed
  By pomp or power, thou seest a MAN
In prince or peasant—slave or lord—
  Pale priest, or swarthy artisan.

Through all disguise, form, place, or name,
  Beneath the flaunting robes of sin,
Through poverty and squalid shame,
  Thou lookest on *the man* within.

On man, as man, retaining yet,
  Howe'er debased, and soiled, and dim,
The crown upon his forehead set—
  The immortal gift of God to him.

And there is reverence in thy look ;
  For that frail form which mortals wear
The Spirit of the Holiest took,
  And veiled His perfect brightness there.

Not from the shallow babbling fount
  Of vain philosophy thou art;
He who of old on Syria's mount
  Thrilled, warmed, by turns, the listener's heart.

In holy words which cannot die,
  In thoughts which angels leaned to know,
Proclaimed thy message from on high—
  Thy mission to a world of woe.

That voice's echo hath not died!
   From the blue lake of Galilee,
And Tabor's lonely mountain side,
   It calls a struggling world to thee.

Thy name and watchword o'er this land
   I hear in every breeze that stirs,
And round a thousand altars stand
   Thy banded party worshippers.

Not to these altars of a day,
   At party's call, my gift I bring;
But on thy olden shrine I lay
   A freeman's dearest offering:—

The voiceless utterance of his will—
   His pledge to Freedom and to Truth,
That manhood's heart remembers still
   The homage of his generous youth.

TO RONGE.

STRIKE home, strong-hearted man! Down to the root
Of old oppression sink the Saxon steel.
Thy work is to hew down. In God's name then
Put nerve into thy task. Let other men
Plant, as they may, that better tree, whose fruit
The wounded bosom of the Church shall heal.
Be thou the image-breaker. Let thy blows
Fall heavy as the Suabian's iron hand,
On crown or crosier, which shall interpose
Between thee and the weal of Father-land.
Leave creeds to closet idlers. First of all,
Shake thou all German dream-land with the fall
Of that accursed tree, whose evil trunk
Was spared of old by Erfurt's stalwart monk.

Fight not with ghosts and shadows. Let us hear
The snap of chain-links. Let our gladdened ear
Catch the pale prisoner's welcome, as the light
Follows thy axe-stroke, through his cell of night.
Be faithful to both worlds; nor think to feed
Earth's starving millions with the husks of creed.
Servant of Him whose mission high and holy
Was to the wronged, the sorrowing, and the lowly,
Thrust not His Eden promise from our sphere,
Distant and dim beyond the blue sky's span;
Like him of Patmos, see it, now and here,—
The New Jerusalem comes down to man!
Be warned by Luther's error. Nor like him,
When the roused Teuton dashes from his limb
The rusted chain of ages, help to bind
His hands, for whom thou claim'st the freedom of the mind

CHALKLEY HALL.*

How bland and sweet the greeting of this breeze
    To him who flies
From crowded street and red wall's weary gleam,
    Till far behind him like a hideous dream
      The close dark city lies!—

Here, while the market murmurs, while men throng
    The marble floor
Of Mammon's altar, from the crush and din
Of the world's madness let me gather in
    My better thoughts once more.

Oh! once again revive, while on my ear
    The cry of Gain
And low hoarse hum of Traffic dies away,
Ye blessed memories of my early day
    Like sere grass wet with rain!—

Once more let God's green earth and sunset air
    Old feelings waken ;
Through weary years of toil and strife and ill,
Oh, let me feel that my good angel still
    Hath not his trust forsaken.

And well do time and place befit my mood:
    Beneath the arms
Of this embracing wood, a good man made
His home, like Abraham resting in the shade
    Of Mamre's lonely palms.

Here, rich with autumn gifts of countless years,
    The virgin soil
Turned from the share he guided, and in rain
And summer sunshine throve the fruits and grain
    Which blessed his honest toil.

Here, from his voyages on the stormy seas,
    Weary and worn,
He came to meet his children, and to bless
The Giver of all good in thankfulness
    And praise for his return.

And here his neighbors gathered in to greet
    Their friend again,
Safe from the wave and the destroying gales,
Which reap untimely green Bermuda's vales,
    And vex the Carib main.

* Chalkley Hall, near Frankford, Pa., the residence of THOMAS CHALKLEY, an eminent
minister of the "Friends" denomination. He was one of the early settlers of the Colony, and
his Journal, which was published in 1749, presents a quaint but beautiful picture of a life
unostentatious and simple goodness. He was the master of a merchant vessel, and, in his
visits to the West Indies and Great Britain, omitted no opportunity to labor for the highest
interests of his fellow-men. During a temporary residence in Philadelphia, in the summer of
38, the quiet and beautiful scenery around the ancient village of Frankford frequently at-
acted me from the heat and bustle of the city.

To hear the good man tell of simple truth,
    Sown in an hour
Of weakness in some far-off Indian isle,
From the parched bosom of a barren soil,
    Raised up in life and power:

How at those gatherings in Barbadian vales,
    A tendering love
Came o'er him, like the gentle rain from heaven,
And words of fitness to his lips were given,
    And strength as from above:

How the sad captive listened to the Word,
    Until his chain
Grew lighter, and his wounded spirit felt
The healing balm of consolation melt
    Upon its lifelong pain:

How the armed warrior sate him down to hear
    Of Peace and Truth,
And the proud ruler and his Creole dame,
Jewelled and gorgeous in her beauty came,
    And fair and bright-eyed youth.

Oh, far away beneath New England's sky,
    Even when a boy,
Following my plough by Merrimack's green shore,
His simple record I have pondered o'er
    With deep and quiet joy.

And hence this scene, in sunset glory warm—
    Its woods around,
Its still stream winding on in light and shade,
Its soft, green meadows and its upland glade—
    To me is holy ground.

And dearer far than haunts where Genius keeps
    His vigils still;
Than that where Avon's son of song is laid,
Or Vaucluse hallowed by its Petrarch's shade,
    Or Virgil's laurelled hill.

To the gray walls of fallen Paraclete,
    To Juliet's urn,
Fair Arno and Sorrento's orange grove,
Where Tasso sang, let young Romance and Love
    Like brother pilgrims turn.

But here a deeper and serener charm
    To all is given;
And blessed memories of the faithful dead
O'er wood and vale and meadow-stream have shed
    The holy hues of Heaven!

TO JOHN PIERPONT.

NOT as a poor requital of the joy
  With which my childhood heard that lay of thine,
  Which, like an echo of the song divine
At Bethlehem breathed above the Holy Boy,
  Bore to my ear the airs of Palestine,—
Not to the poet, but the man I bring
In friendship's fearless trust my offering:
How much it lacks I feel, and thou wilt see,
Yet well I know that thou hast deemed with me
Life all too earnest, and its time too short
For dreamy ease and Fancy's graceful sport;
  And girded for thy constant strife with wrong,
Like Nehemiah fighting while he wrought
  The broken walls of Zion, even thy song
Hath a rude martial tone, a blow in every thought!

THE CYPRESS TREE OF CEYLON.

[Ibn Batuta, the celebrated Mussulman traveler of the fourteenth century, speaks of a Cypress tree in Ceylon, universally held sacred by the natives, the leaves of which were said to
fall only at certain intervals, and he who had the happiness to find and eat one of them, was restored, at once, to youth and vigor. The traveller saw several venerable JOGEES, or saints, sitting silent and motionless under the tree, patiently awaiting the falling of a leaf.]

THEY sat in silent watchfulness
  The sacred cypress tree about,
And, from beneath old wrinkled brows
  Their failing eyes looked out.

Gray Age and Sickness waiting there
  Through weary night and lingering day—
Grim as the idols at their side
  And motionless as they.

Unheeded in the boughs above
  The song of Ceylon's birds was sweet;
Unseen of them the island flowers
  Bloomed brightly at their feet.

O'er them the tropic night-storm swept,
  The thunder crashed on rock and hill;
The cloud-fire on their eyeballs blazed,
  Yet there they waited still!

What was the world without to them?
  The Moslem's sunset-call—the dance
Of Ceylon's maids—the passing gleam
  Of battle-flag and lance?

They waited for that falling leaf,
  Of which the wandering Jogees sing:
Which lends once more to wintry age
  The greenness of its spring.

Oh!—if these poor and blinded ones
  In trustful patience wait to feel
O'er torpid pulse and failing limb
  A youthful freshness steal;

Shall we, who sit beneath that Tree,
  Whose healing leaves of life are shed
In answer to the breath of prayer
  Upon the waiting head:

Not to restore our failing forms,
  And build the spirit's broken shrine,
But, on the fainting soul to shed
  A light and life divine:

Shall we grow weary in our watch,
  And murmur at the long delay?
Impatient of our Father's time
  And His appointed way?

Or, shall the stir of outward things
  Allure and claim the Christian's eye,
When on the heathen watcher's ear
  Their powerless murmurs die?

Alas! a deeper test of faith
  Than prison cell or martyr's stake,
The self-abasing watchfulness
  Of silent prayer may make.

We gird us bravely to rebuke
  Our erring brother in the wrong:
And in the ear of Pride and Power
  Our warning voice is strong.

Easier to smite with Peter's sword,
  Than " watch one hour " in humbling prayer:
Life's " great things," like the Syrian lord
  Our hearts can do and dare.

But oh ! we shrink from Jordan's side,
  From waters which alone can save:
And murmur for Abana's banks
And Pharpar's brighter wave.

Oh, Thou, who in the garden's shade
  Didst wake Thy weary ones again,
Who slumbered at that fearful hour
  Forgetful of thy pain ;

Bend o'er us now, as over them,
　　And set our sleep-bound spirits free,
Nor leave us slumbering in the watch
　　Our souls should keep with Thee !

A DREAM OF SUMMER.

BLAND as the morning breath of June
　　The southwest breezes play;
And, through its haze, the winter noon
　　Seems warm as summer's day.
The snow-plumed Angel of the North
　　Has dropped his icy spear;
Again the mossy earth looks forth,
　　Again the streams gush clear.

The fox his hillside cell forsakes,
　　The muskrat leaves his nook,
The bluebird in the meadow breaks
　　Is singing with the brook.
" Bear up, oh mother Nature ! " cry
　　Bird, breeze, and streamlet free;
" Our winter voices prophesy
　　Of summer days to thee ! "

So, in those winters of the soul,
　　By bitter blasts and drear
O'erswept from Memory's frozen pole,
　　Will sunny days appear.
Reviving Hope and Faith, they show
　　The soul its living powers,
And how beneath the winter's snow
　　Lie germs of summer flowers !

The Night is mother of the Day,
　　The Winter of the Spring,
And ever upon old Decay
　　The greenest mosses cling.
Behind the cloud the starlight lurks,
　　Through showers the sunbeams fall ;
For God, who loveth all His works,
　　Has left His Hope with all !

TO ——,

With a Copy of Woolmans Journal.*

Maiden! with the fair brown
tresses
Shading o'er thy dreamy eye,
Floating on thy thoughtful fore-
head
Cloud wreaths of its sky.

Youthful years and maiden beauty,
Joy with them should still
abide—
Instinct take the place of Duty—
Love, not Reason, guide.

Ever in the New rejoicing,
Kindly beckoning back the Old,
Turning, with a power like Midas,
All things into gold.

And the passing shades of sadness
Wearing even a welcome guise,
As when some bright lake lies open
To the sunny skies;

Every wing of bird above it,
Every light cloud floating on,
Glitters like that flashing mirror
In the self-same sun.

But upon thy youthful forehead
Something like a shadow lies;
And a serious soul is looking
From thy earnest eyes.

With an early introversion,
Through the forms of outward
things,
Seeking for the subtle essence,
And the hidden springs.

Deeper than the gilded surface
Hath thy wakeful vision seen,
Farther than the narrow present
Have thy journeyings been.

Thou hast midst Life's empty
noises
Heard the solemn steps of Time,
And the low mysterious voices
Of another clime.

All the mystery of Being
Hath upon thy spirit pressed—
Thoughts which, like the Deluge
wanderer,
Find no place of rest;

That which mystic Plato pondered
That which Zeno heard with awe
And the star-rapt Zoroaster
In his night-watch saw.

From the doubt and darkness
springing
Of the dim, uncertain Past,
Moving to the dark still shadows
O'er the Future cast,

Early hath Life's mighty question
Thrilled within thy heart of
youth
With a deep and strong beseeching,
What and where is Truth?

Hollow creed and ceremonial,
Whence the ancient life hath
fled,
Idle faith unknown to action,
Dull and cold and dead.

Oracles, whose wire-worked mean-
ings
Only wake a quiet scorn,—
Not from these thy seeking spirit
Hath its answer drawn.

But, like some tired child at even
On thy mother Nature's breast,
Thou, methinks, art vainly seeking
Truth, and peace, and rest.

O'er that mother's rugged feature
Thou art throwing Fancy's veil
Light and soft as woven moon-
beams,
Beautiful and frail!

O'er the rough chart of Existence
Rocks of sin and wastes of woe

* " Get the writings of John Woolman by heart."—*Essays of Elia.*

Soft airs breathe, and green leaves
    tremble,
  And cool fountains flow.

And to thee an answer cometh
  From the earth and from the sky,
And to thee the hills and waters
  And the stars reply.

But a soul-sufficing answer
  Hath no outward origin;
More than Nature's many voices
  May be heard within.

Even as the great Augustine
  Questioned earth and sea and
    sky,*
And the dusty tomes of learning
  And old poesy.

But his earnest spirit needed
  More than outward Nature
    taught—
More than blest the poet's vision
  Or the sage's thought.

Only in the gathered silence
  Of a calm and waiting frame
Light and wisdom as from Heaven
  To the seeker came.

Not to ease and aimless quiet
  Doth that inward answer tend,
But to works of love and duty
  As our beings end,—

Not to idle dreams and trances,
  Length of face, and solemn tone,
But to Faith, in daily striving
  And performance shown.

Earnest toil and strong endeavor
  Of a spirit which within
Wrestles with familiar evil
  And besetting sin;

And without, with tireless vigor,
  Steady heart, and weapon strong,
In the power of truth assailing
  Every form of wrong.

Guided thus, how passing lovely
  Is the track of WOOLMAN's feet!

And his brief and simple record
  How serenely sweet !

O'er life's humblest duties throwing
  Light the earthling never knew,
Freshening all its dark waste places
  As with Hermon's dew.

All which glows in Pascal's pages—
  All which sainted Guion sought,
Or the blue-eyed German Rahel
  Half-unconscious taught:—

Beauty, such as Goethe pictured,
  Such as Shelley dreamed of, shed
Living warmth and starry bright-
    ness
  Round that poor man's head.

Not a vain and cold ideal,
  Not a poet's dream alone,
But a presence warm and real,
  Seen and felt and known.

When the red right hand of slaugh-
    ter
  Moulders with the steel it swung,
When the name of seer and poet
  Dies on Memory's tongue,

All bright thoughts and pure shall
    gather
  Round that meek and suffering
    one—
Glorious, like the seer-seen angel
  Standing in the sun !

Take the good man's book and
    ponder
  What its pages say to thee—
Blessed as the hand of healing
  May its lesson be.

If it only serves to strengthen
  Yearnings for a higher good,
For the fount of living waters
  And diviner food ;

If the pride of human reason
  Feels its meek and still rebuke
Quailing like the eye of Peter
  From the Just One's look!—

* August. Sili* loq. cap. xxxi., " Interrogavi Terram," etc.

If with readier ear thou heedest
  What the Inward Teacher saith,
Listening with a willing spirit
  And a childlike faith,—

Thou mayst live to bless the giver,
  Who himself but frail and weak,

Would at least the highest well
  Of another seek;

And his gift, though poor lowly
  It may seem to other eyes,
Yet may prove an angel holy
  In a pilgrim's guise.

LEGGETT'S MONUMENT.

"Ye build the tombs of the prophets."—*Holy Writ.*

YES—pile the marble o'er him! It is well
  That ye who mocked him in his long stern strife,
  And planted in the pathway of his life
The ploughshares of your hatred hot from hell,
  Who clamored down the bold reformer when
  He pleaded for his captive fellow-men,
Who spurned him in the market-place, and sought
  Within thy walls, St. Tammany, to bind
In party chains the free and honest thought,
  The angel utterance of an upright mind,—
Well is it now that o'er his grave ye raise
The stony tribute of your tardy praise,
For not alone that pile shall tell to Fame
Of the brave heart beneath, but of the builders' shame!

THE ANGELS OF BUENA VISTA.

[A LETTER-WRITER from Mexico states that, at the terrible fight of Buena Vista, Mex
women were seen hovering near the field of death, for the purpose of giving aid and succ
the wounded. One poor woman was found surrounded by the maimed and suffering of
armies, ministering to the wants of AMERICANS as well as MEXICANS, with impartial te
ness.]

SPEAK and tell us, our Ximena, looking northward far away,
O'er the camp of the invaders, o'er the Mexican array,
Who is losing? who is winning? are they far or come they near?
Look abroad, and tell us, sister, whither rolls the storm we hear.

"Down the hills of Angostura still the storm of battle rolls;
Blood is flowing, men are dying; God have mercy on their souls!
Who is losing? who is winning?—" Over hill and over plain,
I see but smoke of cannon clouding through the mountain rain."

Holy Mother! keep our brothers! Look, Ximena, look once more
"Still I see the fearful whirlwind rolling darkly as before,
Bearing on, in strange confusion, friend and foeman, foot and hor
Like some wild and troubled torrent sweeping down its moun
  course."

ok forth once more, Ximena! "Ah! the smoke has rolled away ;
nd I see the Northern rifles gleaming down the ranks of gray.
ark! That sudden blast of bugles! there the troop of Minon wheels ;
here the Northern horses thunder, with the cannon at their heels.

Jesu, pity! how it thickens! now retreat and now advance !
ght against the blazing cannon shivers Puebla's charging lance!
wn they go, the brave young riders ; horse and foot together fall ;
ke a plowshare in the fallow, through them plow the Northern ball."

earer came the storm and nearer, rolling fast and frightful on :
eak, Ximena, speak and tell us, who has lost, and who has won ?
Alas! alas! I know not ; friend and foe together fall,
er the dying rush the living : pray, my sisters, for them all ! "

Lo! the wind the smoke is lifting: Blessed Mother, save my brain!
an see the wounded crawling slowly out from heaps of slain.
w they stagger, blind and bleeding; now they fall, and strive to rise ;
asten, sisters, haste and save them, lest they die before our eyes ! "

Oh my heart's love! oh my dear one! lay thy poor head on my knee;
st thou know the lips that kiss thee ? Canst thou hear me? canst thou
    see ?
, my husband, brave and gentle ! oh, my Bernal, look once more
n the blessed cross before thee! mercy! mercy ! all is o'er ! "

ry thy tears, my poor Ximena; lay thy dear one down to rest;
t his hands be meekly folded, lay the cross upon his breast;
t his dirge be sung hereafter, and his funeral masses said;
-day, thou poor bereaved one, the living ask thy aid.

ose beside her, faintly moaning, fair and young, a soldier lay,
rn with shot and pierced with lances, bleeding slow his life away;
t, as tenderly before him, the lorn Ximena knelt,
e saw the Northern eagle shining on his pistol belt.

ith a stifled cry of horror straight she turned away her head ;
ith a sad and bitter feeling looked she back upon her dead;
t she heard the youth's low moaning, and his struggling breath of
    pain,
nd she raised the cooling water to his parching lips again.

hispered low the dying soldier, pressed her hand and faintly smiled :
as that pitying face his mother's ? did she watch beside her child ?
ll his stranger words with meaning her woman's heart supplied :
ith her kiss upon his forehead, "Mother! " murmured he, and died!

A bitter curse upon them, poor boy, who led thee forth,
om some gentle, sad-eyed mother, weeping, lonely, in the North! "
ake the mournful Mexic woman, as she laid him with her dead,
nd turned to soothe the living, and bind the wounds which bled.

Look forth once more, Ximena! " Like a cloud before the wind
Rolls the battle down the mountains, leaving blood and death behind
Ah! they plead in vain for mercy; in the dust the wounded strive;
Hide your faces, holy angels! oh, thou Christ of God, forgive! "

Sink, oh Night, among thy Mountains! let the cool, gray shadows fall
Dying brothers, fighting demons, drop thy curtain over all!
Through the thickening winter twilight, wide apart the battle rolled,
In its sheath the sabre rested, and the cannon's lips grew cold.

But the noble Mexic women still their holy task pursued,
Through that long, dark night of sorrow, worn and faint and lacking
    food;
Over weak and suffering brothers, with a tender care they hung,
And the dying foeman blessed them in a strange and Northern tongue.

Not wholly lost, oh Father! is this evil world of ours;
Upward, through its blood and ashes, spring afresh the Eden flowers;
From its smoking hell of battle, Love and Pity send their prayer,
And still thy white-winged angels hover dimly in our air!

FORGIVENESS.

My heart was heavy, for its trust had been
    Abused, its kindness answered with foul wrong;
So, turning gloomily from my fellow-men,
    One summer Sabbath day I strolled among
The green mounds of the village burial place;
    Where, pondering how all human love and hate
    Find one sad level—and how, soon or late,
Wronged and wrong-doer, each with meekened face,
    And cold hands folded over a still heart,
Pass the green threshold of our common grave,
    Whither all footsteps tend, whence none depart,
Awed for myself, and pitying my race,
Our common sorrow, like a mighty wave,
Swept all my pride away, and trembling I forgave!

BARCLAY OF URY.

[Among the earliest converts to the doctrines of FRIENDS, in Scotland, was BARCLAY of Ury, an old and distinguished soldier, who had fought under GUSTAVUS ADOLPHUS, in Germany. As a Quaker, he became the object of persecution and abuse at the hands of the magistrates and the populace. None bore the indignities of the mob with greater patience and nobleness of soul than this once proud gentleman and soldier. One of his friends, on an occasion of common rudeness, lamented that he should be treated so harshly in his old age, who had been so honored before. "I find more satisfaction," said BARCLAY, "as well as honor, in being thus insulted for my religious principles, than when, a few years ago, it was usual for the magistrates, as I passed the city of Aberdeen, to meet me on the road and conduct me to public entertainment in their hall, and then escort me out again, to gain my favor."]

Up the streets of Aberdeen,
By the kirk and college green,
 Rode the Laird of Ury;
Close behind him, close beside,
Foul of mouth and evil-eyed,
 Pressed the mob in fury.

Flouted him the drunken churl,
Jeered at him the serving girl,
 Prompt to please her master;
And the begging carlin, late
Fed and clothed at Ury's gate,
 Cursed him as he passed her.

Yet, with calm and stately mien,
Up the streets of Aberdeen
 Came he slowly riding;
And, to all he saw and heard
Answering not with bitter word,
 Turning not for chiding.

Came a troop with broadsword
 swinging,
Bits and bridles sharply ringing,
 Loose and free and froward;
Quoth the foremost, "Ride him
 down!
Push him! prick him! through the
 town
 Drive the Quaker coward!"

But from out the thickening crowd
Cried a sudden voice and loud:
 "Barclay! Ho! a Barclay!"
And the old man at his side,
Saw a comrade, battle tried,
 Scarred and sunburned darkly;

Who with ready weapon bare,
Fronting to the troopers there,
 Cried aloud: "God save us?

Call ye coward him who stood
Ankle deep in Lutzen's blood,
 With the brave Gustavus?"

"Nay, I do not need thy sword,
Comrade mine," said Ury's lord;
 "Put it up I pray thee:
Passive to His holy will,
Trust I in my Master's still,
 Even though He slay me."

"Pledges of thy love and faith,
Proved on many a field of death,
 Not by me are needed."
Marvelled much that henchman
 bold,
That his laird, so stout of old,
 Now so meekly pleaded.

"Woe's the day," he sadly said,
With a slowly shaking head,
 And a look of pity;
"Ury's honest lord reviled,
Mock of knave and sport of child,
 In his own good city!

"Speak the word, and, master
 mine,
As we charged on Tilly's line,
 And his Walloon lancers,
Smiting through their midst we'll
 teach
Civil look and decent speech
 To these boyish prancers!"

"Marvel not, mine ancient friend,
Like beginning, like the end:"
 Quoth the Laird of Ury,
"Is the sinful servant more
Than his gracious Lord who bore
 Bonds and stripes in Jewry?

" Give me joy that in His name
I can bear, with patient frame,
    All these vain ones offer;
While for them He suffereth long,
Shall I answer wrong with wrong,
    Scoffing with the scoffer?

" Happier I, with loss of all,
Hunted, outlawed, held in thrall,
    With few friends to greet me,
Than when reeve and squire were
        seen,
Riding out from Aberdeen,
    With bared heads, to meet me.

" When each good wife, o'er and
        o'er,
Blessed me as I passed her door;
    And the snooded daughter,
Through her casement glancing
        down,
Smiled on him who bore renown
    From red fields of slaughter.

" Hard to feel the stranger's scoff,
Hard the old friend's falling off,
    Hard to learn forgiving:
But the Lord His own rewards,
And his love with theirs accords,
    Warm and fresh and living.

" Through this dark and stormy
        night
Faith beholds a feeble light.
    Up the blackness streaking;
Knowing God's own time is best,
In a patient hope I rest
    For the full day-breaking!"

So the Laird of Ury said,
Turning slow his horse's head
    Toward the Tolbooth prison,
Where, though iron grates,
        heard
Poor disciples of the Word
    Preach of Christ arisen!

Not in vain, Confessor old,
Unto us the tale is told
    Of thy day of trial;
Every age on him, who strays
From its broad and beaten ways,
    Pours its sevenfold vial.

Happy he whose inward ear
Angel comfortings can hear,
    O'er the rabble's laughter;
And, while Hatred's fagots burn
Glimpses through the smoke di-
        cern
    Of the good hereafter.

Knowing this, that never yet
Share of Truth was vainly set
    In the world's wide fallow;
After hands shall sow the seed,
After hands from hill and mead
    Reap the harvests yellow.

Thus, with somewhat of the See
Must the moral pioneer
    From the Future borrow;
Clothe the waste with dreams
        grain,
And, on midnight's sky of rain,
    Paint the golden morrow!

WHAT THE VOICE SAID.

MADDENED by Earth's wrong and evil,
    " Lord!" I cried in sudden ire,
" From thy right hand, clothed with thunder,
    Shake the bolted fire!

" Love is lost, and Faith is dying;
    With the brute the man is sold;
And the dropping blood of labor
    Hardens into gold.

"Here the dying wail of Famine,
 There the battle's groan of pain;
And, in silence, smooth-faced Mammon
 Reaping men like grain.

"'Where is God, that we should fear Him?'
 Thus the earth-born Titans say;
'God! if thou art living, hear us!'
 Thus the weak ones pray.

"Thou, the patient Heaven upbraiding,"
 Spake a solemn Voice within;
"Weary of our Lord's forbearance,
 Art thou free from sin?

"Fearless brow to Him uplifting,
 Canst thou for his thunders call,
Knowing that to guilt's attraction
 Ever more they fall?

"Know'st thou not all germs of evil
 In thy heart await their time?
Not thyself, but God's restraining,
 Stays their growth of crime.

"Could'st thou boast, oh child of weakness!
 O'er the sons of wrong and strife,
Were their strong temptations planted
 In thy path of life?

"Thou hast seen two streamlets gushing
 From one fountain, clear and free,
But by widely varying channels
 Searching for the sea.

"Glideth one through greenest valleys,
 Kissing them with lips still sweet;
One, mad roaring down the mountains,
 Stagnates at their feet.

"Is it choice whereby the Parsee
 Kneels before his mother's fire?
In his black tent did the Tartar
 Choose his wandering sire?

"He alone, whose hand is bounding
 Human power and human will,
Looking through each soul's surrounding,
 Knows its good or ill.

"For thyself, while wrong and sorrow
 Make to thee their strong appeal,
Coward wert thou not to utter
 What the heart must feel.

" Earnest words must needs be spoken
    When the warm heart bleeds or burns
With its scorn of wrong, or pity
    For the wronged, by turns.

' But, by all thy nature's weakness,
    Hidden faults and follies known,
Be thou, in rebuking evil,
    Conscious of thine own.

" Not the less shall stern-eyed Duty
    To thy lips her trumpet set,
But with harsher blasts shall mingle
    Wailings of regret."

Cease not, Voice of holy speaking,
    Teacher sent of God, be near,
Whispering through the day's cool silence,
    Let my spirit hear!

So, when thoughts of evil-doers
    Waken scorn or hatred move,
Shall a mournful fellow-feeling
    Temper all with love.

TO DELAWARE.

Written during the Discussion, in the Legislature of that State in the Winter of 1846-47, of
Bill for the Abolition of Slavery.

THRICE welcome to thy sisters of the East,
    To the strong tillers of a rugged home,
With spray-wet locks to Northern winds released,
    And hardy feet o'er-swept by ocean's foam;
And to the young nymphs of the golden West,
    Whose harvest mantles, fringed with prairie bloom,
Trail in the sunset,— oh, redeemed and blest,
    To the warm welcome of thy sisters come!
Broad Pennsylvania, down her sail-white bay
    Shall give thee joy, and Jersey from her plains,
And the great lakes, where echoes free alway
    Moaned never shoreward with the clank of chains,
Shall weave new sun-bows in their tossing spray,
And all their waves keep grateful holiday.
And, smiling on thee through her mountain rains,
    Vermont shall bless thee; and the Granite peaks,
And vast Katahdin o'er his woods, shall wear
Their snow-crowns brighter in the cold keen air;
    And Massachusetts, with her rugged cheeks
O'errun with grateful tears, shall turn to thee,
    When, at thy bidding, the electric wire
    Shall tremble northward with its words of fire:
Glory and praise to God! another state is free!

WORSHIP.

["Pure religion and undefiled before God and the Father is this, To visit the fatherless and widows in their affliction, and to keep himself unspotted from the world."—*James* i. 27.]

THE Pagan's myths through marble lips are spoken,
  And ghosts of old Beliefs still flit and moan
Round fane and altar overthrown and broken,
  O'er tree-grown barrow and gray ring of stone.

Blind Faith had martyrs in those old high places,
  The Syrian hill grove and the Druid's wood,
With mothers' offering, to the Fiend's embraces,
  Bone of their bone, and blood of their own blood.

Red altars, kindling through that night of error,
  Smoked with warm blood beneath the cruel eye
Of lawless Power and sanguinary Terror,
  Throned on the circle of a pitiless sky;

Beneath whose baleful shadow, overcasting
  All heaven above, and blighting earth below,
The scourge grew red, the lip grew pale with fasting,
  And man's oblation was his fear and woe!

Then through great temples swelled the dismal moaning
  Of dirge-like music and sepulchral prayer;
Pale wizard priests, o'er occult symbols droning,
  Swung their white censers in the burdened air:

As if the pomp of rituals, and the savor
  Of gums and spices, could the Unseen One please;
As if His ear could bend, with childish favor,
  To the poor flattery of the organ keys!

Feet red from war fields trod the church aisles holy,
  With trembling reverence; and the oppressor there,
Kneeling before his priest, abased and lowly,
  Crushed human hearts beneath his knee of prayer.

Not such the service the benignant Father
  Requireth at his earthly children's hands:
Not the poor offering of vain rites, but rather
  The simple duty man from man demands.

For Earth he asks it: the full joy of Heaven
  Knoweth no change of waning or increase;
The great heart of the Infinite beats even,
  Untroubled flows the river of his peace.

He asks no taper lights, on high surrounding
 The priestly altar and the saintly grave,
No dolorous chant nor organ music sounding,
 Nor incense clouding up the twilight nave.

For he whom Jesus loved hath truly spoken:
 The holier worship which he deigns to bless
Restores the lost, and binds the spirit broken,
 And feeds the widow and the fatherless!

Types of our human weakness and our sorrow!
 Who lives unhaunted by his loved ones dead?
Who, with vain longing, seeketh not to borrow
 From stranger eyes the home lights which have fled?

Oh, brother man! fold to thy heart thy brother;
 Where pity dwells, the peace of God is there;
To worship rightly is to love each other,
 Each smile a hymn, each kindly deed a prayer.

Follow with reverent steps the great example
 of him whose holy work was " doing good ";
So shall the wide earth seem our Father's temple,
 Each loving life a psalm of gratitude.

Then shall all shackles fall; the stormy clangor
 Of wild war music o'er the earth shall cease;
Love shall tread out the baleful fire of anger,
 And in its ashes plant the tree of peace!

THE ALBUM.

THE dark-eyed daughters of the Sun,
 At morn and evening hours,
O'er-hung their graceful shrines alone
 With wreaths of dewy flowers.

Not vainly did those fair ones cull
 Their gifts by stream and wood;
The Good is always beautiful,
 The Beautiful is good!

We live not in their simple day,
 Our Northern blood is cold,
And few the offerings which we lay
 On other shrines than Gold.

With Scripture texts to chill and ban
 The heart's fresh morning hours,

The heavy-footed Puritan
    Goes trampling down the flowers;

Nor thinks of Him who sat of old
    Where Syrian lilies grew,
And from their mingling shade and gold
    A holy lesson drew.

Yet lady, shall this book of thine,
    Where Love his gifts has brought,
Become to thee a Persian shrine,
    O'er-hung with flowers of thought.

THE DEMON OF THE STUDY.

THE Brownie sits in the Scotchman's room,
    And eats his meat and drinks his ale,
And beats the maid with her unused broom,
    And the lazy lout with his idle flail,
But he sweeps the floor and threshes the corn,
And hies him away ere the break of dawn.

The shade of Denmark fled from the sun,
    And the Cocklane ghost from the barn-loft cheer,
The fiend of Faust was a faithful one,
    Agrippa's demon wrought in fear,
And the devil of Martin Luther sat
By the stout monk's side in social chat.

The Old Man of the Sea, on the neck of him
    Who seven times crossed the deep,
Twined closely each lean and withered limb,
    Like the nightmare in one's sleep.
But he drank of the wine, and Sinbad cast
The evil weight from his back at last.

But the demon that cometh day by day
    To my quiet room and fireside nook,
Where the casement light falls dim and gray
    On faded painting and ancient book,
Is a sorrier one than any whose names
Are chronicled well by good king James.

No bearer of burdens like Caliban,
    No runner of errands like Ariel,
He comes in the shape of a fat old man,
    Without rap of knuckle or pull of bell:
And whence he comes, or whither he goes,
I know as I do of the wind which blows.

A stout old man with a greasy hat
　　Slouched heavily down to his dark, red nose,
And two gray eyes enveloped in fat,
　　Looking through glasses with iron bows.
Read ye, and heed ye, and ye who can,
Guard well your doors from that old man!

He comes with a careless " how d'ye do,"
　　And seats himself in my elbow chair;
And my morning paper and pamphlet new
　　Fall forthwith under his special care,
And he wipes his glasses and clears nis throat,
And, button by button, unfolds his coat.

And then he reads from paper and book,
　　In a low and husky asthmatic tone,
With the stolid sameness of posture and look
　　Of one who reads to himself alone;
And hour after hour on my senses come
That husky wheeze and that dolorous hum.

The price of stocks, the auction sales,
　　The poet's song and the lover's glee,
The horrible murders, the seaboard gales,
　　The marriage list, and the *jeu d' esprit*,
All reach my ear in the self-same tone,—
I shudder at each, but the fiend reads on!

Oh! sweet as the lapse of water at noon
　　O'er the mossy roots of some forest tree,
The sigh of the wind in the woods of June,
　　Or sound of flutes o'er a moonlit sea,
Or the low soft music, perchance which seems
To float through the slumbering singer's dreams.

So sweet, so dear is the silvery tone
　　Of her in whose features I sometimes look,
As I sit at eve by her side alone,
　　And we read by turns from the self-same book—
Some tale perhaps of the olden time,
Some lover's romance or quaint old rhyme.

Then when the story is one of woe,—
　　Some prisoner's plaint through his dungeon-bar,
Her blue eye glistens with tears, and low
　　Her voice sinks down like a moan afar;
And I seem to hear that prisoner's wail,
And his face looks on me worn and pale.

And when she reads some merrier song,
　　Her voice is glad as an April bird's,

And when the tale is of war and wrong,
  A trumpet's summons is in her words,
And the rush of the hosts I seem to hear,
And see the tossing of plume and spear!—

Oh, pity me then, when, day by day,
  The stout fiend darkens my parlor door;
And reads me perchance the self-same lay
  Which melted in music the night before,
From lips as the lips of Hylas sweet,
And moved like twin roses which zephyrs meet!

I cross my floor with a nervous tread,
  I whistle and laugh and sing and shout,
I flourish my cane above his head,
  And stir up the fire to roast him out;
I topple the chairs, and drum on the pane,
And press my hands on my ears, in vain!

I've studied Glanville and James the wise,
  And wizard black-letter tomes which treat
Of demons of every name and size,
  Which a Christian man is presumed to meet,
But never a hint and never a line
Can I find of a reading fiend like mine.

I've crossed the Psalter with Brady and Tate,
  And laid the Primer above them all,
I've nailed a horseshoe over the grate,
  And hung a wig to my parlor wall
Once worn by a learned Judge, they say,
At Salem court in the witchcraft day!

" *Conjuro te, sceleratissime,*
    Abire ad tuum locum! "—still
Like a visible nightmare he sits by me—
  The exorcism has lost its skill;
And I hear again in my haunted room
The husky wheeze and the dolorous hum!

Ah!—commend me to Mary Magdalen
  With her sevenfold plagues—to the wandering Jew,
To the terrors which haunted Orestes when
  The furies his midnight curtains drew,
But charm him off, ye who charm him can,
That reading demon, that fat old man!

THE PUMPKIN.

Oh! greenly and fair in the lands of the sun,
The vines of the gourd and the rich melon run,
And the rock and the tree and the cottage enfold,
With broad leaves all greenness and blossoms all gold,
Like that which o'er Nineveh's prophet once grew,
While he waited to know that his warning was true,
And longed for the storm-cloud, and listened in vain,
For the rush of the whirlwind and red fire-rain.

On the banks of the Xenil the dark Spanish maiden
Comes up with the fruit of the tangled vine laden;
And the Creole of Cuba laughs out to behold
Through orange-leaves shining the broad spheres of gold;
Yet with dearer delight from his home in the North,
On the fields of his harvest the Yankee looks forth,
Where crook-necks are coiling and yellow fruit shines,
And the sun of September melts down on his vines.

Ah!—on Thanksgiving Day, when from East and from West,
From North and from South come the pilgrim and guest,
When the gray-haired New Englander sees round his board
The old broken links of affection restored,
When the care-wearied man seeks his mother once more,
And the worn matron smiles where the girl smiled before,
What moistens the lip and what brightens the eye?
What calls back the past, like the rich Pumpkin pie?

Oh!—fruit loved of boyhood!—the old days recalling,
When wood-grapes were purpling and brown nuts were falling!
When wild, ugly faces we carved in its skin,
Glaring out through the dark with a candle within!
When we laughed round the corn-heap, with hearts all in tune,
Our chair a broad pumpkin—our lantern the moon,
Telling tales of the fairy who travelled like steam,
In a pumpkin-shell coach, with two rats for her team!

Then thanks for thy present!—none sweeter or better
E'er smoked from an oven or circled a platter!
Fairer hands never wrought at a pastry more fine,
Brighter eyes never watched o'er its baking than thine!
And the prayer, which my mouth is too full to express,
Swells my heart that thy shadow may never be less:
That the days of thy lot may be lengthened below,
And the fame of thy worth like a pumpkin-vine grow,
And thy life be as sweet, and its last sunset sky
Golden-tinted and fair as thy own Pumpkin Pie!

EXTRACT FROM " A NEW ENGLAND LEGEND."

How has New England's romance fled,
    Even as a vision of the morning!
Its rites fordone—its guardians dead—
Its priestesses, bereft of dread,
    Waking the veriest urchin's scorning!—
Gone like the Indian wizard's yell
    And fire-dance round the magic rock,
Forgotten like the Druid's spell
    At moonrise by his holy oak!
No more along the shadowy glen,
Glide the dim ghosts of murdered men;
No more the unquiet church-yard dead
Glimpse upward from their turfy bed,
    Startling the traveller, late and lone;
As, on some night of starless weather,
They silently commune together,
    Each sitting on his own head-stone!
The roofless house, decayed, deserted,
Its living tenants all departed,
No longer rings with midnight revel
Of witch, or ghost, or goblin evil;
No pale, blue flame sends out its flashes
Through creviced roof and shattered sashes!—
The witch-grass round the hazel spring
May sharply to the night-air sing,
But there no more shall withered hags
Refresh at ease their broom-stick nags,
Or taste those hazel-shadowed waters
As beverage meet for Satan's daughters;
No more their mimic tones be heard—
The mew of cat—the chirp of bird,
Shrill blending with the hoarser laughter
Of the fell demon following after!

The cautious good-man nails no more
A horseshoe on his outer door,
Lest some unseemly hag should fit
To his own mouth her bridle-bit—
The good-wife's churn no more refuses
Its wonted culinary uses
Until, with heated needle burned,
The witch has to her place returned!
Our witches are no longer old
And wrinkled beldames, Satan-sold,
But young and gay and laughing creatures,
With the heart's sunshine on their features—

Their sorcery—the light which dances
  Where the raised lid unveils its glances;
Or that low-breathed and gentle tone,
    The music of Love's twilight hours,
Soft, dream-like, as a fairy's moan
    Above her nightly closing flowers,
Sweeter than that which sighed of yore,
Along the charmed Ausonian shore.
Even she, our own weird heroine,
Sole Pythoness of ancient Lynn,
    Sleeps calmly where the living laid her.
And the wide realm of sorcery,
  Left by its latest mistress free,
    Hath found no gray and skilled invader:
So perished Albion's " glammarye,"
    With him in Melrose Abbey sleeping,
  His charmed torch beside his knee,
That even the dead himself might see
    The magic scroll within his keeping.
And now our modern Yankee sees
Nor omens, spells, nor mysteries;
And naught above, below, around,
Of life or death, of sight or sound,
    Whate'er its nature, form, or look,
Excites his terror or surprise—
All seeming to his knowing eyes
Familiar as his " catechise,"
Or " Webster's Spelling Book."

HAMPTON BEACH.

THE sunlight glitters keen and bright,
    Where, miles away,
Lies stretching to my dazzled sight
A luminous belt, a misty light,
Beyond the dark pine bluffs and wastes of sandy gray.

The tremulous shadow of the Sea!
    Against its ground
Of silvery light, rock, hill, and tree,
Still as a picture, clear and free,
With varying outline mark the coast for miles around.

On—on—we tread with loose-flung rein
    Our seaward way;
Through dark-green fields and blossoming grain,
Where the wild brier-rose skirts the lane,
And bends above our heads the flowering locust spray.

Ha! like a kind hand on my brow
Comes this fresh breeze,
Cooling its dull and feverish glow,
While through my being seems to flow
The breath of a new life—the healing of the seas!

Now rest we, where this grassy mound
His feet hath set
In the great waters, which have bound
His granite ankles greenly round
With long and tangled moss, and weeds with cool spray wet.

Good-by to Pain and Care! I take
Mine ease to-day;
Here where these sunny waters break,
And ripples this keen breeze, I shake
All burdens from the heart, all weary thoughts away.

I draw a freer breath—I seem
Like all I see—
Waves in the sun—the white-winged gleam
Of sea-birds in the slanting beam—
And far-off sails which flit before the South wind free.

So when Time's veil shall fall asunder,
The soul may know
No fearful change, nor sudden wonder,
Nor sink the weight of mystery under,
But with the upward rise, and with the vastness grow.

And all we shrink from now may seem
No new revealing;
Familiar as our childhood's stream
Or pleasant memory of a dream,
The loved and cherished Past upon the new life stealing.

Serene and mild the untried light
May have its dawning;
And, as in Summer's northern night
The evening and the dawn unite,
The sunset hues of Time blend with the soul's new morning.

I sit alone: in foam and spray
Wave after wave
Breaks on the rocks which, stern and gray,
Beneath like fallen Titans lay,
Or murmurs hoarse and strong through mossy cleft and cave.

What heed I of the dusty land
And noisy town?
I see the mighty deep expand
From its white line of glimmering sand
To where the blue of heaven on bluer waves shuts down!

In listless quietude of mind,
          I yield to all
The change of cloud and wave and wind,
And passive on the flood reclined,
I wander with the waves, and with them rise and fall.

But look, thou dreamer!—wave and shore
          In shadow lie;
The night-wind warns me back once more
To where my native hilltops o'er
Bends like an arch of fire the glowing sunset sky!

So then, beach, bluff, and wave, farewell!
          I bear with me
No token stone nor glittering shell,
But long and oft shall Memory tell
Of this brief thoughtful hour of musing by the Sea.

LINES

Written on Hearing of the Death of Silas Wright, of New York.

As they who, tossing midst the storm at night,
  While turning shoreward, where a beacon shone,
    Meet the walled blackness of the heaven alone,
So, on the turbulent waves of party tossed,
  In gloom and tempest, men have seen thy light
    Quenched in the darkness. At thy hour of noon,
While life was pleasant to thy undimmed sight,
And, day by day, within thy spirit grew
A holier hope than young Ambition knew,
As through thy rural quiet, not in vain,
Pierced the sharp thrill of Freedom's cry of pain,
  Man of the millions, thou art lost too soon!
Portents at which the bravest stand aghast—
The birth-throes of a Future, strange and vast,
  Alarm the land; yet thou, so wise and strong,
Suddenly summoned to the burial bed,
  Lapped in its slumbers deep and ever long,
Hear'st not the tumult surging overhead.
Who now shall rally Freedom's scattering host?
Who wear the mantle of the leader lost?
Who stay the march of slavery? He, whose voice
  Hath called thee from thy task-field, shall not lack
    Yet bolder champions, to beat bravely back
The wrong which, through His poor ones, reaches Him:
Yet firmer hands shall Freedom's torch-lights trim,
  And wave them high across the abysmal black,
    Till bound, dumb millions there shall see them and rejoice.

LINES

ACCOMPANYING MANUSCRIPTS PRESENTED TO A FRIEND.

'TIS said that in the Holy Land
　The angels of the place have blessed
The pilgrim's bed of desert sand,
　Like Jacob's stone of rest.

That down the hush of Syrian skies
　Some sweet-voiced saint at twilight sings
The song whose holy symphonies
　Are beat by unseen wings;

Still starting from his sandy bed,
　The way-worn wanderer looks to see
The halo of an angel's head
　Shine through the tamarisk tree.

So through the shadows of my way
　Thy smile hath fallen soft and clear,
So at the weary close of day
　Hath seemed thy voice of cheer.

That pilgrim pressing to his goal
　May pause not for the vision's sake,
Yet all fair things within his soul
　The thought of it shall wake;

The graceful palm tree by the well,
　Seen on the far horizon's rim;
The dark eyes of the fleet gazelle,
　Bent timidly on him;

Each pictured saint, whose golden hair
　Streams sunlike through the convent's gloom;
Pale shrines of martyrs young and fair,
　And loving Mary's tomb;

And thus each tint or shade which falls
　From sunset cloud or waving tree,
Along my pilgrim path recalls
　The pleasant thought of thee.

Of one, in sun and shade the same,
　In weal and woe my steady friend,
Whatever by that holy name
　The angels comprehend.

Not blind to faults and follies, thou
  Hast never failed the good to see,
Nor judged by one unseemly bough
  The upward-struggling tree.

These light leaves at thy feet I lay—
  Poor common thoughts on common things,
Which time is shaking, day by day,
  Like feathers from his wings—

Chance shootings from a frail life-tree,
  To nurturing care but little known,
Their good was partly learned of thee,
  Their folly is my own.

That tree still clasps the kindly mould,
  Its leaves still drink the twilight dew,
And weaving its pale green with gold,
  Still shines the sunlight through.

There still the morning zephyrs play.
  And there at times the spring bird sings,
And mossy trunk and fading spray
  Are flowered with glossy wings.

Yet, even in genial sun and rain,
  Root, branch, and leaflet fail and fade,
The wanderer on its lonely plain
  Ere long shall miss its shade.

Oh, friend beloved, whose curious skill
  Keeps bright the last year's leaves and flowers,
With warm, glad summer thoughts to fill
  The cold, dark, winter hours!

Pressed on thy heart, the leaves I bring
  May well defy the wintry cold,
Until, in Heaven's eternal spring,
  Life's fairer ones unfold.

THE REWARD.

Who, looking backward from his manhood's prime,
Sees not the spectre of his misspent time?
  And, through the shade
Of funeral cypress planted thick behind,
Hears no reproachful whisper on the wind
  From his loved dead?

Who bears no trace of passion's evil force?
Who shuns thy sting, oh terrible Remorse?—
  Who does not cast
On the thronged pages of his memory's book,
At times, a sad and half reluctant look,
  Regretful of the Past?

Alas!—the evil which we fain would shun
We do, and leave the wished-for good undone:
  Our strength to-day
Is but to-morrow's weakness, prone to fall;
Poor, blind, unprofitable servants all
  Are we alway.

Yet, who, thus looking backward o'er his years,
Feels not his eyelids wet with grateful tears,
  If he hath been
Permitted, weak and sinful as he was,
To cheer and aid, in some ennobling cause,
  His fellow-men?

If he hath hidden the outcast, or let in
A ray of sunshine to the cell of sin,—
  If he hath lent
Strength to the weak, and, in an hour of need,
Over the suffering, mindless of his creed
  Or home, hath bent,

He has not lived in vain, and while he gives
The praise to Him, in whom he moves and lives,
  With thankful heart;
He gazes backward, and with hope before,
Knowing that from his works he never more
  Can henceforth part.

RAPHAEL.*

I SHALL not soon forget that sight:
 The glow of Autumn's westering day,
A hazy warmth, a dreamy light,
 On Raphael's picture lay.

It was a simple print I saw,
 The fair face of a musing boy;
Yet while I gazed a sense of awe
 Seemed blending with my joy.

* Suggested by a portrait of Raphael, at the age of fifteen, in the possession of Thomas Tracy, of Newburyport.

A simple print:—the graceful flow
   Of boyhood's soft and wavy hair,
And fresh young lip and cheek, and brow
   Unmarked and clear, were there.

Yet through its sweet and calm repose
   I saw the inward spirit shine;
It was as if before me rose
   The white veil of a shrine.

As if, as Gothland's sage has told,
   The hidden life, the man within,
Dissevered from its frame and mould,
   By mortal eye were seen.

Was it the lifting of that eye,
   The waving of that pictured hand?
Loose as a cloud-wreath on the sky,
   I saw the walls expand.

The narrow room had vanished,—space
   Broad, luminous, remained alone,
Through which all hues and shapes of grace
   And beauty looked or shone.

Around the mighty master came
   The marvels which his pencil wrought,
Those miracles of power whose fame
   Is wide as human thought.

There drooped thy more than mortal face,
   Oh Mother, beautiful and mild!
Enfolding in one dear embrace
   Thy Saviour and Thy Child!

The rapt brow of the Desert John;
   The awful glory of that day,
When all the Father's brightness shone
   Through manhood's veil of clay.

And, midst gray prophet forms, and wild
   Dark visions of the days of old,
How sweetly woman's beauty smiled
   Through locks of brown and gold!

There Fornarina's fair young face
   Once more upon her lover shone,
Whose model of an angel's grace
   He borrowed from her own.

Slow passed that vision from my view,
   But not the lesson which it taught;
The soft, calm shadows which it threw
   Still rested on my thought:

The truth, that painter, bard, and sage,
   Even in Earth's cold and changeful clime,
Plant for their deathless heritage
   The fruits and flowers of time.

We shape ourselves the joy or fear
   Of which the coming life is made
And fill our Future's atmosphere
   With sunshine or with shade.

The tissue of the Life to be
   We weave with colors all our own,
And in the field of Destiny
   We reap as we have sown.

Still shall the soul around it call
   The shadows which it gathered here,
And painted on the eternal wall
   The Past shall reappear.

Think ye the notes of holy song
   On Milton's tuneful ear have died?
Think ye that Raphael's angel throng
   Has vanished from his side?

Oh no!—We live our life again:
   Or warmly touched or coldly dim
The pictures of the Past remain,—
   Man's works shall follow him!

LINES

Written on visiting a singular cave in Chester, N. H., known in the vicinity by the name of " The Devil's Den."

THE moon is bright on the rocky hill,
But its dwarfish pines rise gloomily still,—
Fix'd, motionless forms in the silent air,
The moonlight is on them, but darkness is there.
The drowsy flap of the owlet's wing,
And the stream's low gush from its hidden spring,
And the passing breeze, in its flight-betray'd
By the timid shiver of leaf and blade;
Half like a sigh and half a moan,
The ear of the listener catches alone.

A dim cave yawns in the rude hillside,
Like the jaws of a monster open'd wide,
Where a few wild bushes of thorn and fern
Their leaves from the breath of the night-air turn;
And half with twining foliage cover
The mouth of that shadowy cavern over:
Above it, the rock rests gloomy and high
Its rugged outline against the sky,
Which seems as, it opens on either hand,
Like some bright sea leaving a desolate land.

Below it, a stream on its bed of stone
From a rift in the rock comes hurrying down.
Telling forever the same wild tale
Of its loftier home to the lowly vale;
And over its waters an oak is bending,
Its boughs like a skeleton's arms extending—
A naked tree, by the lightning shorn,
With its trunk all bare and its branches torn;
And the rocks beneath it, blacken'd and rent,
Tell where the bolt of the thunder went.

'Tis said that this cave is an evil place—
The chosen haunt of the fallen race;
That the midnight traveller oft hath seen
A red flame tremble its jaws between,
And lighten and quiver the boughs among,
Like the fiery play of a serpent's tongue;
That sounds of fear from its chambers swell—
The ghostly gibber, the fiendish yell;
That bodiless hands at its entrance wave,—
And hence they have named it THE DEMON'S CAVE!

The fears of man to this place have lent
A terror which Nature never meant;
For who hath wander'd, with curious eye,
This dim and shadowy cavern by,
And known, in the sun or starlight, aught
Which might not beseem so lonely a spot,—
The stealthy fox, and the shy raccoon,
The night-bird's wing in the shining moon,
The frog's low croak, and, upon the hill,
The steady chant of the whippoorwill?

Yet is there something to fancy dear
In this silent cave and its lingering fear,—
Something which tells of another age,
Of the wizard's wand, and the Sybil's page,
Of the fairy ring and the haunted glen,
And the restless phantoms of murder'd men,
The grandame's tale and the nurse's song,
The dreams of childhood remember'd long;
And I love even now to list the tale
Of the Demon's Cave, and its haunted vale.

SUICIDE POND.

'is a dark and dismal little pool, and fed by tiny rills,
nd bosom'd in waveless quietude between two barren hills;
here is no tree on its rugged marge, save a willow old and lone,
ike a solitary mourner for its sylvan sisters gone.

he plough of the farmer turneth not the sward of its gloomy shore,
'hich bears even now the same gray moss which in other times it bore;
nd seldom or never the tread of man is heard in that lonely spot,
or with all the dwellers around that pool its story is unforgot.

nd why does the traveller turn aside from that dark and silent pool,
hough the sun be burning above his head, and the willow's shade be
    cool ?
r glance with fear to its shadowy brink, when night rests darkly there,
nd down, through its sullen and evil depths, the stars of the mid-
    night glare ?

errily whistles the cowboy on—but he hushes his music when
e hurries his cows, with a sidelong glance, from that cold forsaken
    glen!
aughing and mirthful the young girl comes, with her gamesome mates,
    from school,
ut her laugh is lost and her lip is white as she passes the haunted pool!

'is said that a young, a beautiful girl, with a brow and with an eye,—
ne like a cloud in the moonlight robed, and one like a star on high!—
ne who was loved by the villagers all, and whose smile was a gift to
    them,
as found one morn in that pool as cold as the water-lily's stem!

y, cold as the rank and wasting weeds, which lie in the pool's dark
    bed,
he villagers found that beautiful one, in the slumber of the dead.
e had strangely whisper'd her dark design in a young companion's
    ear,
ut so wild and vague that the listener smiled and knew not what to
    fear.

nd she went to die in that loathsome pool when the summer day was
    done,
'ith her dark hair curl'd on her pure white brow, and her fairest gar-
    ments on;
'ith the ring on her taper finger still, and her necklace of ocean pearl,
wined as in mockery round the neck of that suicidal girl.

nd why she perish'd so strangely there no mortal tongue can tell—
e told her story to none, and Death retains her secret well!
nd the willow, whose mossy and aged boughs o'er the silent water
    lean,
ke a sad and sorrowful mourner of the beautiful dead, is seen!

But oft, our village maidens say, when the summer evenings fall,
When the frog is calling from his pool to the cricket in the wall;
When the night-hawk's wing dips lightly down to that dull and sleepi

lake,
And slow through its green and stagnant mass the shoreward circl

break—

At a time like this, a misty form—as fog beneath the moon—
Like a meteor glides to the startled view, and vanishes as soon;
Yet weareth it ever a human shape, and ever a human cry
Comes faintly and low on the still night-air, as when the despairing di

---

STANZAS

Suggested by the Letter of a Friend.

I see thee still before me, even
   As when we parted,
When o'er thy blue eye's brilliant heaven
   A tear had started;—
And a slight tremor in thy tone,
Like that of some frail harp string blown
   By fitful breezes, faint and low,
Told, in that brief and sad farewell,
All that affection's heart may tell,
   And more than words can show!

Yet, thou art with the dreamless dead
   Quietly sleeping,
Around the marble at thy head
   The wild grass creeping!—
How many thoughts, which but belong
Unto the living and the young,
   Have whisper'd from my heart of thee,
When thou wast resting calmly there,
Shut from the blessed sun and air—
   From life and love and me!

Why did I leave thee?—Well I knew
   A flower so frail
Might sink beneath the Summer dew,
   Or soft Spring gale:
I knew how delicately wrought,
With feeling and intensest thought,
   Was each sweet lineament of thine;—
And that thy heavenward soul would gain
An early freedom from its chain,
   Was there not many a sign?

There was a brightness in thine eye,
   Yet not of mirth—

A light whose clear intensity
  Was not of earth!
Along thy cheek a deepened red
Told where the feverish hectic fed,
  And, yet, each fearful token gave
A newer and a dearer grace
To the mild beauty of thy face,
  Which spoke not of the grave!

Why did I leave thee ?—Far away
  They told of lands
Glittering with gold, and none to stay
  The gleaner's hands.
For this I left thee—ay, and sold
The *riches of my heart for gold!*
  For yonder mansion's vanity—
For green verandas, hung with flowers,
For marbled fount and orange bowers,
  And grove and flowering tree.

Vain—worthless, all ! The lowliest spot
  Enjoy'd with thee,
A richer and a dearer lot
  Would seem to me:
For well I knew that thou couldst find
Contentment in thy spotless mind
  And in my own unchanging love.
Why did I leave thee ?—Fully mine
The blessing of a heart like thine,
  What could I ask above ?

Mine is a selfish misery—
  I cannot weep
For one supremely blest, like thee,
  With Heaven's sleep ;
The passion and the strife of time
Can never reach that sinless clime,
  Where the redeem'd of spirit dwell!—
Why should I weep that thou art free
From all the grief which maddens me ?—
  Sainted and loved—Farewell!

LINES ON A PORTRAIT.

How beautiful!—That brow of snow,
  That glossy fall of fair brown tresses,
The blue eye's tranquil heaven below,
  The hand whereon the fair cheek presses,
Half-shadow'd by a falling curl
  Which on the temple's light reposes—
Each finger like a line of pearl
  Contrasted with the cheek's pure roses!
There as she sits beneath the shade

By vine and rose-wreath'd arbor made,
Tempering the light which, soft and warm,
Reveals her full and matchless form,
In thoughtful quietude, she seems
Like one of Raphael's pictur'd dreams,
Where blend in one all radiant face
The woman's warmth—the angel's grace!

Well—I can gaze upon it now,
  As on some cloud of autumn's even,
Bathing its pinions in the glow
  And glory of the sunset heaven—
So holy and so far away
  That love without desire is cherish'd,
Like that which lingers o'er the clay
  Whose warm and breathing life has perish'd,
While yet upon its brow is shed
The mournful beauty of the dead!
And I can look on her as one
Too pure for aught save gazing on—
An Idol in some holy place,
Which man may kneel to, not caress—
Or melting tone of music heard
From viewless lip, or unseen bird.

I know her not.   And what is all
  Her beauty to a heart like mine,
While memory yet hath power to call
  Its worship from a stranger-shrine?
Still midst the weary din of life
  The tones I love my ear has met;
Midst lips of scorn and brows of strife
  The smiles I love are lingering yet!
The hearts in sun and shadow known—
The kind hands lingering in our own—
The cords of strong affection spun
By early deeds of kindness done—
The blessed sympathies which bind
The spirit to its kindred mind,—
Oh, who would leave these tokens tried
For all the stranger world beside?

THE MURDERED LADY.

A DARK-HULLED brig at anchor rides
  Within the still and moonlit bay,
And round its black, portentous sides
  The waves like living creatures play!
And close at hand a tall ship lies,
  A voyager from the Spanish Main,
Laden with gold and merchandise—
  She'll ne'er return again!

The fisher in his seaward skiff
  Creeps stealthily along the shore
Within the shadow of the cliff,
  Where keel had never plowed before:
He turns him from that stranger bark
  And hurries down the silvery bay,
Where like a demon still and dark,
  She watches o'er her prey.

     *   *   *   *   *

The midnight came.—A dash of oars
  Broke on the ocean-stillness then,
And swept toward the rocky shores
  The fierce wild forms of outlawed men;—
The tenants of this fearful ship,
  Grouped strangely in the pale moonlight—
Dark, iron brow and bearded lip,
  Ghastly with storm and fight.

They reached the shore,—but who is she,
  The white-robed one they bear along?
She shrieks—she struggles to be free—
  God shield that gentle one from wrong;
It may not be,—those pirate men
  Along the hushed, deserted street
Have borne her to a narrow glen
  Scarce trod by human feet.

     *   *   *   *   *

And there the ruffians murdered her,
  When not an eye, save Heaven's beheld,—
Ask of the shuddering villager
  What sounds upon the night-air swelled:
Woman's long shriek of mortal fear—
  Her wild appeal to hearts of stone,
The oath—the taunt—the brutal jeer—
  The pistol-shot—the groan!

With shout and jest and losel song,
  From savage tongues which knew no rein,
The stained with murder passed along
  And sought their ocean-home again;
And all the night their revel came
  In hoarse and sullen murmurs on,—
A yell rang up—a burst of flame—
  The Spanish ship was gone!

The morning light came red and fast
  Along the still and blushing sea;
The phantoms of the night had passed—
  That ocean-robber—where was she?

Her sails were reaching from the wind,
  Her crimson banner-folds were stirred;
And ever and anon behind
  Her shouting crew were heard

Then came the village-dwellers forth
  And sought with fear the fatal glen;
The stain of blood—the trampled earth—
  Told where the deed of death had been.
They found a grave—a new made one—
  With bloody sabres hollowed out.
And shadowed from the searching sun
  By tall trees round about.

They left the hapless stranger there;
  They knew her sleep would be as well
As if the priest had poured his prayer
  Above her, with the funeral-bell.
The few poor rites which man can pay
  Are felt not by the lonely sleeper;
The deaf, unconscious ear of clay
  Heeds not the living weeper.

They tell a tale—those sea-worn men
  Who dwell along that rocky coast—
Of sights and sounds within the glen,
  Of midnight shriek and gliding ghost.
And oh! if ever from their chill
  And dreamless sleep the dead arise,
That victim of unhallowed ill
  Might wake to human eyes!

They say that often when the morn
  Is struggling with the gloomy even,
And over moon and stars is drawn
  The curtain of a clouded heaven,
Strange sounds swell up the narrow glen,
  As if that robber-crew were there—
The hellish laugh—the shouts of men—
  And woman's dying prayer!

THE WEIRD GATHERING.

A Trumpet in the darkness blown—
  A peal upon the air—
The church-yard answers to its tone
With boding shriek and wail and groan—
  The dead are gliding there!

It rose upon the still midnight,
    A summons long and clear—
The wakeful shuddered with affright—
The dreaming sleeper sprang upright
    And pressed his stunning ear.

The Indian, where his serpent eye
    Beneath the green-wood shone,
Started, and tossed his arms on high,
And answered, with his own wild cry,
    The sky's unearthly tone.

The wild birds rose in startled flocks
    As the long trumpet swelled;
And loudly from their old, gray rocks
The gaunt, fierce wolf and caverned fox
    In mutual terror yelled.

There is a wild and haunted glen
    'Twixt Saugus and Naumkeag—
'Tis said of old that wizard-men
And demons to that spot have been
    To consecrate their league.

A fitting place for such as these—
    That small and sterile plain,
So girt about with tall old trees
Which rock and groan in every breeze,
    Like spirits cursed with pain.

It was the witch's trysting-place,
    The wizard's chosen ground,
Where the accursed of human race
With demons gathered, face to face,
    By the midnight trumpet's sound.

And there that night the trumpet rang
    And rock and hill replied,
And down the glen strange shadows sprang,
Mortal and fiend—a wizard gang—
    Seen dimly side by side.

They gathered there from every land
    That sleepeth in the sun,—
They came with spell and charm in hand,
Waiting their Master's high command—
    Slaves to the Evil One!

From islands of the far-off seas—
    From Hecla's ice and flame—
From where the loud and savage breeze
Growls through the tall Norwegian trees
    Seer, witch, and wizard came!

And from the sunny land of palms
  The negro hag was there—
The Gree-gree, with his Obi charms—
The Indian, with his tattooed arms
  And wild and streaming hair.

The Gypsy, with her fierce, dark eyes,
  The worshipper of flame—
The searcher out of mysteries
Above a human sacrifice—
  All—all—together came!

*   *   *   *   *

Nay, look not down that lighted dell,
  Thou startled traveller!—
Thy christian eye should never dwell
On gaunt, gray witch and fiend of hell
  And evil Trumpeter!

But the traveller turned him from his way,
  For he heard the revelling,
And saw the red light's wizard ray
Among the dark-leafed branches play
  Like an unholy thing

He knelt him on the rocks and cast
  A fearful glance beneath;
Wizard and hag before him passed,
Each wilder, fiercer than the last,—
  His heart grew cold as death!

He saw the dark-browed Trumpeter,
  In human shape was he;
And witch and fiend and sorcerer,
With shriek and laugh and curses, were
  Assembled at his knee.

And lo! beneath his straining glance
  A light form stole along—
Free, as if moving to the dance,
He saw her fairy steps advance
  Toward the evil throng.

The light along her forehead played—
  A wan, unearthly glare;
Her cheek was pale beneath the shade
The wildness of her tresses made,
  Yet nought of fear was there!

Now God have mercy on thy brain,
  Thou stricken traveller!
Look on thy victim once again,
Bethink thee of her wrongs and pain—
  Dost thou remember her ?

The traveller smote his burning brow,
  For he saw the wronged one there—
He knew her by her forehead's snow,
And by her large blue eye below,
  And by her wild, dark hair.

Slowly, yet firm she held her way,—
  The wizard's song grew still—
The sorcerer left his elfish play,
And hideous imp and beldame gray
  Waited the stranger's will.

A voice came up that place of fear—
  The Trumpeter's hoarse tone:
"Speak—who art thou that comest here
With brow baptized and christian ear,
  Unsummoned and alone?"

One moment, and a tremor shook
  Her light and graceful frame,—
It passed, and then her features took
A fiercer and a haughtier look
  As thus her answer came:—

  "Spirits of evil—
    Workers of doom!—
  Lo! to your revel
    For vengeance I come—
  Vengeance on him
    Who hath blighted my fame!

  Fill his cup to the brim
    With a curse without name!
  Let his false heart inherit
    The madness of mine,
  And I yield ye my spirit
    And bow at your shrine!"

A sound—a mingled laugh and yell,
  Went howling fierce and far;
A redder light shone through the dell,
As if the very gates of hell
  Swung suddenly ajar.

"Breathe then thy curse, thou daring one,"
  A low, deep voice replied:
"Whate'er thou askest shall be done,
The burthen of thy doom upon
  The false one shall abide."

The maiden stood erect—her brow
  Grew dark as those around her,
As burned upon her lip that vow
Which christian ear may never know,—
  And the dark fetter bound her!

Ay, there she stood—the holy Heaven
  Was looking down on her—
An angel from her bright home driven—
A spirit lost and doomed and given
  To fiend and sorcerer!

And changed—how changed!—her aspect grew
  Fearful and elfish there;
The warm tinge from her cheek withdrew,
And one dark spot of blood-red hue
  Burned on her forehead fair.

Wild from her eye of madness shone
  The baleful fire within,
As with a shrill and lifted tone
She made her fearful purpose known
  Before the powers of sin:—

      "Let my curse be upon him—
        The faithless of heart!
      Let the smiles that have won him
        In frowning depart!
      Let his last, cherished blossom
        Of sympathy die,
      And the hopes of his bosom
        In shadows go by!
      Ay, curse him—but keep
        The poor boon of his breath
      Till he sigh for the sleep
        And the quiet of death!
      Let a viewless one haunt him
        With whisper and jeer,
      And an evil one daunt him
        With phantoms of fear!
      Be the fiend unforgiving
        That follows his tread!
      Let him walk with the living,
        Yet gaze on the dead!"

She ceased. The doomed one felt the spell
  Already on his brain;
He turned him from the wizard-dell;
He prayed to Heaven; he cursed at hell;—
  He wept—and all in vain.

The night was one of mortal fear;
  The morning rose to him
Dark as the shroudings of a bier,
As if the blessèd atmosphere,
  Like his own soul, was dim.

He passed among his fellow-men
  With wild and dreamy air,
For, whispering in his ear again

The horrors of the midnight glen,
  The demon found him there.

And when he would have knelt and prayed
  Amidst his household band,
An unseen power his spirit stayed,
And on his moving lip was laid
  A hot and burning hand!

The lost one in the solitude
  Of dreams he gazed upon,
And when the holy morning glowed
Her dark eye shone, her wild hair flowed
  Between him and the sun!

His brain grew wild,—and then he died;
  Yet, ere his heart grew cold,
To the gray priest who at his side
The strength of prayer and blessing tried,
  His fearful tale was told.

    *   *   *   *   *

They've bound the witch with many a thong—
  The holy priest is near her;
And ever as she moves along,
A murmur rises fierce and strong
  From those who hate and fear her

She's standing up for sacrifice
  Beneath the gallows-tree;
The silent town beneath her lies,
Above her are the summer skies,
  Far off the quiet sea.

So young—so frail—so very fair—
  Why should the victim die?
Look on her brow!—the red stain there
Burns underneath her tangled hair—
  And mark her fiery eye!

A thousand eyes are looking up
  In scorn and hate to her;
A bony hand hath coiled the rope,
And yawns upon the green hill's slope
  The witch's sepulchre!

Ha! she hath spurned both priest and book—
  Her hand is tossed on high—
Her curse is loud, she will not brook
The impatient crowd's abiding look—
  Hark! how she shrieks to die!

Up—up—one struggle—all is done!
  One groan—the deed is wrought!
Wo for the wronged and fallen one!
Her corse is blackened in the sun,
  Her spirit—trace it not!

THE BLACK FOX.

It was on a cold and cruel night,
  Some fourscore years ago,
The clouds across the winter sky
  Were scudding to and fro;
The air above was cold and keen,
  The earth was white below.

Around an ancient fireplace
  A happy household drew;
The husband and his own goodwife,
  And children not a few;
And bent above the spinning-wheel
  The aged grandame too.

The fire-light reddened all the
    room,
  It rose so high and strong,
And mirth was in each pleasant
    eye
  Within that household throng:
And while the grandame turned
    her wheel
  The good man hummed a song.

At length spoke up a fair-haired
    girl,
  Some seven summers old,
"Now grandame, tell the tale again
  Which yesterday you told;
About the Black Fox and the men
  Who followed him so bold."

"Yes, tell it," said a dark-eyed
    boy,
  And "Tell it," said his brother;
"Just tell the story of the Fox,
  We will not ask another."
And all the children gathered close
  Around their old grandmother

Then lightly in her withered hands
  The grandame turned her reel.
And when the thread was wound
    away
  She set aside her wheel,
And smiled with that peculiar joy
  The old and happy feel.

"'Tis more than sixty years ago
  Since first the Fox was seen—
'Twas in the winter of the year,
  When not a leaf was green,
Save where the dark old hemlock
    stood
  The naked oaks between.

"My father saw the creature first
  One bitter winter's day—
It passed so near that he could se[e]
  Its fiery eyeballs play,
And well he knew an evil thing,
  And foul, had crossed his way.

"A hunter like my father then
  We never more shall see—
The mountain-cat was not mor[e]
    swift
  Of eye and foot than he:
His aim was fatal in the air
  And on the tallest tree.

"Yet close beneath his ready aim
  The Black Fox hurried on,
And when the forest echoes mocke[d]
  The sharp voice of his gun,
The creature gave a frightful yell
  Long, loud, but only one.

"And there was something horribl[e]
  And fiendish in that yell;
Our good old parson heard it once
  And I have heard him tell
That it might well be likened to
  A fearful cry from hell.

"Day after day that Fox was seen
  He prowled our forests through
Still gliding wild and spectre-like
  Before the hunter's view;
And howling louder than the
    storm
  When savagely it blew.

"The Indians, when upon the
    wind
  That howl rose long and clear,

Shook their wild heads mysteri-
ously
And muttered, as in fear;
Or veiled their eyes, as if they knew
An evil thing was near.

"They said it was a Fox accurst
By Hobomocko's will,
That it was once a mighty chief
Whom battle might not kill,
But who, for some unspoken
crime,
Was doomed to wander still.

"That every year, when all the
hills
Were white with winter snow,
And the tide of Salmon River ran
The gathering ice below,
His howl was heard and his form
was seen
Still hurrying to and fro.

"At length two gallant hunter
youths,
The boast and pride of all—
The gayest in the hour of mirth
The first at danger's call,
Our playmates at the village
school,
Our partners at the ball—

"Went forth to hunt the sable Fox
Beside that haunted stream,
Where it so long had glided like
The creature of a dream,
Or like unearthly forms that dance
Under the cold moonbeam!

"They went away one winter day,
When all the air was white,
And thick and hazed with falling
snow,
And blinding to the sight;
They bade us never fear for them,
They would return by night.

"The night fell thick and darkly
down,
And still the storm blew on;
And yet the hunters came not
back,
Their task was yet undone;

Nor came they with their words of
cheer,
Even with the morrow's sun.

"And then our old men shook their
heads,
And the red Indians told
Their tales of evil sorcery
Until our blood ran cold,—
The stories of their Powwow seers,
And withered hags of old.

"They told us that our hunters
Would never more return—
That they would hunt for ever-
more
Through tangled swamp and
fern,
And that their last and dismal fate
No mortal e'er might learn.

"And days and weeks passed
slowly on,
And yet they came not back,
Nor evermore by stream or hill
Was seen that form of black—
Alas! for those who hunted still
Within its fearful track!

"But when the winter passed
away,
And early flowers began
To bloom along the sunned hill-
side,
And where the waters ran,
There came unto my father's door
A melancholy man.

"His form had not the sign of
years,
And yet his locks were white,
And in his deep and restless eye
There was a fearful light;
And from its glance we turned
away
As from an adder's sight.

"We placed our food before that
man,
So haggard and so wild,—
He thrust it from his lips as he
Had been a fretful child;

And when we spoke with words of
    cheer,
    Most bitterly he smiled.

" He smiled, and then a gush of
    tears,
    And then a fierce, wild look,
And then he murmured of the Fox
    Which haunted Salmon Brook,
Until his hearers every one
    With nameless terror shook.

" He turned away with a frightful
    cry,
    And hurried madly on,
As if the dark and spectral thing
    Before his path had gone:
We called him back, but he heeded
    not
    The kind and warning tone.

" He came not back to us again,
    But the Indian hunters said
That far, where the howling wilder-
    ness
    Its leafy tribute shed,
They found our missing hunters—
    Naked and cold and dead.

" Their grave they made beneath
    the shade
    Of the old and solemn wood,
Where oaks by Time alone hewn
    down
For centuries had stood,
And left them without shroud or
    prayer
    In the dark solitude.

" The Indians always shun that
    grave—
    The wild deer treads not there—
The green grass is not trampled
    down
    By catamount or bear—
The soaring wild-bird turns away
    Even in the upper air.

" For people said that every year
    When winter snows are spread
All over the face of the frozen
    earth,
    And the forest leaves are shed,
The Spectre Fox comes forth and
    howls
    Above the hunters' bed."

THE WHITE MOUNTAINS.

GRAY searcher of the upper air!
    There's sunshine on thy ancient walls—
A crown upon the forehead bare—
    A flashing on thy water-falls—
A rainbow glory in the cloud,
Upon thy awful summit bowed,
    Dim relic of the recent storm!
And music, from the leafy shroud
Which wraps in green thy giant form,
Mellowed and softened from above,
    Steals down upon the listening ear,
Sweet as the maiden's dream of love,
    With soft tones melting on her ear,

The time has been, gray mountain, when
    Thy shadows veiled the red man's home;
And over crag and serpent den,
And wild gorge, where the steps of men
    In chase or battle might not come,
The mountain eagle bore on high
    The emblem of the free of soul;

And midway in the fearful sky
Sent back the Indian's battle-cry,
  Or answered to the thunder's roll.

The wigwam fires have all burned out—
  The moccasin hath left no track—
Nor wolf nor wild-deer roam about
  The Saco or the Merrimack.
And thou that liftest up on high
Thine awful barriers to the sky,
  Art not the haunted mount of old,
When on each crag of blasted stone

Some mountain-spirit found a throne,
  And shrieked from out the thick cloud-fold,
And answered to the Thunderer's cry
When rolled the cloud of tempest by,
And jutting rock and riven branch
Went down before the avalanche.

The Father of our people then
  Upon thy awful summit trod,
And the red dwellers of the glen
  Bowed down before the Indian's God.
There, when His shadow veiled the sky,
  The Thunderer's voice was long and loud,
And the red flashes of His eye
  Were pictured on the o'erhanging cloud.

The Spirit moveth there no more,
  The dwellers of the hill have gone,
The sacred groves are trampled o'er,
  And footprints mar the altar-stone,
The white man climbs thy tallest rock
  And hangs him from the mossy steep,
Where, trembling to the cloud-fire's shock,
Thy ancient prison-walls unlock,
And captive waters leap to light,
And dancing down from height to height,
  Pass onward to the far-off deep.

Oh, sacred to the Indian seer,
  Gray altar of the days of old!
Still are thy rugged features dear,
As when unto my infant ear
  The legends of the past were told.
Tales of the downward sweeping flood,
When bowed like reeds thy ancient wood,—
  Of armed hand and spectral form,
Of giants in their misty shroud,
And voices calling long and loud
  In the drear pauses of the storm!

Farewell! The red man's face is turned
  Toward another hunting ground;
For where the council-fire has burned,
  And o'er the sleeping warrior's mound
Another fire is kindled now:
Its light is on the white man's brow!
  The hunter race have passed away—
Ay, vanished like the morning mist,
Or dewdrops by the sunshine kissed,—
  And wherefore should the red man stay?

THE INDIAN'S TALE.

THE War-God did not wake to strife
  The strong men of our forest land,
No red hand grasped the battle-knife
  At Areouski's high command:—
We held no war-dance by the dim
  And red light of the creeping flame;
Nor warrior yell, nor battle hymn
  Upon the midnight breezes came.

There was no portent in the sky,
  No shadow on the round, bright sun,
With light and mirth and melody
  The long, fair summer days came on.
We were a happy people then,
  Rejoicing in our hunter mood
No footprints of the pale-faced men
  Had marred our forest solitude.

The land was ours—this glorious land—
  With all its wealth of wood and streams;
Our warriors strong of heart and hand,
  Our daughters beautiful as dreams.
When wearied at the thirsty noon,
  We knelt us where the spring gushed up,
To taste our Father's blessed boon—
  Unlike the white man's poison cup.

There came unto my father's hut
  A wan, weak creature of distress;
The red man's door is never shut
  Against the lone and shelterless.
And when he knelt before his feet,
  My father led the stranger in;
He gave him of his hunter meat—
  Alas! It was a deadly sin!

The stranger's voice was not like ours—
  His face at first was sadly pale,

Anon 'twas like the yellow flowers
   Which tremble in the meadow gale:
And when he laid him down to die,
   And murmured of his fatherland,
My mother wiped his tearful eye,
   My father held his burning hand!

He died at last—the funeral yell
   Rang upward from his burial sod,
And the old Powwah knelt to tell
   The tidings to the white man's God!
The next day came—my father's brow
   Grew heavy with a fearful pain,
He did not take his hunting-bow—
   He never sought the woods again?

He died even as the white man died;
   My mother, she was smitten too;
My sisters vanished from my side,
   Like diamonds from the sunlit dew.
And then we heard the Powwahs say
   That God had sent his angel forth
To sweep our ancient tribes away,
   And poison and unpeople Earth.

And it was so: from day to day
   The Spirit of the Plague went on—
And those at morning blithe and gay
   Were dying at the set of sun.
They died—our free, bold hunters died—
   The living might not give them graves,
Save when along the water-side
   They cast them to the hurrying waves.

The carrion crow, the ravenous beast,
   Turned loathing from the ghastly dead;
Well might they shun the funeral feast
   By that destroying angel spread!
One after one the red men fell,
   Our gallant war-tribe passed away,
And I alone am left to tell
   The story of its swift decay.

Alone—alone—a withered leaf,
   Yet clinging to its naked bough;
The pale race scorn the aged chief,
   And I will join my fathers now.
The spirits of my people bend
   At midnight from the solemn West,
To me their kindly arms extend,
   To call me to their home of rest!

THE SPECTRE SHIP.

THE morning light is breaking forth
  All over the dark blue sea,
And the waves are changed—they are rich with gold
  As the morning waves should be,
And the rising winds are wandering out
  On their seaward pinions free.

The bark is ready, the sails are set,
  And the boat rocks on the shore—
Say why do the passengers linger yet?
  Is not the farewell o'er?
Do those who enter that gallant ship
  Go forth to return no more?

A wailing rose by the water-side,
  A young, fair girl was there,
With a face as pale as the face of Death
  When its coffin-lid is bare;
And an eye as strangely beautiful
  As a star in the upper air

She leaned on a youthful stranger's arm—
  A tall and silent one—
Who stood in the very midst of the crowd,
  Yet uttered a word to none;
He gazed on the sea and the waiting-ship,
  But he gazed on them alone!

The fair girl leaned on the stranger's arm,
  And she wept as one in fear,
But he heeded not the plaintive moan
  And the dropping of the tear;
His eye was fixed on the stirring sea,
  Cold, darkly and severe!

The boat was filled—the shore was left—
  The farewell word was said—
But the vast crowd lingered still behind
  With an overpowering dread;
They feared that stranger and his bride,
  So pale and like the dead.

And many said that an evil pair
  Among their friends had gone,—
A demon with his human prey,
  From the quiet graveyard drawn;
And a prayer was heard that the innocent
  Might escape the Evil One.

Away—the good ship sped away,
  Out on the broad high seas,
The sun upon her path before—
  Behind, the steady breeze—
And there was naught in sea or sky
  Of fearful auguries.

The day passed on—the sunlight fell
  All slantwise from the west,
And then the heavy clouds of storm
  Sat on the ocean's breast;
And every swelling billow'd mourn'd
  Like a living thing distressed.

The sun went down among the clouds,
  Tinging with sudden gold,
The fall-like shadow of the storm,
  On every mighty fold—
And then the lightning's eye look'd forth
  And the red thunder rolled.

The storm came down upon the sea,
  In its surpassing dread,
Rousing the white and broken surge
  Above its rocky bed,
As if the deep was stirred beneath
  A giant's viewless tread.

All night the hurricane went on,
  And all along the shore
The smothered cry of shipwreck'd men
  Blent with the ocean's roar;
The gray-haired man had scarcely known
  So wild a night before.

Morn rose upon a tossing sea,
  The tempest's work was done,
And freely over land and wave
  Shone out the blessed sun;
But where was she—the merchant bark—
  Where had the good ship gone?

Men gathered on the shore to watch
  The billows' heavy swell,
Hoping, yet fearing much, some frail
  Memorial might tell
The fate of that disastrous ship—
  Of friends they loved so well.

None came—the billows smoothed away,
  And all was strangely calm,
As if the very sea had felt
  A necromancer's charm;

And not a trace was left behind
    Of violence and harm.

The twilight came with sky of gold,
    And curtaining of night—
And then a sudden cry rang out,
    "A ship—the ship in sight!"
And lo! tall masts grew visible
    Within the fading light.

Near and more near the ship came on,
    With all her broad sails spread—
The night grew thick, but a phantom light
    Around her path was shed,
And the gazers shuddered as on she came,
    For against the wind she sped.

They saw by the dim and baleful glare
    Around that voyager thrown,
The upright forms of the well-known crew,
    As paled and fixed as stone;
And they called to them, but no sound came back
    Save the echoed cry alone.

The fearful stranger youth was there,
    And clasped in his embrace
The pale and passing sorrowful
    Gazed wildly in his face,
Like one who had been wakened from
    The silent burial-place.

A shudder ran along the crowd,
    And a holy man knelt there,
On the wet sea-sand, and offered up
    A faint and trembling prayer,
That God would shield his people from
    The spirits of the air!

And lo! the vision passed away—
    The spectre ship—the crew—
The stranger and his pallid bride,
    Departed from their view;
And nought was left upon the waves
    Beneath the arching blue.

It passed away, that vision strange,
    Forever from their sight,
Yet long shall Naumkeag's annals tell
    The story of that night—
The phantom bark—the ghostly crew—
    The pale, encircling light.

THE SPECTRE WARRIORS.

AWAY to your arms! for the foemen are here,
The yell of the red man is loud on the ear!
On—on to the garrison—soldiers away,
The moccasin's track shall be bloody to-day.

The fortress is reached, they have taken their stand,
With war-knife in girdle, and rifle in hand;—
Their wives are behind them, the savage before—
Will the Puritan fail at his hearthstone and door?

There's a yell in the forest, unearthly and dread,
Like the shriek of a fiend o'er the place of the dead;
Again—how it swells through the forest afar—
Have the tribes of the fallen arisen to war?

Ha—look! they are coming—not cautious and slow,
In the serpent-like mood of the blood-seeking foe,
Nor stealing in shadow nor hiding in grass,
But tall and uprightly and sternly they pass.

"Be ready!"—the watchword has passed on the wall—
The maidens have shrunk to the innermost hall—
The rifles are levelled—each head is bowed low—
Each eye fixes steady—God pity the foe!

They are closely at hand! Ha! the red flash has broke
From the garrisoned wall through a curtain of smoke,
There's a yell from the dying—that aiming was true—
The red man no more shall his hunting pursue!

Look, look to the earth, as the smoke rolls away,
Do the dying and dead on the green herbage lay?
What mean those wild glances? no slaughter is there—
The red man has gone like the mist on the air!

Unharmed as the bodiless air he has gone
From the war-knife's edge and the ranger's long gun,
And the Puritan warrior has turned him away
From the weapons of war, and is kneeling to pray!

He fears that the Evil and Dark One is near,
On an errand of wrath, with his phantoms of fear
And he knows that the aim of his rifle is vain—
That the spectres of evil may never be slain!

He knows that the Powwah has cunning and skill
To call up the Spirit of Darkness at will;
To waken the dead in their wilderness-graves,
And summons the demons of forest and waves.

And he layeth the weapons of battle aside,
And forgetteth the strength of his natural pride,
And he kneels with the priest by his garrisoned door,
That the spectres of evil may haunt him no more!

THE LAST NORRIDGEWOCK.

SHE stood beneath the shadow of an oak,
Grim with uncounted winters, and whose boughs
Had sheltered in their youth the giant forms
Of the great chieftain's warriors.   She was fair,
Even to a white man's vision—and she wore
A blended grace and dignity of mien
Which might befit the daughter of a king—
The queenliness of nature.   She had all
The magic of proportion which might haunt
The dream of some rare painter, or steal in
Upon the musings of the sanctuary
Like an unreal vision.   She was dark,—
There was no play of crimson on her cheek,
Yet were her features beautiful.   Her eye
Was clear and wild—and brilliant as a beam
Of the live sunshine ; and her long, dark hair
Sway'd in rich masses to th' unquiet wind.
The West was glad with sunset.   Over all
The green hills and the wilderness there fell
A great and sudden glory.   Half the sky
Was full of glorious tints, as if the home
And fountain of the rainbow were revealed;
And through its depth of beauty looked the star
Of the blest Evening, like an angel's eye.

The Indian watched the sunset, and her eye
Glistened one moment; then a tear fell down,
For she was dreaming of her fallen race—
The mighty who had perished—for her creed
Had taught her that the spirits of the brave
And beautiful were gathered in the West—
The red man's Paradise;—and then she sang
Faintly her song of sorrow, with a low
And half-hushed tone, as if she knew that those
Who listened were unearthly auditors,
And that the dead had bowed themselves to hear.

" The moons of autumn wax and wane, the sound of swelling floods
Is borne upon the mournful wind, and broadly on the woods
The colors of the changing leaves—the fair, frail flowers of frost,
Before the round and yellow sun most beautiful are tossed.
The morning breaketh with a clear, bright pencilling of sky,
And blushes through its golden clouds as the great sun goes by;
And evening lingers in the West—more beautiful than dreams
Which whisper of the Spirit-land, its wilderness and streams!

" A little time—another moon—the forest will be sad—
The streams will mourn the pleasant light which made their journey
    glad;

The morn will faintly lighten up, the sunlight glisten cold,
And wane into the western sky without its autumn gold.
" And yet I weep not for the sign of desolation near—
The ruin of my hunter race may only ask a tear,—
The wailing streams will laugh again, the naked trees put on
The beauty of their summer green beneath the summer sun;
The autumn cloud will yet again its crimson draperies fold,
The star of sunset smile again—a diamond set in gold!
But never for their forest lake, or for their mountain path,
The mighty of our race shall leave the hunting ground of Death.

" I know the tale my fathers told—the legend of their fame—
The glory of our spotless race before the pale ones came—
When asking fellowship of none, by turns the foe of all,
The death-bolts of our vengeance fell, as Heaven's own lightnings fall;
When at the call of Tacomet, my warrior-sire of old,
The war-shout of a thousand men upon the midnight rolled;
And fearless and companionless our warriors strode alone,
And from the big lake to the sea the green earth was their own.

" Where are they now ? Around their changed and stranger-peopled
    home,
Full sadly o'er their thousand graves the flowers of autumn bloom—
The bow of strength is buried with the calumet and spear,
And the spent arrow slumbereth, forgetful of the deer!
The last canoe is rotting by the lake it glideth o'er,
When dark-eyed maidens sweetly sang its welcome from the shore.
The footprints of the hunter race from all the hills have gone—
Their offerings to the Spirit-land have left the altar-stone—
The ashes of the council-fire have no abiding token—
The song of war has died away—the Powwah's charm is broken—
The startling war-whoop cometh not upon the loud, clear air—
The ancient woods are vanishing—the pale men gathered there.

" And who is left to mourn for this ?—a solitary one
Whose life is waning into death like yonder setting sun !
A broken reed, a faded flower, that lingereth behind,
To mourn above its fallen race, and wrestle with the wind !
Lo ! from the Spirit-land I hear the voices of the blest;
The holy faces of the loved are leaning from the West.
The mighty and the beautiful—the peerless ones of old—
They call me to their pleasant sky and to their thrones of gold;
Ere the spoilers' eye hath found me, when there are none to save—
Or the evil-hearted pale-face made the free of soul a slave;
Ere the step of air grow weary, or the sunny eye be dim,
The father of my people is calling me to him."

THE AERIAL OMENS.

A LIGHT is troubling Heaven!—A strange, dull glow
Is trembling like a fiery veil between
The blue sky and the earth; and the far stars
Glimmer but faintly through it.   Day hath left
No traces of its presence, and the blush
With which it welcomed the embrace of Night
Has faded from the sky's blue cheek, as fades
The blush of human beauty when the tone
Or look which woke its evidence of love
Hath passed away forever.   Wherefore then
Burns the strange fire in Heaven?—It is as if
Nature's last curse—the terrible plague of fire,
Were working in her elements, and the sky
Consuming like a vapor.

      Lo—a change!
The fiery flashes sink, and all along
The dim horizon of the fearful North
Rests a broad crimson, like a sea of blood,
Untroubled by a wave.   And lo—above,
Bendeth a luminous arch of pale, pure white,
Clearly contrasted with the blue above,
And the dark red beneath it.   Glorious!
How like a pathway for the sainted ones—
The pure and beautiful intelligences
Who minister in Heaven, and offer up
Their praise as incense; or, like that which rose
Before the pilgrim-prophet, when the tread
Of the most holy angels brightened it,
And in his dream the haunted sleeper saw
The ascending and descending of the blest!
Another change.   Strange, fiery forms uprise
On the wide arch, and take the throngful shape
Of warriors gathering to the strife on high,
A dreadful marching of infernal shapes,
Beings of fire with plumes of bloody red,
With banners flapping o'er their crowded ranks,
And long swords quivering up against the sky!
And now they meet and mingle; and the ear
Listens with painful earnestness to catch
The ring of cloven helmets and the groan
Of the down-trodden.   But there comes no sound,
Save a low, sullen rush upon the air,
Such as the unseen wings of spirits make,
Sweeping the void above us.   All is still.
Yet falls each red sword fiercely, and the hoof
Of the wild steed is crushing on the breast
Of the o'erthrown and vanquished.   'Tis a strange

And awful conflict—an unearthly war!
It is as if the dead had risen up
To battle with each other—the stern strife
Of spirits visible to mortal eyes.

Steed, plume, and warrior vanish one by one,
Wavering and changing to unshapely flame;
And now across the red and fearful sky
A long bright flame is trembling, like the sword
Of the great Angel at the guarded gate
Of Paradise, when all the sacred groves
And beautiful flowers of Eden-land blushed red
Beneath its awful shadow; and the eye
Of the lone outcast quailed before its glare,
As from the immediate questioning of God.

And men are gazing on that troubled sky
With most unwonted earnestness, and fair
And beautiful brows are reddening in the light
Of that strange vision of the upper air;
Even as the dwellers of Jerusalem,
The leaguered of the Roman, when the sky
Of Palestine was thronged with fiery shapes,
And from Antonio's tower the mailed Jew
Saw his own image pictured in the air,
Contending with the heathen; and the priest
Beside the Temple's altar veiled his face
From that most horrid phantasy, and held
The censer of his worship with a hand
Shaken by terror's palsy.

                    It has passed—
And Heaven again is quiet; and its stars
Smile down serenely. There is not a stain
Upon its dream-like loveliness of blue—
No token of the fiery mystery
Which made the evening fearful. But the hearts
Of those who gazed upon it, yet retained
The shadow of its awe—the chilling fear
Of its ill-boding aspect. It is deemed
A revelation of the things to come—
Of war and its calamities—the storm
Of the pitched battle, and the midnight strife
Of heathen inroad—the devouring flame,
The dripping tomahawk, the naked knife,
The swart hand twining with the silken locks
Of the fair girl—the torture, and the bonds
Of perilous captivity with those
Who know not mercy, and with whom revenge
Is sweeter than the cherished gift of life.

MEMORIALS.

LUCY HOOPER.*

THEY tell me, Lucy, thou art dead—
 That all of thee we loved and cherished,
 Has with the summer roses perished:
And left, as its young beauty fled,
An ashen memory in its stead—
 The twilight of a parted day
  Whose fading light is cold and vain:
  The heart's faint echo of a strain
Of low, sweet music passed away.
That true and loving heart—that gift
 Of a mind, earnest, clear, profound,
Bestowing, with a glad unthrift,
 Its sunny light on all around,
Affinities which only could
Cleave to the pure, the true, and good;
 And sympathies which found no rest,
 Save with the loveliest and best.
Of them—of thee remains there naught
 But sorrow in the mourner's breast?—
A shadow in the land of thought?
No!—Even *my* weak and trembling faith
 Can lift for thee the veil which doubt
 And human fear have drawn about
The all-awaiting scene of death.
Even as thou wast I see thee still;
And, save the absence of all ill,
And pain and weariness, which here
Summoned the sigh or wrung the tear,
The same as when, two summers back,
Beside our childhood's Merrimack,
I saw thy dark eye wander o'er
Stream, sunny upland, rocky shore,
And heard thy low, soft voice alone
Midst lapse of waters, and the tone
Of pine leaves by the west-wind blown,
There's not a charm of soul or brow—
 Of all we knew and loved in thee—
But lives in holier beauty now,
 Baptized in immortality!
Not mine the sad and freezing dream

---

* Died at Brooklyn, L. I., on the 1st of 8th mo., 1841, aged twenty-four years.

Of souls that, with their earthly mould,
 Cast off the loves and joys of old—
Unbodied—like a pale moonbeam,
 As pure, as passionless, and cold;
Nor mine the hope of Indra's son,
 Of slumbering in oblivion's rest,
Life's myriads blending into one—
 In blank annihilation blest;
Dust-atoms of the infinite—
Sparks scattered from the central light,
And winning back through mortal pain
Their old unconsciousness again.
No!—I have FRIENDS in Spirit Land—
Not shadows in a shadowy band,
 Not *others*, but *themselves* are they.
And still I think of them the same
As when the Master's summons came;
Their change—the holy morn-light breaking
Upon the dream-worn sleeper, waking—
 A change from twilight into day.
They've laid thee midst the household graves,
 Where father, brother, sister lie;
Below thee sweep the dark blue waves,
 Above thee bends the summer sky.
Thy own loved church in sadness read
Her solemn ritual o'er thy head,
And blessed and hallowed with her prayer
The turf laid lightly o'er thee there.
That church, whose rites and liturgy,
Sublime and old, were truth to thee,
Undoubted to thy bosom taken,
As symbols of a faith unshaken.
Even I, of simple views, could feel
The beauty of thy trust and zeal;
And, owning not thy creed, could see
How deep a truth it seemed to thee,
And how thy fervent heart had thrown
O'er all, a coloring of its own,
And kindled up, intense and warm,
A life in every rite and form,
As, when on Chebar's banks of old,
The Hebrew's gorgeous vision rolled,
A spirit filled the vast machine—
A life "within the wheels" was seen.

Farewell! A little time, and we
 Who knew thee well, and loved thee here,
One after one shall follow thee
 As pilgrims through the gate of fear,
Which opens on eternity.
Yet shall we cherish not the less
 All that is left our hearts meanwhile;

The memory of thy loveliness
  Shall round our weary pathway smile,
Like moonlight when the sun has set—
A sweet and tender radiance yet.
Thoughts of thy clear-eyed sense of duty,
  Thy generous scorn of all things wrong—
The truth, the strength, the graceful beauty
  Which blended in thy song.
All lovely things by thee beloved,
  Shall whisper to our hearts of thee:
These green hills, where thy childhood roved—
  Yon river winding to the sea—
The sunset light of autumn eves
  Reflecting on the deep, still floods,
Cloud, crimson sky, and trembling leaves
  Of rainbow-tinted woods,—
These, in our view, shall henceforth take
A tenderer meaning for thy sake;
And all thou loved'st of earth and sky,
Seem sacred to thy memory.

CHANNING.

NOT vainly did old poets tell,
  Nor vainly did old genius paint
God's great and crowning miracle—
  The hero and the saint!

For even in a faithless day
  Can we our sainted ones discern;
And feel, while with them on the way,
  Our hearts within us burn.

And thus the common tongue and pen
  Which, world-wide, echo CHANNING'S fame,
As one of Heaven's anointed men,
  Have sanctified his name.

In vain shall Rome her portals bar,
  And shut from him her saintly prize,
Whom, in the world's great calendar,
  All men shall canonize.

By Narragansett's sunny bay,
  Beneath his green embowering wood,
To me it seems but yesterday
  Since at his side I stood.

The slopes lay green with summer rains,
  The western wind blew fresh and free,

And glimmered down the orchard lanes
  The white surf of the sea.

With us was one, who, calm and true,
  Life's highest purpose understood,
And like his blessed Master knew
  The joy of doing good.

Unlearned, unknown to lettered fame,
  Yet on the lips of England's poor
And toiling millions dwelt his name,
  With blessings evermore.

Unknown to power or place, yet where
  The sun looks o'er the Carib sea,
It blended with the freeman's prayer
  And song of jubilee.

He told of England's sin and wrong—
  The ills her suffering children know—
The squalor of the city's throng—
  The green field's want and woe.

O'er Channing's face the tenderness
  Of sympathetic sorrow stole
Like a still shadow, passionless,
  The sorrow of the soul.

But, when the generous Briton told
  How hearts were answering to his own,
And Freedom's rising murmur rolled
  Up to the dull-eared throne,

I saw, methought, a glad surprise
  Thrill through that frail and pain-worn frame
And kindling in those deep, calm eyes
  A still and earnest flame.

His few, brief words were such as move
  The human heart—the Faith-sown seeds
Which ripen in the soil of love
  To high heroic deeds.

No bars of sect or clime were felt—
  The Babel strife of tongues had ceased,—
And at one common altar knelt
  The Quaker and the priest.

And not in vain: with strength renewed,
  And zeal refreshed, and hope less dim,

For that brief meeting, each pursued
    The path allotted him.

How echoes yet each Western hill
    And vale with Channing's dying word !
How are the hearts of freemen still
    By that great warning stirred!

The stranger treads his native soil,
    And pleads with zeal unfelt before
The honest right of British toil,
    The claim of England's poor.

Before him time-wrought barriers fall,
    Old fears subside, old hatreds melt,
And, stretching o'er the sea's blue wall,
    The Saxon greets the Celt.

The yoeman on the Scottish lines,
    The Sheffield grinder, worn and grim,
The delver in the Cornwall mines,
    Look up with hope to him.

Swart smiters of the glowing steel,
    Dark feeders of the forge's flame,
Pale watchers at the loom and wheel,
    Repeat his honored name.

And thus the influence of that hour
    Of converse on Rhode Island's strand,
Lives in the calm, resistless power
    Which moves our father-land.

God blesses still the generous thought,
    And still the fitting word He speeds,
And Truth, at His requiring taught,
    He quickens into deeds.

Where is the victory of the grave ?
    What dust upon the spirit lies ?
God keeps the sacred life He gave—
    The prophet never dies !

TO THE MEMORY OF CHARLES B. STORRS,

Late President of Western Reserve College.

Thou hast fallen in thine armor,
  Thou martyr of the Lord!
With thy last breath crying—
  "Onward!"
    And thy hand upon the sword.
The haughty heart derideth,
  And the sinful lip reviles,
But the blessing of the perishing
  Around thy pillow smiles!

When to our cup of trembling
  The added drop is given,
And the long suspended thunder
  Falls terribly from Heaven,—
When a new and fearful freedom
  Is proffered of the Lord
To the slow consuming Famine—
  The Pestilence and Sword!

When the refuges of Falsehood
  Shall be swept away in wrath,
And the temple shall be shaken,
  With its idol, to the earth,—
Shall not thy words of warning
  Be all remembered then?
And thy now unheeded message
  Burn in the hearts of men?

Oppression's hand may scatter
  Its nettles on thy tomb,
And even Christian bosoms
  Deny thy memory room;
For lying lips shall torture
  Thy mercy into crime,
And the slanderer shall flourish
  As the bay-tree for a time.

But, where the south wind lingers
  On Carolina's pines,
Or, falls the careless sunbeam
  Down Georgia's golden mines,—
Where now beneath his burden
  The toiling slave is driven,—
Where now a tyrant's mockery
  Is offered unto Heaven,—

Where Mammon hath its altars
  Wet o'er with human blood,
And pride and lust debases
  The workmanship of God—
There shall thy praise be spoken,
  Redeemed from Falsehood's ban,
When the fetters shall be broken,
  And the *slave* shall be a *man!*

Joy to thy spirit, brother!
  A thousand hearts are warm—
A thousand kindred bosoms
  Are baring to the storm.
What though red-handed Violence
  With secret Fraud combine,
The wall of fire is round us—
  Our Present Help was thine!

Lo—the waking up of nations,
  From Slavery's fatal sleep—
The murmur of a Universe—
  Deep calling unto Deep!
Joy to thy spirit, brother!
  On every wind of heaven
The onward cheer and summons
  Of Freedom's voice is given!

Glory to God forever!
  Beyond the despot's will
The soul of Freedom liveth
  Imperishable still.
The words which thou hast uttered
  Are of that soul a part,
And the good seed thou hast scattered
  Is springing from the heart.

In the evil days before us,
  And the trials yet to come—
In the shadow of the prison,
  Or the cruel martyrdom—
We will think of thee, O, brother!
  And thy sainted name shall be
In the blessing of the captive,
  And the Anthem of the free.

LINES

On the Death of S. Oliver Torry, Secretary of the Boston Young Men's Anti-Slavery Society

GONE before us, O our brother,
  To the spirit-land!
Vainly look we for another
  In thy place to stand.
Who shall offer youth and beauty
On the wasting shrine
Of a stern and lofty duty,
  With a faith like thine?

Oh! thy gentle smile of greeting
  Who again shall see?
Who amidst the solemn meeting
  Gaze again on thee?—
Who, when peril gathers o'er us,
  Wear so calm a brow?
Who, with evil men before us,
  So serene as thou?

Early hath the spoiler found thee,
  Brother of our love!
Autumn's faded earth around thee,
  And its storms above!
Evermore that turf lie lightly,
  And, with future showers,
O'er thy slumbers fresh and
    brightly
  Blow the summer flowers!

In the locks thy forehead gracing,
  Not a silvery streak;
Nor a line of sorrow's tracing
  On thy fair young cheek;

Eyes of light and lips of roses,
  Such as Hylas wore—
Over all that curtain closes,
  Which shall rise no more!

Will the vigil Love is keeping
  Round that grave of thine,
Mournfully, like Jazer weeping
  Over Sibmah's vine *—
Will the pleasant memories, swell
    ing
  Gentle hearts, of thee,
In the spirit's distant dwelling
  All unheeded be?

If the spirit ever gazes,
  From its journeyings, back;
If the immortal ever traces
  O'er its mortal track;
Wilt thou not, O brother, meet u
  Sometimes on our way,
And, in hours of sadness, greet u
  As a spirit may?

Peace be with thee, O our brother
  In the spirit-land!
Vainly look we for another
  In thy place to stand.
Unto Truth and Freedom giving
  All thy early powers,
Be thy virtues with the living,
  And thy spirit ours!

A LAMENT.

"The parted spirit,
Knoweth it not our sorrow?   Answereth not
Its blessing to our tears?"

THE circle is broken—one seat is forsaken,—
One bud from the tree of our friendship is shaken—
One heart from among us no longer shall thrill
With joy in our gladness, or grief in our ill.

* "O vine of Sibmah! I will weep for thee with the weeping of Jazer!"—*Jeremiah* xlvi
32.

Weep!—lonely and lowly, are slumbering now
The light of her glances, the pride of her brow,
Weep!—sadly and long shall we listen in vain
To hear the soft tones of her welcome again.

Give our tears to the dead! For humanity's claim
From its silence and darkness is ever the same;
The hope of that World whose existence is bliss
May not stifle the tears of the mourners of this.

For, oh! if one glance the freed spirit can throw
On the scene of its troubled probation below,
Than the pride of the marble—the pomp of the dead—
To that glance will be dearer the tears which we shed.

Oh, who can forget the mild light of her smile,
Over lips moved with music and feeling the while—
The eye's deep enchantment, dark, dream-like, and clear,
In the glow of its gladness—the shade of its tears.

And the charm of her features, while over the whole
Played the hues of the heart and the sunshine of soul,—
And the tones of her voice, like the music which seems
Murmured low in our ears by the Angel of dreams!

But holier and dearer our memories hold
Those treasures of feeling, more precious than gold—
The love and the kindness and pity which gave
Fresh flowers for the bridal, green wreaths for the grave!

The heart ever open to Charity's claim,
Unmoved from its purpose by censure and blame,
While vainly alike on her eye and her ear
Fell the scorn of the heartless, the jesting and jeer.

How true to our hearts was that beautiful sleeper!
With smiles for the joyful, with tears for the weeper!—
Yet, evermore prompt, whether mournful or gay,
With warnings in love to the passing astray.

For, though spotless herself, she could sorrow for them
Who sullied with evil the spirit's pure gem;
And a sigh or a tear could the erring reprove,
And the sting of reproof was still tempered by love.

As a cloud of the sunset, slow melting in heaven,
As a star that is lost when the daylight is given,
As a glad dream of slumber, which wakens in bliss,
She hath passed to the world of the holy from this.

DANIEL WHEELER.

[DANIEL WHEELER, a minister of the Society of Friends, and who had labored in the caus
of his Divine Master in Great Britain, Russia, and the islands of the Pacific, died in New York
in the spring of 1840, while on a religious visit to this country.]

OH, dearly loved
And worthy of our love !—No more
Thy aged form shall rise before
The hushed and waiting worshipper,
In meek obedience utterance giving
To words of truth, so fresh and living,
That, even to the inward sense,
They bore unquestioned evidence
Of an anointed Messenger !
Or, bowing down thy silver hair
In reverent awfulness of prayer—
The world, its time and sense, shut out—
The brightness of Faith's holy trance
Gathered upon thy countenance,
As if each lingering cloud of doubt—
The cold, dark shadows resting here
In Time's unluminous atmosphere—
Were lifted by an angel's hand,
And through them on thy spiritual eye
Shone down the blessedness on high,
The glory of the Better Land !

The oak has fallen !
While, meet for no good work, the vine
May yet its worthless branches twine.
Who knoweth not that with thee fell
A great man in our Israel ?
Fallen, while thy loins were girded still,
Thy feet with Zion's dews still wet,
And in thy hand retaining yet
The pilgrim's staff and scallop shell !
Unharmed and safe, where, wild and free,
Across the Neva's cold morass
The breezes from the Frozen Sea
With winter's arrowy keenness pass ;
Or, where the unwarning tropic gale
Smote to the waves thy tattered sail,
Or, where the noon-hour's fervid heat

Against Tahiti's mountains beat ;
The same mysterious hand which gave
Deliverance upon land and wave,
Tempered for thee the blasts which blew
Ladoga's frozen surface o'er,
And blessed for thee the baleful dew
Of evening upon Eimeo's shore,

Beneath this sunny heaven of ours,
Midst our soft airs and opening flowers
  Hath given thee a grave !

His will be done,
Who seeth not as man, whose way
  Is not as ours !—'Tis well with thee !
Nor anxious doubt nor dark dismay
Disquieted thy closing day,
But, evermore, thy soul could say,
  " My Father careth still for me ! "
Called from thy hearth and home—from her,
  The last bud on thy household tree,
The last dear one to minister
  In duty and in love to thee,
From all which nature holdeth dear,
  Feeble with years and worn with pain,
  To seek our distant land again,
Bound in the spirit, yet unknowing
  The things which should befall thee here,
  Whether for labor or for death,
In childlike trust serenely going
  To that last trial of thy faith !

Oh, far away,
Where never shines our Northern star
  On that dark waste which Balboa saw
From Darien's mountains stretching far,
So strange, heaven broad, and lone, that there
With forehead to its damp wind bare
  He bent his mailed knee in awe ;
In many an isle whose coral feet
The surges of that ocean beat,
In thy palm shadows, Oahu,
  And Honolulu's silver bay,
Amidst Owhyhee's hills of blue,
  And Taro-plains of Tooboonai,
Are gentle hearts, which long shall be
Sad as our own at thought of thee,—
Worn sowers of Truth's holy seed,
Whose souls in weariness and need
Were strengthened and refreshed by thine,
For, blessed by our Father's hand,
  Was thy deep love and tender care,
  Thy ministry and fervent prayer—
Grateful as Eschol's clustered vine
To Israel in a weary land !

And they who drew
By thousands round thee, in the hour
  Of prayerful waiting, hushed and deep
  That He who bade the islands keep

Silence before Him, might renew
    Their strength with His unslumbering power,
They too shall mourn that thou art gone,
    That never more thy aged lip
Shall soothe the weak, the erring warn,
Of those who first, rejoicing, heard
Through thee the Gospel's glorious word—
    Seals of thy true apostleship.
And, if the brightest diadem,
    Whose gems of glory purely burn
    Around the ransomed ones in bliss,
Be evermore reserved for them
    Who here, through toil and sorrow, turn
    Many to righteousness.—
May we not think of thee, as wearing
That star-like crown of light, and bearing,
Amidst Heaven's white and blissful band,
The fadeless palm-branch in thy hand ;
    And joining with a seraph's tongue
    In that new song the elders sung,
Ascribing to its blessed Giver
Thanksgiving, love, and praise forever!

        Farewell!
And though the ways of Zion mourn
When her strong ones are called away,
Who like thyself have calmly borne
The heat and burden of the day,
Yet He who slumbereth not nor sleepeth
His ancient watch around us keepeth;
Still sent from His creating hand,
New witnesses for Truth shall stand—
New instruments to sound abroad
The Gospel of a risen Lord ;
    To gather to the fold once more,
The desolate and gone astray,
The scattered of a cloudy day,
    And Zion's broken walls restored!
And, through the travail and the toil
    Of true obedience, minister
Beauty for ashes, and the oil
    Of joy for mourning, unto her!
So shall her holy bounds increase
With walls of praise and gates of peace:
So shall the Vine, which martyr tears
And blood sustained in other years,
    With fresher life be clothed upon ;
And to the world in beauty show.
Like the rose-plant of Jericho,
    And glorious as Lebanon!

DANIEL NEALL.

I.

FRIEND of the Slave, and yet the friend of all;
　　Lover of peace, yet ever foremost, when
　　The need of battling Freedom called for men
To plant the banner on the outer wall;
Gentle and kindly, ever at distress
Melted to more than woman's tenderness,
Yet firm and steadfast, at his duty's post
Fronting the violence of a maddened host,
Like some gray rock from which the waves are tossed!
Knowing his deeds of love, men questioned not
　　The faith of one whose walk and word were right—
Who tranquilly in Life's great task-field wrought
And, side by side with evil, scarcely caught
　　A stain upon his pilgrim garb of white:
Prompt to redress another's wrong, his own
Leaving to Time and Truth and Penitence alone.

II.

Such was our friend.   Formed on the good old plan,
A true and brave and downright honest man!—
He blew no trumpet in the market-place,
Nor in the church with hypocritic face
Supplied with cant the lack of Christian grace;
Loathing pretense, he did with cheerful will
What others talked of while their hands were still:
And, while "Lord, Lord!" the pious tyrants cried,
Who, in the poor, their Master crucified,
His daily prayer, far better understood
In acts than words, was simply DOING GOOD.
So calm, so constant was his rectitude,
That, by his loss alone we know its worth,
And feel how true a man has walked with us on earth.

TO MY FRIEND ON THE DEATH OF HIS SISTER.*

THINE is a grief, the death of which another
　　　　May never know;
Yet, o'er the waters, O, my stricken brother!
　　　　To thee I go.

---

* SOPHIA STURGE, sister of JOSEPH STURGE, of Birmingham, the President of the British Complete Suffrage Association, died in the 6th mo., 1845. She was the colleague, counselor, and ever ready helpmate of her brother in all his vast designs of beneficence. The Birmingham *Pilot* says of her: " Never, perhaps, were the active and passive virtues of the human character more harmoniously and beautifully blended, than in this excellent woman."

I lean my heart unto thee, sadly folding
    Thy hand in mine;
With even the weakness of my soul upholding
    The strength of thine.

I never knew, like thee, the dear departed;
    I stood not by
When, in calm trust, the pure and tranquil-hearted
    Lay down to die.

And on thy ears my words of weak condoling
    Must vainly fall:
The funeral bell which in thy heart is tolling,
    Sounds over all!

I will not mock thee with the poor world's common
    And heartless phrase,
Nor wrong the memory of a sainted woman
    With idle praise.

With silence only as their benediction,
    God's angels come
Where, in the shadow of a great affliction,
    The soul sits dumb!

Yet, would I say what thy own heart approveth:
    Our Father's will,
Calling to Him the dear one whom He loveth,
    Is mercy still.

Not upon thee or thine the solemn angel
    Hath evil wrought:
Her funeral anthem is a glad evangel—
    The good die not!

God calls our loved ones, but we lose not wholly
    What He hath given;
They live on earth, in thought and deed, as truly
    As in His heaven.

And she is with thee; in thy path of trial
    She walketh yet;
Stil with the baptism of thy self-denial
    Her locks are wet.

Up, then, my brother! Lo, the fields of harvest
    Lie white in view!
She lives and loves thee, and the God thou servest
    To both is true.

Thrust in thy sickle!—England's toil-worn peasants
    Thy call abide;
And she thou mourn'st, a pure and holy presence,
    Shall glean beside!

GONE.

ANOTHER hand is beckoning us,
    Another call is given;
And glows once more with Angel-steps
    The path which reaches Heaven.

Our young and gentle friend whose smile
    Made brighter summer hours,
Amid the frosts of autumn time,
    Has left us, with the flowers.

No paling of the cheek of bloom
    Forewarned us of decay;
No shadow from the Silent Land
    Fell around our sister's way.

The light of her young life went down,
    As sinks behind the hill
The glory of a setting star—
    Clear, suddenly, and still.

As pure and sweet, her fair brow seemed—
    Eternal as the sky;
And like the brook's low song, her voice—
    A sound which could not die.

And half we deemed she needed not
    The changing of her sphere,
To give to Heaven a Shining One,
    Who walked an Angel here.

The blessing of her quiet life
    Fell on us like the dew;
And good thoughts, where her footsteps pressed,
    Like fairy blossoms grew.

Sweet promptings unto kindest deeds
    Were in her very look;
We read her face, as one who reads
    A true and holy book,

The measure of a blessed hymn,
    To which our hearts could move;
The breathing of an inward psalm;
    A canticle of love.

We miss her in the place of prayer,
    And by the hearth-fire's light;
We pause beside her door to hear
    Once more her sweet "Good-night!"

There seems a shadow on the day,
   Her smile no longer cheers;
A dimness on the stars of night,
   Like eyes that look through tears.

Alone unto our Father's will
   One thought hath reconciled;
That He whose love exceedeth ours
   Hath taken home His child.

Fold her, oh Father! in thine arms,
   And let her henceforth be
A messenger of love between
   Our human hearts and Thee.

Still let her mild rebuking stand
   Between us and the wrong,
And her dear memory serve to make
   Our faith in Goodness strong.

And grant that she who, trembling, here
   Distrusted all her powers,
May welcome to her holier home
   The well beloved of ours.

TO THE MEMORY OF J. O. ROCKWELL.

THE turf is smooth above him! and this rain
Will moisten the rent roots, and summon back
The perishing life of its green-bladed grass,
And the crush'd flower will lift its head again
Smilingly unto Heaven, as if it kept
No vigil with the dead.

                     Well—it is meet
That the green grass should tremble, and the flowers
Blow wild about his resting-place.   His mind
Was in itself a flower, but half disclosed—
A bud of blessed promise, which the storm
Visited rudely, and the passer by
Smote down in wantonness.—But we may trust
That it hath found a dwelling, where the sun
Of a more holy clime will visit it,
And the pure dews of mercy will descend,
Through Heaven's own atmosphere, upon its head.

   His form is now before me, with no trace
Of death in its fine lineaments, and there
Is a faint crimson on his youthful cheek,
And his free lip is softening with the smile

Which in his eye is kindling.   I can feel
The parting pressure of his hand, and hear
His last " *God bless you !* "—Strange—that he is there
Distinct before me like a breathing thing,
Even when I know that he is with the dead,
And that the damp earth hides him.   I would not
Think of him otherwise—his image lives
Within my memory as he seem'd before
The curse of blighted feeling, and the toil
And fever of an uncongenial strife, had left
Their traces on his aspect.

                Peace to him!
He wrestled nobly with the weariness
And trials of our being—smiling on,
While poison mingled with his springs of life
And wearing a calm brow, while on his heart
Anguish was resting like a hand of fire—
Until at last the agony of thought
Grew insupportable, and madness came
Darkly upon him,—*and the sufferer died !*

Nor died he unlamented!   To his grave
The beautiful and gifted shall go up,
And muse upon the sleeper.   And young lips
Shall murmur in the broken tones of grief—
His own sweet melodies—and if the ear
Of the freed spirit heedeth aught beneath
The brightness of its new inheritance,
It may be joyful to the parted one
To feel that Earth remembers him in love.

THE UNQUIET SLEEPER.

THE Hunter went forth with his dog and gun,
In the earliest glow of the golden sun ;—
The trees of the forest bent over his way,
In the changeful colors of Autumn gay ;
For a frost had fallen the night before
On the quiet greenness which Nature wore.

A bitter frost !—for the night was chill,
And starry dark, and the wind was still,
And so when the sun looked out on the hills,
On the stricken woods and the frosted rills,
The unvaried green of the landscape fled,
And a wild, rich robe was given instead.

We know not whither the Hunter went,
Or how the last of his days was spent ;

For the moon drew nigh—but he came not back,
Weary and faint from his forest track;
And his wife sat down to her frugal board,
Beside the empty seat of her lord.

And the day passed on, and the sun came down
To the hills of the west, like an angel's crown,
The shadows lengthened from wood and hill,
The mist crept up from the meadow-rill,
Till the broad sun sank, and the red light rolled
All over the west, like a wave of gold!

Yet he came not back—though the stars gave forth
Their wizard light to the silent Earth;
And his wife looked out from the lattice dim
In the earnest manner of fear for him;
And his fair-haired child on the door-stone stood
To welcome his father back from the wood!

He came not back!—yet they found him soon,
In the burning light of the morrow's noon,
In the fixed and visionless sleep of death,
Where the red leaves fell at the soft wind's breath;
And the dog, whose step in the chase was fleet,
Crouched silent and sad at the Hunter's feet.

He slept in death;—but his sleep was one
Which his neighbors shuddered to look upon;
For his brow was black, and his open eye
Was red with the sign of agony:
And they thought, as they gazed on his features grim,
That an evil deed had been done on him.

They buried him where his fathers laid,
By the mossy mounds in the graveyard shade,
Yet whispers of doubt passed over the dead,
And beldames muttered while prayers were said;
And the hand of the sexton shook as he pressed
The damp earth down on the Hunter's breast.

The season passed—and the Autumn rain
And the colored forests returned again;
'Twas the very eve that the Hunter died,
The winds wail'd over the bare hillside,
And the wreathing limbs of the forest shook
The red leaves over the swollen brook.

There came a sound on the night-air then,
Like a spirit-shriek, to the homes of men,
And louder and shriller it rose again,
Like the fearful cry of the mad with pain;

And trembled alike the timid and brave,
For they knew that it came from the Hunter's grave!

And every year when Autumn flings
Its beautiful robe on created things,
When Piscataqua's tide is turbid with rain
And Cocheco's woods are yellow again,
That cry is heard from the graveyard earth,
Like the howl of a demon struggling forth!

SONGS OF LABOR

AND OTHER POEMS.

DEDICATION.

I WOULD the gift I offer here
    Might graces from thy favor take,
And, seen through Friendship's atmosphere,
On softened lines and coloring, wear
The unaccustomed light of beauty, for thy sake.

Few leaves of Fancy's spring remain :
    But what I have I give to thee,—
The o'er-sunned bloom of summer's plain,
And paler flowers, the latter rain
Calls from the westering slope of life's autumnal lea.

Above the fallen groves of green,
    Where youth's enchanted forest stood,
The dry and wasting roots between,
A sober after-growth is seen,
As springs the pine where falls the gay-leafed maple wood!

Yet birds will sing, and breezes play
    Their leaf-harps in the sombre-tree;
And through the bleak and wintry day
It keeps its steady green alway,—
So even my after-thoughts may have a charm for thee.

Art's perfect forms no moral need,
    And beauty is its own excuse;*
But for the dull and flowerless weed
Some healing virtue still must plead,
And the rough ore must find its honors in its use.

So haply these, my simple lays
    Of homely toil, may serve to show
The orchard bloom and tasselled maize
That skirt and gladden duty's ways,
The unsung beauty hid life's common things below!

* For the idea of this line, I am indebted to Emerson, in his inimitable sonnet to the Rhodora :—

" If eyes were made for seeing,
Then beauty is its own excuse for being."

Haply from them the toiler, bent
   Above his forge or plough, may gain
A manlier spirit of content,
And feel that life is wisest spent
Where the strong working hand makes strong the working
   brain.

The doom which to the guilty pair
   Without the walls of Eden came,
Transforming sinless ease to care
And rugged toil, no more shall bear
The burden of old crime, or mark of primal shame.

A blessing now—a curse no more;
   Since He, whose name we breathe with awe,
The coarse mechanic vesture wore,—
A poor man toiling with the poor,
In labor, as in prayer, fulfilling the same law.

THE SHIP-BUILDERS.

THE sky is ruddy in the East,
   The earth is gray below,
And, spectral in the river-mist,
   The ship's white timbers show.
Then let the sounds of measured stroke
   And grating saw begin;
The broad-axe to the gnarléd oak,
   The mallet to the pin!

Hark!—roars the bellows, blast on blast
   The sooty smithy jars,
And fire-sparks, rising far and fast,
   Are fading with the stars.
All day for us the smith shall stand
   Beside that flashing forge;
All day for us his heavy hand
   The groaning anvil scourge.

From far-off hills, the panting team
   For us is toiling near;
For us the raftsmen down the stream
   Their island barges steer.
Rings out for us the axeman's stroke
   In forests old and still,—
For us the century-circled oak
   Falls crashing down his hill.

Up—up!—in nobler toil than ours
   No craftsmen bear a part:

We make of nature's giant powers
    The slaves of human Art.
Lay rib to rib and beam to beam,
    And drive the treenails free;
Nor faithless joint nor yawning seam
    Shall tempt the searching sea!

Where'er the keel of our good ship
    The sea's rough field shall plough—
Where'er her tossing spars shall drip
    With salt-spray caught below—
That ship must heed her master's beck,
    Her helm obey his hand,
And seamen tread her reeling deck
    As if they trod the land.

Her oaken ribs the vulture-beak
    Of Northern ice may peel;
The sunken rock and coral peak
    May grate along her keel;
And know we well the painted shell
    We give to wind and wave,
Must float, the sailor's citadel,
    Or sink, the sailor's grave!

Oh!—strike away the bars and blocks,
    And set the good ship free!
Why lingers on these dusty rocks
    The young bride of the sea?
Look! how she moves adown the grooves
    In graceful beauty now!
How lowly on the breast she loves
    Sinks down her virgin prow!

God bless her! wheresoe'er the breeze
    Her snowy wing shall fan,
Aside the frozen Hebrides,
    Or sultry Hindostan!
Where'er, in mart or on the main
    With peaceful flag unfurled,
She helps to wind the silken chain
    Of commerce round the world!

Speed on the ship!—But let her bear
    No merchandise of sin,
No groaning cargo of despair
    Her roomy hold within.
No Lethean drug for Eastern lands,
    Nor poison-draught for ours;
But honest fruits of toiling hands
    And Nature's sun and showers.

Be hers the Prairie's golden grain,
  The Desert's golden sand,
The clustered fruits of sunny Spain,
  The spice of Morning-land!
Her pathway on the open main
  May blessings follow free,
And glad hearts welcome back again
  Her white sails from the sea!

THE SHOEMAKERS.

Ho! workers of the old time styled
  The Gentle Craft of Leather!
Young brothers of the ancient guild,
  Stand forth once more together!
Call out again your long array,
  In the olden merry manner!
Once more, on gay St. Crispin's day,
  Fling out your blazoned banner!

Rap, rap! upon the well worn stone
  How falls the polished hammer!
Rap, rap! the measured sound has grown
  A quick and merry clamor.
Now shape the sole! now deftly curl
  The glossy vamp around it,
And bless the while the bright-eyed girl
  Whose gentle fingers bound it!

For you, along the Spanish main
  A hundred keels are ploughing;
For you, the Indian on the plain
  His lasso-coil is throwing;
For you, deep glens with hemlock dark
  The woodman's fire is lighting;
For you, upon the oak's gray bark
  The woodman's axe is smiting.

For you, from Carolina's pine
  The rosin-gum is stealing;
For you, the dark-eyed Florentine
  Her silken skein is reeling;
For you, the dizzy goat-herd roams
  His rugged Alpine ledges ;
For you, round all her shepherd homes,
  Bloom England's thorny hedges.

The foremost still, by day or night,
  On moated mound or heather,
Where'er the need of trampled right
  Brought toiling men together;

Where the free burghers from the wall
    Defied the mail-clad master,
Than yours, at Freedom's trumpet-call,
    No craftsmen rallied faster.

Let foplings sneer, let fools deride—
    Ye heed no idle scorner;
Free hands and hearts are still your pride,
    And duty done, your honor.
Ye dare to trust, for honest fame,
    The jury Time empanels,
And leave to truth each noble name
    Which glorifies your annals.

Thy songs, Hans Sachs, are living yet,
    In strong and hearty German;
And Bloomfield's lay, and Gifford's wit,
    And patriot fame of Sherman;
Still from his book, a mystic seer,
    The soul of Behmen teaches,
And England's priestcraft shakes to hear
    Of Fox's leathern breeches.

The foot is yours; where'er it falls,
    It treads your well-wrought leather,
On earthen floor, in marble halls,
    On carpet, or on heather.
Still there the sweetest charm is found
    Of matron grace or vestal's,
As Hebe's foot bore nectar round
    Among the old celestials!

Rap! rap!—your stout and bluff brogan,
    With footsteps slow and weary,
May wander where the sky's blue span
    Shuts down upon the prairie.
On Beauty's foot, your slippers glance,
    By Saratoga's fountains,
Or twinkle down the summer dance
    Beneath the Crystal Mountains!

The red brick to the mason's hand,
    The brown earth to the tiller's,
The shoe in yours shall wealth command,
    Like fairy Cinderella's!
As they who shunned the household maid
    Beheld the crown upon her,
So all shall see your toil repaid
    With hearth and home and honor.

Then let the toast be freely quaffed,
    In water cool and brimming—

" All honor to the good old Craft,
  Its merry men and women ! "
Call out again your long array,
  In the old time's pleasant manner;
Once more, on gay St. Crispin's day,
  Fling out his blazoned banner!

THE DROVERS.

THROUGH heat and cold, and shower and sun
  Still onward cheerly driving!
There's life alone in duty done,
  And rest alone in striving.
But see! the day is closing cool,
  The woods are dim before us;
The white fog of the wayside pool
  Is creeping slowly o'er us.

The night is falling, comrades mine,
  Our foot-sore beasts are weary,
And through yon elms the tavern sign
  Looks out upon us cheery.
The landlord beckons from his door,
  His beechen fire is glowing;
These ample barns, with feed in store,
  Are filled to overflowing.

From many a valley frowned across
  By brows of rugged mountains;
From hillsides where, through spongy moss,
  Gush out the river fountains;
From quiet farm-fields, green and low,
  And bright with blooming clover;
From vales of corn the wandering crow
  No richer hovers over;

Day after day our way has been,
  O'er many a hill and hollow;
By lake and stream, by wood and glen,
  Our stately drove we follow.
Through dust-clouds rising thick and dun,
  As smoke and battle o'er us,
Their white horns glisten in the sun,
  Like plumes and crests before us.

We see them slowly climb the hill,
  As slow behind it sinking;
Or, thronging close, from roadside rill,
  Or sunny lakelet, drinking.

Now crowding in the narrow road,
  In thick and struggling masses,
They glare upon the teamster's load,
  Or rattling coach that passes.

Anon, with toss of horn and tail,
  And paw of hoof, and bellow,
They leap some farmer's broken pale,
  O'er meadow-close or fallow.
Forth comes the startled good-man; forth
  Wife, children, house-dog, sally,
Till once more on their dusty path
  The baffled truants rally.

We drive no starvelings, scraggy grown,
  Loose-legged, and ribbed and bony,
Like those who grind their noses down
  On pastures bare and stony—
Lank oxen, rough as Indian dogs,
  And cows too lean for shadows,
Disputing feebly with the frogs
  The crop of saw-grass meadows!

In our good drove, so sleek and fair,
  No bones of leanness rattle;
No tottering hide-bound ghosts are there,
  Or Pharaoh's evil cattle.
Each stately beeve bespeaks the hand
  That fed him unrepining;
The fatness of a goodly land
  In each dun hide is shining.

We've sought them where, in warmest nooks,
  The freshest feed is growing,
By sweetest springs and clearest brooks
  Through honeysuckle flowing:
Wherever hillsides, sloping south,
  Are bright with early grasses,
Or, tracking green the lowland's drouth,
  The mountain streamlet passes.

But now the day is closing cool,
  The woods are dim before us,
The white fog of the wayside pool
  Is creeping slowly o'er us.
The cricket to the frog's bassoon
  His shrillest time is keeping;
The sickle of yon setting moon
  The meadow-mist is reaping.

The night is falling, comrades mine,
  Our foot-sore beasts are weary,

And through yon elms the tavern sign
   Looks out upon us cheery.
To-morrow, eastward with our charge
   We'll go to meet the dawning,
Ere yet the pines of Kéarsarge
   Have seen the sun of morning.

When snow-flakes o'er the frozen earth.
   Instead of birds, are flitting;
When children throng the glowing hearth,
   And quiet wives are knitting;
While in the fire-light strong and clear
   Young eyes of pleasure glisten,
To tales of all we see and hear
   The ears of home shall listen.

By many a Northern lake and hill,
   From many a mountain pasture,
Shall Fancy play the Drover still,
   And speed the long night faster.
Then let us on, through shower and sun,
   And heat and cold, be driving;
There's life alone in duty done,
   And rest alone in striving.

THE FISHERMEN.

Hurrah! the seaward breezes
   Sweep down the bay amain;
Heave up, my lads, the anchor!
   Run up the sail again!
Leave to the lubber landsmen
   The rail-car and the steed;
The stars of heaven shall guide us,
   The breath of heaven shall speed.

From the hill-top looks the steeple,
   And the lighthouse from the sand;
And the scattered pines are waving
   Their farewell from the land.
One glance, my lads, behind us,
   For the homes we leave one sigh,
Ere we take the change and chances
   Of the ocean and the sky.

Now brothers, for the icebergs
   Of frozen Labrador,
Floating spectral in the moonshine,
   Along the low, black shore!

Where like snow the gannet's feathers
  Of Brador's rocks are shed,
And the noisy murr are flying,
  Like black scuds, overhead;

Where in mist the rock is hiding,
  And the sharp reef lurks below,
And the white squall smites in summer,
  And the autumn tempests blow;
Where, through gray and rolling vapor,
  From evening unto morn,
A thousand boats are hailing,
  Horn answering unto horn.

Hurrah! for the Red Island,
  With the white cross on its crown!
Hurrah! for Meccatina,
  And its mountains bare and brown!
Where the Caribou's tall antlers
  O'er the dwarf-wood freely toss,
And the footstep of the Mickmack
  Has no sound upon the moss.

There we'll drop our lines, and gather
  Old Ocean's treasures in,
Where'er the mottled mackerel
  Turns up a steel-dark fin.
The sea's our field of harvest,
  Its scaly tribes our grain;
We'll reap the teeming waters
  As at home they reap the plain!

Our wet hands spread the carpet,
  And light the hearth of home;
From our fish, as in the old time,
  The silver coin shall come.
As the demon fled the chamber
  Where the fish of Tobit lay,
So ours from all our dwellings
  Shall frighten Want away.

Though the mist upon our jackets
  In the bitter air congeals,
And our lines wined stiff and slowly
  From off the frozen reels;
Though the fog be dark around us,
  And the storm blow high and loud,
We will whistle down the wild wind,
  And laugh beneath the cloud!

In the darkness as in daylight,
  On the water as on land,

God's eye is looking on us,
 And beneath us is his hand!
Death will find us soon or later,
 On the deck or in the cot;
And we cannot meet him better
 Than in working out our lot.

Hurrah!—hurrah!—the west wind
 Comes freshening down the bay,
The rising sails are filling—
 Give way, my lads, give way!
Leave the coward landsman clinging
 To the dull earth, like a weed—
The stars of heaven shall guide us,
 The breath of heaven shall speed!

THE HUSKERS.

It was late in mild October, and the long autumnal rain
Had left the summer harvest-fields all green with grass again;
The first sharp frosts had fallen, leaving all the woodlands gay
With the hues of summer's rainbow, or the meadow-flowers of May.

Through a thin, dry mist, that morning, the sun rose broad and red,
At first a rayless disc of fire, he brightened as he sped;
Yet, even his noontide glory fell chastened and subdued,
On the corn-fields and the orchards, and softly pictured wood.

And all that quiet afternoon, slow sloping to the night,
He wove with golden shuttle the haze with yellow light;
Slanting through the painted beeches, he glorified the hill;
And, beneath it, pond and meadow lay brighter, greener still.

And shouting boys in woodland haunts caught glimpses of that sky,
Flecked by the many-tinted leaves, and laughed, they knew not why;
And schoolgirls, gay with aster-flowers, beside the meadow brooks,
Mingled the glow of autumn with the sunshine of sweet looks.

From spire and barn, looked westerly the patient weather-cocks;
But even the birches on the hill stood motionless as rocks.
No sound was in the woodlands, save the squirrel's dropping shell,
And the yellow leaves among the boughs, low rustling as they fell

The summer grains were harvested; the stubble-fields lay dry,
Where June winds rolled, in light and shade, the pale-green waves of rye;
But still, on gentle hill-slopes, in valleys fringed with wood,
Ungathered, bleaching in the sun, the heavy corn crop stood.

Bent low, by autumn's wind and rain, through husks that, dry and sere,
Unfolded from their ripened charge, shone out the yellow ear;
Beneath, the turnip lay concealed, in many a verdant fold,
And glistened in the slanting light the pumpkin's sphere of gold.

There wrought the busy harvesters; and many a creaking wain
Bore slowly to the long barn-floor its load of husk and grain;
Till broad and red, as when he rose, the sun sank down, at last,
And like a merry guest's farewell, the day in brightness passed.

And lo! as through the western pines, on meadow, stream and pond,
Flamed the red radiance of a sky, set all afire beyond,
Slowly o'er the Eastern sea-bluffs a milder glory shone,
And the sunset and the moonrise were mingled into one!

As thus into the quiet night the twilight lapsed away,
And deeper in the brightening moon the tranquil shadows lay;
From many a brown old farmhouse, and hamlet without name,
Their milking and their home-tasks done, the merry huskers came.

Swung o'er the heaped-up harvest, from pitchforks in the mow,
Shone dimly down the lanterns on the pleasant scene below;
The growing pile of husks behind, the golden ears before,
And laughing eyes and busy hands and brown cheeks glimmering o'er.

Half hidden in a quiet nook, serene of look and heart,
Talking their old times over, the old men sat apart;
While, up and down the unhusked pile, or nestling in its shade,
At hide-and-seek, with laugh and shout, the happy children played.

Urged by the good host's daughter, a maiden young and fair,
Lifting to light her sweet blue eyes and pride of soft brown hair,
The master of the village school, sleek of hair and smooth of tongue,
To the quaint tune of some old psalm, a husking-ballad sung.

THE CORN SONG.

HEAP high the farmer's wintry hoard!
    Heap high the golden corn!
No richer gift has Autumn poured
    From out her lavish horn!

Let other lands, exulting, glean
    The apple from the pine,
The orange from its glossy green,
    The cluster from the vine;

We better love the hardy gift
    Our rugged vales bestow,
To cheer us when the storm shall drift
    Our harvest-fields with snow.

Through vales of grass and meads of flowers,
   Our ploughs their furrows made,
While on the hills the sun and showers
   Of changeful April played.

We dropped the seed o'er hill and plain,
   Beneath the sun of May,
And frightened from our sprouting grain
   The robber crows away.

All through the long, bright days of June,
   Its leaves grew green and fair,
And waved in hot midsummer's noon
   Its soft and yellow hair.

And now, with Autumn's moonlit eves,
   Its harvest time has come,
We pluck away the frosted leaves,
   And bear the treasure home.

There, richer than the fabled gift
   Apollo showered of old,
Fair hands the broken grain shall sift,
   And knead its meal of gold.

Let vapid idlers loll in silk,
   Around their costly board;
Give us the bowl of samp and milk,
   By homespun beauty poured!

Where'er the wide old kitchen hearth
   Sends up its smoky curls,
Who will not thank the kindly earth,
   And bless our farmer girls!

Then shame on all the proud and vain,
   Whose folly laughs to scorn
The blessing of our hardy grain,
   Our wealth of golden corn!

Let earth withhold her goodly root,
   Let mildew blight the rye,
Give to the worm the orchard's fruit,
   The wheat-field to the fly:

But let the good old crop adorn
   The hills our fathers trod;
Still let us, for his golden corn,
   Send up our thanks to God!

THE LUMBERMEN.

WILDLY round our woodland quarters,
　　Sad-voiced Autumn grieves;
Thickly down these swelling waters
　　Float his fallen leaves.

Through the tall and naked timber,
　　Column-like and old,
Gleam the sunsets of November,
　　From their skies of gold.

O'er us, to the southland heading,
　　Screams the gray wild-goose;
On the night-frost sounds the treading
　　Of the brindled moose.
Noiseless creeping, while we're sleeping,
　　Frost his task-work plies;
Soon, his icy bridges heaping,
　　Shall our log-piles rise.

When, with sounds of smothered thunder,
　　On some night of rain,
Lake and river break asunder
　　Winter's weakened chain,
Down the wild March flood shall bear them
　　To the saw-mill's wheel,
Or where Steam, the slave, shall tear them
　　With his teeth of steel.

Be it starlight, be it moonlight,
　　In these vales below,
When the earliest beams of sunlight
　　Streak the mountain's snow,
Crisps the hoar-frost, keen and early,
　　To our hurrying feet,
And the forest echoes clearly
　　All our blows repeat.

Where the crystal Ambijejis
　　Stretches broad and clear,
And Millnoket's pine-black ridge
　　Hide the browsing deer:
Where, through lakes and wide morasses,
　　Or through rocky walls,
Swift and strong, Penobscot passes
　　White with foamy falls;

Where, through clouds, are glimpses given
　　Of Katahdin's sides, —

Rock and forest piled to heaven,
　　Torn and ploughed by slides!
Far below, the Indian trapping,
　　In the sunshine warm;
Far above, the snow-cloud wrapping
　　Half the peak in storm!

Where are mossy carpets better
　　Than the Persian weaves,
And than Eastern perfumes sweeter
　　Seem the fading leaves;
And a music wild and solemn,
　　From the pine-tree's height,
Rolls its vast and sea-like volume
　　On the wind of night;

Make we here our camp of winter;
　　And, through sleet and snow,
Pitchy knot and beechen splinter
　　On our hearth shall glow.
Here, with mirth to lighten duty,
　　We shall lack alone
Woman's smile and girlhood's beauty,
　　Childhood's lisping tone.

But their hearth is brighter burning
　　For our toil to-day;
And the welcome of returning
　　Shall our loss repay,
When, like seamen from the waters,
　　From the woods we come,
Greeting sisters, wives, and daughters,
　　Angels of our home!

Not for us the measured ringing
　　From the village spire,
Not for us the Sabbath singing
　　Of the sweet-voiced choir:
Ours the old, majestic temple,
　　Where God's brightness shines
Down the dome so grand and ample,
　　Propped by lofty pines!

Through each branch-enwoven skylight,
　　Speaks He in the breeze,
As of old beneath the twilight
　　Of lost Eden's trees!
For his ear, the inward feeling
　　Needs no outward tongue;
He can see the spirit kneeling
　　While the axe is swung.

Heeding truth alone, and turning
   From the false and dim,
Lamp of toil or altar burning
   Are alike to Him.
Strike, then, comrades!—Trade is waiting
   On our rugged toil;
Far ships waiting for the freighting
   Of our woodland spoil!

Ships, whose traffic links these highlands,
   Bleak and cold, of ours,
With the citron planted islands
   Of a clime of flowers;
To our frosts the tribute bringing
   Of eternal heats;
In our lap of winter flinging
   Tropic fruits and sweets,

Cheerily, on the axe of labor,
   Let the sunbeams dance,
Better than the flash of sabre
   Or the gleam of lance!
Strike!—With every blow is given
   Freer sun and sky,
And the long-hid earth to heaven
   Looks, with wondering eye!

Loud behind us grow the murmurs
   Of the age to come;
Clang of smiths, and tread of farmers,
   Bearing harvest-home!
Here her virgin lap with treasures
   Shall the green earth fill;
Waving wheat and golden maize-ears
   Crown each beechen hill.

Keep who will the city's alleys,
   Take the smooth-shorn plain,—
Give to us the cedar valleys,
   Rocks and hills of Maine!
In our North-land, wild and woody,
   Let us still have part;
Rugged nurse and mother sturdy,
   Hold us to thy heart!

O! our free hearts beat the warmer
   For thy breath of snow;
And our tread is all the firmer
   For thy rocks below.
Freedom, hand in hand with labor,
   Walketh strong and brave;

On the forehead of his neighbor
No man writeth Slave!

Lo, the day breaks! old Katahdin's
Pine-trees show its fires,
While from these dim forest gardens
Rise their blackened spires.
Up, my comrades! up and doing!
Manhood's rugged play
Still renewing, bravely hewing
Through the world our way?

MISCELLANEOUS.

THE LAKE-SIDE.

THE shadows round the inland sea
  Are deepening into night;
Slow, up the slopes of Ossipee,
  They chase the lessening light.
Tired of the long day's blinding heat,
  I rest my languid eye,
Lake of the Hills! where, cool and sweet,
  Thy sunset waters lie!

Along the sky, in wavy lines,
  O'er isle and reach and bay,
Green-belted with eternal pines,
  The mountains stretch away.
Below, the maple masses sleep
  Where shore with water blends,
While midway on the tranquil deep
  The evening light descends.

So seemed it when yon hill's red crown,
  Of old, the Indian trod,
And, through the sunset air, looked down
  Upon the Smile of God.*
To him of light and shade the laws
  No forest sceptic taught;
Their living and eternal Cause
  His truer instinct sought.

He saw these mountains in the light
  Which now across them shines;
This lake, in summer sunset bright,
  Walled round with sombering pines.
God near him seemed; from earth and skies
  His loving voice he heard,
As, face to face in Paradise,
  Man stood before the Lord.

Thanks, oh, our Father! that, like him,
  Thy tender love I see,

* Winnipiseogee : "Smile of the Great Spirit."

286

In radiant hill and woodland dim,
　　And tinted sunset sea.
For not in mockery dost Thou fill
　　Our earth with light and grace;
Thou hid'st no dark and cruel will
　　Behind Thy smiling face!

THE HILL-TOP.

THE burly driver at my side,
　　We slowly climbed the hill,
Whose summit, in the hot noontide,
　　Seemed rising, rising still.
At last, our short noon-shadows hid
　　The top-stone, bare and brown,
From whence, like Gizeh's pyramid,
　　The rough mass slanted down.

I felt the cool breath of the North;
　　Between me and the sun,
O'er deep, still lake, and ridgy earth,
　　I saw the cloud-shades run.
Before me, stretched for glistening miles,
　　Lay mountain-girdled Squam;
Like green-winged birds, the leafy isles
　　Upon its bosom swam.

And, glimmering through the sun-haze warm,
　　Far as the eye could roam,
Dark billows of an earthquake storm
　　Beflecked with clouds like foam,
Their vales in misty shadow deep,
　　Their rugged peaks in shine,
I saw the mountain ranges sweep
　　The horizon's northern line.

There towered Chocorua's peak ; and west,
　　Moosehillock's woods were seen,
With many a nameless slide-scarred crest
　　And pine-dark gorge between.
Beyond them, like a sun-rimmed cloud,
　　The great Notch mountains shone,
Watched over by the solemn-browed,
　　And awful face of stone!

"A good look-off!" the driver spake:
　　"About this time, last year,
I drove a party to the Lake,
　　And stopped, at evening, here.

'Twas duskish down below; but all
   These hills stood in the sun,
Till, dipped behind yon purple wall,
   He left them, one by one.

" A lady, who, from Thornton hill,
   Had held her place outside,
And, as a pleasant woman will,
   Had cheered the long, dull ride,
Besought me, with so sweet a smile,
   That—though I hate delays—
I could not choose but rest awhile—
   (These women have such ways!)

" On yonder mossy ledge she sat,
   Her sketch upon her knees,
A stray brown lock beneath her hat
   Unrolling in the breeze;
Her sweet face, in the sunset light
   Upraised and glorified,—
I never saw a prettier sight
   In all my mountain ride.

" As good as fair; it seemed her joy
   To comfort and to give;
My poor, sick wife, and crippled boy,
   Will bless her while they live!"
The tremor in the driver's tone
   His manhood did not shame:
"I dare say, sir, you may have known—"
   He named a well-known name.

Then sank the pyramidal mounds,
   The blue lake fled away;
For mountain-scope a parlor's bounds,
   A lighted hearth for day!
From lonely years and weary miles
   The shadows fell apart;
Kind voices cheered, sweet human smiles
   Shone warm into my heart.

We journeyed on; but earth and sky
   Had power to charm no more;
Still dreamed my inward-turning eye
   The dream of memory o'er.
Ah! human kindness, human love—
   To few who seek denied—
Too late we learn to prize above
   The whole round world beside!

ON RECEIVING AN EAGLE'S QUILL FROM LAKE SUPERIOR.

ALL day the darkness and the cold
  Upon my heart have lain,
Like shadows on the winter sky,
  Like frost upon the pane;

But now my torpid fancy wakes,
  And, on thy Eagle's plume,
Rides forth, like Sinbad on his bird,
  Or witch upon her broom!

Below me roar the rocking pines,
  Before me spreads the lake,
Whose long and solemn-sounding waves
  Against the sunset break.

I hear the wild Rice-Eater thresh
  The grain he has not sown;
I see, with flashing scythe of fire,
  The prairie harvest mown!

I hear the far-off voyager's horn;
  I see the Yankee's trail—
His foot on every mountain-pass,
  On every stream his sail.

By forest, lake and water-fall,
  I see his pedler show;
The mighty mingling with the mean,
  The lofty with the low.

He's whittling by St. Mary's Falls,
  Upon his loaded wain;
He's measuring o'er the Pictured Rocks,
  With eager eyes of gain.

I hear the mattock in the mine,
  The axe-stroke in the dell,
The clamor from the Indian lodge,
  The Jesuit chapel bell!

I see the swarthy trappers come
  From Mississippi's springs;
And war-chiefs with their painted brows,
  And crests of eagle wings.

Behind the scared squaw's birch canoe,
  The steamer smokes and raves;

And city lots are staked for sale
   Above old Indian graves.

I hear the tread of pioneer,
   Of nations yet to be;
The first low wash of waves, where soon
   Shall roll a human sea.

The rudiments of empire here
   Are plastic yet and warm ;
The chaos of a mighty world
   Is rounded into form!

Each rude and jostling fragment soon
   Its fitting place shall find—
The raw material of a State,
   Its muscle and its mind!

And, westering still, the star which leads
   The New World in its train
Has tipped with fire the icy spears
   Of many a mountain chain.

The snowy cones of Oregon
   Are kindling on its way ;
And California's golden sands
   Gleam brighter in its ray!

Then, blessings on thy eagle quill,
   As, wandering far and wide,
I thank thee for this twilight dream
   And Fancy's airy ride!

Yet, welcomer than regal plumes,
   Which Western trappers find,
Thy free and pleasant thoughts, chance-sown,
   Like feathers on the wind.

Thy symbol be the mountain-bird,
   Whose glistening quill I hold ;
Thy home the ample air of hope,
   And memory's sunset gold !

In thee, let joy with duty join,
   And strength unite with love,
The eagle's pinions folding round
   The warm heart of the dove !

So, when in darkness sleeps the vale
   Where still the blind bird clings,
The sunshine of the upper sky
   Shall glitter on thy wings !

MEMORIES.

A BEAUTIFUL and happy girl,
 With step as light as summer air,
Eyes glad with smiles, and brow of pearl,
Shadowed by many a careless curl
 Of unconfined and flowing hair ;
A seeming child in everything,
 Save thoughtful brow and ripening charms,
As Nature wears the smile of Spring
 When sinking into Summer's arms.

A mind rejoicing in the light
 Which melted through its graceful bower,
Leaf after leaf, dew-moist and bright,
And stainless in its holy white,
 Unfolding like a morning flower:
A heart, which, like a fine-toned lute,
 With every breath of feeling woke,
And, even when the tongue was mute,
 From eye and lip in music spoke.

How thrills once more the lengthening chain
 Of memory, at the thought of thee !
Old hopes which long in dust have lain
Old dreams, come thronging back again,
 And boyhood lives again in me;
I feel its glow upon my cheek,
 Its fulness of the heart is mine,
As when I leaned to hear thee speak,
 Or raised my doubtful eye to thine.

I hear again thy low replies,
 I feel thy arm within my own,
And timidly again uprise
The fringéd lids of hazel eyes,
 With soft brown tresses overblown.
Ah ! memories of sweet summer eves,
 Of moonlit wave and willowy way,
Of stars and flowers, and dewy leaves,
 And smiles and tones more dear than they ?

Ere this, thy quiet eye has smiled
 My picture of thy youth to see,
When, half a woman, half a child,
Thy very artlessness beguiled,
 And folly's self seemed wise in thee;
I too can smile, when o'er that hour
 The lights of memory backward stream,
Yet feel the while that manhood's power
 Is vainer than my boyhood's dream.

Years have passed on, and left their trace
   Of graver care and deeper thought;
And unto me the calm, cold face
Of manhood, and to thee the grace
   Of woman's pensive beauty brought.
More wide, perchance, for blame than praise,
   The schoolboy's humble name has flown;
Thine, in the green and quiet ways
   Of unobtrusive goodness known.

And wider yet in thought and deed
   Diverge our pathways, one in youth;
Thine the Genevan's sternest creed,
While answers to my spirit's need
   The Derby dalesman's simple truth.
For thee, the priestly rite and prayer,
   And holy day, and solemn psalm;
For me, the silent reverence where
   My brethren gather, slow and calm.

Yet hath thy spirit left on me
   An impress Time has worn not out,
And something of myself in thee,
A shadow from the past, I see,
   Lingering, even yet, thy way about;
Not wholly can the heart unlearn
   That lesson of its better hours,
Not yet has Time's dull footstep worn
   To common dust that path of flowers.

Thus, while at times before our eyes
   The shadows melt, and fall apart,
And, smiling through them, round us lies
The warm light of our morning skies—
   The Indian Summer of the heart!—
In secret sympathies of mind,
   In founts of feeling which retain
Their pure, fresh flow, we yet may find
   Our early dreams not wholly vain!

THE LEGEND OF ST. MARK.*

THE day is closing dark and cold,
   With roaring blast and sleety showers;
And through the dusk the lilacs wear
   The bloom of snow, instead of flowers.

* This legend is the subject of a celebrated picture by Tintoretto, of which Mr. Rogers possesses the original sketch. The slave lies on the ground, amid a crowd of spectators, who look on, animated by all the various emotions of sympathy, rage, terror; a woman, in front, with a child in her arms, has always been admired for the lifelike vivacity of her attitude and expression. The executioner holds up the broken implements; St. Mark, with a headlong movement, seems to rush down from heaven in haste to save his worshiper. The dramatic grouping in this picture is wonderful; the coloring, in its gorgeous depth and harmony, is, in Mr. Rogers's sketch, finer than in the picture.—*Mrs. Jamieson's Poetry of Sacred and Legendary Art*, vol. i. p. 121.

I turn me from the gloom without,
  To ponder o'er a tale of old,
A legend of the age of Faith,
  By dreaming monk or abbess told.

On Tintoretto's canvas lives
  That fancy of a loving heart,
In graceful lines and shapes of power,
  And hues immortal as his art.

In Provence (so the story runs)
  There lived a lord, to whom, as slave,
A peasant boy of tender years
  The chance of trade or conquest gave.

Forth-looking from the castle tower,
  Beyond the hills with almonds dark,
The straining eye could scarce discern
  The chapel of the good St. Mark.

And there, when bitter word or fare
  The service of the youth repaid,
By stealth, before that holy shrine,
  For grace to bear his wrong, he prayed.

The steed stamped at the castle gate,
  The boar-hunt sounded on the hill;
Why stayed the Baron from the chase,
  With looks so stern, and words so ill?

" Go, bind yon slave! and let him learn,
  By scathe of fire and strain of cord,
How ill they speed who give dead saints
  The homage due their living lord!"

They bound him on the fearful rack,
  When, through the dungeon's vaulted dark,
He saw the light of shining robes,
  And knew the face of good St. Mark.

Then sank the iron rack apart,
  The cords released their cruel clasp,
The pincers, with their teeth of fire,
  Fell broken from the torturer's grasp.

And lo! before the Youth and Saint,
  Barred door and wall of stone gave way;
And up from bondage and the night
  They passed to freedom and the day!

O, dreaming monk! thy tale is true;—
  O, painter! true thy pencil's art;

In tones of hope and prophecy,
  Ye whisper to my listening heart!

Unheard no burdened heart's appeal
  Moans up to God's inclining ear;
Unheeded by his tender eye,
  Falls to the earth no sufferer's tear.

For still the Lord alone is God!
  The pomp and power of tyrant man
Are scattered at his lightest breath,
  Like chaff before the winnower's fan.

Not always shall the slave uplift
  His heavy hands to Heaven in vain;
God's angel, like the good St. Mark,
  Comes shining down to break his chain!

O, weary ones! ye may not see
  Your helpers in their downward flight;
Nor hear the sound of silver wings
  Slow beating through the hush of night!

But not the less gray Dothan shone,
  With sunbright watches bending low,
That Fear's dim eye beheld alone
  The spear-heads of the Syrian foe.

There are, who, like the Seer of old,
  Can see the helpers God has sent,
And how life's rugged mountain-side
  Is white with many an angel tent!

They hear the heralds whom our Lord
  Sends down his pathway to prepare ;
And light, from others hidden, shines
  On their high place of faith and prayer.

Let such, for earth's despairing ones,
  Hopeless, yet longing to be free,
Breathe once again the Prophet's prayer :
  "Lord, ope their eyes, that they may see!"

THE WELL OF LOCH MAREE.*

CALM on the breast of Loch Maree
   A little isle reposes;
A shadow woven of the oak
   And willow o'er it closes.

Within, a Druid's mound is seen,
   Set round with stony warders;
A fountain, gushing through the turf,
   Flows o'er its grassy borders.

And whoso bathes therein his brow,
   With care or madness burning,
Feels once again his healthful thought
   And sense of peace returning.

O ! restless heart and fevered brain,
   Unquiet and unstable,
That holy well of Loch Maree
   Is more than idle fable !

Life's changes vex, its discords stun,
   Its glaring sunshine blindeth,
And blest is he who on his way
   That fount of healing findeth !

The shadows of a humbled will
   And contrite heart are o'er it:
Go, read its legend—" TRUST IN GOD "—
   On Faith's white stones before it.

TO MY SISTER:

WITH A COPY OF " SUPERNATURALISM IN NEW ENGLAND."

DEAR SISTER !—while the wise and sage
Turn coldly from my playful page,
And count it strange that ripened age
   Should stoop to boyhood's folly;
I know that thou wilt judge aright
Of all which makes the heart more light,
Or lends one star-gleam to the night
   Of clouded Melancholy.

Away with the weary cares and themes !—
Swing wide the moonlit gate of dreams !

* Pennant, in his "Voyage to the Hebrides," describes the holy well of Loch Maree, the waters of which were supposed to effect a miraculous cure of melancholy, trouble, and insanity.

Leave free once more the land which teems
   With wonders and romances!
Where thou, with clear discerning eyes,
Shalt rightly read the truth which lies
Beneath the quaintly masking guise
   Of wild and wizard fancies.

Lo! once again our feet we set
On still green wood-paths, twilight wet,
By lonely brooks, whose waters fret
   The roots of spectral beeches;
Again the hearth-fire glimmers o'er
Home's whitewashed wall and painted floor,
And young eyes widening to the lore
   Of faëry-folks and witches.

Dear heart!—the legend is not vain
Which lights that holy hearth again,
And, calling back from care and pain,
   And death's funereal sadness,
Draws round its old familiar blaze
The clustering groups of happier days,
And lends to sober manhood's gaze
   A glimpse of childish gladness.

And, knowing how my life hath been
A weary work of tongue and pen,
A long, harsh strife, with strong-willed men
   Thou wilt not chide my turning,
To con, at times, an idle rhyme,
To pluck a flower from childhood's clime,
Or listen, at Life's noonday chime,
   For the sweet bells of Morning!

AUTUMN THOUGHTS.

From "Margaret Smith's Journal."

Gone hath the Spring, with all its flowers,
   And gone the Summer's pomp and show,
And Autumn, in his leafless bowers,
   Is waiting for the Winter's snow.

I said to Earth, so cold and gray,
   "An emblem of myself thou art:"
"Not so," the Earth did seem to say,
   "For Spring shall warm my frozen heart."

I soothe my wintry sleep with dreams
   Of warmer sun and softer rain,

And wait to hear the sound of streams
  And songs of merry birds again.

But thou, from whom the Spring hath gone,
  For whom the flowers no longer blow,
Who standest blighted and forlorn,
  Like Autumn waiting for the snow:

No hope is thine of sunnier hours,
  Thy Winter shall no more depart;
No Spring revive thy wasted flowers,
  Nor Summer warm thy frozen heart.

CALEF IN BOSTON, 1692.

In the solemn days of old,
  Two men met in Boston town—
One a tradesman frank and bold,
  One a preacher of renown.

Cried the last, in bitter tone—
  "Poisoner of the wells of truth!
Satan's hireling, thou hast sown
  With his tares the heart of youth!"

Spake the simple tradesman then—
  "God be judge 'twixt thou and I;
All thou knowest of truth hath been
  Unto men like thee a lie.

"Falsehoods which we spurn to-day
  Were the truths of long ago;
Let the dead boughs fall away,
  Fresher shall the living grow.

"God is good and God is light.
  In this faith I rest secure;
Evil can but serve the right,
  Over all shall love endure.

"Of your spectral puppet play
  I have traced the cunning wires;
Come what will, I needs must say,
  God is true, and ye are liars."

When the thought of man is free,
  Error fears its lightest tones;
So the priest cried, "Sadducee!"
  And the people took up stones.

In the ancient burying-ground,
   Side by side the twain now lie—
One with humble grassy mound,
   One with marbles pale and high.

But the Lord hath blest the seed
   Which that tradesman scattered then.
And the preacher's spectral creed
   Chills no more the blood of men.

Let us trust, to one is known
   Perfect love which casts out fear,
While the other's joys atone
   For the wrong he suffered here.

TO PIUS IX.*

THE cannon's brazen lips are cold;
   No red shell blazes down the air;
And street and tower, and temple old,
   Are silent as despair.

The Lombard stands no more at bay—
   Rome's fresh young life has bled in vain;
The ravens scattered by the day
   Come back with night again.

Now, while the fratricides of France
   Are treading on the neck of Rome,
Hider at Gaeta—seize thy chance!
   Coward and cruel, come!

Creep now from Naples' bloody skirt;
   Thy mummer's part was acted well,
While Rome, with steel and fire begirt,
   Before thy crusade fell!

Her death-groans answered to thy prayer;
   Thy chant, the drum and bugle-call;
Thy lights, the burning villa's glare;
   Thy beads, the shell and ball!

Let Austria clear thy way, with hands
   Foul from Ancona's cruel sack,

---

* The writer of these lines is no enemy of Catholics. He has, on more than one occasion, exposed himself to the censures of his Protestant brethren, by his strenuous endeavors to procure indemnification for the owners of the convent destroyed near Boston. He defended the cause of the Irish patriots long before it had become popular in this country ; and he was one of the first to urge the most liberal aid to the suffering and starving population of the Catholic island. The severity of his language finds its ample apology in the reluctant confession of one of the most eminent Romish priests, the eloquent and devoted Father Ventura.

And Naples, with his dastard bands
  Of murderers, lead thee back!

Rome's lips are dumb; the orphan's wail,
  The mother's shriek, thou may'st not hear,
Above the faithless Frenchman's hail,
  The unsexed shaveling's cheer!

Go, bind on Rome her cast-off weight,
  The double curse of crook and crown,
Though woman's scorn and manhood's hate
  From wall and roof flash down!

Nor heed those blood-stains on the wall,
  Not Tiber's flood can wash away,
Where, in thy stately Quirinal,
  Thy mangled victims lay!

Let the world murmur; let its cry
  Of horror and disgust be heard;—
Truth stands alone; thy coward lie
  Is backed by lance and sword!

The cannon of St. Angelo,
  And chanting priest and clanging bell,
And beat of drum and bugle blow,
  Shall greet thy coming well!

Let lips of iron and tongues of slaves
  Fit welcome give thee;—for her part,
Rome, frowning o'er her new-made graves,
  Shall curse thee from her heart!

No wreaths of sad Campagna's flowers
  Shall childhood in thy pathway fling;
No garlands from their ravaged bowers
  Shall Terni's maidens bring;

But, hateful as that tyrant old,
  The mocking witness of his crime,
In thee shall loathing eyes behold
  The Nero of our time!

Stand where Rome's blood was freest shed,
  Mock Heaven with impious thanks, and call
Its curses on the patriot dead,
  Its blessings on the Gaul!

Or sit upon thy throne of lies,
  A poor, mean idol, blood-besmeared,
Whom even its worshippers despise—
  Unhonored, unrevered!

Yet, Scandal of the World! from thee
    One needful truth mankind shall learn—
That kings and priests to Liberty
    And God are false in turn.

Earth wearies of them; and the long
    Meek sufferance of the Heavens doth fail;
Woe for weak tyrants, when the strong
    Wake, struggle, and prevail! ·

Not vainly Roman hearts have bled
    To feed the Crozier and the Crown,
If, roused thereby, the world shall tread
    The twin-born vampires down!

ELLIOTT.*

HANDS off! thou tythe-fat plunderer! play
    No trick of priestcraft here!
Back, puny lordling! darest thou lay
    A hand on Elliott's bier?
Alive, your rank and pomp, as dust,
    Beneath his feet he trod:
He knew the locust swarm that cursed
    The harvest-fields of God.

On these pale lips, the smothered thought
    Which England's millions feel,
A fierce and fearful splendor caught,
    As from his forge the steel.
Strong-armed as Thor—a shower of fire
    His smitten anvil flung;
God's curse, Earth's wrong, dumb Hunger's ire—
    He gave them all a tongue!

Then let the poor man's horny hands
    Bear up the mighty dead,
And labor's swart and stalwart bands
    Behind as mourners tread.
Leave cant and craft their baptized bounds,
    Leave rank its minster floor;
Give England's green and daisied grounds
    The poet of the poor!

* Ebenezer Elliott, the intelligence of whose death has recently reached us, was to the artisans of England what Burns was to the peasantry of Scotland. His "Corn-law Rhymes" contributed not a little to that overwhelming tide of popular opinion and feeling which resulted in the repeal of the tax on bread. Well has the eloquent author of "The Reforms and Reformers of Great Britain" said of him: "Not corn-law repealers alone, but all Britons who moisten their scanty bread with the sweat of the brow, are largely indebted to his inspiring lays for the mighty bound which the laboring mind of England has taken in our day."

Lay down upon his Sheaf's green verge
  That brave old heart of oak,
With fitting dirge from sounding forge,
  And pall of furnace smoke!
Where whirls the stone its dizzy rounds,
  And axe and sledge are swung,
And, timing to their stormy sounds,
  His stormy lays are sung.

Then let the peasant's step be heard,
  The grinder chant his rhyme;
Nor patron's praise nor dainty word
  Befits the man or time.
No soft lament nor dreamer's sigh
  For him whose words were dread—
The Runic rhyme and spell whereby
  The foodless poor were fed!

Pile up thy tombs of rank and pride,
  O England, as thou wilt!
With pomp to nameless worth denied,
  Emblazon titled guilt!
No part or lot in these we claim;
  But, o'er the sounding wave,
A common right to Elliott's name,
  A free hold in his grave!

ICHABOD!

So fallen! so lost! the light withdrawn
    Which once he wore!
The glory from his gray hairs gone
    Forevermore!

Revile him not—the Tempter hath
    A snare for all;
And pitying tears, not scorn and wrath,
    Befit his fall!

Oh! dumb be passion's stormy rage
    When he who might
Have lighted up and led his age,
    Falls back in night.

Scorn! would the angels laugh, to mark
    A bright soul driven,
Fiend-goaded, down the endless dark,
    From hope and heaven?

Let not the land, once proud of him,
    Insult him now,
Nor brand with deeper shame his dim,
    Dishonored brow.

But let its humbled sons, instead,
    From sea to lake,
A long lament, as for the dead,
    In sadness make.

Of all we loved and honored, naught
    Save power remains—
A fallen angel's pride of thought,
    Still strong in chains.

All else is gone; from those great eyes
    The soul has fled:
When faith is lost, when honor dies,
    The man is dead!

Then, pay the reverence of old days
    To his dead fame;
Walk backward, with averted gaze,
    And hide the shame!

THE CHRISTIAN TOURISTS.*

No aimless wanderers, by the fiend Unrest
    Goaded from shore to shore;
No schoolmen, turning, in their classic quest,
    The leaves of empire o'er.
Simple of faith, and bearing in their hearts
    The love of man and God,
Isles of old song, the Moslem's ancient marts,
And Scythia's steppes, they trod.

Where the long shadows of the fir and pine
    In the night sun are cast,
And the deep heart of many a norland mine
    Quakes at each riving blast;
Where, in barbaric grandeur, Moskwa stands,
    A baptized Scythian queen,
With Europe's arts and Asia's jewelled hands,
    The North and East between!

Where still, through vales of Grecian fable, stray
    The classic forms of yore,

* The reader of the Biography of the late William Allen, the philanthropic associate of Clarkson and Romilly, cannot fail to admire his simple and beautiful record of a tour through Europe in the years 1818 and 1819, in the company of his American friend, Stephen Grellett.

And Beauty smiles, new risen from the spray,
  And Dian weeps once more ;
Where every tongue in Smyrna's mart resounds!
  And Stamboul from the sea
Lifts her tall minarets over burial-grounds
  Black with the cypress tree!

From Malta's temples to the gates of Rome,
  Following the track of Paul,
And where the Alps gird round the Switzer's home
  Their vast, eternal wall;
They paused not by the ruins of old time,
  They scanned no pictures rare,
Nor lingered where the snow-locked mountains climb
  The cold abyss of air!

But unto prisons, where men lay in chains,
  To haunts where Hunger pined,
To kings and courts forgetful of the pains
  And wants of human kind,
Scattering sweet words, and quiet deeds of good,
  Along their way, like flowers,
Or, pleading as Christ's freemen only could
  With princes and with powers;

Their single aim the purpose to fulfil
  Of Truth, from day to day,
Simply obedient to its guiding will,
  They held their pilgrim way.
Yet dream not, hence, the beautiful and old,
  Were wasted on their sight,
Who in the school of Christ had learned to hold
  All outward things aright.

Not less to them the breath of vineyards blown
  From off the Cyprian shore,
Not less for them the Alps in sunset shone,
  That man they valued more.
A life of beauty lends to all it sees
  The beauty of its thought;
And fairest forms and sweetest harmonies
  Make glad its way, unsought.

In sweet accordancy of praise and love,
  The singing waters run;
And sunset mountains wear in light above
  The smile of duty done;
Sure stands the promise—ever to the meek
  A heritage is given:
Nor lose they Earth who, single-hearted, seek
  The righteousness of Heaven!

THE MEN OF OLD.

WELL speed thy mission, bold Iconoclast!
 Yet all unworthy of its trust thou art,
  If, with dry eye, and cold, unloving heart,
Thou tread'st the solemn Pantheon of the Past,
 By the great Future's dazzling hope made blind
 To all the beauty, power, and truth, behind.
Not without reverent awe shouldst thou put by
 The cypress branches and the amaranth blooms,
  Where, with clasped hands of prayer, upon their tombs
The effigies of old confessors lie,
God's witnesses; the voices of his will,
Heard in the slow march of the centuries still!
Such were the men at whose rebuking frown,
Dark with God's wrath, the tyrant's knee went down;
Such from the terrors of the guilty drew
The vassal's freedom and the poor man's due.

St. Anselm (may he rest forevermore
 In Heaven's sweet peace!) forbade, of old, the sale
 Of men as slaves, and from the sacred pale
Hurled the Northumbrian buyers of the poor.
To ransom souls from bonds and evil fate
St. Ambrose melted down the sacred plate—
Image of saint, the chalice, and the pix,
Crosses of gold, and silver candlesticks.
" MAN IS WORTH MORE THAN TEMPLES ! " he replied
To such as came his holy work to chide.
And brave Cesarius, stripping altars bare,
 And coining from the Abbey's golden hoard
The captive's freedom, answered to the prayer
 Or threat of those whose fierce zeal for the Lord
Stifled their love of man—" An earthen dish
 The last sad supper of the Master bore:
Most miserable sinners! do ye wish
 More than your Lord, and grudge his dying poor
What your own pride and not his need requires ?
 Souls, than these shining gauds, He values more ;
Mercy, not sacrifice, his heart desires ! "
O faithful worthies! resting far behind
In your dark ages, since ye fell asleep,
Much has been done for truth and human kind—
Shadows are scattered wherein ye groped blind ;
Man claims his birthright, freer pulses leap
Through peoples driven in your day like sheep ;
Yet, like your own, our age's sphere of light,
Though widening still, is walled around by night;
 With slow, reluctant eye, the Church has read,
Sceptic at heart, the lessons of its Head ;

Counting, too oft, its living members less
Than the wall's garnish and the pulpit's dress;
World-moving zeal, with power to bless and feed
Life's fainting pilgrims, to their utter need,
Instead of bread, holds out the stone of creed;
Sect builds and worships where its wealth and pride
And vanity stand shrined and deified,
Careless that in the shadow of its walls
God's living temple into ruin falls.
We need, methinks, the prophet-hero still,
Saints true of life, and martyrs strong of will,
To tread the land, even now, as Xavier trod
    The streets of Goa, barefoot, with his bell,
Proclaiming freedom in the name of God,
    And startling tyrants with the fear of hell!
    Soft words, smooth prophecies, are doubtless well;
But to rebuke the age's popular crime,
We need the souls of fire, the hearts of that old time!

THE PEACE CONVENTION AT BRUSSELS.

STILL in thy streets, oh Paris! doth the stain
Of blood defy the cleansing autumn rain;
Still breaks the smoke Messina's ruins through,
And Naples mourns that new Bartholomew,
When squalid beggary, for a dole of bread,
At a crowned murderer's beck of license fed
The yawning trenches with her noble dead;
Still, doomed Vienna, through thy stately halls
The shell goes crashing and the red shot falls,
And, leagued to crush thee, on the Danube's side,
The bearded Croat and Bosniak spearmen ride;
Still in that vale where Himalaya's snow
Melts round the cornfields and the vines below,
The Sikh's hot cannon, answering ball for ball,
Flames in the breach of Moultan's shattered wall;
On Chenab's side the vulture seeks the slain,
And Sutlej paints with blood its banks again.
" What folly, then," the faithless critic cries,
With sneering lip, and wise, world-knowing eyes,
" While fort to fort, and post to post, repeat
The ceaseless challenge of the war-drum's beat,
And round the green earth, to the church-bell's chime,
The morning drum-roll of the camp keeps time,
To dream of peace amidst a world in arms,
Of swords to ploughshares changed by scriptural charms,
Of nations, drunken with the wine of blood,
Staggering to take the Pledge of Brotherhood,
Like tipplers answering Father Mathew's call—
The sullen Spaniard, and the mad-cap Gaul,

The bulldog Briton, yielding but with life,
The Yankee swaggering with his bowie knife,
The Russ, from banquets with the vulture shared
The blood still dripping from his amber beard,
Quitting their mad Berserker dance, to hear
The dull, meek droning of a drab-coat seer;
Leaving the sport of Presidents and Kings,
Where men for dice each titled gambler flings,
To meet alternate on the Seine and Thames,
For tea and gossip, like old country dames!
No! let the cravens plead the weakling's cant,
Let Cobden cipher, and let Vincent rant,
Let Sturge preach peace to democratic throngs,
And Burritt, stammering through his hundred tongues,
Repeat, in all, his ghostly lessons o'er,
Timed to the pauses of the battery's roar;
Check Ban or Kaiser with the barricade
Of ' Olive-leaves ' and Resolutions made,
Spike guns with pointed scripture-texts, and hope
To capsize navies with a windy trope;
Still shall the glory and the pomp of War
Along their train the shouting millions draw;
Still dusty Labor to the passing Brave
His cap shall doff, and Beauty's kerchief wave;
Still shall the bard to Valor tune his song,
Still Hero-worship kneel before the Strong;
Rosy and sleek, the sable-gowned divine,
O'er his third bottle of suggestive wine,
To plumed and sworded auditors, shall prove
Their trade accordant with the Law of Love;
And Church for State, and State for Church, shall fight,
And both agree, that Might alone is Right! "
Despite of sneers like these, oh, faithful few,
Who dare to hold God's word and witness true,
Whose clear-eyed faith transcends our evil time,
And, o'er the present wilderness of crime,
Sees the calm future, with its robes of green,
Its fleece-flecked mountains, and soft streams between,—
Still keep the path which duty bids ye tread,
Though worldly wisdom shake the cautious head;
No truth from Heaven descends upon our sphere,
Without the greeting of the sceptic's sneer;
Denied and mocked at, till its blessings fall,
Common as dew and sunshine, over all.

Then, o'er Earth's war-field, till the strife shall cease,
Like Morven's harpers, sing your song of peace;
As in old fable rang the Thracian's lyre,
Midst howl of fiends and roar of penal fire,
Till the fierce din to pleasing murmurs fell,
And love subdued the maddened heart of hell.

Lend, once again, that holy song a tongue,
Which the glad angels of the Advent sung,
Their cradle-anthem for the Saviour's birth,
Glory to God, and peace unto the earth!
Through the mad discord send that calming word
Which wind and wave on wild Genesareth heard,
Lift in Christ's name his Cross against the Sword!
Not vain the vision which the prophets saw,
Skirting with green the fiery waste of war,
Through the hot sand-gleam, looming soft and calm
On the sky's rim, the fountain-shading palm.
Still lives for Earth, which fiends so long have trod,
The great hope resting on the truth of God—
Evil shall cease and Violence pass away,
And the tired world breathe free through a long Sabbath
    day.

THE WISH OF TO-DAY.

I ASK not now for gold to gild
    With mocking shine a weary frame;
The yearning of the mind is stilled—
    I ask not now for Fame.

A rose-cloud, dimly seen above,
    Melting in heaven's blue depths away—
O! sweet, fond dream of human Love!
    For thee I may not pray.

But, bowed in lowliness of mind,
    I make my humble wishes known—
I only ask a will resigned,
    O Father, to thine own!

To-day, beneath thy chastening eye,
    I crave alone for peace and rest,
Submissive in thy hand to lie,
    And feel that it is best.

A marvel seems the Universe,
    A miracle our Life and Death;
A mystery which I cannot pierce,
    Around, above, beneath.

In vain I task my aching brain,
    In vain the sage's thought I scan
I only feel how weak and vain,
    How poor and blind, is man.

And now my spirit sighs for home,
    And longs for light whereby to see,

And, like a weary child, would come,
　O Father, unto Thee!

Though oft, like letters traced on sand,
　My weak resolves have passed away,
In mercy lend thy helping hand
　Unto my prayer to-day!

OUR STATE.

THE South-land boasts its teeming cane,
The prairied West its heavy grain,
And sunset's radiant gates unfold
On rising marts and sands of gold!

Rough, bleak and hard, our little State
Is scant of soil, of limits strait;
Her yellow sands are sands alone,
Her only mines are ice and stone.

From Autumn frost to April rain,
Too long her Winter woods complain;
From budding flower to falling leaf,
Her Summer time is all too brief.

Yet, on her rocks, and on her sands,
And wintry hills, the school-house stands,
And what her rugged soil denies,
The harvest of the mind supplies.

The riches of the commonwealth
Are free, strong minds, and hearts of health;
And more to her than gold or grain,
The cunning hand and cultured brain.

For well she keeps her ancient stock,
The stubborn strength of Pilgrim Rock;
And still maintains, with milder laws,
And clearer light, the Good Old Cause!

Nor heeds the sceptic's puny hands,
While near her school the church spire stands;
Nor fears the blinded bigot's rule,
While near her church-spire stands the school!

ALL'S WELL.

THE clouds, which rise with thunder, slake
　Our thirsty souls with rain;
The blow most dreaded falls to break
　From off our limbs a chain;

And wrongs of man to man but make
  The love of God more plain.
As through the shadowy lens of even
The eye looks farthest into heaven,
On gleams of star and depths of blue
The glaring sunshine never knew!

SEED TIME AND HARVEST.

As o'er his furrowed fields which lie
Beneath a coldly-dropping sky
Yet chill with winter's melted snow,
The husbandman goes forth to sow;

Thus, Freedom, on the bitter blast
The ventures of thy seed we cast,
And trust to warmer sun and rain,
To swell the germ, and fill the grain.

Who calls thy glorious service hard?
Who deems it not its own reward?
Who, for its trials, counts it less
A cause of praise and thankfulness?

It may not be our lot to wield
The sickle in the ripened field;
Nor ours to hear, on summer eves,
The reaper's song among the sheaves;

Yet where our duty's task is wrought
In unison with God's great thought,
The near and future blend in one,
And whatsoe'er is willed is done!

And ours the grateful service whence
Comes, day by day, the recompense;
The hope, the trust, the purpose stayed
The fountain and the noonday shade.

And were this life the utmost span,
The only end and aim of man,
Better the toil of fields like these
Than waking dream and slothful ease.

But life, though falling like our grain,
Like that revives and springs again;
And, early called, how blest are they
Who wait in heaven their harvest-day!

TO A. K.

On Receiving a Basket of Sea-Mosses.

Thanks for thy gift
Of ocean flowers,
Born where the golden drift
Of the slant sunshine falls
Down the green, tremulous walls
Of water, to the cool, still coral bowers,
Where, under rainbows of perpetual showers,
God's gardens of the deep
His patient angels keep;
Gladdening the dim, strange solitude
With fairest forms and hues, and thus
Forever teaching us
The lesson which the many-colored skies,
The flowers, and leaves, and painted butterflies,
The deer's branched antlers, the gay bird that flings
The tropic sunshine from its golden wings,
The brightness of the human countenance,
Its play of smiles, the magic of a glance,
Forevermore repeat,
In varied tones and sweet,
That beauty, in and of itself, is good.

O, kind and generous friend, o'er whom
The sunset hues of Time are cast,
Painting, upon the overpast
And scattered clouds of noonday sorrow,
The promise of a fairer morrow,
An earnest of the better life to come;
The binding of the spirit broken,
The warning to the erring spoken,
The comfort of the sad,
The eye to see, the hand to cull
Of common things the beautiful,
The absent heart made glad
By simple gift or graceful token
Of love it needs as daily food,
All own one Source, and all are good !
Hence, tracking sunny cove and reach,
Where spent waves glimmer up the beach,
And toss their gifts of weed and shell
From foamy curve and combing swell,
No unbefitting task was thine
To weave these flowers so soft and fair
In unison with his design,
Who loveth beauty everywhere;
And makes in every zone and clime,
In ocean and in upper air,
" All things beautiful in their time."

For not alone in tones of awe and power
          He speaks to man;
The cloudy horror of the thunder-shower
          His rainbows span;
          And, where the caravan
Winds o'er the desert, leaving, as in air
The crane-flock leaves, no trace of passage there
          He gives the weary eye
The palm-leaf shadow for the hot noon hour
          And on its branches dry
Calls out the acacia's flowers;
          And, where the dark shaft pierces down
          Beneath the mountain roots,
Seen by the miner's lamp alone,
          The star-like crystal shoots;
          So, where, the winds and waves below,
          The coral-branchéd gardens grow,
          His climbing weeds and mosses show,
          Like foliage, on each stony bough,
          Of varied hues more strangely gay
Than forest leaves in autumn's day;—
          Thus evermore,
          On sky, and wave, and shore,
An all-pervading beauty seems to say:
God's love and power are one: and they
Who, like the thunder of a sultry day,
          Smite to restore,
And they, who, like the gentle wind, uplift
The petals of the dew-wet flowers, and drift
          Their perfume on the air,
Alike may serve Him, each, with their own gift,
          Making their lives a prayer!

THE CURSE OF THE CHARTER-BREAKERS.

[The rights and liberties affirmed by MAGNA CHARTA were deemed of such importance, in the thirteenth century, that the bishops, twice a year, with tapers burning, and in their pontifical robes, pronounced, in the presence of the king and the representatives of the estates of England, the greater excommunication against the infringer of that instrument. The imposing ceremony took place in the great Hall of Westminster. A copy of the curse, as pronounced in 1253, declares that, "By the authority of Almighty God, and the blessed Apostles and Martyrs, and all the saints in heaven, all those who violate the English liberties, and secretly or openly, by deed, word, or counsel, do make statutes, *or observe them being made*, against said liberties, are accursed and sequestered from the company of heaven and the sacraments of the Holy Church."

WILLIAM PENN, in his admirable political pamphlet, "England's Present Interest Considered," alluding to the curse of the Charter-breakers, says: "I am no Roman Catholic, and little value their other curses; yet I declare I would not for the world incur this curse, as every man deservedly doth, who offers violence to the fundamental freedom thereby repeated and confirmed."]

          IN Westminster's royal halls,
          Robed in their pontificals,
          England's ancient prelates stood
          For the people's right and good.

Closed around the waiting crowd,
Dark and still, like winter's cloud;
King and council, lord and knight,
Squire and yeoman, stood in sight—

Stood to hear the priest rehearse,
In God's name, the Church's curse,
By the tapers round them lit,
Slowly, sternly uttering it.

" Right of voice in framing laws,
Right of peers to try each cause;
Peasant homestead, mean and small
Sacred as the monarch's hall—

" Whoso lays his hand on these,
England's ancient liberties—
Whoso breaks, by word or deed,
England's vow at Runnymede—

" Be he Prince or belted knight,
Whatsoe'er his rank or might,
If the highest, then the worst,
Let him live and die accursed.

" Thou, who to thy Church hast given
Keys alike, of hell and heaven,
Make our word and witness sure,
Let the curse we speak endure!"

Silent, while that curse was said,
Every bare and listening head
Bowed in reverent awe, and then
All the people said, Amen!

Seven times the bells have tolled,
For the centuries gray and old,
Since that stoled and mitred band
Cursed the tyrants of their land.

Since the priesthood, like a tower,
Stood between the poor and power;
And the wronged and trodden down
Blessed the abbot's shaven crown.

Gone, thank God, their wizard spell,
Lost, their keys of heaven and hell;
Yet I sigh for men as bold
As those bearded priests of old.

Now, too oft the priesthood wait
At the threshold of the state—

Waiting for the beck and nod
Of its power as law and God.

Fraud exults, while solemn words
Sanctify his stolen hoards;
Slavery laughs, while ghostly lips
Bless his manacles and whips.

Not on them the poor rely,
Not to them looks liberty,
Who with fawning falsehood cower
To the wrong, when clothed with power.

Oh! to see them meanly cling,
Round the master, round the king,
Sported with, and sold and bought—
Pitifuller sight is not!

Tell me not that this must be:
God's true priest is always free;
Free, the needed truth to speak,
Right the wronged, and raise the weak.

Not to fawn on wealth and state,
Leaving Lazarus at the gate—
Not to peddle creeds like wares—
Not to mutter hireling prayers—

Not to paint the new life's bliss
On the sable ground of this—
Golden streets for idle knave,
Sabbath rest for weary slave!

Not for words and works like these,
Priest of God, thy mission is;
But to make earth's desert glad,
In its Eden greenness clad;

And to level manhood bring
Lord and peasant, serf and king;
And the Christ of God to find
In the humblest of thy kind!

Thine to work as well as pray
Clearing thorny wrongs away;
Plucking up the weeds of sin,
Letting heaven's warm sunshine in—

Watching on the hills of faith;
Listening what the spirit saith,
Of the dim-seen light afar,
Growing like a nearing star,

God's interpreter art thou,
To the waiting ones below;
'Twixt them and its light midway
Heralding the better day—

Catching gleams of temple spires,
Hearing notes of angel choirs,
Where, as yet unseen of them,
Comes the New Jerusalem!

Like the seer of Patmos gazing,
On the glory downward blazing;
Till upon Earth's grateful sod
Rests the City of our God!

THE SLAVES OF MARTINIQUE.

SUGGESTED BY A DAGUERREOTYPE FROM A FRENCH ENGRAVING.

BEAMS of noon, like burning lances, through the tree-tops flash and glisten,
As she stands before her lover, with raised face to look and listen.

Dark, but comely, like the maiden in the ancient Jewish song:
Scarcely has the toil of task-fields done her graceful beauty wrong.

He, the strong one and the manly, with the vassal's garb and hue,
Holding still his spirit's birthright, to his higher nature true;

Hiding deep the strengthening purpose of a freeman in his heart,
As the greegree holds his Fetich from the white man's gaze apart.

Ever foremost of his comrades, when the driver's morning horn
Calls away to stifling mill-house, to the fields of cane and corn;

Fall the keen and burning lashes, never on his back or limb;
Scarce with look or word of censure, turns the driver unto him.

Yet, his brow is always thoughtful and his eye is hard and stern;
Slavery's last and humblest lesson, he has never deigned to learn.

And, at evening, when his comrades dance before their master's door,
Folding arms and knitting forehead, stands he silent evermore.

God be praised for every instinct which rebels against a lot,
Where the brute survives the human and man's upright form is not!

As the serpent-like bejuco winds his spiral fold on fold,
Round the tall and stately ceiba, till it withers in its hold;—

Slow decays the forest monarch, closer girds the fell embrace,
Till the tree is seen no longer and the vine is in his place—

So a base and bestial nature round the vassal's manhood twines,
And the spirit wastes beneath it, like the ceiba choked with vines.

God is Love, saith the Evangel; and our world of woe and sin
Is made light and happy only when a Love is shining in

Ye whose lives are free as sunshine, finding wheresoe'er ye roam,
Smiles of welcome, looks of kindness, making all the world like home;

In the veins of whose affections kindred blood is but a part,
Of one kindly current throbbing from the universal heart;

Can ye know the deeper meaning of a love in Slavery nursed,
Last flower of a lost Eden, blooming in that Soil accursed?

Love of Home, and Love of Woman!—dear to all, but doubly dear
To the heart whose pulses elsewhere measure only hate and fear.

All around the desert circles, underneath a brazen sky,
Only one green spot remaining where the dew is never dry!

From the horror of that desert, from its atmosphere of hell,
Turns the fainting spirit thither, as the diver seeks his bell.

'Tis the fervid tropic noontime; faint and low the sea-waves beat;
Hazy rise the inland mountains through the glimmer of the heat,—

Where, through mingled leaves and blossoms arrowy sunbeams flash
    and glisten,
Speaks her lover to the slave girl, and she lifts her head to listen :—

" We shall live as slaves no longer!   Freedom's hour is close at hand!
Rocks her bark upon the waters, rests the boat upon the strand!

" I have seen the Haytien Captain; I have seen his swarthy crew,
Haters of the pallid faces, to their race and color true.

" They have sworn to wait our coming till the night has passed its noon,
And the gray and darkening waters roll above the sunken moon!"

Oh! the blessed hope of freedom! how with joy and glad surprise,
For an instant throbs her bosom, for an instant beam her eyes!

But she looks across the valley, where her mother's hut is seen,
Through the snowy bloom of coffee and the lemon leaves so green

And she answers, sad and earnest: "It were wrong for thee to stay;
God hath heard thy prayer for freedom, and his finger points the way.

" Well I know with what endurance, for the sake of me and mine,
Thou hast borne too long a burden, never meant for souls like thine.

" Go; and at the hour of midnight, when our last farewell is o'er,
Kneeling on our place of parting, I will bless thee from the shore.

" But for me, my mother, lying on her sick bed all the day,
Lifts her weary head to watch me, coming through the twilight gray.

" Should I leave her sick and helpless, even freedom, shared with thee,
Would be sadder far than bondage, lonely toil, and stripes to me.

" For my heart would die within me, and my brain would soon be wild :
I should hear my mother calling through the twilight for her child!

Blazing upward from the ocean, shines the sun of morning time,
Through the coffee trees in blossom, and green hedges of the lime.

Side by side, amidst the slave gang, toil the lover and the maid ;
Wherefore looks he o'er the waters, leaning forward on his spade?

Sadly looks he, deeply sighs he : 'tis the Haytien's sail he sees,
Like a white cloud of the mountains, driven seaward by the breeze!

But his arm a light hand presses, and he hears a low voice call :
Hate of Slavery, hope of Freedom, Love is mightier than all.

THE CRISIS.

WRITTEN ON LEARNING THE TERMS OF THE TREATY WITH MEXICO.

ACROSS the Stony Mountains, o'er the desert's drouth and sand,
The circles of our empire touch the Western Ocean's strand;
From slumberous Timpanogos to Gila, wild and free,
Flowing down from Neuvo Leon to California's sea;
And from the mountains of the East to Santa Rosa's shore,
The eagles of Mexitli shall beat the air no more.

O Vale of Rio Bravo!   Let thy simple children weep;
Close watch about their holy fire let maids of Pecos keep;
Let Taos send her cry across Sierra Madre's pines,
And Algodones toll her bells amidst her corn and vines;
For lo! the pale land-seekers come, with eager eyes of gain,
Wide scattering, like the bison herds on broad Salada's plain.

Let Sacramento's herdsmen heed what sound the winds bring down,
Of footsteps on the crisping snow, from cold Nevada's crown!
Full hot and fast the Saxon rides, with rein of travel slack,
And, bending o'er his saddle, leaves the sunrise at his back ;
By many a lonely river and gorge of fir and pine,
On many a wintry hilltop his nightly camp-fires shine.

O countrymen and brothers! that land of lake and plain,
Of salt wastes alternating with valleys fat with grain;
Of mountains white with winter, looking downward, cold, serene,
On their feet with spring-vines tangled and lapped in softest green;
Swift through those black volcanic gates, o'er many a sunny vale,
Wind-like the Arapahoe sweeps the bison's dusty trail!

Great spaces yet untravelled, great lakes whose mystic shores
The Saxon rifle never heard, nor dip of Saxon oars;
Great herds that wander all unwatched, wild steeds that none have
    tamed,
Strange fish in unknown streams, and birds the Saxon never named;
Deep mines, dark mountain crucibles, where Nature's chemic powers
Work out the Great Designer's will:—all these ye say are ours!

Forever ours! for good or ill, on us the burden lies;
God's balance, watched by angels, is hung across the skies.
Shall Justice, Truth, and Freedom, turn the poised and trembling scale?
Or shall the Evil triumph, and robber Wrong prevail?
Shall the broad land o'er which our flag in starry splendor waves,
Forego through us its freedom, and bear the tread of slaves?

The day is breaking in the East, of which the prophets told,
And brightens up the sky of Time the Christian Age of Gold:
Old Might to Right is yielding, battle blade to clerkly pen,
Earth's monarchs are her peoples, and her serfs stand up as men;
The isles rejoice together, in a day are nations born,
And the slave walks free in Tunis, and by Stamboul's Golden Horn!

Is this, O countrymen of mine! a day for us to sow
The soil of new-gained empire with slavery's seeds of woe?
To feed with our fresh life-blood the old world's cast-off crime,
Dropped, like some monstrous early birth, from the tired lap of Time?
To run anew the evil race the old lost nations ran,
And die like them of unbelief of God, and wrong of man?

Great Heaven! Is this our mission? End in this the prayers and tears,
The toil, the strife, the watchings of our younger, better years?
Still, as the old world rolls in light, shall ours in shadow turn,
A beamless Chaos, cursed of God, through outer darkness borne?
Where the far nations looked for light, a blackness in the air?
Where for words of hope they listened, the long wail of despair?

The Crisis presses on us; face to face with us it stands,
With solemn lips of question, like the Sphinx in Egypt's sands!
This day we fashion Destiny, our web of Fate we spin;
This day for all hereafter choose we holiness or sin;
Even now from starry Gerizim, or Ebal's cloudy crown,
We call the dews of blessing or the bolts of cursing down!

By all for which the martyrs bore their agony and shame;
By all the warning words of truth with which the prophets came;

By the Future which awaits us; by all the hopes which cast
Their faint and trembling beams across the blackness of the Past;
And by the blessed thought of Him who for Earth's freedom died,
O, my people! O, my brothers! let us choose the righteous side.

So shall the Northern pioneer go joyful on his way,
To wed Penobscot's waters to San Francisco's bay;
To make the rugged places smooth, and sow the vales with grain;
And bear, with Liberty and Law, the Bible in his train:
The mighty West shall bless the East, and sea shall answer sea,
And mountain unto mountain call: PRAISE GOD, FOR WE ARE FREE!

THE KNIGHT OF ST. JOHN.

ERE down yon blue Carpathian hills
　　The sun shall sink again!
Farewell to life and all its ills,
　　Farewell to cell and chain.

These prison shades are dark and cold,—
　　But, darker far than they,
The shadow of a sorrow old
　　Is on my heart alway.

For since the day when Warkworth wood
　　Closed o'er my steed and I,
An alien from my name and blood,
　　A weed cast out to die,—

When, looking back in sunset light,
　　I saw her turret gleam,
And from its casement, far and white,
　　Her sign of farewell stream,

Like one who from some desert shore
　　Doth home's green isles descry,
And, vainly longing, gazes o'er
　　The waste of wave and sky;

So from the desert of my fate
　　I gaze across the past;
Forever on life's dial-plate
　　The shade is backward cast!

I've wandered wide from shore to shore,
　　I've knelt at many a shrine;
And bowed me to the rocky floor
　　Where Bethlehem's tapers shine;

And by the Holy Sepulchre
   I've pledged my knightly sword
To Christ, his blessed Church, and her,
   The Mother of our Lord.

Oh, vain the vow, and vain the strife!
   How vain do all things seem!
My soul is in the past, and life
   To-day is but a dream!

In vain the penance strange and long,
   And hard for flesh to bear;
The prayer, the fasting, and the thong,
   And sackcloth shirt of hair.

The eyes of memory will not sleep,—
   Its ears are open still;
And vigils with the past they keep
   Against my feeble will.

And still the loves and joys of old
   Do evermore uprise;
I see the flow of locks of gold,
   The shine of loving eyes!

Ah me! upon another's breast
   Those golden locks recline;
I see upon another rest
   The glance that once was mine!

" O faithless Priest!—O perjured knight!"
   I hear the Master cry;
" Shut out the vision from thy sight,
   Let Earth and Nature die!

"The Church of God is now thy spouse,
   And thou the bridegroom art;
Then let the burden of thy vows
   Crush down thy human heart!"

In vain! This heart its grief must know
   Till life itself hath ceased,
And falls beneath the self-same blow,
   The lover and the priest!

O pitying Mother! souls of light,
   And saints, and martyrs old!
Pray for a weak and sinful knight,
   A suffering man uphold.

Then let the Paynim work his will,
   And death unbind my chain,
Ere down yon blue Carpathian hill
   The sun shall fall again.

THE HOLY LAND.

FROM LAMARTINE.

I HAVE not felt o'er seas of sand,
  The rocking of the desert bark;
Nor laved at Hebron's fount my hand,
  By Hebron's palm-trees cool and dark
Nor pitched my tent at even-fall,
  On dust where Job of old has lain,
Nor dreamed beneath its canvas wall,
  The dream of Jacob o'er again.

One vast world-page remains unread;
  How shine the stars in Chaldea's sky,
How sounds the reverent pilgrim's tread,
  How beats the heart with God so nigh!—
How round gray arch and column lone
  The spirit of the old time broods,
And sighs in all the winds that moan
  Along the sandy solitudes!

In thy tall cedars, Lebanon,
  I have not heard the nation's cries
Nor seen thy eagles stooping down
  Where buried Tyre in ruin lies.
The Christian's prayer I have not said,
  In Tadmor's temples of decay,
Nor startled with my dreary tread,
  The waste where Memnon's empire lay.

Nor have I, from thy hallowed tide,
  O, Jordan! heard the low lament,
Like that sad wail along thy side,
  Which Israel's mournful prophet sent!
Nor thrilled within that grotto lone,
  Where deep in night, the Bard of Kings
Felt hands of fire direct his own,
  And sweep for God the conscious strings.

I have not climbed to Olivet,
  Nor laid me where my Saviour lay,
And left his trace of tears as yet
  By angel eyes unwept away;
Nor watched at midnight's solemn time,
  The garden where His prayer and groan,
Wrung by His sorrow and our crime,
  Rose to One listening ear alone.

I have not kissed the rock-hewn grot,
  Where in His Mother's arms He lay,

Nor knelt upon the sacred spot
   Where last His footsteps pressed the clay;
Nor looked on that sad mountain head,
   Nor smote my sinful breast, where wide
His arms to fold the world He spread,
   And bowed His head to bless—and died!

MOUNT AGIOCHOOK.

GRAY searcher of the upper air!
   There's sunshine on thy ancient walls
A crown upon thy forehead bare—
   A flashing on thy water-falls—
A rainbow glory in the cloud,
Upon thine awful summit bowed,
   Dim relic of the recent storm!
And music, from the leafy shroud
Which wraps in green thy giant form,
Mellowed and softened from above,
   Steals down upon the listening ear,
Sweet as the maiden's dream of love,
   With soft tones melting on her ear.

The time has been, gray mountain, when
   Thy shadows veiled the red man's home;
And over crag and serpent den,
   And wild gorge, where the steps of men
   In chase or battle might not come,
The mountain eagle bore on high
   The emblem of the free of soul;
And midway in the fearful sky
Sent back the Indian's battle-cry,
   Or answered to the thunder's roll.

The wigwam fires have all burned out—
   The moccasin hath left no track—
Nor wolf nor wild-deer roam about
   The Saco or the Merrimack.
And thou that liftest up on high
Thine awful barriers to the sky,
   Art not the haunted mount of old,
When on each crag of blasted stone
Some mountain-spirit found a throne,
   And shrieked from out the thick cloud-fold,
And answered to the Thunderer's cry
When rolled the cloud of tempest by,
And jutting rock and riven branch
Went down before the avalanche.

The Father of our people then
   Upon thy awful summit trod,

And the red dwellers of the glen
   Bowed down before the Indian's God.
There, when His shadow veiled the sky,
   The Thunderer's voice was long and loud,
And the red flashes of His eye
   Were pictured on the o'erhanging cloud.

The Spirit moveth there no more,
   The dwellers of the hill have gone,
The sacred groves are trampled o'er,
   And footprints mar the altar-stone.
The white man climbs thy tallest rock
   And hangs him from the mossy steep,
Where, trembling to the cloud-fire's shock,
Thy ancient prison-walls unlock,
And captive waters leap to light,
And dancing down from height to height,
   Pass onward to the far-off deep.

Oh, sacred to the Indian seer,
   Gray altar of the days of old!
Still are thy rugged features dear,
As when unto my infant ear
   The legends of the past were told.
Tales of the downward sweeping flood,
When bowed like reeds thy ancient wood,—
   Of armed hand and spectral form,
Of giants in their misty shroud,
And voices calling long and loud
   In the drear pauses of the storm!
Farewell! The red man's face is turned
   Toward another hunting-ground;
For where the council-fire has burned,
   And o'er the sleeping warrior's mound
Another fire is kindled now:
Its light is on the white man's brow!
   The hunter race have passed away—
Ay, vanished like the morning mist,
Or dewdrops by the sunshine kissed,—
   And wherefore should the red man stay?

METACOM.

RED as the banner which enshrouds
   The warrior-dead when strife is done,
A broken mass of crimson clouds
   Hung over the departed sun.
The shadow of the western hill
Crept swiftly down, and darkly still,

As if a sullen wave of night
Were rushing on the pale twilight,
The forest-openings grew more dim,
   As glimpses of the arching blue
   And waking stars came softly through
The rifts of many a giant limb.
Above the wet and tangled swamp
White vapors gathered thick and damp,
And through their cloudy curtaining
Flapped many a brown and dusky wing—
Pinions that fan the moonless dun,
But fold them at the rising sun!

Beneath the closing veil of night,
   And leafy bough and curling fog,
With his few warriors ranged in sight—
Scarred relics of his latest fight—
   Rested the fiery Wampanoag.
He leaned upon his loaded gun,
Warm with its recent work of death,
And, save the struggling of his breath
That, slow and hard, and long-suppressed
Shook the damp folds around his breast,
An eye, that was unused to scan
The sterner moods of that dark man,
Had deemed his tall and silent form
With hidden passion fierce and warm,
With that fixed eye, as still and dark
As clouds which veil their lightning-spark—
That of some forest-champion
Whom sudden death had passed upon—
A giant frozen into stone.
Son of the thronéd Sachem,—thou,
   The sternest of the forest kings,—
Shall the scorned pale-one trample now,
Unambushed, on thy mountain's brow—
Yea, drive his vile and hated plough
   Among thy nation's holy things,
Crushing the warrior-skeleton
In scorn beneath his arméd heel,
And not a hand be left to deal
A kindred vengeance fiercely back,
And cross in blood the Spoiler's track?

He started,—for a sudden shot
   Came booming through the forest-trees—
The thunder of the fierce Yengeese:
It passed away, and injured not,
But, to the Sachem's brow it brought
The token of his lion thought.
He stood erect—his dark eye burned,
As if to meteor-brightness turned;

And o'er his forehead passed the frown
Of an archangel stricken down,
Ruined and lost, yet chainless still—
Weakened of power but strong of will
It passed—a sudden tremor came
Like ague o'er his giant frame,—
It was not terror—he had stood
   For hours, with death in grim attendance,
When moccasins grew stiff with blood,
   And through the clearing's midnight flame,
Dark, as a storm, the Pequod came,
   His red right arm their strong dependence—
When thrilling through the forest gloom
The onset cry of "Metacom!"
   Rang on the red and smoky air!—
No—it was agony which passed
Upon his soul—the strong man's last
And fearful struggle with despair.

He turned him to his trustiest one—
The old and war-tried Annawon—
"Brother"—the favored warrior stood
In hushed and listening attitude—
"This night the Vision-Spirit hath
Unrolled the scroll of fate before me;
And ere the sunrise cometh, Death
Will wave his dusky pinion o'er me!
Nay, start not—well I know thy faith:
Thy weapon now may keep its sheath;
But when the bodeful morning breaks,
And the green forest widely wakes
   Unto the roar of Yengeese thunder,
Then, trusted brother, be it thine
To burst upon the foeman's line
And rend his serried strength asunder.
Perchance thyself and yet a few
Of faithful ones may struggle through,
And, rallying on the wooded plain,
Offer up in Yengeese blood
An offering to the Indian's God."

Another shot—a sharp, quick yell,
   And then the stifled groan of pain,
Told that another red man fell,—
   And blazed a sudden light again
Across that kingly brow and eye,
Like lightning on a clouded sky,—
And a low growl, like that which thrills
The hunter of the Eastern hills,
   Burst through clenched teeth and rigid lip—
And when the Monarch spoke again,
His deep voice shook beneath its rein,

And wrath and grief held fellowship.
"Brother! methought when as but now
I pondered on my nation's wrong,
With sadness on his shadowy brow
　My father's spirit passed along!
He pointed to the far southwest,
　Where sunset's gold was growing dim,
　And seemed to beckon me to him,
And to the forests of the blest!—
My father loved the Yengeese, when
They were but children, shelterless;
For his great spirit at distress
Melted to woman's tenderness—
Nor was it given him to know
　That children whom he cherished then
Would rise at length, like arméd men,
To work his people's overthrow.
Yet thus it is;—the God before
　Whose awful shrine the pale ones bow
Hath frowned upon and given o'er
　The red man to the stranger now!—
A few more moons, and there will be
No gathering to the council-tree;
The scorched earth, the blackened log,
　The naked bones of warriors slain,
　Be the sole relics which remain
Of the once mighty Wampanoag!
The forests of our hunting-land,
　With all their old and solemn green,
Will bow before the Spoiler's axe,
The plough displace the hunter's tracks,
And the tall Yengeese altar stand
　Where the Great Spirit's shrine hath been.

"Yet, brother, from this awful hour
The dying curse of Metacom
Shall linger with abiding power
　Upon the spoilers of my home.
　The fearful veil of things to come
　By Kitchtan's hand is lifted from
The shadows of the embryo years;
　And I can see more clearly through
Than ever visioned Powwow did,
For all the future comes unbid
　Yet welcome to my trancéd view,
As battle-yell to warrior's ears!
From stream and lake and hunting-hill
　Our tribes may vanish like a dream,
　And even my dark curse may seem
Like idle winds when Heaven is still—
　No bodeful harbinger of ill,

But fiercer than the downright thunder
When yawns the mountain-rock asunder,
And riven pine and knotted oak
Are reeling to the fearful stroke,
    That curse shall work its master's will!
The bed of yon blue mountain stream
Shall pour a darker tide than rain—
The sea shall catch its blood-red stain,
And broadly on its banks shall gleam
    The steel of those who should be brothers—
Yea, those whom once fond parent nursed
Shall meet in strife, like fiends accursed,
And trample down the once loved form,
While yet with breathing passion warm,
    As fiercely as they would another's!"

The morning star sat dimly on
The lighted eastern horizon—
The deadly glare of levelled gun
    Came streaking through the twilight haze,
    And naked to its reddest blaze
A hundred warriors sprang in view:
    One dark red arm was tossed on high—
One giant shout came hoarsely through
    The clangor and the charging cry,
Just as across the scattering gloom,
Red as the naked hand of Doom,
    The Yengeese volley hurtled by—
The arm—the voice of Metacom!—
    One piercing shriek—one vengeful yell,
Sent like an arrow to the sky,
    Told when the hunter-monarch fell!

THE FRATRICIDE.

In the recently published "History of Wyoming,"—a valley rendered classic ground by the
poetry of Campbell,—in an account of the attack of Brandt and Butler on the settlements in
1778, a fearful circumstance is mentioned. A tory, who had joined the Indians and British,
discovered his own brother, whilst pursuing the Americans, and, deaf to his entreaties, deliber-
ately presented his rifle and shot him dead on the spot. The murderer fled to Canada.

HE stood on the brow of the well-known hill,
Its few gray oaks moan'd over him still—
The last of that forest which cast the gloom
Of its shadow at eve o'er his childhood's home;
And the beautiful valley beneath him lay
With its quivering leaves, and its streams at play,
And the sunshine over it all the while
Like the golden shower of the Eastern isle.

He knew the rock with its fingering vine,
And its gray top touch'd by the slant sunshine,

And the delicate stream which crept beneath
Soft as the flow of an infant's breath;
And the flowers which lean'd to the West wind's sigh,
Kissing each ripple which glided by;
And he knew every valley and wooded swell,
For the visions of childhood are treasured well.

Why shook the old man as his eye glanced down
That narrow ravine where the rude cliffs frown,
With their shaggy brows and their teeth of stone,
And their grim shade back from the sunlight thrown?
What saw he there save the dreary glen,
Where the shy fox crept from the eye of men,
And the great owl sat in the leafy limb
That the hateful sun might not look on him?

Fix'd, glassy, and strange was that old man's eye,
As if a spectre were stealing by,
And glared it still on that narrow dell
Where thicker and browner the twilight fell;
Yet at every sigh of the fitful wind,
Or stirring of leaves in the wood behind,
His wild glance wander'd the landscape o'er,
Then fix'd on that desolate dell once more.

Oh, who shall tell of the thoughts which ran
Through the dizzied brain of that gray old man?
His childhood's home—and his father's toil—
And his sister's kiss—and his mother's smile—
And his brother's laughter and gamesome mirth,
At the village school and the winter hearth—
The beautiful thoughts of his early time,
Ere his heart grew dark with its later crime.

And darker and wilder his visions came
Of the deadly feud and the midnight flame,
Of the Indian's knife with its slaughter red,
Of the ghastly forms of the scalpless dead,
Of his own fierce deeds in that fearful hour
When the terrible Brandt was forth in power,—
And he clasp'd his hands o'er his burning eye
To shadow the vision which glided by.

It came with the rush of the battle-storm—
With a brother's shaken and kneeling form,
And his prayer for life when a brother's arm
Was lifted above him for mortal harm,
And the fiendish curse, and the groan of death,
And the welling of blood, and the gurgling breath,
And the scalp torn off while each nerve could feel
The wrenching hand and the jagged steel!

And the old man groan'd—for he saw, again,
The mangled corse of his kinsman slain,
As it lay where his hand had hurl'd it then,
At the shadow'd foot of that fearful glen!—
And it rose erect, with the death-pang grim,
And pointed its bloodied finger at him!—
And his heart grew cold—and the curse of Cain
Burn'd like a fire in the old man's brain.

Oh, had he not seen that spectre rise
On the blue of the cold Canadian skies?—
From the lakes which sleep in the ancient wood,
It had risen to whisper its tale of blood,
And follow'd his bark to the sombre shore,
And glared by night through the wigwam door;
And here—on his own familiar hill—
It rose on his haunted vision still!

Whose corse was that which the morrow's sun,
Through the opening boughs, look'd calmly on?
There where those who bent o'er that rigid face
Who well in its darken'd lines might trace
The features of him who, a traitor, fled
From a brother whose blood himself had shed,
And there—on the spot where he strangely died—
They made the grave of the Fratricide!

ISABELLA OF AUSTRIA.

"Isabella, Infanta of Parma, and consort of Joseph of Austria, predicted her own death, immediately after her marriage with the Emperor. Amidst the gayety and splendor of Vienna and Presburg, she was reserved and melancholy; she believed that Heaven had given her a view of the future, and that her child, the namesake of the great Maria Theresa, would perish with her. Her prediction was fulfilled."

Midst the palace-bowers of Hungary,—imperial Presburg's pride,—
With the noble-born and beautiful assembled at her side,
She stood, beneath the summer heaven,—the soft winds sighing on,
Stirring the green and arching boughs, like dancers in the sun.
The beautiful pomegranate's gold, the snowy orange-bloom,
The lotus and the creeping vine, the rose's meek perfume,
The willow crossing with its green some statue's marble hair,—
All that might charm th' exquisite sense, or light the soul, was there.

But she—a monarch's treasured one—lean'd gloomily apart,
With her dark eye tearfully cast down and a shadow on her heart.
Young, beautiful, and dearly loved, what sorrow hath she known?
Are not the hearts and swords of all held sacred as her own?
Is not her lord the kingliest in battle-field or bower?
The foremost in the council-hall, or at the banquet hour?

Is not his love as pure and deep as his own Danube's tide?
And wherefore in her princely home weeps Isabel, his bride?

She raised her jewell'd hand and flung her veiling tresses back,
Bathing its snowy tapering within their glossy black.—
A tear fell on the orange leaves; rich gem and mimic blossom,
And fringed robe shook fearfully upon her sighing bosom:
"Smile on, smile on," she murmur'd low, "for all is joy around,
Shadow and sunshine, stainless sky, soft airs and blossom'd ground;
'Tis meet the light of heart should smile when nature's brow is fair,
And melody and fragrance meet, twin sisters of the air!

"But ask not me to share with you the beauty of the scene—
The fountain-fall, mosaic walk, and tessellated green;
And point not to the mild blue sky, or glorious summer sun:
I know how very fair is all the hand of God hath done—
The hills, the sky, the sunlit cloud, the fountain leaping forth,
The swaying trees, the scented flowers, the dark green robes of earth—
I love them still; yet I have learn'd to turn aside from all,
And never more my heart must own their sweet but fatal thrall!

"And I could love the noble one whose mighty name I bear,
And closer to my bursting heart his hallow'd image wear;
And I could watch our sweet young flower, unfolding day by day,
And taste of that unearthly bliss which mothers only may;
But no, I may not cling to earth—that voice is in my ear,
That shadow lingers by my side—the death-wail and the bier,
The cold and starless night of death where day may never beam,
The silence and the loathsomeness, the sleep which hath no dream!

"O God! to leave this fair bright world, and, more than all, to know
The moment when the Spectral One shall deal his fearful blow;
To know the day, the very hour; to feel the tide roll on;
To shudder at the gloom before, and weep the sunshine gone;
To count the days, the few short days, of light and life and breath,—
Between me and the noisome grave—the voiceless home of death,—
Alas!—if, knowing, feeling this, I murmur at my doom,
Let not thy frowning, O my God! lend darkness to the tomb.

"Oh, I have borne my spirit up, and smiled amid the chill
Remembrance of my certain doom, which lingers with me still:
I would not cloud our fair child's brow, nor let a teardrop dim
The eye that met my wedded lord's, lest it should sadden him.
But there are moments when the gush of feeling hath its way;
That hidden tide of unnamed woe nor fear nor love may stay.
Smile on, smile on, light-hearted ones, your sun of joy is high;
Smile on, and leave the doom'd of Heaven alone to weep and die."

*   *   *   *   *   *

A funeral chant was wailing through Vienna's holy pile;
A coffin with its gorgeous pall was borne along the aisle;

The banners of a kingly race waved high above the dead;
A mighty band of mourners came—a king was at its head,
A youthful king, with mournful tread and dim and tearful eye—
He had not dream'd that one so pure as his fair bride could die;
And sad and wild above the throng the funeral anthem rung:
"Mourn for the hope of Austria!   Mourn for the loved and young!"

The wail went up from other lands—the valleys of the Hun,
Fair Parma with its orange bowers and hills of vine and sun;
The lilies of imperial France droop'd as the sound went by,
The long lament of cloister'd Spain was mingled with the cry;
The dwellers in Colorno's halls, the Slowak at his cave,
The bow'd at the Escurial, the Magyar sternly brave—
All wept the early-stricken flower, and burst from every tongue:
"Mourn for the dark-eyed Isabel!   Mourn for the loved and young!"

STANZAS.

" Art thou beautiful?—Live, then, in accordance with the curious make and frame of thy
creation; and let the beauty of thy person teach thee to beautify thy mind with holiness, the
ornament of the beloved of God."—*William Penn.*

BIND up thy tresses, thou beautiful one,
Of brown in the shadow and gold in the sun!
Free should their delicate lustre be thrown
O'er a forehead more pure than the Parian stone—
Shaming the light of those Orient pearls
Which bind o'er its whiteness thy soft wreathing curls.

Smile—for thy glance on the mirror is thrown,
And the face of an angel is meeting thine own!
Beautiful creature—I marvel not
That thy cheek a lovelier tint hath caught;
And the kindling light of thine eye hath told
Of a dearer wealth than the miser's gold.

Away, away—there is danger here—
A terrible phantom is bending near;
Ghastly and sunken, his rayless eye
Scowls on thy loveliness scornfully—
With no human look—with no human breath,
He stands beside thee,—the haunter, DEATH!

Fly! but, alas! he will follow still,
Like a moonlight shadow, beyond thy will;
In thy noonday walk—in thy midnight sleep,
Close at thy hand will that phantom keep—
Still in thine ear shall his whispers be—
Woe, that such phantom should follow thee!

In the lighted hall where the dancers go,
Like beautiful spirits, to and fro;
When thy fair arms glance in their stainless white,
Like ivory bathed in still moonlight;
And not one star in the holy sky
Hath a clearer light than thine own blue eye!

Oh, then—even then—he will follow thee,
As the ripple follows the bark at sea;
In the soften'd light—in the turning dance—
He will fix on thine his dead, cold glance—
The chill of his breath on thy cheek shall linger,
And thy warm blood shrink from his icy finger!

And yet there is hope.   Embrace it now,
While thy soul is open as thy brow;
While thy heart is fresh—while its feelings still
Gush clear as the unsoil'd mountain-rill—
And thy smiles are free as the airs of spring,
Greeting and blessing each breathing thing.

When the after cares of thy life shall come,
When the bud shall wither before its bloom;
When thy soul is sick of the emptiness
And changeful fashion of human bliss;
And the weary torpor of blighted feeling
Over thy heart as ice is stealing—

Then, when thy spirit is turn'd above,
By the mild rebuke of the Chastener's love;
When the hope of that joy in thy heart is stirred
Which eye hath not seen, nor ear hath heard,—
THEN will that phantom of darkness be
Gladness, and Promise, and Bliss to thee.

THE MISSIONARY.

" It is an awful, an arduous thing to root out every affection for earthly things, so as to live
only for another world.   I am now far, very far, from you all ; and as often as I look around
and see the Indian scenery, I sigh to think of the distance which separates us."—*Letters of
Henry Martyn from India.*

" SAY, whose is this fair picture, which the light
From the unshutter'd window rests upon
Even as a lingering halo ?—Beautiful!
The keen, fine eye of manhood, and a lip
Lovely as that of Hylas, and impress'd
With the bright signet of some brilliant thought—
That broad expanse of forehead, clear and high,
Mark'd visibly with the characters of mind,
And the free locks around it, raven black,
Luxuriant and unsilver'd—who was he ?"

A friend, a more than brother. In the spring
And glory of his being he went forth
From the embraces of devoted friends,
From ease and quiet happiness, from more—
From the warm heart that loved him with a love
Holier than earthly passion, and to whom
The beauty of his spirit shone above
The charms of perishing nature. He went forth
Strengthen'd to suffer—gifted to subdue
The might of human passion—to pass on
Quietly to the sacrifice of all
The lofty hopes of boyhood, and to turn
The high ambition written on that brow,
From its first dream of power and human fame,
Unto a task of seeming lowliness,—
Yet Godlike in its purpose. He went forth
To bind the broken spirit—to pluck back
The heathen from the wheel of Juggernaut—
To place the spiritual image of a God
Holy and just and true, before the eye
Of the dark-minded Brahmin—and unseal
The holy pages of the Book of Life,
Fraught with sublimer mysteries than all
The sacred tomes of Vedas—to unbind
The widow from her sacrifice—and save
The perishing infant from the worshipp'd river!
"And, lady, where is he ? " He slumbers well
Beneath the shadow of an Indian palm.
There is no stone above his grave. The wind,
Hot from the desert, as it stirs the leaves
Of neighboring bananas, sighs alone
Over his place of slumber.

                 " God forbid
That he should die alone! "—Nay, not alone.
His God was with him in that last dread hour—
His great arm underneath him, and His smile
Melting into a spirit full of peace.
And one kind friend, a human friend, was near—
One whom his teachings and his earnest prayers
Had snatch'd as from the burning. He alone
Felt the last pressure of his failing hand,
Caught the last glimpses of his closing eye,
And laid the green turf over him with tears,
And left him with his God.

                 " And was it well,
Dear lady, that this noble mind should cast
Its rich gifts on the waters ?—That a heart
Full of all gentleness and truth and love
Should wither on the suicidal shrine
Of a mistaken duty ? If I read

Aright the fine intelligence which fills
That amplitude of brow, and gazes out
Like an indwelling spirit from that eye,
He might have borne him loftily among
The proudest of his land, and with a step
Unfaltering ever, steadfast and secure,
Gone up the paths of greatness,—bearing still
A sister spirit with him, as some star,
Preëminent in Heaven, leads steadily up
A kindred watcher, with its fainter beams
Baptized in its great glory. Was it well
That all this promise of the heart and mind
Should perish from the earth, and leave no trace,
Unfolding like the Cereus of the clime
Which hath its sepulchre, but in the night
Of pagan desolation—was it well?"

Thy will be done, O Father!—it *was* well.
What are the honors of a perishing world
Grasp'd by a palsied finger ?—the applause
Of the unthoughtful multitude which greets
The dull ear of decay ?—the wealth that loads
The bier with costly drapery, and shines
In tinsel on the coffin, and builds up
The cold substantial monument ? Can these
Bear up the sinking spirit in that hour
When heart and flesh are failing, and the grave
Is opening under us ? Oh, dearer then
The memory of a kind deed done to him
Who was our enemy, one grateful tear
In the meek eye of virtuous suffering,
One smile call'd up by unseen charity
On the wan cheek of hunger, or one prayer
Breathed from the bosom of the penitent—
The stain'd with crime and outcast, unto whom
Our mild rebuke and tenderness of love
A merciful God hath bless'd.

                              "But, lady, say,
Did he not sometimes almost sink beneath
The burden of his toil, and turn aside
To weep above his sacrifice, and cast
A sorrowing glance upon his childhood's home—
Still green in memory ? Clung not to his heart
Something of earthly hope uncrucified,
Of earthly thought unchasten'd ? Did he bring
Life's warm affections to the sacrifice—
Its loves, hopes, sorrows—and become as one
Knowing no kindred but a perishing world,
No love but of the sin-endangered soul,
No hope but of the winning back to life
Of the dead nations, and no passing thought

Save of the errand wherewith he was sent
As to a martyrdom ? ''

       Nay, though the heart
Be consecrated to the holiest work
Vouchsafed to mortal effort, there will be
Ties of the earth around it, and, through all
Its perilous devotion, it must keep
Its own humanity. And it is well.
Else why wept He, who with our nature veil'd
The spirit of a God, o'er lost Jerusalem,
And the cold grave of Lazarus ? And why
In the dim garden rose his earnest prayer,
That from his lips the cup of suffering
Might pass, if it were possible ?

       My friend
Was of a gentle nature, and his heart
Gush'd like a river-fountain of the hills,
Ceaseless and lavish, at a kindly smile,
A word of welcome, or a tone of love.
Freely his letters to his friends disclosed
His yearnings for the quiet haunts of home—
For love and its companionship, and all
The blessings left behind him; yet above
Its sorrows and its clouds his spirit rose,
Tearful and yet triumphant, taking hold
Of the eternal promises of God,
And steadfast in its faith. Here are some lines
Penn'd in his lonely mission-house, and sent
To a dear friend of his who even now
Lingers above them with a mournful joy.
Holding them well nigh sacred—as a leaf
Pluck'd from the record of a breaking heart:

An Evening In Burmah.

A night of wonder !—piled afar
 With ebon feet and crests of snow,
Like Himalaya's peaks, which bar
The sunset and the sunset's star
 From half the shadow'd vale below,
Volumed and vast the dense clouds lie,
And over them, and down the sky,
 Broadly and pale the lightnings go.

Above, the pleasant moon is seen,
 Pale journeyer to her own loved West!
Like some bright spirit sent between
The earth and heaven, she seems to lean
 Wearily on the cloud and rest;

And light from her unsullied brow
That gloomy cloud is gathering now
   Along each wreath'd and whitening crest.

And what a strength of light and shade
   Is checkering all the earth below!—
And, through the jungle's verdant braid
Of tangled vine and wild reed made,
   What blossoms in the moonlight glow!—
The Indian rose's loveliness,
The ceiba with its crimson dress,
   The myrtle with its bloom of snow.

And flitting in the fragrant air,
   Or nestling in the shadowy trees,
A thousand bright-hued birds are there—
Strange plumage quivering, wild and rare,
   With every faintly-breathing breeze:
And, wet with dew from roses shed,
The Bulbul droops her weary head,
   Forgetful of her melodies.

Uprising from the orange leaves
   The tall pagoda's turrets glow;
O'er graceful shaft and fretted caves
Its verdant web the myrtle weaves,
   And hangs in flowering wreaths below;
And where the cluster'd palms eclipse
The moonbeams, from its marble lips
   The fountain's silver waters flow.

Yes, all is lovely—earth and air—
   As aught beneath the sky may be:
And yet my thoughts are wandering where
My native rocks lie bleak and bare—
   A weary way beyond the sea.
The yearning spirit is not here;
It lingers on a spot more dear
   Than India's brightest bowers to me.

Methinks I tread the well-known street—
   The tree my childhood loved is there,
Its bare-worn roots are at my feet,
And through its open boughs I meet
   White glimpses of the place of prayer—
And unforgotten eyes again
Are glancing through the cottage pane,
   Than Asia's lustrous eyes more fair.

What though, with every fitful gush
   Of night-wind, spicy odors come;

And hues of beauty glow and flush
From matted vine and wild rose-bush;
   And music's sweetest, faintest hum
Steals through the moonlight, as in dreams,—
Afar from all my spirit seems
   Amid the dearer scenes of HOME!

A holy name—the name of home!—
   Yet where, O wandering heart, is thine?
Here where the dusky heathen come
To bow before the deaf and dumb,
   Dead idols of their own design,
Where deep in Ganges' worshipp'd tide
The infant sinks—and on its side
   The widow's funeral altars shine!

Here, where 'mid light and song and flowers
   The priceless soul in ruin lies—
Lost—dead to all those better powers
Which link a fallen world like ours
   To God's own holy Paradise;
Where open sin and hideous crime
Are like the foliage of their clime—
   The unshorn growth of centuries!

Turn, then, my heart—thy home is here;
   No other now remains for thee:—
The smile of love, and friendship's tear,
The tones that melted on thine ear,
   The mutual thrill of sympathy,
The welcome of the household band,
The pressure of the lip and hand,
   Thou mayest not hear, nor feel, nor see.

God of my spirit!—Thou, alone,
   Who watchest o'er my pillowed head,
Whose ear is open to the moan
And sorrowing of thy child, hast known
   The grief which at my heart has fed,—
The struggle of my soul to rise
Above its earth-born sympathies,—
   The tears of many a sleepless bed!

Oh, be Thine arm, as it hath been,
   In every test of heart and faith—
The Tempter's doubt—the wiles of men—
The heathen's scoff—the bosom sin—
   A helper and a stay beneath,
A strength in weakness 'mid the strife
And anguish of my wasting life—
   My solace and my hope in death!

MASSACHUSETTS.

Written on hearing that the Resolutions of the Legislature of Massachusetts on the subject of Slavery, presented by Hon. C. CUSHING to the House of Representatives of the United States, have been laid on the table unread and unreferred, under the infamous rule of "PAT-TON'S RESOLUTION."

AND have they spurn'd *thy* word,
    Thou of the old THIRTEEN!
Whose soil, where Freedom's blood first pour'd
    Hath yet a darker green ?
Tread the weak Southron's pride and lust
Thy name and councils in the dust ?

And have they closed thy mouth,
    And fix'd the padlock fast ?
Slave of the mean and tyrant South !
    Is this thy fate at last ?
Old Massachusetts ! can it be
That thus thy sons must speak of thee ?

Call from the Capitol
    Thy chosen ones again—
Unmeet for them the base control
    Of Slavery's curbing rein !
Unmeet for necks like theirs to feel
The chafing of the despot's heel !

Call back to Quincy's shade
    That steadfast son of thine ;
Go—if thy homage must be paid
    To Slavery's pagod-shrine,
Seek out some meaner offering than
The free-born soul of that old man.

Call that true spirit back,
    So eloquent and young ;
In his own vale of Merrimack
    No chains are on his tongue !
Better to breathe its cold, keen air,
Than wear the Southron's shackle there.

Ay, let them hasten home,
    And render up their trust ;
Through them the Pilgrim-state is dumb,
    Her proud lip in the dust !
Her counsels and her gentlest word
Of warning spurn'd aside, unheard !

Let them come back, and shake
    The base dust from their feet ;

And with their tale of outrage wake
 The free hearts whom they meet;
And show before indignant men
The scars where Slavery's chain has been.

Back from the Capitol—
 It is no place for thee!
Beneath the arch of Heaven's blue wall
 Thy voice may still be free!
What power shall chain thy spirit there,
In God's free sun and freer air?

A voice is calling thee,
 From all the martyr-graves
Of those stern men, in death made free,
 Who could not live as slaves.
The slumberings of thy honor'd dead
Are for thy sake disquieted!

The curse of Slavery comes
 Still nearer, day by day;
Shall thy pure altars and thy homes
 Become the Spoiler's prey?
Shall the dull tread of fetter'd slaves
Sound o'er thy old and holy graves?

Pride of the old THIRTEEN!
 That curse may yet be stay'd—
Stand thou, in Freedom's strength, between
 The living and the dead:
Stand forth, for God and Liberty
In one strong effort worthy thee!

Once more let Faneuil Hall
 By freemen's feet be trod,
And give the echoes of its wall
 Once more to Freedom's God!
And in the midst, unseen, shall stand
The mighty fathers of thy land.

Thy gather'd sons shall feel
 The soul of Adams near,
And Otis with his fiery zeal.
 And Warren's onward cheer;
And heart to heart shall thrill as when
They moved and spake as living men.

Fling, from thy Capitol,
 Thy banner to the light,
And, o'er thy Charter's sacred scroll,
 For Freedom and the Right,

Breathe once again thy vows, unbroken—
Speak once again as thou hast spoken.

On thy bleak hills, speak out!
    A WORLD thy words shall hear;
And they who listen round about,
    In friendship, or in fear,
Shall know thee still, when sorest tried,
"Unshaken and unterrified!" *

TO THE MEMORY OF THOMAS SHIPLEY.

President of the Pennsylvania Abolition Society, who died on the 17th of the 9th month, 1826, a devoted Christian and Philanthropist.

GONE to the Heavenly Father's rest!
    The flowers of Eden round thee blowing!
And on thine ear the murmurs blest
    Of Shiloah's waters softly flowing!
Beneath that Tree of Life which gives
To all the earth its healing leaves!
In the white robe of angels clad!
    And wandering by that sacred river,
Whose streams of holiness make glad
    The city of our God forever!

Gentlest of spirits!—not for thee
    Our tears are shed—our sighs are given:
Why mourn to know thou art a free
    Partaker of the joys of Heaven?
Finish'd thy work, and kept thy faith
In Christian firmness unto death:
And beautiful as sky and earth,
    When Autumn's sun is downward going,
The blessed memory of thy worth
Around thy place of slumber glowing!

But woe for us! who linger still
    With feebler strength and hearts less lowly,
And minds less steadfast to the will
    Of Him whose every work is holy.
For not like thine, is crucified
The spirit of our human pride:
And at the bondman's tale of woe,
    And for the outcast and forsaken,
Not warm like thine, but cold and slow,
    Our weaker sympathies awaken.

* " Massachusetts has held her way right onward, unshaken, unseduced, unterrified."—*Speech of C. Cushing in the House of Representatives of the United States,* 1836.

Darkly upon our struggling way
   The storm of human hate is sweeping;
Hunted and branded, and a prey,
   Our watch amidst the darkness keeping!
Oh! for that hidden strength which can
Nerve unto death the inner man!
Oh! for thy spirit, tried and true,
   And constant in the hour of trial,
Prepare to suffer, or to do,
   In meekness and in self-denial.

Oh! for that spirit, meek and mild,
   Derided, spurn'd, yet uncomplaining—
By man deserted and reviled,
   Yet faithful to its trust remaining.
Still prompt and resolute to save
From scourge and chain the hunted slave!
Unwavering in the Truth's defence,
   Even where the fires of Hate are burning,
The unquailing eye of innocence
   Alone upon the oppressor turning!

O loved of thousands! to thy grave,
   Sorrowing of heart, thy brethren bore thee!
The poor man and the rescued slave
   Wept as the broken earth closed o'er thee—
And grateful tears, like summer rain,
Quicken'd its dying grass again!
And there, as to some pilgrim-shrine,
   Shall come the outcast and the lowly,
Of gentle deeds and words of thine
   Recalling memories sweet and holy!

Oh! for the death the righteous die!
   And end, like Autumn's day declining,
On human hearts, as on the sky,
   With holier, tenderer beauty shining;
As to the parting soul were given
The radiance of an opening Heaven!
As if that pure and blessed light,
   From off the Eternal altar flowing,
Were bathing, in its upward flight,
   The spirit to its worship going!

A SUMMONS.

Lines written on the adoption of Pinckney's Resolutions, in the House of Representatives, and the passage of Calhoun's " Bill of Abominations " to a second reading, in the Senate of the United States.

Now, by our fathers' ashes! where's the spirit
   Of the true-hearted and the unshackled gone?
Sons of old freemen, do we but inherit
               Their *names* alone?

Is the old Pilgrim spirit quench'd within us?
   Stoops the proud manhood of our souls so low,
That Mammon's lure or Party's wile can win us
        To silence now?

No. When our land to ruin's brink is verging,
   In God's name, let us speak while there is time!
Now, when the padlocks for our lips are forging,
        SILENCE IS CRIME!

What! shall we henceforth humbly ask as favors
   Rights all our own? In madness shall we barter,
For treacherous peace, the FREEDOM Nature gave us,
        God and our charter?

Here shall the statesman seek the free to fetter?
   Here Lynch law light its horrid fires on high?
And, in the church, their proud and skill'd abettor,
        Make truth a lie?

Torture the pages of the hallow'd Bible,
   To sanction crime, and robbery, and blood?
And, in Oppression's hateful service, libel
        Both man and God?

Shall our New England stand erect no longer,
   But stoop in chains upon her downward way,
Thicker to gather on her limbs and stronger
        Day after day?

Oh, no; methinks from all her wild, green mountains—
   From valleys where her slumbering fathers lie—
From her blue rivers and her welling fountains,
        And clear, cold sky—

From her rough coast, and isles, which hungry Ocean
   Gnaws with his surges—from the fisher's skiff,
With white sail swaying to the billows' motion
        Round rock and cliff—

From the free fire-side of her unbought farmer—
   From her free laborer at his loom and wheel—
From the brown smith-shop, where, beneath the hammer,
        Rings the red steel—

From each and all, if God hath not forsaken
   Our land, and left us to an evil choice,
Loud as the summer thunderbolt shall waken
        A PEOPLE'S VOICE!

Startling and stern! the Northern winds shall bear it
 Over Potomac's to St. Mary's wave;
And buried Freedom shall awake to hear it
   Within her grave.

Oh, let that voice go forth!   The bondman sighing
 By Santee's wave, in Mississippi's cane,
Shall feel the hope, within his bosom dying,
   Revive again.

Let it go forth!   The millions who are gazing
 Sadly upon us from afar, shall smile,
And unto God devout thanksgiving raising,
   Bless us the while.

Oh, for your ancient freedom, pure and holy,
 For the deliverance of a groaning earth,
For the wrong d captive, bleeding, crush'd, and lowly,
   Let it go forth!

Sons of the best of fathers! will ye falter
 With all they left ye peril'd and at stake?
Ho! once again on Freedom's holy altar
   The fire awake!

Prayer-strengthen'd for the trial, come together,
 Put on the harness for the moral fight,
And, with the blessing of your heavenly Father,
   MAINTAIN THE RIGHT!

THE EXILE'S DEPARTURE.*

FOND scenes, which delighted my youthful existence,
 With feelings of sorrow I bid ye adieu—
A lasting adieu! for now, dim in the distance,
 The shores of Hibernia recede from my view.
Farewell to the cliffs, tempest-beaten and gray,
 Which guard the lov'd shores of my own native land;
Farewell to the village and sail-shadow'd bay,
 The forest-crown'd hill and the water-wash'd strand.

I've fought for my country—I've braved all the dangers
 That throng round the path of the warrior in strife;
I now must depart to a nation of strangers,
 And pass in seclusion the remnant of life:
Far, far, from the friends to my bosom most dear,
 With none to support me in peril and pain,
And none but the stranger to drop the sad tear,
 On the grave where the heart-broken Exile is lain.

* The first of Whittier's poems, ever printed in the Newburyport *Free Press*, June 8, 1826.

Friends of my youth! I must leave you forever,
  And hasten to dwell in a region unknown:—
Yet time cannot change, nor the broad ocean sever,
  Hearts firmly united and tried as our own.
Ah, no! though I wander, all sad and forlorn,
  In a far distant land, yet shall memory trace,
When far o'er the ocean's white surges I'm borne,
  The scenes of past pleasures,—my own native place.

Farewell, shores of Erin, green land of my fathers—
  Once more, and forever, a mournful adieu!
For round thy dim headlands the ocean-mist gathers,
  And shrouds the fair isle I no longer can view.
I go—but wherever my footsteps I bend,
  For freedom and peace to my own native isle,
And contentment and joy to each warm-hearted friend,
  Shall be the heart's prayer of the lonely Exile!

THE DEITY.*

1 Kings xix. 11.

THE prophet stood
On the dark mount, and saw the tempest cloud
Pour the fierce whirlwind from its dark reservoir
Of congregated gloom.   The mountain oak,
Torn from the earth, heav'd high its roots where once
Its branches wav'd.   The fir-tree's shapely form,
Smcte by the tempest, lash'd the mountain's side.
—Yet, calm in conscious purity, the seer
Beheld the scene of desolation—for
Th' Eternal Spirit mov'd not in the storm!

The tempest ceas'd!—the cavern'd earthquake burst
Forth from its prison, and the mountain rock'd
E'en to its base: the topmost crags were thrown,
With fearful crashing, down its shuddering sides.
—Unaw'd the prophet saw and heard— he felt
Not in the earthquake mov'd the God of Heaven!

The murmurs died away!—and from the height
(Rent by the storm, and shattered by the shock),
Rose far and clear a pyramid of flame,
Mighty and vast!—the startled mountain deer
Shrunk from its glare and cower'd within the shade,
The wild fowl shriek'd!—Yet, even then, the seer
Untrembling stood, and mark'd the fearful glow—
For Israel's God came not within the flame!

* Whittier's second poem, printed in the Newburyport *Free Press*, June 22, 1826.

The fiery beacon sunk !— a *still small voice*
Now caught the prophet's ear.   Its awful tones,
Unlike to human sounds, at once conveyed
Deep awe and reverence to his pious heart.
Then bow'd the holy man! his face he veil'd
Within his mantle, and in meekness owned
The presence of his God—discern'd not in
The storm, the earthquake, or the mighty flame,
But in the *still small voice !*